The
NORTHWEST
NATURE GUIDE

The
NORTHWEST
NATURE GUIDE

*Where to go and what to see
month by month in Oregon,
Washington, and British Columbia*

JAMES LUTHER DAVIS

TIMBER PRESS
Portland · London

Dedicated to Harry Nehls,
who has contributed more to Oregon birding,
and taught me more about Oregon's birds,
than anyone else I've known.

Frontispiece: Great blue heron at Reifel Refuge BC

Every effort has been made to ensure all information in this book is correct and up to date, but addresses, phone numbers, Web sites, e-mail addresses, hours of operations, and other specific directions may change. The author and publisher can take no responsibility for the misidentification of mushrooms or plants by the users of this book or for any illness that might result from their consumption or from any attempted remedies. If there is any doubt whatsoever about the identity and edibility of a mushroom or plant, do not eat it. Users should exercise caution when driving and hiking in wilderness areas; the maps in this book are limited in detail.

Maps by Erik Goetze, The Art of Geography
All photographs by the author

This revised, expanded work incorporates portions of the book published in 1996 by Fulcrum Publishing as *Seasonal Guide to the Natural Year: A Month by Month Guide to Natural Events*.

Published in 2009 by Timber Press, Inc.

The Haseltine Building
133 S.W. Second Avenue, Suite 450
Portland, Oregon 97204-3527
www.timberpress.com

2 The Quadrant
135 Salusbury Road
London NW6 6RJ
www.timberpress.co.uk

Second printing 2009
Printed in China
Designed by Susan Applegate

Library of Congress Cataloging-in-Publication Data

Davis, James L. (James Luther), 1949–
    The Northwest nature guide: where to go and what to see month by month in Oregon, Washington, and British Columbia/James Luther Davis.
        p. cm.
    Includes bibliographical references and index.
    ISBN-13: 978-0-88192-867-9
    1. Natural history—Oregon—Guidebooks. 2. Natural history—Washington (State)—Guidebooks. 3. Natural history—British Columbia—Guidebooks. 4. Oregon—Guidebooks. 5. Washington (State)—Guidebooks. 6. British Columbia—Guidebooks. I. Title.
    QH105.O7D38 2009
    508.795—dc22   2008009642

CONTENTS

MAPS

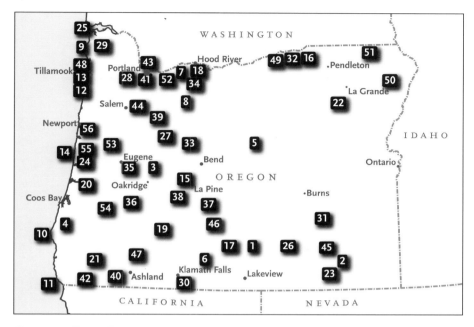

Oregon Best Bets

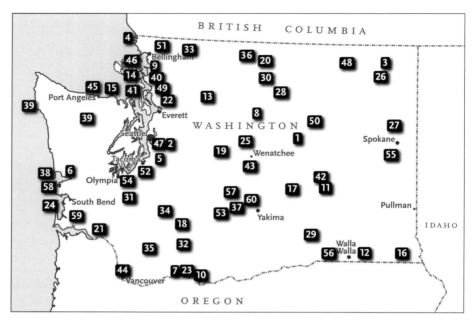

Washington Best Bets

1. Banks Lake
2. Mercer Slough Nature Park
3. Big Meadow Lake
4. Birch Bay State Park
5. Black River Riparian Forest
6. Bowerman Basin and Grays Harbor
7. Catherine Creek
8. Chelan Ridge
9. Chuckanut Drive
10. Columbia Hills State Park
11. Columbia National Wildlife Refuge
12. Coppei Creek
13. Darrington
14. Deception Pass State Park, Washington Park, and Anacortes
15. Dungeness National Wildlife Refuge and Ediz Hook
16. Fields Spring State Park
17. Ginkgo Petrified Forest State Park
18. Goat Rocks Wilderness Area
19. Gold Creek Pond
20. Hart's Pass
21. Julia Butler Hansen Refuge for the Columbia White-Tailed Deer
22. Kayak Point Regional Park
23. Klickitat Wildlife Area
24. Leadbetter Point
25. Leavenworth National Fish Hatchery and Wenatchee River
26. Little Pend Oreille National Wildlife Refuge
27. Little Spokane River Natural Area and Riverside State Park
28. Loup Loup Campground
29. McNary National Wildlife Refuge
30. Methow Valley
31. Mima Mounds Natural Area Preserve
32. Mount Adams and Bird Creek Meadows
33. Mount Baker
34. Mount Rainier National Park
35. Mount St. Helens National Volcanic Monument
36. North Cascades National Park
37. Oak Creek and Clemen Mountain wildlife areas
38. Ocean Shores peninsula
39. Olympic National Park
40. Padilla Bay
41. Port Townsend
42. Potholes Reservoir
43. Red Top Mountain
44. Ridgefield National Wildlife Refuge and Vancouver Lake
45. Salt Creek County Park
46. San Juan Islands
47. Seattle sites
48. Sherman Pass
49. Skagit Wildlife Area and Skagit Flats
50. Steamboat Rock State Park
51. Sumas
52. Tacoma Nature Center
53. Timberwolf Mountain and Rimrock Lake
54. Tumwater Falls
55. Turnbull National Wildlife Refuge
56. Walla Walla Valley and Touchet
57. Wenas Creek
58. Westport
59. Willapa Bay
60. Yakima River Canyon

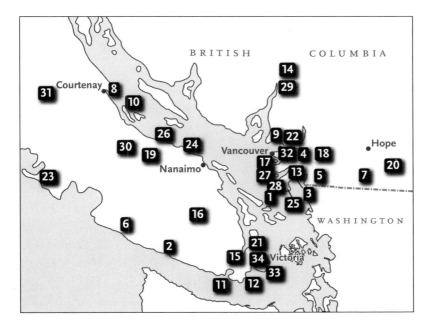

Southwest British Columbia Best Bets

INTRODUCTION

Ahh, another day in paradise. If you've lived in the Pacific Northwest for long you've probably figured out that you reside in one of the greatest places on Earth. Yet, like urbanites in any developed country, we Northwesterners spend so much of our time in environments of our own creation and on schedules of our own design that we are out of touch with the natural world and its rhythms. Many people feel this isolation and seek a greater understanding and a greater connection with nature. Interest in outdoor activities, wildlife, and environmental issues is high in the Northwest with a disproportionately large number of people in the region belonging to conservation and natural history organizations, compared with the rest of North America. Over the years names such as Cascadia or Ecotopia have been used to emphasize our regional identity.

This book will help you have outstanding experiences in the natural world. Most of these experiences involve observing native animals in their natural habitats. However, some are about plants, and a few deal with physical elements of the earth. I hope that by using this book you will have outdoor adventures that leave you feeling revitalized and inspired, with a renewed sense of wonder and appreciation for nature. You may even have some experiences that can best be described as spiritual. Ultimately, I hope that those who use this book are moved to do all they can to protect our planet and its awesome diversity of living things.

This book covers all of Oregon and Washington and the part of British Columbia within 150 miles of Victoria. Although this southwestern section represents a small part of the vast province of British Columbia, it includes

The rocky shore from Yachats to Cape Perpetua has many wildlife watching sites.

11

some of the richest wildlife habitats and the majority of the province's human population. Southwestern BC was also included because many of its residents regularly visit Oregon and Washington and, conversely, Victoria and Vancouver are extremely popular destinations for Oregonians and Washingtonians. In addition, the inclusion of southwestern BC makes sense biologically, and the plants and animals certainly don't recognize any political boundaries. Throughout this book "our region" means Oregon, Washington, and southwestern BC, and "we" means residents of our region.

Since timing is so important in nature, this book takes you through the year month by month and for each month describes four main wildlife attractions or natural events that are exceptional during that month. The first part of these chapters gives you background information on the chapter's topic to increase your understanding, appreciation, and enjoyment of the event. This is followed by detailed directions to specific places or Best Bets throughout the region. Each month also has some Nature Nuggets, briefer mentions of other natural happenings, and an additional section—a closer look—about a general topic pertinent to that month. A list of abbreviations used in the book and US-to-metric conversion tables appear at the end of this introduction.

Although many animal activities and natural events do occur with surprising regularity, wildlife and nature are unpredictable. While I can't guarantee you'll see a particular animal in a particular place, if you follow the suggestions in this guide and use good wildlife-watching techniques, your chances will be very good. Be prepared to miss some of the things that you have gone to see, and just relax and enjoy your time in that place. Be patient, flexible, and observant, and you will probably see things that you did not expect. Keep in mind that change is fundamental to the natural world as well as to our human contrivances. Areas may change because of natural processes or human intervention; roads and signs may be different than when this book went to print. Make each trip an adventure.

I chose these sites not only because they are fairly predictable for viewing wildlife, but also because they are great places to visit in general. Most of the sites are very scenic, and many have some historical and cultural features. Some places are good for seeing certain animals, gulls at a sewage plant for example, but you would probably not go to them for any reason other than to see that animal. These places are not included. Why go to a yucky place when you can go to more scenic places to see the same thing? Site selection in this book is for the overall experience and not just one specific target animal. Different habitats and areas of the Northwest are represented, so you will become familiar with the broad landscape of our region as you use this book.

The Salish Sea

One of the largest physical features in our part of the world is the vast, complex, inland sea consisting of Puget Sound, the Strait of Georgia, the Strait of Juan de Fuca, and the numerous other interconnected inlets, channels, passages, straits, and bays. Unfortunately, this ecosystem has no common name, making it very wordy and awkward to refer to in its entirety. Phrases such as "Puget Sound and adjacent waters," although used, certainly don't help much. Confusion even exists about the exact boundaries of Puget Sound itself. It would be great to have a good, simple name, perhaps with some meaning, that could be used for the whole "greater Puget Sound and adjacent waters super-estuary ecosystem." An interesting tidbit: Canadian publications usually call it Juan de Fuca Strait, whereas American publications call it Strait of Juan de Fuca.

Were there names for this ecosystem before the Europeans came? Some authors state that the original Native American name for this inland sea was Whulge or Whulch. Most authorities believe these names referred to only a specific bay or channel, and the first human inhabitants did not have one name for the whole sea. This makes sense because they certainly didn't have any maps showing the whole thing or nice photos from space. There do not seem to be any advocates for establishing the name Whulge. However, a name that has been gathering support since the 1990s is Salish Sea. The majority of Native Americans living adjacent to these waters belonged to the linguistic group called the Coast Salish. Salish is the native word many of these people called themselves. It is not a derogatory English or Spanish name made up by Europeans. Since I first became aware of this term in 1992, I have noticed it being used more and more, often by people involved in environmental education or natural history. I have used the term *Salish Sea* throughout this book.

Wildlife-Watching Secrets

You may be in the right place at the right time, but unless you know some basic techniques for finding and watching wild animals, you may be out of luck. Mammals, especially, are usually hard to see. Even some birds, the most conspicuous type of wildlife, will be sometimes difficult to find. Here are some tips gathered from naturalists, wildlife photographers, and hunters.

BE INVISIBLE The most important technique is to make yourself "not there." We call this "the routine of invisibility" in our park programs. Animals know humans are around because they hear and see us. It is not as common for an animal to actually smell people before it sees or hears them, but that is another way mammals can tell we are present. We can't do much about our smell, but we can reduce our movement and sound.

What an animal does when it notices we are coming varies. Because birds can fly and we are not good at jumping into the air and grabbing them, many birds in trees or flying overhead don't react much to people not directly threatening them. This is one reason why birdwatching is so popular; you can actually see birds easily. Mammals, on the other hand, "disappear" before we even know they are there. They may hide or slowly slip away. Often mammals hide by "freezing," and because their coloring blends so well with their habitat, people walk right by them. Mammals will usually run away only as a last ditch escape, and when they are moving is when we notice them most easily.

To see mammals, and more birds, reptiles, and amphibians, we need to be quiet and still. The goal is to see or hear the animal before it sees or hears you—at least to see the animal when it freezes and before it leaves. You are playing a different kind of freeze tag, one without touching. In our programs we call our quiet walk "the fox walk," and we listen with "deer ears." Sometime when you are in a park with trails, sit or stand quietly by a trail and try to notice other hikers coming before you can see them. How far in advance did you know the hikers were coming before they noticed you? It is easy to understand how animals can avoid being seen by people.

Our outings are usually social events and, regardless of good intentions, more people mean more noise. A general rule: the smaller the group, the better the wildlife watching. Of course, if a family is on vacation the parents are not going to leave the kids in the motel so they can go see bighorn sheep.

It isn't often that we change our social outings for wildlife watching, so it is more realistic to think about generating enthusiasm for the fun of becoming sneaky explorers stalking wild animals. Everyone should try to make themselves the smallest, stillest, quietest, most uninteresting blob they can. Then everyone turns their senses on "max."

TIME OF DAY Dawn and dusk are usually the best times to see animals because this is when many of them are active (they are crepuscular). This also is about the only time you can see nocturnal animals. Unless you are looking for basking reptiles and insects, the middle of a warm, sunny day is generally not a good time to see wildlife. However, a warm sunny day in the spring is ideal for wildflowers, butterflies, and some birds. The time of year, of course, is very important, and that is what this book is all about.

HABITAT AND HABITS Know the habitat of the animals you seek; that is, know what animals live in the habitat you are visiting. Each species is usually found in its preferred habitat, so knowing that habitat allows you to concentrate your efforts in the right place. Some habitats are harder to tell apart than others, but the more experience you have, the more you will become "habitat aware."

The animal's behaviors are important for knowing where and when to look. If you have found some trees recently cut down by beaver, come back with a big flashlight before sunset, hide where you can see the area, then wait and watch for the critter. Find out as much as you can about the animal you want to see. Where does it nest or roost? What does it eat? When does it look for food? What noises does it make? Learning about animal tracks and signs can be extremely helpful. If you know an animal is using a particular path regularly, that's the place to hide and watch. Knowing the habits and habitat of an animal can also help with identification.

YOUR CAR IS YOUR BLIND As incongruous as it may seem, cars make excellent wildlife observation blinds. Many animals are not frightened by the shape of a car but quickly flee when they see the silhouette of a standing human. Car blinds work especially well when driving the roads in a typical national wildlife refuge. Some refuges have created auto tour routes and use wonderfully funny signs to tell you to stay in your car while driving on the route. The auto tour route at Ridgefield National Wildlife Refuge is an excellent example, providing great wildlife viewing while reducing disturbance to the animals. In some situations, such as when watching sage-grouse, getting out of your car will frighten away the animals.

Wildlife-Watching Etiquette

It is important to be an ethical wildlife watcher and not harm or harass the very animals we enjoy seeing. If you can tell you are affecting an animal's behavior, back off—you're getting too close. Ideally, you should not alarm an animal so much that it flees. Nests are especially sensitive; please stay away from any known or suspected nesting areas.

Do not try to pet or handle a wild animal unless you know that neither you nor the animal can be hurt, such as touching a sea star in a tidepool or picking up a sow bug. If in doubt—hands off. Do not feed wildlife except in unharmful situations, such as feeding seeds to backyard birds or providing suet at a feeder. In particular, do not feed human food to mammals, especially in parks that specifically ask visitors not to, despite the powerful temptation and poor examples of others. This rule is for your own safety as well as for the animal's welfare. Every year people are injured, some even killed, as a result of deer being fed in parks.

Please respect private property and do not trespass. The sites in this book are on public land or on private land where visitation is allowed or invited. When on public land please follow all appropriate rules and regulations and leave every place you visit cleaner than when you found it. Stay on roads and trails designated for public use, and be aware that many national wildlife refuges have some areas with seasonal closures.

More Helpful Advice

Don't hesitate to ask others for advice or help. If you see someone prowling around headquarters at Malheur National Wildlife Refuge with binoculars, they probably will be delighted to tell you about what they have seen. Ask the staff at national parks, state or provincial parks, national forests, and wildlife refuges about good wildlife-watching opportunities—you might get a hot, new viewing tip.

BOOKS AND MAPS Your trusty field guides are a major part of a naturalist's equipment. I have provided a comprehensive bibliography of the most useful Northwest natural history field guides, along with comments, at the end of the book. Field guides are essential for identification unless you are lucky enough to be accompanied by someone who knows the local flora and fauna. Being with an expert or near-expert is one advantage of going on guided nature walks in parks or on organized field trips with an Audubon Society or, in Canada, with a field naturalists club (suggestions for finding these are in Resources).

The DeLorme atlases for each state have become almost de rigueur among US naturalists and agency personnel. These are excellent maps for areas outside of cities and are invaluable for finding the sites in Oregon and Washington. An atlas for British Columbia that is not as detailed but is very useful and identifies many wildlife viewing sites is *Southwestern British Columbia Recreational Atlas*, published by PTC Phototype Composing Ltd. of Victoria in conjunction with BC Environment. It is sometimes hard to find good maps of BC in the States. I have found Davenport Maps (Custom Drafting, Ltd.) and the BCAA maps (Canadian Cartographics, Ltd.) to be excellent.

FEES The Northwest Forest Pass is now required for parking in many areas in most of the national forests in Oregon and Washington. Washington requires an annual Vehicle Use Permit decal to park in any of the state wildlife areas. Purchase your pass in advance—wherever hunting and fishing licenses are sold and at other places listed on Washington Department of Fish and Wildlife's Web site—because they are not available at the sites where they are required. Some national wildlife refuges now have an entrance or parking fee. These fee systems may change, so check the current situation when planning trips to state, provincial, or federal lands. The America the Beautiful recreation pass became available in the United States in January 2007. This annual pass covers entrance and standard amenity fees at all national parks and monuments, national forests, wildlife refuges, Bureau of Land Management sites, and others. These state and federal passes probably will change in coming years so be sure to check before planning trips.

Both Oregon and Washington have a state Sno-Park program whereby the state plows and maintains many parking areas that provide access to winter recreation throughout the state. To park in these areas you must display a current Sno-Park permit. Permits are available for the day or the season. Each state honors the Sno-Park permit from the other state (even Idaho), but your permit must match the state of your license plate. Sno-Park permits are available at sporting goods stores, downhill ski areas, and in many stores on mountain roads. In Washington they are also available online and at state parks listed on the Internet. In Oregon they are for sale, in addition to the retail outlets, at any DMV office.

PERSONAL SAFETY Using this book will result in traveling during different times of the year, so take the normal precautions for extended travel and for being outside a lot. Many of the sites described in this book are in remote, rural country—be well prepared for travel in these areas. This includes proper clothing (always assume the weather will change for the worse in the Northwest), food and water, first aid kit, and auto safety equipment. Although an excellent time for wildlife viewing, winter travel is potentially hazardous to the traveler. All sites in this book are normally accessible by regular passenger car (or on foot), but mention is made of some roads where high clearance is desirable. In warm months always have insect repellent with you; northwestern mosquitoes can hold their own against Alaskan brutes any time.

Wildlife watchers need to be aware of hunting seasons, both for personal safety and for the best viewing opportunities. Hunting seasons generally take place between September and January but vary from place to place, species to species, and year to year. Hunting takes place on about half of all US national wildlife refuges. It is worth a little research to avoid hunting days. Hunting regulations and schedules are usually available in sporting goods stores by August, and are also available on the Internet.

Abbreviations

Here are the abbreviations (US unless otherwise indicated) used throughout the book:

BLM	Bureau of Land Management
FR	Forest Road (in US National Forests)
NF	National Forest
NFH and FH	(National) Fish Hatchery
NM	National Monument
NP	National Park (US and BC)
NPS	National Park Service
NWR	National Wildlife Refuge
NWRS	National Wildlife Refuge System
ODFW	Oregon Department of Fish and Wildlife
PP	Provincial Park (BC)
RP	Regional Park (US and BC)
SP	State Park
USFS	US Forest Service
USFWS	US Fish and Wildlife Service
WDFW	Washington Department of Fish and Wildlife

Common conversions

Those of you who frequently travel between the US and Canada are probably accustomed to converting units of measure and may have your own tricks. This table is for making approximate conversions from US units to Canadian (metric) units.

APPROXIMATE CONVERSIONS

US UNIT	CANADIAN UNIT (METRIC)
miles × 1.6	kilometers
feet × 0.3	meters
yards × 0.9	meters
inches × 2.5	centimeters
acre × 0.4	hectare
square miles × 2.6	square kilometers
pounds × 0.45	kilograms

APPROXIMATE TEMPERATURE EQUIVALENTS

FAHRENHEIT	CELSIUS
100	37
90	32
80	27
70	21
60	16
50	10
40	4
32	0
20	−7

ABOUT BINOCULARS

Binoculars are the most important piece of equipment for wildlife watching, in addition to the right clothing. Although they are fairly common, I have learned after 30 years of leading nature programs and teaching classes that many people who own binoculars don't know how to use them correctly. Some people are flabbergasted to learn that there actually is anything to learn about using binoculars. I regularly have people tell me they can't see anything through binoculars only to have them gasp in amazement when they are shown how to do it correctly. I have, therefore, been going over the four steps for adjusting binoculars before every program for over a decade. Some experienced birders pooh-pooh my doing this, but every time I do at least one person says something like, "Oh my goodness, I can't believe it. I've never seen this before."

How to Use Binoculars

To get the most out of your binoculars, you need to know how to adjust them properly. Here are instructions for making these adjustments, including the tricky adjustable eyepiece. Because binoculars need to be adjusted for each person, sharing binoculars is usually not practical.

EYECUPS Modern binoculars have soft rubber eyecups on the eyepieces that fold down to adjust for eyeglasses. If you use binoculars with your glasses on, fold the eyecups down so the end of the eyepiece is as flat as possible. Put the flat eyepiece right on the lens of your glasses when using the binoculars.

If you aren't wearing glasses, leave the eyecups extended. Some binoculars have eyecups that screw in to get flat for glasses.

THE HINGE The two halves of the binoculars are joined together in the center with a hinge so you can set them the right distance apart for your eyes. While looking through the binoculars, move the two sides in and out until you have one large, clear, circular field of view. If you get dark patches or crescents in the center or on the sides, they are too close together or too far apart. You will never see two circles as in cartoons. Keep fiddling with them until you get the best field of view, and don't be afraid to keep adjusting them throughout the day.

THE CENTRAL FOCUS Hold the binoculars in both hands and use a big finger to turn the wheel in the center—the central focus. To get the sharpest, clearest image you can, turn the wheel back and forth every time you look at something new. However, your eyes are probably not exactly the same, and you'll need to make one more adjustment to see as well as you can with your binoculars.

THE ADJUSTABLE EYEPIECE This is the most confusing thing about using binoculars. It is almost never explained on birdwatching or other nature walks and is poorly explained in the instructions that come with binoculars (yes, there were some).

When you use the central focus, you focus the two sides of the binoculars at the same time. Your eyes, however, are probably not identical—you'll need to use the adjustable eyepiece, the one that turns, to adjust your binoculars so that both eyes are in focus at the same time. On most binoculars the right eyepiece is the adjustable eyepiece; I've written these directions with that assumption. On the underside of this eyepiece is a scale marked +, 0, − and a reference mark on the binoculars' frame next to the scale. Find the adjustable eyepiece and turn it. Find the scale on the underside and set it at 0.

Pick something, like a sign, that is 50 to 200 yards away and sharp and clear to look at.

Make the other adjustments and focus on the sign with the central focus as best as you can.

Close your right eye and use the central focus to get the left eye's image as sharp as possible. You are looking through only the left side of your binoculars. "Left eye—central focus."

When the left eye image is sharp, close your left eye and open your right eye. Don't touch the central focus. You are now looking through only the right side of your binoculars. Turn the adjustable eyepiece back and forth with your right hand until you get the sharpest image you can in your right eye. You are matching your right eye to the left eye. "Right eye—right eyepiece."

After you get the right eye sharp, open your left eye and the object should be in sharp focus in both eyes. To check, focus on something else with the central focus, and then alternate looking with one eye and then the other. The image should be identical and in focus in both eyes. Sometimes you just have to fiddle a bit with the central focus and the adjustable eyepiece until you get them right. The point is that every time you focus with the central focus, both of your eyes are in the same sharp focus.

When you have the adjustable eyepiece in the correct position, look at the scale and remember that setting. This is your basic setting for those binoculars—always start there. Many people find that their eyes change from time to time, so don't hesitate to keep fiddling with it to get the best image you can. Remember: Left eye—central focus, then right eye—right eyepiece.

To ease discomfort from the binocular strap, always put it behind any collars or hoods on your shirts and jackets. You can also buy wide, soft straps that are much more comfortable than what usually comes with binoculars at camera stores. If straps bother you, you can find alternative strap setups at stores that specialize in binoculars or at online dealers. Be sure to get cleaning supplies for the lenses and use them. A nice pair of binoculars will open up a new world to you; you can also take them to sporting events and concerts.

Buying Binoculars

Good binoculars are now available at a lower cost than 10 years ago, but cost and quality are related. The big difference today is that many mid-priced binoculars have excellent quality, but are not outrageously expensive. More important than cost, however, is having the right kind and knowing how to use them.

All binoculars have two numbers, such as 7×35, 8×40, or 7×26. The first number is the magnification; the second number is the diameter of the objective lens (the big lens) in millimeters. The magnification (power) determines how large the image appears, and the size of the objective lens determines how much light gets to your eye. Contrary to prevailing attitudes and some sales pitches, more power is not better.

Here are my tips for buying binoculars:

- Never buy any kind of zoom binoculars or so-called focus-free binoculars.
- Don't buy binoculars over 8 power unless you're experienced and know you can use and need 10 power. Do not get binoculars over 10 power.
- Don't buy any binoculars under $60.
- Don't buy any binoculars you haven't looked through and tested.
- Binoculars made by well-known camera and optics companies are the safest bet. Examples in the moderate price range: Bushnell, Nikon, Pentax, Canon, Fuji, and Eagle Optics.
- I recommend full-sized binoculars, not compacts. The second number will be larger than 30 on full-sized binoculars; that is, 7×35, 8×40. Full-sized binoculars let in more light, giving the best image. Compacts should not be over 8 power (6 or 7 is better) and should be at least 25 mm.
- I recommend 8×40 or 8×42 binoculars. Other good models: 7×35 or 8×36. It's possible to get decent 7 and 8 power binoculars in the $70 to $150 range. Many excellent binoculars are available for under $350. When choosing between binoculars by the major brands in the $200 to $350 range, personal preference will be the major factor. A number of waterproof binoculars are now available at lower cost. Waterproof binoculars tend to be more rugged and, given our Northwest weather, are a good choice. Shop around and try different ones at stores with knowledgeable staff.

In general, children under the age of six are not able to use binoculars, and toy binoculars are useless. Make little-kid binoculars out of toilet paper tubes covered with black duct tape and then taped together. Add a black shoelace for the strap. Cool.

JANUARY

WINTERING RAPTORS

When most people think of winter, images of bare trees, snowy lifeless land-scapes, and a pervading stillness come to mind. Many are surprised to find that the dead of winter is actually the liveliest time of the year for some kinds of wildlife. At least, that's the case in the Pacific Northwest, where our winters are mild because of the moderating influence of the Pacific Ocean. We do have our cold spells, especially east of the Cascades, but by and large we are downright balmy compared to the Midwest or certainly compared to the Arctic tundra. It was hard for me to get used to this idea when I first moved here from warmer climates, but for many animals this is the south to which they come for the winter.

Two major groups of birds that are more numerous and conspicuous in the winter are waterfowl and raptors. Waterfowl are the subject of several other chapters; here we will discuss wintering raptors. *Raptor* is synonymous with *bird of prey*, which has a precise meaning to biologists, naturalists, and bird-ers. Birds of prey are predators—they eat other animals for their food. But not all birds that are predators are birds of prey, a confusing state of affairs. Examples of predators include loons, pelicans, shrikes, and the many bug-eating birds. Yet none of these is ever considered a bird of prey. To be a bird of prey a bird must be a member of either one of these orders or groups of birds: the owls or the hawks.

The owls are a very homogeneous group; all owls are called owls and look unmistakably like owls, a very distinctive look indeed. The hawk order, how-ever, is much more diverse (and confusing) and includes birds called hawks, eagles, falcons, kites, and harriers, as well as a few others. Vultures had been considered raptors for decades, but the results of recent genetic research has

Trumpeter swans near Willapa Bay

25

reclassified them as (are you ready?) storks. Well, they are not really storks, of course—they are their own family—but their closest relatives are storks and ibis. However, birders usually still include vultures when discussing raptor identification because vultures look so similar to eagles. While most people can tell a vulture from an ibis, distinguishing a turkey vulture from a golden eagle or dark red-tailed hawk can be a problem. This shocking reclassification applies to only the New World Vultures, "our" vultures living in the Americas. The Old World Vultures are still classified as raptors in the large hawk order.

Birds of prey are easily recognized by their talons—big claws for catching and killing prey—and their distinctive hooked, sharp beaks, which they use for tearing their prey apart. Despite the similarities between owls and hawks, these two groups of birds are not closely related. They have evolved independently to have the same adaptations because they do the same thing, not because one group has inherited characteristics from the other. Owls and hawks are an excellent example of what is called convergent evolution. They are two unrelated types of animals converging on a similar body style and set of adaptations because of similar lifestyles and selective pressures.

Most birds of prey eat rodents and play an important ecological role in helping regulate the numbers of these prolific mammals. Until recently, this clear benefit to humans went ignored, and these birds were relentlessly persecuted by people who saw them as vicious killers competing for game or threatening their domestic animals. Fortunately, raptors are heavily protected today by state and federal laws, and there has been a dramatic increase in the enforcement of these laws.

Fourteen species of owls and 18 species of hawks regularly occur in our region. Of these, four species are almost never seen except during the winter: the rough-legged hawk, the merlin, the gyrfalcon, and the snowy owl. The rough-legged hawk and merlin may arrive fairly early in the fall and stay late into spring. A few merlin even stay and nest. But the gyrfalcon and snowy owl are truly birds of the far north and come this far south only in winter. How many show up in our region in any one winter will vary from year to year, but we always get a few somewhere. How many of them travel to various points south is influenced by declines in prey populations, severe winter weather, and probably other factors we don't understand. More of both are seen the farther north you go—the fields around Boundary Bay usually having the most individuals. When one shows up in a particular place, it is hot news and will be on the nearest rare bird alert.

Most other birds of prey, especially owls, are year-round or permanent residents in our region. However, many raptors are more conspicuous in the winter for several reasons. A significant influx of winter visitors makes bald eagles and peregrine falcons more abundant. Raptors also generally move from the colder east side of the Cascades to milder western agricultural lands, where rodents and rabbits are abundant. Some raptors are easier to see in winter because of a change in their behaviors. For example, sharp-shinned and Cooper's hawks stalk bird feeders in winter for easy pickings. Goshawks get "pushed down" out of the mountains by severe weather. And birds of prey are easier to see because the deciduous trees have lost their leaves. Even common, permanent residents, such as red-tailed hawks and kestrels become more conspicuous during the wintertime.

Trying to see an owl always presents a challenge. In the winter you have a much better chance of spotting an owl roosting (sleeping or resting for an extended period) during the day in a bare deciduous tree. Your most likely winter owl sighting will be a great horned owl hunkered down in a tree for the day. Look for what appears to be a rugby ball sitting vertically on a branch near the trunk of a big tree. In many areas west of the Cascades, short-eared owls are more conspicuous during winter because they are fairly diurnal. The one owl that is really a winter specialty is the snowy owl. The Best Bets describe where to look for these visitors from the Arctic.

Spotting wintering hawks can be as easy as driving through farmland. A trip down I-5 in the Willamette Valley or through the Skagit Flats in January can easily produce a dozen red-tailed hawks and a few rough-legged hawks in less than an hour. Pastures, farm fields or grasslands, and perching areas, such as power poles, fence poles, and trees are potentially good habitat for finding birds of prey. Weather won't affect your chances of seeing raptors much unless it's really windy or a blasting storm. A typical Northwest winter day west of the Cascades, overcast with intermittent drizzle and temperatures in the 30s or 40s, is just fine for finding raptors.

A few raptor locations stand out because of the high concentrations and variety of species. Most of these locations are in areas where you drive roads and look for birds perched on nearby poles. Stay in your car as much as possible—in many cases you'll be able to see the bird just as well from your car as you will if you get out. In fact if you do get out, you'll probably scare the bird away if it's close. And let's face it, if you're winter birdwatching it's nice staying in the warm car. Of course at times you'll have to jump out to watch a flying bird or get a scope set up for birds at a distance, but in these cases you probably won't be close enough to scare the birds. Always try to minimize your impact on the animals, especially during cold weather when the animals must conserve energy to stay warm.

The target birds for our Best Bets are the four winter specialties—the rough-legged hawk, the merlin, the gyrfalcon, and the snowy owl. While out looking for these birds expect to see plenty of our common year-round hawks: red-tailed, sharp-shinned, and Cooper's hawks; northern harrier; American kestrel; and, east of the Cascades, golden eagle. Not common but possible in small numbers in the right place are peregrine and prairie falcons and in Oregon, white-tailed kite and red-shouldered hawk. The most difficult to see is the goshawk; consider any sighting of this bird a lucky gift. What many consider the most spectacular raptor, the bald eagle, is covered in its own chapter.

▶ WINTERING RAPTORS BEST BETS OREGON

Broad floodplains that are mainly used as pastures today often occur where the Oregon coastal rivers flow out of the Coast Range and meet the sea. These pastures are full of rodents and are attractive to raptors. The most famous for birds is Nehalem Meadows. Drive south on US Hwy 101 from the small town of Nehalem and cross the Nehalem River. As soon as you cross the river turn right onto Tideland Rd. Follow Tideland as it turns and takes you back under the bridge you were just on. Tideland Rd winds through the pastureland known to Oregon birders as the Nehalem Meadows until it intersects State Hwy 53, which can be taken back to US 101 (turn right) making a loop trip.

Search the trees and the power and fence poles and, of course, keep your eyes on the sky as you drive through the meadows. This is the kind of birder's driving that turns passengers' knuckles white, so try to make it look as if you're also keeping your eye on the road. These pastures are one of the most reliable spots in the state for seeing white-tailed kites, a "California bird" that just barely makes it into the Northwest. Other noteworthy species that have been seen here at times include merlin, peregrine falcon, and even a few sightings of gyrfalcon.

Regardless of the raptor action, be sure to stop at the wastewater treatment plant at 14000 Tideland Rd to check out the waterfowl, gulls, and shorebirds. Birders are welcome on the plant grounds. Park outside the fence near the RV dump site, as out of the way as you can, and walk in the main gate. If the main gate is locked use the "birdwatcher's gate" to the side. Be respectful of the facility, of course, and realize that you are at a sewage treatment plant, which is a potential biohazard. In other words, don't touch stuff and poke in the muck.

Snowy owls are unpredictable, but they are most commonly seen on Clatsop Spit, site of the south jetty of the Columbia River. This area is part of Fort Stevens SP, about halfway between Seaside and Astoria. From US 101 turn west onto Ridge Rd into the park, drive past the main camping area, and follow signs to the south jetty. Parking area C is the closest to the jetty itself and has an observation tower. Parking lot D, at the end of the road, is the area where snowy owls, and a few gyrfalcons, have been seen in past years. If either bird is at the jetty, the Portland Audubon rare bird alert will probably have information. In both places park the car and search on foot.

The Klamath Basin in the dead of winter is peak time for bald eagles and rough-legged hawks. You'll also see plenty of red-tailed hawks, kestrels, and northern harriers around, plus a few golden eagles, prairie falcons, merlins, Cooper's hawks, sharp-shinned hawks, and ferruginous hawks. This is a good place to practice distinguishing between the two buteos—the red-tailed and the rough-legged hawks. Buteos are the large soaring hawks and the individual variation within each species can make telling them apart a real challenge. A map and more information are in February (Bald Eagles).

▶ WINTERING RAPTORS BEST BETS WASHINGTON

Washington birders seem to agree that the hot spot in their state for winter raptors is western Skagit County, especially the Skagit and Samish flats. In the broadest terms the Skagit Flats are Fir Island and the farm fields north of Fir Island and south of State Hwy 20, west of Interstate 5 and the town of Mount Vernon. Part of Fir Island is the Skagit WA, famous for snow geese. To get to the Skagit Flats take the Conway exit (Exit 221) from I-5, and head west on Fir Island Rd. You can explore the farm roads north and south of Fir Island Rd, including Wylie Rd, which leads into the Skagit WA managed by WDFW. You'll need a WDFW annual vehicle use permit to park in this and other state wildlife areas. These permits are sold wherever hunting and fishing licenses are sold and at other places listed on WDFW's Web site. In the Skagit Flats, including Fir Island, you can usually see the birds that you would find in the wildlife area by driving the public roads through the farmlands, making the parking permit unnecessary.

As you drive west on Fir Island Rd, it eventually turns right and heads north to intersect Best Rd. Turn left onto Best and take it north across the North Fork Skagit River, and enter the farmlands between the Skagit River and Hwy 20. The roads in this area form a basic grid. You can just cruise around the area looking for raptors as well as swans, snow geese, and other waterfowl. The main roads to drive are Best, Calhoun, McLean, Bradshaw, and Beaver Marsh. These are busy farm roads so watch carefully for other cars, and pull far over to the side if you stop. Birders can drive local residents crazy with thoughtless driving.

The Samish Flats is north of Hwy 20, gen-

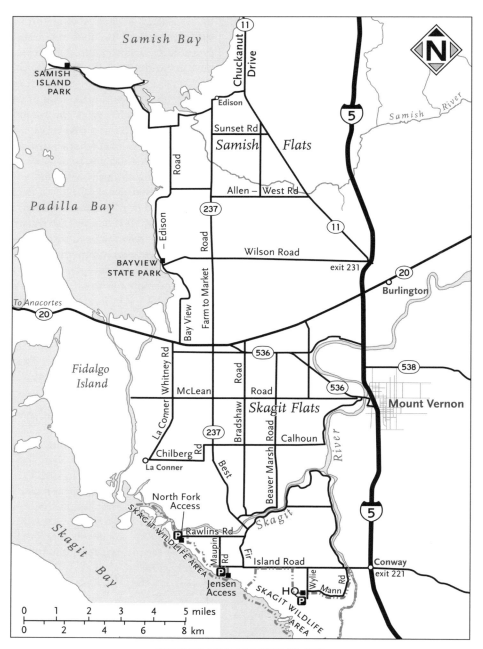

SKAGIT AND SAMISH FLATS

erally the area within the 4 miles south of the hamlet of Edison. From the Skagit Flats drive north on Best Rd, which crosses Hwy 20 and becomes State Hwy 237. Highway 237 is also called Farm to Market Rd and takes you into the heart of the Samish Flats. Again, the roads form a grid. West of Farm to Market Rd is Bay View—Edison, Samish Island, and D'Arcy roads. To the east are Sunset, Field, and Thomas roads. You can eventually work your way east to Chuckanut Dr (State Hwy 11), and then drive either south toward Mount Vernon or north to Bellingham on the gorgeous Chuckanut Scenic Drive.

The most common raptors in both areas are red-tailed and rough-legged hawks, bald eagles, and northern harriers. Other regulars, in small numbers, are peregrine falcons, kestrels, merlins, Cooper's hawks, and barn and short-eared owls. Less predictable, but possible, species are great horned and barred owl, golden eagle, prairie falcon, snowy owl, and the much sought-after gyrfalcon. The Seattle Audubon rare bird alert will have information about gyrfalcons and snowy owls if they are in the area. It was a thrill to finally see my first gyrfalcon on Samish Island Rd, right where the rare bird alert said it would be.

Two areas in eastern Washington are noted for their winter raptors. The Walla Walla Valley south of State Hwy 12, between Walla Walla and the little town of Touchet, is mainly alfalfa fields with the Walla Walla River winding through them. The alfalfa fields provide lots of rodents, and the cottonwoods along the river provide the nesting and roosting sites for plenty of raptors. You can wander around on any of the roads in the area, but here is one route that provides a raptor alternative to driving Hwy 12 to Walla Walla.

Starting at the Columbia River on Hwy 12, head east toward Walla Walla. You'll drive by the Wallula Unit of McNary NWR, a good spot for waterfowl. In about 6 miles turn south onto Byrnes Rd. This junction, at milepost 314 across from the Nine Mile Ranch, is well signed. Stay on Byrnes, part gravel and part paved, until it rejoins Hwy 12 just west of Touchet. Just after you pass the "Entering Touchet" sign and a grain elevator, turn south (right) onto Balm Rd (signed). Take Balm until you have to turn left, and then drive to the stop sign on the Touchet-Gardena Rd (signed "Tou. Gard. Road"). Turn right and head south until you come to Gardena Rd, and then turn left and take it east. It twists and turns a bit, but just stay on the main road and, presto, it will become Frog Hollow Rd.

Take Frog Hollow (what a great name; I wish I lived on a Frog Hollow Rd) about 8 miles east to Last Chance Rd, and then take it north, back to Hwy 12. Watch for raptors along this route, the most common being the red-tailed, rough-legged, and northern harrier trio. I've never seen as many harriers at one time as I've seen on this route. After you return to Hwy 12 you can continue east to the very charming and picturesque college town of Walla Walla.

For east side snowy owls try the irrigated fields east of Potholes Reservoir. The Potholes region is excellent for waterfowl, but here's the deal on the owls. State Hwy 17 goes southeast from the town of Moses Lake. In this area the east-west roads are numbered and the north-south roads are named with letters. Heading southeast on Hwy 17 from Moses Lake, turn right and head south on M SE. Cruise slowly as far as 5 SE, then turn right onto 5 SE and go to L SE, and then turn right to head north. Drive a couple of miles north on L SE, turn right on 3 SE, and return to M SE. Pretty confusing with all these letters and numbers, eh? You are just driving a rectangle drawn by roads M, 5,

L, and 3. Don't worry—on a map it's obvious, and even if you get off a bit it doesn't matter. Scan the cut fields looking for owls perched on irrigation equipment or the cement sides of irrigation ditches.

You can also try another area with the same habitat north of Interstate 90. Drive back toward Moses Lake on Hwy 17 until you cross I-90. Right away you'll come to 1 NE. Turn right and take 1 NE to L NE, turn left and cruise north on L NE searching that area. Special thanks to Washington birder Mike Denny for the tip on this area. If snowy owls are in the area, it will probably be reported on Tweeters or southeastern Washington's rare bird alert.

▶ WINTERING RAPTORS BEST BETS BRITISH COLUMBIA

A similar situation exists in the farmlands north of Boundary Bay, an extraordinary area just north of the US-Canada border, which has the highest density of wintering birds of prey in Canada. Highway 99, the main highway to Vancouver, goes through the area. South of Hwy 99, and parallel to most of it, is Ladner Trunk Rd which is also Hwy 10. Take Exit 20 off Hwy 99 to get onto Ladner Trunk Rd. Note that at this interchange, Hwy 10 crosses to the north side of Hwy 99. To stay south of Hwy 99 and continue east from this point, Ladner Trunk Rd changes names and becomes Hornby Dr. You want to stay on Hornby and Ladner Trunk south of Hwy 99 as you travel east and west through the area.

Six numbered streets—64th, 72nd, 88th, 96th, 104th and 112th—head south through the farmlands from Ladner Trunk or Hornby and end at the dike on the northern shore of Boundary Bay. A map of this area is in August (Fall Shorebird Migration). It's worth driving through all these streets looking for raptors. This area, one of the Northwest's best for winter birding, is also great for gulls, waterfowl, and shorebirds. Some years dozens of snowy owls are spotted. The dike at the end of 88th to 112th provides the best views of waterfowl and shorebirds. Come during high tide for all the birds except the raptors.

WILDLIFE WATCHING ON SKIS

It used to be when winter and heavy snows came to the mountains, the number of humans out and about was pretty small. For the most part, human activity became as dormant as most of the plants and animals. Things sure are different now. In my lifetime two recreational activities have totally changed the face of winter in most mountains that have reliable snowfall—skiing and snowmobiling. I'm lumping together downhill and cross-country skiing, snowboarding, and snowshoeing as skiing because it was the downhill skiing boom of the 1960s that started the winter recreation industry. Many people probably wouldn't consider any of these as part of a natural cycle, but here in the Northwest, winter brings these activities as surely as it brings waterfowl and bald eagles.

The best way to travel on snow to see wildlife, and evidence of wildlife, is on cross-country skis or snowshoes. Cross-country skiing and snowshoeing are the winter equivalents of hiking and can provide unique opportunities for seeing wildlife activity. Of course, you have to practice basic wildlife-watching techniques and be a sneaky skier just as you would be if you were walking. This chapter describes the most common wildlife and signs of wildlife that people see when cross-country skiing or snowshoeing in our region's mountains, although downhill skiers and snowboarders will see some of these animals as well. I consider snowmobiles and wildlife viewing as basically incompatible.

The majority of skiing takes place in coniferous forests above about 4000 feet, and the wildlife in these forests is very similar throughout our region. Because we're dealing with wildlife that is active in winter, we are pretty much limited to the birds and the mammals. Birds are easy to spot any time of year, but mammals are more often known by the signs they leave: tracks, scat, trails, digging, evidence of eating, and sometimes even a part of an animal, like an antler. In general, the lower you are in elevation and the more forested the area you are skiing in, the more wildlife and wildlife signs you will see. Of course, your chances to see wildlife improve the farther you get from snowmobiles, roads, and other humans. January and February are the best time for cross-country skiing in the Northwest, although December and March may be excellent in some years.

The corvids, the family of jays and crows, are very conspicuous almost any time of year. They are intelligent, aggressive, noisy, and bold. Being generalists, corvids will eat a variety of foods and can adapt quickly to new food sources. They have learned that humans often leave edible waste behind them and will carefully check spots where skiers have stopped to eat or where there is human garbage. In our northwestern mountains you'll regularly see four members of this family in winter: the Steller's jay, the gray jay, the Clark's nutcracker, and the common raven.

The blue and black Steller's jay is about the most conspicuous bird of western coniferous forests and readily makes its presence known with its loud, raucous calls. These crested jays range from sea level to timberline, but generally you will see fewer of them the higher you are in the mountains. At higher elevations the Steller's jay is "replaced" by its relatives, the gray jay and the Clark's nutcracker. People often confuse these two high mountain jays. Both are called camp robbers because they will readily snatch food from snacking humans. However, the gray jay is particularly astounding in its boldness and will grab food from picnic tables, packs, tents, people's hands, and even pans on a stove. In winter gray jays travel in flocks and have certainly figured out where the skiers eat. Whenever I stop to eat lunch while cross-country skiing in Oregon, a flock of gray jays will show up to join the meal.

The Clark's nutcracker is named after William Clark of the Lewis and Clark Expedition, who was the first to describe the bird for science. They are more reserved than gray jays in their camp robbing but much noisier and easier to identify with their bold black and white markings in their wings and tail. Clark's nutcrackers are more common the higher and farther east you go. These handsome jays are famous for burying tremendous numbers of seeds for the winter, especially seeds from whitebark pine. They forget where some of their seeds are stashed, making them critically important as planters of the pines.

The common raven is the most wary of the corvids you'll see while in the mountains in winter. Ravens are much too careful to come and snatch food from your hand, but they will keep track of your comings and goings and may check out places where food scraps have been left. However, ravens are big-time scavengers and will be out looking for dead animals. You may see them soaring overhead like a hawk or perched near the top of a tree, checking out the situation. Being one of North America's smartest birds, along with cousin crow, they may display some unusual behaviors, and their range of harsh, raspy, croaky, and rattle-like calls is quite entertaining.

Chickadees announce their presence with their distinctive "chick-a-dee-dee" calls, one of the most common sounds in the woods in winter. Of the three types of chickadees in our region, the most common chickadee companion in our mountains is, of course, the mountain chickadee. Don't you wish all bird names made so much sense? You can tell mountain chickadees from other chickadees by the white line above their eye that breaks up their black cap. But look carefully; the line is sometimes small and hard to see. Chickadees are very active as they search for spiders and insect eggs, larvae, or pupae and are not shy. It is often easy to get close to chickadees and to attract them by imitating their calls or making little "pishing" noises.

Nuthatches are close relatives of the chickadees. Of the three types of nuthatches, the red-breasted nuthatch is more commonly seen and heard than the others. The high, nasal "beep-beep-beep" of the red-breasted nuthatch sounds like a little electric bicycle horn in the distance and is another of the very familiar sounds in northwestern coniferous forests. Nuthatches are well known for their tendency to descend tree trunks upside down as they glean for bugs. This behavior is a good clue for identification. Chickadees and nuthatches often flock together, along with kinglets, and sometimes warblers and downy woodpeckers. These mixed "balls o' birds" of the hyper little insect eaters are a common occurrence in winter woodlands. When you come upon such a mixed flock, be sure to look them over because you never know how many different species you may have.

Woodpeckers eat insect larvae that are living under the bark of dead and dying trees. Because of this year-round food source, many woodpeckers don't have to migrate and are common winter birds. While skiing you can expect to see the downy and its larger look-alike, the hairy woodpecker, and the northern flicker. In lodgepole pine forests you'll sometimes encounter the black-backed woodpecker and in ponderosa pine forests, the white-headed woodpecker. Traveling farther north into British Columbia will improve your chances of seeing the rarer three-toed woodpecker. You may see sapsuckers and the pileated woodpecker, largest woodpecker in North America, but these are more common at lower elevations.

Several finches and sparrows are common breeders in the mountains and are often present in the winter, although they commonly descend to lower elevations if conditions are too harsh. Such birds are called altitudinal migrants—their movement depends on the recent weather. Dark-eyed juncos, evening grosbeaks, pine siskins, and red crossbills are the most common of these mountain seed eaters. Seeing a flock of juncos flying away from you as they flash their white tail feathers is a common winter sight. Red crossbills are the most unpredictable of these four because they travel long distances searching for good seed crops.

With mammals, you're more likely to see their tracks or signs than to see the animals themselves. Interest in nature awareness and the skills of animal tracking has undergone a resurgence, and books by Tom Brown and Jon Young have helped to boost the rebirth. Jon Young, one of Tom's protégés, established the Wilderness Awareness School in Washington, and the Northwest is now a center of the "tracking renaissance." There are many good books on this skill, but nothing beats the experience of "dirt time," getting out in the wild by yourself or with a mentor and studying the real thing.

In some ways, snow tracking is easier than other types of tracking. It may be more difficult to see clear footprints in snow, but it is easier to see the overall pattern of tracks. The number of possible mammals in any one area in the winter is not that large, so reading the pattern of the gait and the general shape of the tracks is often enough to identify the animal. It's really fun when you can tell what the animal was doing and sometimes even see a little story unfold involving more than one animal. I'll never forget seeing a long, clear trail of a snowshoe hare and then discovering where a bobcat came along, discovered the trail, and trotted off to see if it could get a meal.

One of the most common tracks seen is indeed that of the snowshoe hare, named for its huge hind feet that are heavily furred for travel over snow. The distinctive tracks with two large snowshoe-shaped prints in front and two smaller, round prints just behind them are easy to recognize with practice. This hare is sometimes called the varying hare because in most of its range its coat changes color from brown in the summer to white in the winter. Rabbits and hares never hibernate so they are active all winter searching for food.

Most people recognize the familiar tracks of deer with their two side-by-side, curved hoof prints for each foot. Unfortunately, other hoofed mammals have tracks that look very similar to deer tracks so you may not be able to tell, even armed with books, if your animal is a deer, bighorn sheep, or mountain goat. Of course, this is where knowing the habits and habitats of the different animals helps. Most places you will be skiing; any tracks that look like deer will be deer. If they look like deer but are bigger, especially wider, you have elk tracks. However, if you're in the Selkirk Mountains of northeastern Washington and southeastern British Columbia and you find really big "deer" tracks, you could have moose tracks.

At the other size extreme are the tiny footprints of mice and shrews, which are both active in the winter. Let's face it, telling apart the small and similar tracks of mice, voles, and shrews may require more study and practice than most folks will invest. But yay for squirrels. The tracks of tree squirrels are plenty big to see and are very common. Because squirrels are active during the day you might actually get a look at one. Tree squirrel tracks look like little rabbit tracks with the long, narrow prints of the hind feet in front of the small, round prints of the front feet. The big difference between rabbit and squirrel tracks is that the round front foot tracks tend to be even with each other in squirrel tracks but staggered, one farther back, in rabbit tracks.

As you might guess, tree squirrel tracks usually start and end at the base of a tree. There are three tree squirrels you could encounter: the chickaree or Douglas squirrel; the red squirrel; and the uncommon western gray squirrel. The chickaree (Douglas squirrel) is the most likely one in the Cascades, Olympics, and Coast Mountains. East of the Cascades and Coast Mountains, and interestingly on Vancouver Island, the red squirrel replaces its close relative the chickaree. The large, handsome western gray squirrel is much less common and fairly restricted to proper habitat on the eastern slope of the Cascades in the US.

Coyote and fox prints are a good possibility, but their tracks look like those of our domestic dogs. Sometimes you'll find scat on the trail, which can be very helpful for telling dog sign from the wild canids. Your friends may laugh as you kneel in the snow to examine dog poop. No doubt you have had experience examining dog scat on your lawn, and you know that dog poop basically looks like dog food, just a bit reformed. Coyote or fox scat, on the other hand, looks quite different with fur, bones, seeds, insect parts, or any combination of these in it.

When trying to distinguish dog tracks from coyote or fox tracks, think of the difference in the behavior of these animals. The dog tracks will usually run all over the place, in circles and back and forth and all around people's tracks. The tracks of foxes and coyotes will not be intertwined with people's tracks and will look like the animal knows where it's going and what it's doing. Let's face it: the dog's tracks just look goofy. The wild canid's tracks will usually be in a straight line and will often follow a natural feature such as a hedgerow, the base of a cliff, or a stream. Telling fox and coyote apart is tough to do in snow, but coyotes are much more common in more places.

Other possible mammal tracks include those of weasels, river otter, beaver, porcupine, bear, bobcat, and mountain lion. At lower elevations raccoon, skunk, and opossum are possible, but these animals generally stay below the snow line.

WILDLIFE WATCHING ON SKIS BEST BETS

You'll find numerous commercial guide books as well as a variety of maps that cover the fabulous cross-country skiing and snowshoeing opportunities in the Northwest. Unfortunately, trail maps and other printed information tend to be locally produced and are not easy to obtain. Often information for a particular area in a national forest is available only at the district ranger station. In addition to the Web sites, contact the headquarters for any specific national forests in which you are interested.

▶ WILDLIFE WATCHING ON SKIS BEST BETS OREGON

The Deschutes and Mount Hood national forests have the most cross-country ski areas in Oregon. Check with the Deschutes National Forest headquarters in Bend and the Mount Hood information center in Welches for maps and the latest information. The Umpqua and the Willamette National forests also may have maps.

The Santiam Pass Winter Recreation Area off US Hwy 20 near the Hoodoo downhill ski area is partially in the Deschutes National Forest and partially in the Willamette National Forest. Over the years trails in this area have been good for woodpeckers, including the uncommon black-backed and three-toed woodpeckers. Another well-known area shared by the two national forests is the Willamette Pass–Odell Lake area. It has a variety of cross-country ski trails, as well as a small downhill area. Odell Lake Lodge Resort serves as a center for this area. Another major cross-country ski area where black-backed woodpeckers have been reliable is the Swampy Lakes area on Century Dr, about 16 miles west of Bend in the Deschutes National Forest. The gray jays here are the boldest I've ever seen; they have the shelters under close surveillance and show up quickly when the gorp appears.

▶ WILDLIFE WATCHING ON SKIS BEST BETS WASHINGTON

Washington's Methow Valley has become the Northwest's cross-country skiing paradise. Amazingly, this fairly isolated valley has one of the largest cross-country ski trail systems in North America. The nonprofit Methow Valley Sport Trails Association, which is the information center for skiing, snowshoeing, and other recreation in the valley, maintains the 124 miles of machine-groomed trails. A variety of lodging, from deluxe resort to camping, is available, and a central reservation center is available for the whole valley. The Methow Valley is home to Washington's largest mule deer herd so the chances of seeing deer are excellent. Coyotes are heard regularly at night and are seen occasionally along the river bottoms. Skiers have even sighted mountain lions.

Mount Rainier NP is a popular area for cross-country skiing, snowshoeing, and for the really hearty, snow camping. The heavily used Paradise Visitor Center is the center for daytime activities. Year-round lodging is available at Longmire, and other trails are in that area. More isolated and better for wildlife viewing is the less frequently used northwestern corner of the park where people ski up the Carbon River, some as far as Mowich Lake. Contact the park for current information and recommendations for areas. Skiers sometimes see elk in the lower river bottoms.

The Gifford Pinchot National Forest, especially the Wind River and Mount Adams districts, has produced a lot of printed materials on winter recreation over the years. One of the most popular areas in the GP is the Upper Wind River Winter Sports Area. It has a large area of improved cross-country ski routes, without snowmobiles, based out of the Oldman Pass Sno-Park. The Wind River Valley is winter range for deer and elk so your chances of spotting a few are good here. One disadvantage to the Wind River area is low eleva-tion (3000 feet) so the season isn't long, and conditions are good during only the coldest weather and after ample snowfall at low elevations. Contact the Wind River district office about conditions before going.

Washington has an extensive non-motorized sports Sno-Parks system of about 40 Sno-Parks where snowmobiles are not allowed and where trails are marked or groomed for cross-country skiing and snowshoeing. Some of these areas, the ones with the most trails and grooming, have a fee in addition to the Sno-Park permit. Another group of Sno-Parks does allow snowmobiles, so make sure you know which is which. A directory of sites and downloadable trail maps are at the Office of Winter Recreation's Web site. You can also buy a brochure, *Groomed Cross-Country Ski Trails Guide*, at a number of private vendors that are also listed on the Web site. One disadvantage to some of the Sno-Parks is their proximity to highways and their popularity; the traffic and human activity will keep some animals away. Some of the non-motorized Sno-Parks also have dog sledding. As much as I like huskies, they are probably not your best companions for wildlife watching. But I can see making a special trip to one of these parks just for the entertainment value of seeing some dog sleds in action.

▶ WILDLIFE WATCHING ON SKIS BEST BETS BRITISH COLUMBIA

Southwestern British Columbia's mainland has three provincial parks that offer cross-country skiing with opportunities for viewing wildlife: Cypress, Mount Seymour, and Garibaldi. Farther to the east is Manning PP. The BC Parks Web site includes information on these parks as well as printable high-quality maps.

Manning PP, 130 miles east of Vancouver in the Cascade Mountains, is a favorite for cross-country skiing. Manning has a wide range of skiing possibilities, from beginning and intermediate groomed trails to backcountry overnight adventuring. For those not wanting to spend winter nights in the woods there is the resort area with lodging, restaurant, store, and equipment rentals. There is also a small downhill ski area, ice skating rink, and snow playgrounds for kids. As in all BC Parks the developed ski areas and resort are managed by a private concessionaire, in this case Manning Park Resort. As usual, you will see the most wildlife away from the action around the resort. The area recommended the most for wildlife is Strawberry Flats.

Just north of Vancouver are Mount Seymour and Cypress provincial parks. Cypress has the most groomed ski trails of the two and both have backcountry skiing for experienced skiers. Both also have downhill ski areas. Neither park is big, by Canadian standards, and cross-country areas are not extensive, but both areas are popular because they are close to the Vancouver metropolitan area. Despite heavy use, Canadian naturalists still recommend them for winter wildlife viewing.

Garibaldi PP has extensive backcountry skiing and snowshoeing possibilities but no groomed trails. All the main trails in the park are available for skiing and snowshoeing but are only suitable for more experienced skiers with alpine touring or telemark skis. Snowshoes are probably more suitable than skis in most of the park. Most skiing is done in the Diamond Head Area in the southwestern corner of the park where marked trails and shel-

ters are available. Red Heather Ridge is a good day trip, suitable for intermediates, and it has a small day shelter. This trail continues to an overnight shelter at Elfin Lakes, which can be used as a base camp for skiing other areas in this part of the park, but this is definitely a snow camping trip for those who know what they're doing.

On Vancouver Island Mount Washington Ski Resort is a major ski area on the border of Strathcona PP, the largest park on the island. Although the downhill resort area is all hustle and bustle, the Raven Lodge serves as a base for cross-country skiing and snowshoeing into the wonderfully named Forbidden Plateau area in Strathcona, a wilderness area with no motorized vehicles. Mount Washington Resort grooms 35 miles of cross-country ski trails that require a fee to use, but the rest of the area is free backcountry skiing or snowshoeing. To get to Mount Washington head northwest on the Inland Island Hwy 19 out of Courtenay, take the Strathcona Pkwy exit (Exit 130), and then follow the signs.

SWANS

When I first moved to the Northwest and saw swans I was astounded. I had never lived in a place where you could regularly see these magnificent birds. I haven't quite gotten used to them yet—they still seem exotic and special, much too extraordinary to be called a common winter resident, which is what they are in much of our region. Many people don't realize how big swans are, but with an average weight just under 30 pounds and a record of 38 pounds for males, the trumpeter swan may well be the heaviest flying animal in the world (the kori bustard and mute swan are the other contenders). Not many birds have a wingspan greater than the 8-foot wingspan of trumpeters. They truly deserve our respect and admiration.

Of the seven species of swans in the world, three live in North America, including the Pacific Northwest. The tundra swan (formerly called whistling swan) and the trumpeter swan are native. The mute swan from Europe has been introduced in many places and is now established in parts of the eastern United States and on southern Vancouver Island. The mute swan, considered a deleterious species, is actually being controlled in some states. Because mute swans are not native or well established and occur in very limited areas, they are not included here.

Tundra and trumpeter swans are very difficult to tell apart and often occur together, so you'll need to carefully read your field guides and get some practice before you can separate them consistently. One reliable way to tell tundras and trumpeters apart is by their voices, but that takes plenty of practice in the field and the birds have to oblige by calling. Birdsong CDs may help. The trumpeter got its name from its loud, low, bugle-like call. Both swans have extra long tracheas (windpipes) that have big loops like a brass horn, which give them a more resonant call.

The simplest field mark on the tundra is a yellow spot in front of the eye. If you see the yellow spot, you know it is a tundra swan. However, some tundras do not have the spot. The yellow spot means something only when it's there. The lack of yellow does not help with identification.

An odd characteristic that I have found useful is the way the two swans hold their long necks. Tundra swans have the basic profile of a goose; their neck just comes out the front of their body and curves up. However, trumpeters will sometimes curve their neck back and lay it on top of their back like a rubber hose. The neck goes back a bit then rises straight up, making it look as though the trumpeter's neck is coming straight up out of its back. I know this sounds pretty strange, and, of course, its neck isn't coming out of its back, but once you see this effect you'll get the idea. They seem to do this more when they're in the water instead of standing around on land. When alert they stick their neck up straight just like the tundra swans do.

Swans exhibit what we would consider model family values. Swans generally mate for life and appear to be very loyal. Both members of the pair select the nest site and build the nest, often using the same site from year to year. Although the female does most of the incubating, the male remains close and guards his mate and the nest. Swans are very territorial—they will defend a large area from other swans and are very aggressive toward intruders, including people.

When the four or five young hatch, both parents attend to them and are very protective. The family unit stays together for the rest of the breeding season and migrates together to wintering grounds. Young swans learn their migration routes on these first flights with their parents. Swans are very strong flyers, some migrating 8000 miles a year, round trip. Some tundras may fly as much as 1000 miles at a time without stopping.

Of the two, the tundra swan is now the most numerous and widespread, outnumbering the trumpeter by about six to one. However, trumpeters are much more common on Vancouver Island. Tundra swans nest in the Arctic tundra and in northern marshes from Alaska across North America to Baffin Island. During migration they can show up almost anywhere in our region in bays, marshes, and lakes. Significant numbers of wintering tundra swans are regularly found in the Puget Sound area, in the lower Columbia River and parts of the Willamette Valley, and at many wildlife refuges east of the Cascades, such as Umatilla, Summer Lake, and the Klamath Basin. Some are also found in coastal bays in Oregon.

The trumpeter swan has had a dramatic and all too familiar history. Before the European invasion, trumpeter swans were widespread and abundant, nesting across half of Canada and Alaska and in at least a dozen of the contiguous states. Like the American bison, they were hunted to the brink of extinction. In the United States in 1932 there were fewer than 70 left, living in the Yellowstone area. Red Rock Lakes National Wildlife Refuge was established in Montana to protect this last remnant population. This group survived and grew until it reached the maximum number the area could support. Some of the swans were then taken from Red Rock Lakes and transplanted into other wildlife refuges in the west, including Malheur NWR in Oregon and Turnbull NWR in Washington.

The transplants had varying success, and for awhile the future for trumpeters remained bleak. However, in the 1950s other populations of trumpeters were discovered in Alaska and northwestern Canada, where 75% of the world's trumpeters breed today. With protection, habitat management, and the swans' adaptation to winter feeding on farmlands, the population has risen to a high of 35,000 in 2005. They have been off the Endangered Species List since 1968.

▶ SWANS BEST BETS OREGON

Tundra swans are common winter residents in much of Oregon, and many of the wildlife refuges in the state will have wintering swans. The biggest population spends the winter in the lower Columbia River, from Portland to the mouth, and at Ridgefield NWR in Washington, just across the Columbia River from Sauvie Island in Oregon. The birds treat Ridgefield, Sauvie Island, and other nearby wetlands as parts of one big system and go back and forth between them. The number of trumpeter swans seen mixed in with tundras has increased since the 1990s. If you are up for an identification challenge, get out your spotting scope and look them over carefully.

You'll occasionally see tundra swans in marshes, flooded fields, and lakes throughout much of the Willamette Valley, especially the northern end, as well as in the Fernhill Wetlands south of Forest Grove. They also occur up and down the coast in estuaries, especially in the Siuslaw River Estuary at Florence.

To get to the Suislaw River estuary, from the north on US Hwy 101, drive through the town of Florence, and then cross the Siuslaw River on the bridge. About 0.75 mile south of the river, turn right onto South Jetty Rd (signed, fee). Follow it as it goes west and then turns to head north. At 4.25 miles from US 101 there is a parking area on your left (with outhouses), where you can scope the area to the east of the road. Tundra swans winter here in large numbers, and the area is also good for other waterfowl and raptors in winter and migrating shorebirds in the fall. Continue north 5.5 miles to the parking area on your right where you can look out over the estuary. From here continue to drive north, and then west onto the jetty road. Keep driving until it gets too rough or too crowded to continue. Park carefully—be sure other cars can get by and you

have room to maneuver when you leave. Don't get stuck in the sand. You can walk out the jetty as far as you want, but the surface continues to worsen as you go.

Trumpeter swans occur in small numbers and are unpredictable in most of Oregon. A few trumpeters can turn up wherever you see lots of tundra swans, particularly during migration, so check groups of swans carefully. In general, the farther north you go, the better your chance of seeing trumpeters. Small numbers have been seen in the Willamette Valley in recent years. The two most reliable places to see trumpeter swans in Oregon are Malheur NWR and Summer Lake WA.

Malheur NWR is unusual because it has the only year-round population of trumpeter swans in Oregon. Some of the first trumpeter swans that were taken from Red Rocks Lakes NWR and introduced to other wildlife refuges were released at Malheur NWR, where their descendants live today. Because they are from the nonmigratory population at Red Rocks, they are there all year. Efforts have been made to get some of these swans migrating to Summer Lake for the winter where conditions are a bit milder.

Summer Lake WA, managed by ODFW, has a small number of trumpeter swans in the winter but is better known for its large number of wintering tundra swans. The best times to visit are in winter—from the end of hunting season in late January until March 15—and early fall—from August 15 until hunting season begins (usually the second weekend in October). During other times various roads and areas are closed because of nesting activity or hunting. February is the best time to see both swan species, as well as a good variety of other waterfowl and some wintering raptors.

Before you plan a trip check with the wildlife area to get hunting and closure dates.

Summer Lake WA and the tiny town of Summer Lake are about halfway between the towns of Lakeview and La Pine, on State Hwy 31 in south central Oregon. Summer Lake has a store, gas station, motel, and cafe. The headquarters for the wildlife area is across the street from the cafe and motel. Here you will find maps, a restroom, and, if you're lucky, a staff member who can give you the latest tips on where to find swans and other wildlife.

Road closures are always a possibility because of weather or maintenance, but the main tour route road is usually open and in good condition. Remember, when driving through a wildlife area or refuge your car is your blind, and the birds will be less frightened if you stay in it. If you drive the tour route loop as described, counterclockwise, you'll see most birds on the outside of the loop, on your right.

From headquarters take the tour route road (Lint Canal Rd) which heads east, with a few bends, for a couple of miles. The road then turns left and heads north until it joins County Rd A-17. Turn left onto A-17 and head west until you rejoin Hwy 31 near the roadside rest. Cruise the tour route road in standard birdwatching style, going slowly while looking very carefully in all directions and making your passengers nervous. In the first part of the tour route there are two roads that head south on Windbreak Dike and Bullgate Dike, and then dead end. It's worth going down these roads if there's plenty of water and the area "looks birdy." Sometimes these roads are closed.

▶ SWANS BEST BETS WASHINGTON

Ridgefield NWR is a reliable place to see lots of tundra swans and often a few trumpeters. The refuge's excellent auto tour route and the education program to get people to stay in their cars has tremendously improved wildlife viewing in the River S Unit. The last few winters when I've driven the route I've seen 700 to 900 swans right out the car window. Folks have gotten with the program. I can tell the birds like the new plan and are more relaxed.

You can park and get out at a couple of places, mainly at the observation blind. This is a must stop regardless of whether someone just needs to use the fancy outhouse there. Aided with a scope, the parking area offers good views of surrounding areas. A short, level path leads to the new blind, which has outstanding views. The path goes through a nice stretch of riparian forest that can be very lively with songbirds.

To get to the refuge take the Interstate 5 Ridgefield exit (Exit 14), about 13 miles north of the Columbia River, and then head west on State Hwy 501. As you come into the town of Ridgefield you'll notice that the north–south cross streets are numbered. To get to the River S Unit, the area with the most wetlands and most waterbirds (and hunting at times), turn left and head south on South 9th St. In a few blocks 9th St turns into Hillhurst as it climbs the hill south of town. In just under one mile you'll see a dirt road to the right with a refuge sign and an automatic gate. Be sure to note the posted hours and don't get locked in. Take this dirt road, which becomes the auto tour route, through the River S Unit. At the start of the tour route are vault toilets, an informational kiosk, and hunters' check station. You'll usually see a clipboard hanging from the check station, in an obvious location, where people can record their wildlife sightings as well as their attempts at outdoor humor. It's pretty easy to

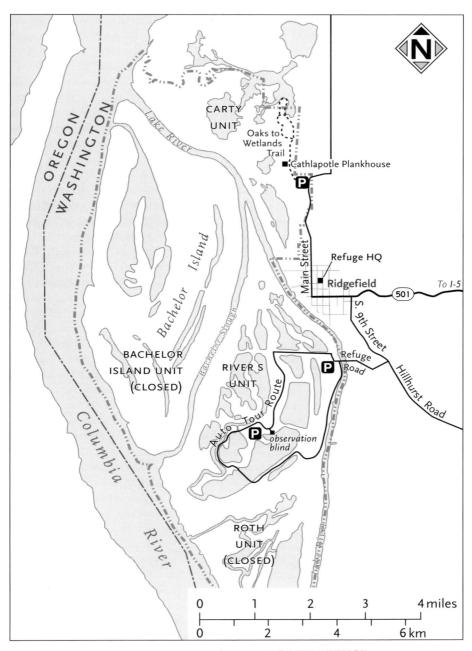

OREGON

WASHINGTON

Lake River

CARTY
UNIT

Oaks to
Wetlands
Trail

■Cathlapotle Plankhouse

P

Bachelor Island

Bachelor Slough

BACHELOR
ISLAND UNIT
(CLOSED)

RIVER S
UNIT

Auto Tour Route

Columbia River

Main Street

Refuge HQ

■ Ridgefield

501

To I-5

S. 9th Street

Refuge Road

Hillhurst Road

P

P

observation
blind

ROTH
UNIT
(CLOSED)

Lake River

| 0 | 1 | 2 | 3 | 4 miles |
| 0 | 2 | 4 | 6 km |

RIDGEFIELD NATIONAL WILDLIFE REFUGE

tell which entries are by the knowledgeable wildlife watchers and which ones are by folks who haven't been outside much.

About 3000 tundra and a few trumpeter swans hang out in the myriad of marshes, islands, and sandbars in the estuary of the Columbia River between Longview, Washington, and Astoria, Oregon. Almost 40,000 acres of this area is included in the Julia Butler Hansen Refuge for the Columbian White-Tailed Deer and Lewis and Clark National Wildlife Refuge, but most of this acreage is actually out in the river and accessible only by boat. Part of the J. B. Hansen Refuge is on the mainland, however, and you can sometimes see swans when driving Steamboat Slough Rd through the refuge.

Both swans are found in Willapa Bay, north of the mouth of the Columbia, which is covered in April (Brant Migration). On the Columbia, south of Willapa Bay, is the town of Ilwaco. Just north of Ilwaco on State Hwy 103 is Black Lake, which often has Trumpeter swans.

A mixed population of tundra and trumpeter swans spends the winter in western Skagit County, one of the Northwest's best winter birding areas and the best place for seeing both species in good numbers. Swans can be found in or near the Skagit WA or in the fields of the Skagit and Samish flats, especially during high tides. Another area in Skagit County that has been a big favorite of trumpeters for years is around Clear Lake, northeast of Mount Vernon.

Near both the town and body of water called Clear Lake are three good areas to check for trumpeter swans. First let's go to Beaver Lake. From I-5 take the College Way (State Hwy 538) exit (Exit 227), and then head east through Mount Vernon. In 3.5 miles turn left and drive north on State Hwy 9 toward Sedro-Woolley. After 2.6 miles turn right and head

south on Beaver Lake Rd. A WDFW access area, with a small boat launch and parking, is one mile farther at the south end of Beaver Lake. From here you can see the entire lake.

The second spot is Clear Lake itself in the town of Clear Lake. Return the way you came, but just before you get back to Hwy 9, turn right onto South Front St and head north into town. The lake will be on your right. The best viewing place is from Clear Lake Park, in the town of Clear Lake, on the shores of Clear Lake. After checking out the Clear Lake-named things, get back on Hwy 9 headed north.

But don't go too far. Access to the third swan site is just a few blocks north of the town's center on Frances Rd. Actually, Frances Rd is on your left; Old Day Creek Rd is on your right. Turn left to head west on Frances Rd, and drive just 0.75 mile until Frances takes a turn to the left. You'll see DeBay Isle Rd angled a bit to the right. This new reserve opened to the public in 2001. You should be able to drive down DeBay Isle Rd during open hours, but if you are stopped by a locked gate, park near the intersection with Frances Rd and walk down the road. When you leave this area you can make a return loop back to Mount Vernon and I-5. Continue on Frances, which eventually turns left and heads south, and then turns into LaVenture Rd, which will take you back to College Way. You could spot more swans, plenty of other waterfowl, and raptors as you drive through the Skagit River bottomlands on Frances Rd.

Both swans are scattered throughout the Puget Sound area and can be found in river mouths and bays or in fields feeding on grain. Tundras regularly winter in some of the wetlands in eastern Washington such as the Potholes Reservoir area and McNary NWR, but if these areas freeze up, the swans will head south or to the Columbia River at places like Umatilla NWR.

▶ SWANS BEST BETS BRITISH COLUMBIA

Almost one third of the world's trumpeter swans winter on Vancouver Island and along the coasts of the Strait of Georgia. Trumpeters can be seen in many of the island's estuaries and other wetlands, but two places really stand out as Best Bets.

The largest single group of wintering trumpeter swans in the world, as many as 3000 and increasing, spends the winter in Comox Harbor and the farmlands of the Comox Valley. Because this population is globally significant, the Canadian Wildlife Service, Ducks Unlimited Canada, other conservation groups, and local farmers have established the Comox Valley Waterfowl Management Project. The project has been a great success and the community takes great pride in "its swans."

The swans can be seen in Comox Harbor or in farm fields north of Comox. Harbor viewing is best during high tide; the higher the better. There are three places for viewing the harbor although you will sometimes be quite far from the birds. Two are along the southwest shore where the Island Highway (Hwy 19A) runs parallel to the shore. The first is in the small town of Royston from Marine Dr. Get onto Marine Dr at its intersection with Hwy 19A or take any of the streets in central Royston north from Hwy 19A to Marine Dr. Cruise Marine Dr until you find a good place to park and view the harbor. The second place is just over one mile northwest of Royston off Hwy 19A. At the intersection with Fraser and Millard streets, turn right onto Millard and drive until it intersects Sandpiper Rd at the edge of the harbor. Park here—there are actually benches for birdwatchers.

The third spot is a viewing platform with interpretive signs at the far northwestern end of the harbor where the Courtenay River enters. In Courtenay Hwy 19A crosses the river and intersects Comox Rd, which heads east to the town of Comox. In less than 0.25 mile toward Comox from this main intersection, you'll see the viewing platform.

The swans feed in many of the farm fields in the valley, but two seem to be favorites. Comox Bay farm is on Comox Rd, just east of Hwy 19A after crossing the Courtenay River. In 1998 the Pacific Estuary Conservation Program and affiliates purchased this farm, formerly Farquharson Farm, to protect prime waterfowl habitat.

The other popular fields are along Knight Rd, northeast of Comox. To get on the best section of Knight Rd take Comox Rd into Comox. Just after the main part of town turn left onto Pritchard Rd and drive just over 2 miles until it intersects Knight Rd. Turn right and watch the fields to your right as you drive along Knight. An interesting way to return to Comox is to take Knight until it turns into Lazo Rd, stopping at Point Holmes to look for waterbirds and seals. A quick side trip to Kye Bay, off Knight Rd, might also provide some good sightings. Take Lazo back into town, possibly stopping at Goose Spit, covered in April (Brant Migration).

Martindale Flats, a favored area by local birders for swans, other waterfowl, and raptors, is about 8 miles north of Victoria, east of Butchart Gardens. Martindale Rd and Island View Rd are less than one mile apart and both head due east from Hwy 17. Fields on both sides of both roads can be outstanding for birding, especially when flooded. Island View Rd ends at Island View Beach Park, which provides excellent views of waterfowl and seabirds in Cordova Bay.

On the mainland, the farm fields around Delta and Ladner, south of Vancouver, are a regular winter hangout for both swans. You can explore any of the roads in the area that go through farmland, but two spots are particularly worth checking. Drive the roads south of the Ladner Trunk Rd north of Boundary Bay—a map of the area is in August (Fall Shorebird Migration)—or visit the George C. Reifel Migratory Bird Sanctuary on Westham Island. The swans have developed quite a taste for fermenting pieces of potatoes left in the fields after harvesting.

FROZEN WATERFALLS

Life depends on water, so it's no surprise that water has always been a powerful symbol to humans. Moving water possesses a particularly strong fascination to people; many can watch transfixed, for long periods of time, waves breaking on a shore or a stream flowing over its rocky bed. It's to be expected, then, that people love waterfalls. Here is moving water at its most dramatic—plunging into space or cascading over rocks, constantly changing its shape yet maintaining a character unique to that waterfall. And what could be more exhilarating than getting blasted by the spray of a big waterfall on a hot day?

The Pacific Northwest is the perfect place for waterfalls because we've got plenty of what it takes to make them—lots of water and lots of high places for it to fall from. If you want to become a serious waterfall watcher, you'll need *Waterfall Lover's Guide—Pacific Northwest* (4th ed.) by Gregory Plumb. This book describes (are you ready?) 634 waterfalls in Oregon, Washington, and Idaho. Included are directions on how to get to them all.

Waterfalls are always changing because the amount of water varies, but a much more dramatic change can take place during the coldest winter weather. Waterfalls can freeze, sometimes completely, into fantastic natural ice sculptures. With larger waterfalls some water usually keeps flowing, while an amazing assortment of ice collects on the surrounding cliffs and in the path of the fall itself. Spray from the falls forms beautiful, delicate crystals on nearby rocks or plants. It is a unique and ephemeral winter display that doesn't happen every year for most falls. One thing you can count on when you go out in freezing weather to look at frozen waterfalls—no crowds. But surprisingly many people actually do bundle up and face the cold to see and photograph this event. The ideal time to go is on a sunny day with the temperature just below freezing and very little wind, after a stretch of really cold temperatures.

The Columbia River Gorge and Silver Falls SP have more impressive, accessible waterfalls in a small area than anywhere else in North America. They also are exceptionally beautiful places with many other natural attractions besides their waterfalls. You can usually get to these waterfalls in freezing winter weather without risking your life on dangerous icy roads. Always a big plus in my book.

The Columbia River is the largest river in volume in the New World that flows into the Pacific Ocean. This huge river has maintained its channel despite the Cascade Mountains rising up around it. The Columbia River Gorge is one of the great scenic wonders of North America, and fortunately it is now protected, to a degree, by the 1986 legislation that established the Columbia River Gorge National Scenic Area, the first in the nation. People seem to appreciate how astounding the Columbia River and its gorge really are after that designation. The Gorge, as it is commonly known, is appreciated for its geology, scenery, wildlife, wildflowers, economic importance, human history, and recreational uses and is the subject of many fine books. For now the question is, Why so many waterfalls in the Gorge?

The Oregon side of the 80-mile long Columbia River Gorge has at least 50 recognized, accessible waterfalls. To understand why there are so many, we need to look at the geologic past and how the Gorge was formed. An ancient Columbia River flowed west to the ocean at least 40 million years ago, long before the Cascade Mountains were formed. About 15 million years ago, huge cracks opened in the earth's crust near the Oregon, Washington, and Idaho border and massive flows of lava poured out, eventually covering 60,000 square miles of eastern Washington and northeastern Oregon and even reaching the coast. These flows, called the Columbia River Basalts, piled up like a giant layer cake, one on top of the other giving the cliffs their characteristic layered look. At Multnomah Falls you can clearly see six different layers and near Bridal Veil geologists have found 16 exposed layers.

Earth movement and volcanic activity that occurred over the next several million years uplifted the land and formed the Cascades. The Columbia River continued to carve its valley through the layers of basalt as fast as the land rose around it. By the time the Pleistocene Epoch started, about 2 million years ago, the Columbia River had carved a deep V-shaped valley down through the rising layers of basalt.

Toward the end of the Pleistocene, about 15,000 years ago, a series of cataclysmic floods blasted through the Gorge and scoured out everything except the hard basalt. The result was a broad, U-shaped valley with steep cliffs. The side streams flowing into the Columbia River Valley then ended abruptly at cliff faces and plunged to the river below. Our present-day waterfall paradise was born. The amazing story of these floods, called the Bretz Floods to honor geologist Harlan Bretz who first proposed their occurrence, can be found in several books and videos. How come there are so few waterfalls on the Washington side of the Gorge? There were more, but the layers of rock in the Gorge are tilted slightly southward. This has resulted in many landslides on the Washington side that have destroyed the cliff faces and their waterfalls.

▶ FROZEN WATERFALLS BEST BETS OREGON

Thanks to this unique set of circumstances we now have the ultimate waterfall-watching site for any time of year. In the 13 miles between Corbett and Ainsworth SP, you can see five major waterfalls between 150- and 620-feet high within a very short walk from your car. Another six big falls, all over 100 feet, can be seen by driving 10 more miles and taking short hikes, the longest being 3.5 miles round trip.

Interstate 84 goes through The Gorge and in places is paralleled by the old Columbia River Scenic Highway, an engineering marvel of its time and a fascinating story in itself. At some exits you can leave I-84 and get on the Historic Columbia River Highway, often called the Scenic Highway or just the old highway. Not all exits are complete interchanges with access and exits in both directions. The five biggest and easiest falls to see are all on the Scenic Highway between the Corbett exit (Exit 22), and the Dodson/Ainsworth SP exit (Exit 35), both complete interchanges.

From Portland, take the Corbett exit, drive up the cliff to the town of Corbett and turn left onto the Scenic Highway in Corbett. Head east and in 2 miles you'll reach the Women's Forum SP where you can get the classic scenic view up the Gorge. One mile farther east and you'll reach Vista House Visitor Center on Crown Point. From Vista House, head east on the Scenic Highway and watch for signs for the various waterfall areas. The Big Five going from west to east are Latourell Falls, Bridal Veil Falls, Wahkeena Falls, Multnomah Falls, and Horsetail Falls. Multnomah Falls is the second highest year-round waterfall in the United States and the busiest tourist attraction in Oregon. At its base is a visitor area with a Forest Service interpretive center, restrooms, a restaurant and a snack bar, and a gift shop. Summer weekends are crowded.

My picks for the next most spectacular falls within easy hiking distance are Upper Latourell Falls, Triple Falls, Ponytail Falls, Elowah Falls, Wahclella Falls, Metlako Falls, and Punch Bowl Falls. All are located between Corbett and Cascade Locks.

Silver Falls SP is Oregon's largest state park. It is 25 miles east of Salem in the foothills of the Cascades. The same lava flows that created the Gorge also formed the bedrock of Silver Falls, again creating the right conditions for many waterfalls. The Trail of Ten Falls is just under

7 miles long and has views of 10 waterfalls, half of them over 100-feet high. From Salem take State Hwy 22 east, then turn onto State Hwy 214 and take it to the park. The main visitor facilities are at the Nature Lodge built by the Civilian Conservation Corps and located near South Falls, the highest in the park. Follow signs to the lodge or the day use area. At the lodge you can get the park map that shows the trails and the waterfalls. A shorter route of 2.5 miles from the Winter Falls parking area will take you by five falls. If it is cold enough to freeze waterfalls then some of the trails will be impassable, even with snowshoes.

▶ FROZEN WATERFALLS BEST BETS WASHINGTON

Unfortunately, the best areas in Washington for concentrations of waterfalls are where roads are usually closed in winter and access is just too dangerous, if not impossible.

JANUARY'S NATURE NUGGETS

JANUARY SKIES The cold skies of winter, when less moisture, pollen, and pollution are in the air, are the clearest. Winter is also the time when the region of the sky most astronomers consider the richest is in full view. In winter you can actually see all the constellations if you stay up all night, but for practical purposes those constellations typically thought of as the winter constellations are those that are high in the sky and easily seen between about 7 p.m. and 9 p.m. The most well known is Orion, one of the most distinct and easiest to identify, and the constellation with the brightest stars. If you use Orion's belt as a pointer, toward the horizon you will see Sirius, brightest star in the sky (after our sun) and part of Canis Major (the Big Dog). Other classic winter constellations are Taurus, Gemini, Auriga (the Charioteer), and Perseus. In addition, you can see the circumpolar constellations that are visible almost all year—the Big and Little Dipper, Cassiopeia, Cepheus, Cygnus, and Draco. The largest meteor shower of the year is the Quadrantids. It occurs January 1–4, before dawn, and appears to be coming from the constellation Boötes. There's a challenge for the hearty folks who don't mind standing around outside at the coldest hour in the coldest month of the year.

SMELT Late January and early February are the peak of the smelt run in the Columbia. These little fish have many names: Columbia River smelt, candlefish, the Native American eulachon (pronounced YOU-la-kon), and the slang hooligan. These prolific fish return by the millions to spawn in tributaries of the lower Columbia and provide an unequaled feast for dozens of predators who join in the mass, multi-species, feeding frenzy. Clouds of gulls swarm over spawning areas and are joined by other fish-eating birds such as cormorants, mergansers, and a few loons and grebes. California sea lions and harbor seals swim up the river to join the gluttony. Humans also catch them, sometimes to eat but mainly for bait or animal food. Just which tributaries of the lower Columbia the smelt will use varies from year to year and includes the Kalama, Lewis, and Sandy rivers. However, the best bet most years is the Cowlitz River where the town of Kelso, Washington, apparently has proclaimed itself the Smelt Capital of the World. In the town of Kelso take Allen St west to cross the Cowlitz River, and then turn right and drive north on State Hwy 411, which parallels the river. You could see the birds and people fishing anywhere along the river from Kelso to Castle Rock, Washington.

STARLINGS Although they are scorned by most birders, European starlings form some of the largest flocks of birds you'll ever see when they gather to roost in winter. Drive over the Broadway Bridge in Portland around sunset during the winter and you may see tens of thousands of starlings settling on the bridge for the night. Be sure your windshield wipers are working and have lots of fluid.

WINTER SURVIVAL: A CLOSER LOOK

For animals living in temperate climates, the greatest challenge is often surviving the winter. Problems caused by the colder temperatures are made worse by the concurrent decrease in the food supply. The population of almost every northwest animal is at its lowest at the end of winter after various types of winter mortality have taken their toll. How do the survivors make it?

Where an animal lives will determine the temperature extremes it will have to endure to survive. Animals living in the ocean have it the easiest—the ocean off our coast varies only about 5°F in a year and it never freezes. Most marine animals really don't need any special adaptations for winter weather. The same is true for animals living in large bodies of freshwater that do not freeze. In contrast, animals living high in the mountains or in the eastern parts of Oregon, Washington, and British Columbia may have to endure weeks of temperatures well below freezing. With different kinds of animals living in a variety of habitats, it's not surprising that adaptations for winter survival vary.

To understand these differences, let's clarify what is meant by cold-blooded and warm-blooded, terms that are often poorly understood and inaccurate. Animals that are commonly referred to as cold-blooded, such as reptiles, fish, and insects, are animals that do not produce much heat inside their bodies and whose body temperatures are usually the same as, and change with, their surroundings. They are able to regulate their body temperatures to some extent by moving to different parts of their environment or by behaviors such as basking in the sun. For the most part, though, they are thermal slaves of their environment. Biologists call these animals ectothermic, which means "outside heat."

The animals we call warm-blooded are quite different. Biologists call these animals endothermic ("inside heat"). Endotherms have high rates of metabolism and produce a lot of heat inside their bodies, which is kept in by insulation. They maintain a constant body temperature that is usually quite high in comparison to their environment. In a way, they have freed themselves from the thermal restraints of their environment—but at a cost. Warm-blooded animals equal in body mass to cold-blooded animals will need at least 10 times the food and oxygen to stay alive. It's life in the fast lane and they can't get out.

So why be an endotherm if it means you must constantly work harder to get more food and oxygen? The advantage is that your activity level can be independent of the temperature of your environment. As the temperature drops and an ectotherm gets colder, its bodily functions slow down until it can't even move. In contrast, when the environment gets colder, either at night or during the winter, an endotherm can remain active and take advantage of whatever food is available, including tasty ectotherms too cold to move. Endothermy has allowed some animals to live in the coldest places on Earth, including the polar ice caps.

So who are these amazing endotherms? An outing in cold winter weather makes it obvious—usually the only active animals you will see are birds and mammals. Although some other animals generate considerable heat inside their bodies at certain times, birds and mammals are the only animals that are endothermic all the time. Insulation is the clue: feathers on birds, and fur or thick layers of fat on mammals. Ectotherms don't need insulation and, indeed, none of them have any. You can't keep your pet turtle warm by wrapping it in a blanket.

Based on this difference in metabolism, ectotherms and endotherms adapt to cold weather differently. Ectotherms don't have much choice. As their environment gets colder, so do they. The ectotherms' metabolism and actions keeps slowing down until they become torpid, a state of suspended animation. This would seem disastrous, but it actually works quite well because an animal in a state of torpor needs very little oxygen or food to stay alive. This explains how air-breathing animals like frogs and turtles can spend the winter in the bottom of a pond. They need so little oxygen in their torpid condition that they can get what they need from the surrounding water through their skin. Stored reserves, such as fat, provide the small amounts of energy and nutrients they need. So the basic winter survival strategy for ectotherms is eat hearty while there's plenty of food and you can move around to get it, store as much food as you can in your body; and find a good safe place when it gets too cold to move.

It's basically a pork-up and chill-out life cycle. A good safe place would be one where the temperature doesn't get too low for too long and where predators (endotherms, naturally) can't eat them. This is the most common way the majority of the earth's animals, which are ectotherms, survive the winter. They just get colder and colder and become less and less active until they are in a dormant state just above freezing. But there is a limit to how low their temperature can drop.

The bottom line for surviving the cold is that an animal can't freeze solid. Animals are mostly water and if it freezes solid, the formation of ice ruptures cells and kills the animal. This means that if an ectotherm gets much below 32°F for too long, it will die. Or so biologists thought for years. Scientists have only recently discovered that the wood frog, garter snake, and some insects can actually freeze solid for brief periods of time and then thaw out and still be alive. Exactly how these animals can do this is not entirely known, but we do know that some animals produce natural antifreeze compounds that can stop ice from forming in the blood and tissues. Some animals (for example,

Arctic and Antarctic fish) have even evolved to be active and live out their lives at near to slightly below freezing temperatures through physiological adaptations including these antifreeze compounds and special enzymes that are active at very low temperatures.

The simplest way for any animal, warm- or cold-blooded, to survive the cold is to avoid it entirely. A mobile animal can just leave and go to a warmer place. Birds, with their amazing flying abilities, are the most famous for their migrations, many flying thousands of miles every year. Other kinds of animals also migrate. One of the best known in our region is the gray whale. There is even an insect, the monarch butterfly, which migrates up to 4000 miles round trip.

Many animals, especially mountain dwellers, do not make long migrations but instead make shorter seasonal movements to avoid the harshest weather or to seek food. Deer, elk, bighorn sheep, and mountain goats descend from higher elevations to wintering grounds. Some of our more common winter feeder birds—juncos, pine siskins, evening grosbeaks, and varied thrushes—are summer breeders in the mountains but drop down to lower elevations as the snow piles up and the seeds get scarce. How many show up in downslope towns will vary with winter conditions in the mountains.

An animal doesn't have to travel a long distance to avoid the coldest temperatures. It may be many degrees warmer, not to mention drier and out of the wind, just a foot below the earth's surface. Many animals use burrows, cavities in logs and trees, or cracks and caves in rocks for winter shelter. Snow is a good insulator, and quite a few animals like gophers, mice, pikas, and soil invertebrates remain active under a protective blanket of snow. A thick conifer covered with snow provides excellent shelter for birds, which roost inside.

One question that might occur to the observant outdoor enthusiast in the winter is, Where are all the bugs? Insects are the most abundant life form on the planet and are very conspicuous most of the year, but seem to disappear completely in winter. In the milder western lowlands of our region the eager naturalist can still find plenty of arthropod action in winter, but in the mountains and on the east side, it's bugless. Ancient people wondered about this and the disappearance of many birds and came up with a host of interesting explanations, including animals transforming from one species into another, including humans, and inanimate objects such as dirt and rocks turning into animals.

The actual explanation is quite simple. Most insects, and many other arthropods, don't even try to survive the winter as adults. The adults die in the fall and the species overwinters in one of the other stages in the insect life cycle, most commonly as eggs, but also as larvae or pupae depending on the species. Insect eggs are extremely tough and can withstand more severe conditions than the adults, as can the larvae and pupae of many species. Some insects, which overwinter as adults, can keep ice from forming in their bodies at temperatures of −40°F. And some insects can actually freeze solid and survive, although we don't know how widespread this ability is.

Endotherms—birds and mammals—have a different problem than the ectotherms. The body temperature of an endotherm remains the same because their insulation keeps the heat generated by their high rate of metabolism inside their body. Their main problem becomes getting enough calories to keep their internal furnace burning. Of course, if they have the ability they can migrate to warmer places. Endotherms migrate not so much because the weather is cold but because the food supply becomes inadequate.

Non-migrating endotherms have several adaptations for surviving the cold. Mammals are well known for their thicker winter coats. In winter we often see birds fluffed up and poofy, making the thickest layer of dead air space possible in their "down parka." To increase heat production endotherms can actually increase their metabolism. The most obvious sign of this is shivering—small, rapid, repetitive muscle contractions that generate heat. But this requires energy.

A change in diet can provide the extra calories needed to stay warm. Fat has twice the calories per ounce compared to carbohydrates, and some animals seek foods higher in calories, hence the popularity of suet bird feeders in winter. Stored food reserves often make the difference in winter survival, and many birds and mammals fatten themselves as much as possible in preparation. Some animals store food outside their bodies: tree squirrels and jays bury nuts, honey bees store honey, and pikas make hay for their winter food supply.

To conserve energy endotherms can seek shelter and become inactive during the coldest times. Many mammals spend time sleeping during the winter, the most famous example being bears which spend long periods of time in a very deep sleep. The most extreme adaptation of endotherms to cold is to actually get out of the fast lane of endothermy and "go ecto;" that is, hibernate. During hibernation it is as if the thermostat in the animal's brain has been set to a lower temperature. As with ectotherms, the animal's entire metabolism, including heart rate, breathing, and urine production, slows to a level that just barely sustains life. The animal can't move, but then it doesn't need all that food to stay active and warm. If it can store enough fat and get in the right shelter, it can just wait out the winter and return to full activity when spring, warmer temperatures, and food arrive. Some hibernating rodents will actually arouse occasionally during warmer times in winter and eat stored seeds in their burrow or even go out and forage.

True hibernation is uncommon. Some bats and rodents, particularly ground squirrels, are the most common and well-known hibernators. Scientists disagree as to what constitutes true hibernation as opposed to what is just torpidity, dormancy, or deep sleep. Hence, bears and some other mammals are called hibernators by some but not by others. The situation with birds is even hazier and seems to mainly be a question of terminology. The only bird that is regularly called a true hibernator is the poorwill, which occurs in our region. Several species of hummingbirds are known to enter a torpid state on cold nights but will arouse quickly.

Regardless of how they do it, enough members of each population of animals must survive the winter to reproduce and repopulate the available habitat the next spring and summer. Changes in one species affects the other members of its community. Fluctuations in animal populations are part of the complex interactions among animals and between animals and their habitats.

FEBRUARY

BALD EAGLES

Not everyone will be thrilled by the sight of a sparrow in breeding plumage or an immature warbler, but everyone seems to be impressed by the sight of an adult bald eagle. Winter eagle watching has become a popular activity in our region and with good reason—the Northwest has the best spots for seeing bald eagles outside of Alaska.

The recovery of the bald eagle is one of the best examples of the success of the Endangered Species Act. Eagles suffered from the triple threat of shooting, habitat destruction, and pesticides. Fortunately, the bald eagle now stands as a symbol of what we can do to protect and restore an animal threatened with extinction. Because of the protections and funding provided by the Endangered Species Act, bald eagles have bounced back and are no longer classified as endangered species and are not in immediate danger of extinction. Improved regulation of some pesticides, most notably DDT, and better enforcement of laws protecting eagles from shooting have left habitat destruction as their biggest threat. Fortunately, habitat protection improved in the 1980s and 1990s, and in many Oregon and Washington cities it is no longer big news to spot an eagle, like it was in the 1970s. Many of us think that we are now seeing a generation of bald eagles nesting in cities that grew up "just outside of town" and are more tolerant of human activities. Bald eagles may prove themselves to be as adaptable as osprey.

Oregon and Washington have always had more bald eagles than any of the other lower 48 states. Bald eagles were never actually classified as endangered in our states, but were classified as threatened. In 1980 there were about 160 nesting pairs of bald eagles in Oregon and Washington combined. The estimate today is just over 1000 nesting pairs. In the winter as many as 4000

Bald eagles at the Skagit Flats

additional eagles come down from Canada and Alaska to join the resident birds. When I started birding I wondered if I would ever see a bald eagle before they were extinct. Now I see them almost every day I go to work at Smith and Bybee Wetlands, right in Portland. That's what I consider really good news.

British Columbia's bald eagle population is in even better shape. Current estimates are that coastal British Columbia alone has at least 4500 breeding pairs of bald eagles and the winter population reaches 30,000 individuals.

While you can see bald eagles any time of year in the Northwest, observing these birds in winter is much easier because thousands of additional birds are present and many of them gather in large numbers in traditional wintering grounds. Bare deciduous trees also contribute to ease of observation. Eagles concentrate in certain areas for the winter because of food availability and good roosting sites where they can sleep or rest. Their main food is either fish or waterfowl so they are most common along rivers with a salmon run or around large wetlands where thousands of ducks and geese spend the winter. They are also scavengers; you might come upon them feasting on roadkill, especially freshly killed deer.

Another very good reason for eagle watching in the winter is that the eagles are not being disturbed during the critical nesting season. It is still important, however, to disturb the birds as little as possible, regardless of time of year. When observing perched eagles in winter, avoid doing anything that will make them fly, causing them to expend critical energy reserves.

Novice eagle watchers are usually puzzled to see many bald eagles that aren't bald—they don't have a white head. Bald eagles do not get their beautiful all-white head and tail until they are mature at four or five years old. Before this age, the young eagles are primarily dark brown all over. As they get older, they begin to get mottled with varying amounts of white before they get their adult plumage of dark blackish-brown with the bright white tail and head. Incidentally, no one ever thought that bald eagles were really bald as in the hairless pate of a man. At the time when American colonists named these birds, the term *balled* or *balde* meant white or white-headed, not hairless.

In many areas it's difficult for western eagle watchers to distinguish immature bald from immature golden eagles, which are very similar in appearance. The easiest way to tell them apart is by the distribution of white on the dark body. Immature golden eagles usually have patches of white that are neat and tidy and concentrated in two areas: the base of the primaries and the base of the tail. By contrast, immature bald eagles can have splotches of white anywhere on their body or wings; they are much messier looking. As they get older some young bald eagles get a lot of white on the underside of their body giving them a "white shield for a breast" look. This is very confusing the first time you see it.

▶ BALD EAGLES BEST BETS OREGON

The best bald eagle spot in the contiguous United States is the Klamath Basin. As many as 1000 bald eagles are in the basin at times in the winter. A new refuge was added to the complex of refuges in the basin in 1978 to protect an area of old growth forest that is a vitally important roost for the birds. The Klamath Basin has become famous for its bald eagles primarily because of the annual Klamath Basin Bald Eagle Conference, which started in 1979.

After 25 years the conference developed into a major community event and now has a new name—the Klamath Basin Winter Wings Festival. The festival is run by Klamath Wingwatchers, a nonprofit organization dedicated to the wildlife of the Klamath Basin. This is a great example of ecotourism benefiting the economy of a community and the local wildlife resources. Among the activities are speakers, films, workshops, music, art exhibits, a photography contest, and, of course, field trips to see eagles and other birds. The conference also brings together wildlife experts and enthusiasts. One year Roger Tory Peterson showed up and probably autographed a million copies of his field guides. At this time of year the K-Basin is also one of the best spots in the Northwest for wintering waterfowl and raptors. The highlight of any eagle-watching trip to the area is the morning flyout from the major roost in Bear Valley NWR.

The birding will be fantastic (and hunting over) anytime in February before the festival, if you prefer no crowds and exploring on your own. Here is what I consider the basic tour of the Klamath Basin. You can make this tour in winter for raptors and waterfowl, in March or early April for huge numbers of migrating waterfowl, or later in the spring (end of April to early June) for a good variety of waterfowl, raptors, shorebirds, herons, and songbirds. No two ways about it, the five national wildlife refuges in the basin plus the state's Klamath WA make this one of the West's all-around greatest birding spots just about any time.

Let's start with the bald eagle flyout. The catch is that you have to be at the site before sunrise. Oh come on, it's not that bad because it's winter and sunrise is late. Check the weather section of a local newspaper for the sunrise and plan to leave downtown Klamath Falls about an hour or 45 minutes before that time. Head south on US Hwy 97 from Klamath Falls (Main St in downtown becomes 97) for 13 miles. Just south of the little town of Worden you'll pass Township Rd on your left. Turn right onto the next road you come to on the right; the sign reads "To Ashland and Keno." Cross the railroad tracks on this paved road, and then immediately turn left onto a dirt road. In about 100 yards the road forks; go right staying on the main road. Drive west

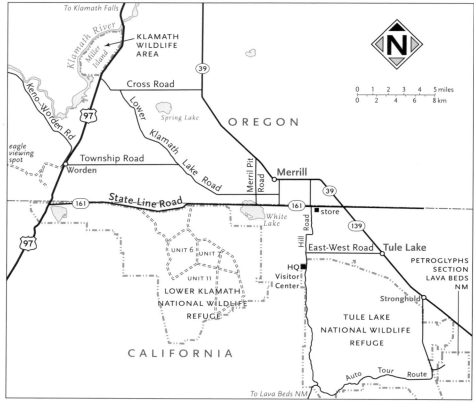

KLAMATH BASIN

on this dirt road for about 0.5 mile to a stretch of the road that is very straight, and then pull over as far as you can and park. Stand by your car and watch toward the hills to the northwest. As it gets light you should begin to see bald eagles and rough-legged hawks fly right over your head and off to the sides. People have seen as many as 300 eagles in a morning.

When you're ready to move on, turn your car around and go back to US 97. Turn left and head north the way you came, but get ready to turn right onto Township Rd which comes up immediately. Township Rd is a great road for a slow cruise through the farmland and along the northern border of the Lower Klamath

NWR. You'll see more eagles and rough-legged hawks, as well as red-tailed hawks, American kestrels, and northern harriers. Township Rd will intersect Lower Klamath Lake Rd; the street sign reads "L. Lake Road." Turn right and head toward the small town of Merrill. This route does not take you into Merrill, a good stop for a hot meal if you want to make a little detour. To continue our birding route, do not go to Merrill but instead watch for Merrill Pit Rd, where you'll turn right and go south on Merrill Pit Rd until it ends at State Line Rd, State Hwy 161. Turn left onto State Line Rd driving east about 4 miles, and you'll reach the intersection with Hill Rd where there is a small store. Turn right and go south about 4 miles to the visitor center and headquarters for the Klamath Basin refuges. The visitor center has displays, a slide show, maps, checklists, restrooms, and friendly staff who can answer questions and give you some current information on birds.

You can make a loop from here that takes you through wetlands and then to a unique rock formation with petroglyphs. If you don't want to take this loop, return north to State Line Rd and skip to the next paragraph. To make the loop, from the visitor center take the auto tour route through Tule Lake NWR to the petroglyphs area of Lava Beds National Monument. You'll see an amazing cliff pocketed with hundreds of holes of varying sizes. Scan these holes with your binoculars—barn owls and prairie falcons often use them for nesting and roosting. After checking out the cliff and the petroglyphs, continue on the road, up and over the petroglyph hill. Turn left when you come to an intersection, and then drive to State Hwy 139. Turn left to head north on Hwy 139 to the intersection with State Line Rd (Hwy 161) where you'll turn left and head west.

To view the main part of the Lower Klamath NWR, go west on State Line Rd about 7.5 miles from the store at Hill Rd. There is a signed entrance for the refuge on the south side of the road. Proceed into the refuge and follow the auto tour route, but veer to the left when you come to the first fork. At the next intersection turn right. Ask at headquarters which roads are open and where the best viewing is. Once I had a great view of a couple of river otters here that were hauled out on shore and lying right next to each other, looking like they were trying to keep each other warm. They were so big and fat they looked like little seals.

When you return to State Line Rd, turn left to head west to US 97, where you'll turn right to go back to Klamath Falls. If you have the time, check out the Klamath WA (Miller Island Unit) owned by ODFW. In March during spring waterfowl migration Miller Island is known for the large flocks of Ross's geese that stop there. To see Miller Island, turn left onto Miller Island Rd which is just south of where US 97 crosses the railroad tracks, about 5 miles south of Klamath Falls. It's just one road, with a few dead end spurs, going through the wildlife area. After Miller Island it's a short drive back to your starting point in Klamath Falls.

Residents of the Portland area have a couple of nearby places for viewing eagles: Sauvie Island and Ridgefield NWR (coming up in Washington Best Bets). Sauvie Island, the large island in the confluence of the Willamette and Columbia rivers, is well known to Portlanders for bicycling, boating, going to the beach, and buying fresh produce. It is also one of the best and most visited birding spots in northwestern Oregon. About half of the island is the Sauvie Island WA, managed by ODFW. You must have a Sauvie Island parking permit to park on ODFW land, which includes the three places described here. You can buy a permit for the day or for the year at the Cracker Barrel store as you first come onto the island, as well as at other retail outlets back in town. A map of Sauvie Island is in October (Sandhill Cranes).

Before the wonderful recovery of the eagle population, you had to be in a certain place at sunrise to ensure you would see a few bald eagles on the island. Now it's pretty easy to see numerous bald eagles by cruising the main roads watching for perched eagles in the bare trees, and then stopping at three main wildlife-watching spots. As you come off the Sauvie Island Bridge you will be headed north on Sauvie Island Rd. In 2 miles you'll reach the intersection with Reeder Rd; turn right onto Reeder. You will pass Oak Island Rd, a good birding road in general, and in 3 miles watch for a parking area on your left—Coon Point. Park here and you'll see a long ramp going up to the top of a big dike. Walk to the top of the dike where you'll have a fantastic view over a big chunk of the island. From this vantage point you'll see geese, ducks, raptors, and maybe cranes and swans. And of course, some bald eagles. The best place to look is in the big trees on the other side of the body of water right in front of you. This is to the northwest, but it's easy to lose your compass bearings on the island. You'll see some great blue heron nests in the closest grove of big cottonwoods, and a few eagles are usually perched in the same trees. If you don't see them there just keep scanning the trees to the right of the heron nests. This spot is a great place to hang out, check out the ducks, and keep scanning in all directions.

From Coon Point get back onto Reeder Rd and continue the direction you were going until you get to Gillihan Rd. Turn left to remain on Reeder Rd and drive another 3 miles, watching for another parking area on your left. You'll see a wooden wildlife-viewing platform, which has a view over a wetland area where you can scan the possible perches and watch the sky.

The third spot is the end of Rentenaar Rd. Continue on Reeder Rd about 2.5 miles to the intersection of Reeder and Rentenaar roads. The small building here is a hunting check station, which should be closed and not in use in February. Stop here in the parking area for the check station and look across Rentenaar Rd to the north for some big nests in the cottonwoods growing between the fields. Bald eagles have been nesting in this area for several years, and chances are good you will find an active nest and some eagles. After looking this area over get back on Rentenaar and continue driving to the end of the road. Warning: this road regularly gets flooded. Proceed with caution and drive carefully through any water on the road. You may not make it to the end. If you do, park and once again walk to the top of the dike. You now have another fabulous vantage point to look for bald eagles, other raptors, sandhill cranes, snow geese, Canada geese, tundra swans, and a whole mess of ducks. You will head back the same way so you can check the other two areas again.

▶ BALD EAGLES BEST BETS WASHINGTON

Every year, starting in November, about 500 bald eagles come to the upper Skagit River to eat spawning chum salmon. Numbers build through January and then eagles slowly start departing until they have dispersed by mid-March. Several nesting pairs remain in the area all year. As in Klamath Falls, local eagle enthusiasts have started an annual festival. The Upper Skagit Bald Eagle Festival, a weekend at the end of January or in early February, is a major community event. The Skagit River Bald Eagle Awareness Team (SRBEAT) is the private, nonprofit organization that runs the festival and operates the Skagit River Bald Eagle Interpretive Center in Rockport.

The center of the eagle gathering is along the Skagit River between the towns of Rockport and Marblemount on State Hwy 20, the North Cascades Highway. Starting in Rockport you can walk from the Skagit River Bald Eagle Interpretive Center on Alfred St to Howard Miller Steelhead County Park. You can view the river to look for eagles from the park or walk onto the bridge over the Skagit for State Route 530 and look upstream and downstream from this vantage point. A sidewalk on the bridge makes it safe for pedestrian eagle watchers, but be sure to stay on the sidewalk.

Another choice spot is upstream from Rockport on Hwy 20 at the milepost 100 rest area, next to the Skagit River. The third and last stop on the regular eagle route is the Marblemount Fish Hatchery farther upstream. In Marblemount cross the Skagit River bridge, drive past the boat launch, and then go over the Cascade River bridge to the hatchery on the Rockport-Cascade Rd. If you are interested in hatchery operations there are tours on weekends during prime eagle time, but people mainly come here to park in the public parking area and scan the area around the hatchery for eagles and the many other waterbirds that hang out here.

The dramatically increasing popularity of eagle watching on the Skagit could disturb the birds; please stay in the parking and viewing areas at these spots, and do not try to get closer. Presently, people are allowed to boat down the Skagit through the area to see the eagles during the middle of the day when they are not actively feeding. Commercial outfitters in the area offer eagle viewing trips. All boaters must stay in their boats while in the area and are asked to float quietly with as little movement as possible.

The San Juan Islands have had the highest density of nesting bald eagles in Washington. As is the common pattern in the Pacific Northwest, these year-round residents are joined by others in the winter. If you spend any time in the San Juans, you are bound to see some bald eagles. The easiest way to see them is from the Washington State ferries that serve the islands. Also, don't forget the Skagit and Samish flats described in January (Wintering Raptors). Given the possibilities for other exciting raptors here, bald eagles would be considered rather ordinary in "the flats."

▶ BALD EAGLES BEST BETS BRITISH COLUMBIA

As you head farther north, especially along the coast, you run into more and more bald eagles. Hence, seeing a bald eagle in British Columbia is almost considered ho-hum. In fact, in 1994 the Squamish River Valley near Brackendale broke the world record for the most bald eagles counted in one area in one day: 3766. This beats the record of 3495 by well-publicized Chilkat, Alaska, and has even led some Canadian naturalists to gloat, a shocking development from a group known for their politeness and decorum. This ultimate eagle winter gathering is the result of a winter run of chum salmon in the Squamish River, just like the Skagit River. The heart of the action is between the small towns of Squamish and Brackendale, about 40 miles north of Vancouver on Hwy 99, the Sea to Sky Highway. The 20th annual Brackendale Winter Eagle Festival and Count was celebrated in 2006. The festival is the entire month of January and offers a variety of events including natural history, art, theater, and music. Headquarters for the festival is the unique Brackendale Art Gallery Theatre Teahouse founded by Thor Froslev, originator of the festival (www.brackendale artgallery.com).

For the best eagle viewing, exit Hwy 99 just north of Squamish at Centennial St. Go left on Centennial and in a short distance turn right onto Government Rd. You will cross the Mamquam River, a tributary of the Squamish River, then drive north toward Brackendale, parallel with the Squamish River. You could see bald eagles anywhere along this route, but in about one mile from Mamquam River you will be in "eagle run," the area with the best viewing. You will soon come to the obvious eagle viewing spot across the road from an Easter Seal camp. Viewing is from the top of the dike, and from this point you are looking west across the Squamish River into Brackendale Eagles PP, established specifically as a wintering area for the eagles. The park is essentially a wilderness area with restricted access; none at all in the winter. January is the best time to see the bald eagles here, but plenty hang around into February.

In 2005 Vancouver had at least 12 active bald eagle nests, including four in Stanley Park and three in residential yards. In Stanley Park, the Dining Pavilion Nest, as it is known, is on the top of a huge Douglas-fir tree between the Dining Pavilion and Malkin Bowl, home of summer concerts. The report on the nesting bald eagles of Vancouver by the Stanley Park Ecological Society states, "The eagles have a bird's-eye view of concerts and plays for much of their time in the nest. The tree is in a grassy maintained area of Stanley Park and frequently has sunbathers and picnics on the grass beneath the nest." If you can't find bald eagles in British Columbia, you aren't looking.

WINTERING WATERFOWL

With its mild winters, thousands of miles of coastline, numerous bays and estuaries, and freshwater wetlands, the Pacific Northwest is a waterbird's winter wonderland. Not just ducks, but other waterbirds like loons, grebes, and gulls, find the trip to our coast perfectly adequate for escaping the rigors of winter in their breeding grounds without the longer and more dangerous flight to Latin America.

The bottom line for survival of waterbirds is ice, or the lack of it. As long as there is enough open water for feeding, drinking, and safety from predators, waterbirds can withstand very low temperatures. After all, they do have the original down parkas. But when the water freezes solid, it's time to go. How far a particular bird migrates each year will vary somewhat with the weather, but ancient routes and destinations are well established. In our region, the abundance and distribution of wintering waterbirds in the area east of the Cascades can vary a lot from year to year, or even week to week. The ocean, however, never freezes, and the western parts of our states and province are the winter home of millions of waterfowl and other waterbirds every year.

What's the difference between the terms *waterbird* and *waterfowl*? Waterbird is a general term, which varies in usage, but usually refers to any bird that can swim: a duck, loon, cormorant, gull, or coot. Sometimes people also use the term for waders, such as herons and sandpipers. Waterfowl, on the other hand, is very specific and means the group or order of birds that consist of the ducks, geese and swans. Swans and geese have their own chapters, so here we'll concentrate on ducks.

Winter waterfowl first start arriving in September, making for generally good waterfowl watching from October through spring migration. But a little problem gets in the way—hunting season. Waterfowl hunting usually starts the second week of October and goes well into January. Breaks in the hunting during this period offer some good waterfowl watching, but you have to know the right places and the right times. Many people just wait until the hunting is over before doing serious waterfowl watching.

Ducks are some of the most familiar and well-known birds to North Americans. I'll bet most kids can recognize and name a duck before any other type of bird. And no wonder; ducks are distinctive-looking animals and are very popular—everybody knows what a duck looks like. However, what most people don't realize is how many different kinds of ducks there are. The Northwest has 28 species of ducks that regularly occur and that's not counting geese and swans.

With so many kinds, it's easy to get your ducks mixed up. Fortunately, most ducks are easy to identify. If you get a good look at a male duck you should be able to identify him with any good field guide. The females are much harder to identify because they are very plain and look a lot more like each other. Learn your males first, and then try your hand at the females. Be aware of what is known as the "eclipse plumage," the non-breeding-plumage ducks have for a few months right after the breeding season. During this period in summer and fall the birds go through a complete molt into a new breeding plumage. While "in eclipse" and molting, the males look like the females and everyone is pretty much a mess, making this the hardest time to identify ducks. This molting process is so variable that very few books show eclipse plumages.

One way to sort out the ducks is to know the main groups or subfamilies to which they belong. Puddle ducks or dabbling ducks rarely dive or swim underwater. They feed from the surface by sticking their heads underwater to reach for plants or animal food and often tip up, with their tails pointing toward the sky. Our common puddle ducks are mallard, northern pintail, northern shoveler, gadwall, American wigeon, and green-winged teal. The Eurasian wigeon is also here every winter but in very small numbers. The blue-winged and cinnamon teal are unusual because they come here to nest and are our only puddle ducks more common here in the summer. The beautiful wood duck is in a group of its own, but its behavior is similar to that of a puddle duck. Wood ducks are year-round residents but much more conspicuous in the winter.

The diving ducks actively dive from the surface and swim underwater after food. Like puddle ducks, they eat both plants and animals, but diving ducks eat a higher proportion of animal foods. Many of these ducks have bold black and white patterns. They are usually seen in deeper water than the puddle ducks, and they have to run along the surface to take off—the puddle ducks seem to just jump into the air. Our diving ducks are the lesser scaup, the greater scaup, the ring-necked duck, the canvasback, the redhead, the bufflehead, the common goldeneye, and the Barrow's goldeneye. The goldeneyes are much more localized than the others and more common to the north. The redhead is not common in our region.

Some of the diving ducks are often called sea ducks because they are usually seen in salt water, mostly in bays but also out past the breakers in the ocean. Our sea ducks that winter along the coast are the surf scoter, the white-winged scoter, the black scoter, the harlequin duck, and the long-tailed duck (formerly oldsquaw). The long-tailed duck is another winter visitor that is more localized and much more common farther north.

Another small group of ducks is the three mergansers—common, red-breasted and hooded—all highly adapted for swimming after and grabbing fish underwater. A merganser is easy to recognize by its unique bill, which is narrow, hooked, and lined with toothlike serrations that gives it the nickname "sawbill." In a group by itself is the little, plump ruddy duck, which is a common winter visitor west of the Cascades and a common breeder east of the mountains.

It is amazing that you can see most of these in one day. Finding ducks in winter in the Northwest is about as easy as finding water. Almost any good wetland habitat with open water will have some waterfowl. The west side of our region, with milder and more consistent weather, has more birds and is more predictable than the east side. Since a majority of the national wildlife refuges were established primarily to protect habitat for waterfowl, almost any refuge is an excellent place to look for wintering waterfowl. Our many coastal bays and estuaries and the Salish Sea provide a tremendous number of opportunities for viewing waterfowl.

▶ WINTERING WATERFOWL BEST BETS OREGON

Any estuary in Oregon has good waterfowl potential, but two favorites are Tillamook and Yaquina bays. US Hwy 101 borders the eastern edge of Tillamook Bay for several miles from the small town of Bay City to the tiny settlement of Barview. In several places along this stretch of US 101, you can pull over to view the birds in Tillamook Bay. Use good judgment and watch carefully for traffic—101 is a very busy highway. The north jetty of Tillamook Bay, called Barview Jetty, still has an intact road from repair work done in 1991. The road is slowly washing away, but at this writing enough remains that you can walk toward the end. You'll usually see more birds inside the channel than outside of the jetty, but check both areas for waterfowl, alcids, loons, and gulls. To reach the jetty drive west through

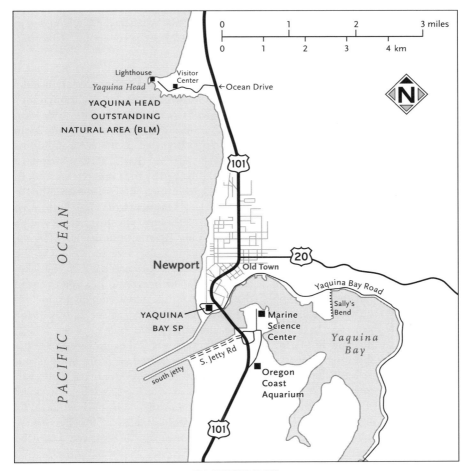

YAQUINA BAY

Barview Jetty County Park (possible fee) to a parking area at the base of the jetty. The road to the county park intersects US 101 in the tiny settlement of Barview, just over one mile north of the small town of Garibaldi. There are signs for the park.

Yaquina Bay and the Newport area are one of Oregon's best birding sites as well as the center for many other recreational activities. It is the home of the excellent Oregon Coast Aquarium and the Hatfield Marine Science Center and the departure point for whale watching and pelagic birding boat trips. The three best winter viewing spots around Yaquina Bay for many kinds of waterbirds—waterfowl, loons, grebes, gulls, shorebirds, and alcids—are the south jetty, the marine center shoreline, and Sally's Bend.

You can drive on the south jetty of Yaquina Bay for quite a distance, but eventually you will have to decide when it's too rough and to park and walk. You'll see a variety of waterfowl and seabirds from this jetty. Head south on US 101 out of Newport, drive over the bay on the Yaquina Bay Bridge, and as soon as you come off the bridge, turn right following the signs for the Oregon Coast Aquarium and the Hatfield Marine Science Center. Coming off US 101, you will curve around to your right and head back north. Do not stay on this road as it goes under the bridge and to the science center and aquarium, but instead turn left onto 26th St. Drive west on 26th St—it becomes the road going out onto the jetty. The road worsens as you go, stop when you know you can get back out.

The second area, near the Hatfield Marine Science Center, is the bay shore, which is also a great area for shorebirds. To reach the marine science center from the central part of Newport, drive south on US 101 and over the bay bridge. After you come off the bridge, turn right on Abalone St and follow the signs to the Hatfield Marine Science Center. Park in the main parking lot. From the northeast corner of the parking lot, a trail heads east and

gives you access and views to much more of the bay. High tide is best. While you're in this area you can visit the Marine Science Center or the Oregon Coast Aquarium.

The third part of Yaquina Bay is the area known as Sally's Bend, accessible from the north side of the bay in the old waterfront part of town. Take the main road, Yaquina Bay Rd, and head east toward Toledo. About 10 miles out of town you'll see huge storage tanks for natural gas on your right. Near the tanks is a dirt road that goes to a public dock for fishing and viewing. This is an excellent spot to scope the bay for birds. Waterfowl often hang out in the area just east of the viewpoint. Afternoon birding is best.

Three areas east of the Cascades are usually excellent for winter waterfowl, although they are subject to freezing, as are all east-side locations. Summer Lake and the Klamath Basin are described in other chapters. An additional spot in the Klamath Basin is Lake Ewauna, a small lake formed by the Link River just south of the old downtown part of Klamath Falls. To view the lake head south on Main St through downtown Klamath Falls. Just before you go over the Link River and under US Hwy 97, turn left onto Conger Ave and take it to the parking area for the small park on the lakeshore. At the main viewing area you can scan the lake for puddle and diving ducks, including goldeneyes. You'll also see gulls, Canada geese, and often a bald eagle or two.

The third area is at the opposite end of the state. Near Hermiston are Cold Springs and Umatilla national wildlife refuges. Both usually have lots of waterfowl, and the birds travel between the two areas. Parts of Umatilla NWR include the Columbia River so when everywhere else freezes up, the birds can usually be found on the river.

To get to Cold Springs NWR starting from downtown Hermiston take Main St east until it angles off to the northeast and becomes State Hwy 207. Go about 3 miles and just past the fire station turn right to head east on Punkin Center Rd (also called County Rd 1250) following signs to Cold Springs Reservoir. Turn east on Punkin Center Rd and in 2 miles it will turn to dirt and a bit farther it forks. Turn to the right, over the train tracks, and into the refuge. The road goes over the dam and then follows the south shore of the reservoir. As you cross the dam you can see lots of birds from your car. Along the road are several places to park and walk to the lakeshore for viewing. The area is also good for raptors and wintering songbirds, which like the thick stands of cottonwood, willow, and Russian olive.

Umatilla NWR is spread out along the Columbia on the Washington and Oregon sides. The refuge has different units, but the easiest viewing is from the auto tour route in the McCormack Slough area, which also has a small information center. From Interstate 84, just east of Boardman, take the exit for US 730 to Walla Walla. In 3.5 miles turn left to head north on Paterson Ferry Rd (there is a sign for the refuge). In 1.5 miles you'll come to the information center; check to see if printed information is available. Outhouses are also available. The auto tour route starts here, crosses McCormack Slough, and then winds through some other wetland areas and large irrigated crop circles. No, not the ones aliens leave; the kind farmers make. You may find yourself among geese, which often forage in fallow winter fields.

▶ WINTERING WATERFOWL BEST BETS WASHINGTON

The array of bays and coves along the vast shoreline of the mainland and the islands in the Salish Sea present an overwhelming range of possibilities. Some of the better spots described in other chapters are Ediz Hook, Skagit Bay, Birch Bay, Kayak Point, and Padilla Bay.

Dungeness NWR includes Dungeness Spit, the largest natural sand spit in the United States. The calm waters, beaches, and tideflats caused by this 5.5-mile spit next to the Dungeness River Estuary provides outstanding habitat for waterfowl, shorebirds, and many other birds. Hiking is permitted all the way to the tip, but a walk along any portion of the spit will provide some excellent wildlife views. The trail to the spit passes through a forest, which can be very lively with songbirds, including red crossbills and Hutton's vireos—often hard-to-find birds.

Finding Dungeness NWR is easy; the way is well signed. From US 101, about 10 miles east of Port Angeles (4 miles west of Sequim),

go north on Kitchen Dick Rd. You'll make a short jog to the right on Lotzgesell Rd then turn left and drive through Dungeness Recreation Area, a large Clallam County park, to get to the parking area for the refuge and the trailhead. You can usually find maps and bird checklists here, as well as the fee station for visiting the refuge. The trail will take you through the coniferous forest to the bluff overlooking the spit. From here you'll get an idea of where the most birds are hanging out and can plan where to go on the spit. It's a pretty steep trail down to the spit. You'll usually see a sample of the different species of birds present without having to walk very far out on the spit. Allow four hours to take the trail to the end, where you'll feel as if you're standing in the middle of the Strait of Juan de Fuca.

In eastern Washington wetlands may freeze completely during some winters, in which case the waterfowl will be on the Columbia River or farther south. McNary NWR is just southeast of the confluence of the Snake and Columbia rivers, near the town of Burbank, and usually remains open all winter. From US Hwy 12 turn east onto Maple St where a sign directs you to refuge headquarters in 0.25 mile. From headquarters, where maps should be available, continue east on Maple a bit, then turn left to head north on Lake Rd. Soon after turning onto Lake Rd, you'll reach a small parking area on your right where you can check Burbank Slough, usually loaded with ducks. Be sure to also check the area where Humorist Rd crosses the slough. In your car, head south on Lake Rd until you come to Humorist, and turn left and head east until you cross the slough again. Several parking areas are near the crossing, but birds are often close to the road so do as much viewing as you can from your car while on Humorist (which has little traffic). Then continue east a short distance uphill, where you'll be able to see more of the slough and more distant birds without scaring them away. Be on the lookout for white pelicans—McNary is one of the most predictable places to see these unique birds in Washington, although they may not be around during the coldest months.

The Wallula Unit of McNary NWR is 11 miles south of Burbank at the confluence of the Walla Walla River and the Columbia. The best viewing is on the north side. From US 12, just north of its junction with US 730, turn east onto North Shore Rd. This is the first road north of the Walla Walla River and is also signed "Madame Dorian Park." Take the left fork immediately after getting on North Shore Rd and head east. In just under 0.5 mile you'll reach an overlook where maps may be available. Here you'll get your first good view of a lake that is usually loaded with birds. Continue along North Shore Rd for more good views of the lake for another 0.5 mile. After 2 miles you'll have good views of fields that are planted with food crops for waterfowl. Because the fields are usually flooded in the winter, they are often as popular with waterfowl as the lake.

▶ WINTERING WATERFOWL BEST BETS BRITISH COLUMBIA

Vancouver is almost surrounded by water, and the Fraser River delta looks like a peninsula sticking out into the Strait of Georgia. With all this water it is not surprising that the Georgia Depression, the name for this ecoprovince, has the most moderate climate and the mildest winters in Canada. Sounds like a winter paradise for waterfowl and other waterbirds, and indeed it is. The waters around Vancouver and Boundary Bay have the largest concentration of wintering waterfowl in Canada, and every year this ecoprovince has the highest number of species on the annual Christmas Bird Count. No surprise then that many areas around Vancouver and Victoria offer fabulous winter waterfowl watching.

Stanley Park, in downtown Vancouver, is a huge park with a bird list of an astonishing 230 species. The park is surrounded by Burrard Inlet and English Bay, both swarming not only with scads of ducks but also loons, grebes, cormorants, gulls, and pigeon guillemots. The outer perimeter of Stanley Park is a seawall with a walkway that offers outstanding views. The area offshore from Ferguson Point, on the west side of the park, seems to be one of the best views. This is right near the Teahouse Restaurant and Third Beach, which has parking, restrooms, and easy access to the walk.

A wonderful example of wildlife in a city is Lost Lagoon Lake in Stanley Park, one of the best spots for ducks in the area. You can look at thousands of scaup, goldeneye, buffle-head, ring-necked, and other diving ducks in the water with the skyline of downtown Vancouver in the background. Don't be surprised if a bald eagle flies over also. Parking near Lost Lagoon Lake can be a challenge, and parking in the park is metered, so have plenty of Loonies (Canadian one-dollar coins) with you. If you have taken the perimeter road (one way) around the park to Third Beach and Ferguson Point, you can continue from there to North Lagoon Dr, where you'll turn left and drive along the north shore of the lake. There are parking spots along this road, which is not heavily used in the winter. After parking you can walk around the lake, going to the west away from the traffic. Take the stone bridge over the lake's outlet at the west end to the south shore trail. There are some feeders in the bushes around the bridge, and the area is usually hopping with sparrows, juncos, chickadees, and towhees. The Stanley Park Ecology Society is in the Nature House (an old boat house) tucked into the southeast shore of the lagoon. If you walk along the south shore, where you have the best light, you will reach the Nature House just before you get to Georgia St. Nature House hours vary with the seasons. For information about Nature House hours and programs, and about the Ecology Society, go to www.stanleyparkecology.ca.

In North Vancouver (where motel rates are much lower than in downtown) you can see the same birds at Ambleside Park, which offers easy parking in an uncrowded setting. Head toward West Vancouver on Marine Dr from the Lions Gate Bridge. Drive past the big Park Royal Shopping Center and watch for 13th St. Turn left onto 13th St, cross the railroad tracks, and then turn left again into Ambleside Park. Drive as far as you can back toward the Lions Gate Bridge and park in the farthest east parking area. In front of you will be Burrard Inlet (saltwater) and behind you a pond (freshwater), offering a nice variety of ducks, gulls, and possible loons, grebes, and cormorants.

Many other areas around Vancouver are good for winter waterbirds. Some other Best Bets south of Vancouver are Iona Island, Boundary Bay, George C. Reifel Migratory Bird Sanctuary, and Roberts Bank Coalport.

Near Victoria are three Best Bets: the Victoria breakwater, Martindale Flats, and Esquimalt and Witty's lagoons. The breakwater along the southeastern shoreline of Victoria is described in Great Gangs of Gulls and Martindale Flats is described in January (Swans). You can get to Esquimalt and Witty's lagoons on the same route. Esquimalt is an easy "spot them from the car" place. At Witty's Lagoon you'll walk through a variety of habitats to the lagoon—it's much more of a nature hike. You should stop at Esquimalt Lagoon first, and then decide whether to continue to Witty's Lagoon or head somewhere else.

To get to Esquimalt Lagoon head east from Victoria on Trans-Canada Highway 1 for about 4 miles. Exit at Helmcken Rd and head south (away from the hospital) to the Island Highway (Hwy 1A). Turn right and head west on Hwy 1A. Stay on it as it curves around to the left through a confusing series of intersections. After about one mile from Helmcken you will pass a landmark, the Six Mile Pub. Continue on 1A past the pub for another mile, and then turn left onto Ocean Blvd, following signs for Fort Rodd Hill Park. Drive past Fort Rodd Hill Park staying on Ocean and following signs to Esquimalt Lagoon. About 2 miles from Hwy 1A, you'll drive onto the sand spit that separates the lagoon from the Juan de Fuca Strait. Drive down the spit and, scanning both sides, carefully pull over any place that looks interesting. There should be a good variety of loons, grebes, and gulls, in addition to waterfowl. You may also see one of the mute swans, an introduced invasive species that has become established on the southern end of Vancouver Island.

To continue to Witty's Lagoon, drive south on Ocean to the end of the spit, and then turn right onto Lagoon Rd. In about 0.5 mile, turn left onto Mitchosin Rd and head south. In a little over 2 miles you'll reach the parking area and entrance for Witty's Lagoon RP. If the visitor center is open, you can get a map and a bird checklist. Picnic tables and outhouses are available. The park also has large, beautiful madrone trees, which are called arbutus trees in Canada. Take the trail down toward the lagoon and go right and over the footbridge, taking the trail that goes near the south shore of the lagoon to the spit that separates Witty's Lagoon from Parry Bay. You'll pass through several habitats and could see a good variety of land birds—the park's checklist is just over 120 species. As you near the spit you'll find several places where you can search both the lagoon and the waters of Parry Bay for water-birds. To return to Victoria, take Mitchosin road north back the way you came.

NATIONAL WILDLIFE REFUGES: A CLOSER LOOK

It happens every time I take a birding class on our first field trip to a national wildlife refuge. At some point I mention that during hunting season some areas are closed to birdwatching because of hunting. "What, hunting? On a wildlife refuge? How can that be?" Some people are surprised, others outraged, to learn that hunting is allowed on a wildlife refuge. Part of the confusion lies in the word "refuge," which means a protected place and in common usage is pretty much synonymous with "sanctuary." However, different kinds of refuges exist. A national wildlife refuge is a specific type of federal land managed by the USFWS with very specific management objectives. Regulated hunting is allowed on about half of the national wildlife refuges where it is considered compatible with the management goals and objectives of the refuge.

Comments about hunting on national wildlife refuges often reveal confusion and misunderstanding about the history and purposes of the NWRS. A brief overview of its history can help clarify.

The earliest stages of what would be called the conservation movement began in the 1870s. The extinction of the passenger pigeon and near extinction of the American bison, both unbelievably abundant just a few decades earlier, were some of America's first wake-up calls to the destruction of our natural resources. Some of the earliest actions taken were the establishment of Yellowstone NP in 1872, the passage of the first state game laws, and the creation of state game departments. Early conservationists such as Teddy

Roosevelt, Gifford Pinchot, George Grinnell, and John Muir began to influence political leaders and the general public. By World War I a broad-based, popular conservation movement was under way along with a growing awareness of the impact of human activities on wildlife and nature.

An important landmark was the establishment of the first national wildlife refuge in 1903 by President Theodore Roosevelt. Like most of the early conservation activists, Teddy was a sportsman—his interest in wildlife was tied to his love of hunting. Throughout the history of wildlife conservation in the United States and Canada, many of the most important people and groups have been hunters (and anglers). The most familiar case of sportsmen helping wildlife conservation is the Migratory Bird Hunting and Conservation Stamp, usually called the Duck Stamp. The Duck Stamp Act in 1934 established the process by which hunters buy the current year's Duck Stamp to legally hunt waterfowl in the United States. The money goes into the Migratory Bird Conservation Fund, which is used to acquire land for national wildlife refuges.

The Duck Stamp program was extremely important for the acquisition of land in the beginning of the NWRS. However, over time additional and greater sources of funds for refuge acquisition have been developed. Since the early 1960s duck stamp funds have accounted for about a fifth of the total money used to buy land. In addition, the direct purchase of land is not the main avenue for refuge land acquisition. Most of the land in the NWRS has been simply reclassified from land already in the public domain.

Getting the land for the refuges is one cost, but equally important is the money needed to operate, maintain, and improve the refuges already in the system. Since 1961 the funds for refuge maintenance, administration, operations, and law enforcement have come from general taxpayer receipts at the level of about $300 million a year.

The total funding for the system is inadequate. A 1992 report by the Commission on New Directions for the NWRS said the system "suffers chronic fiscal starvation and administrative neglect." The situation has improved little since then. In the last few decades the NWRS has accumulated a $2.5 billion backlog of deferred maintenance and operations. The amount of funding per acre for the smaller National Park System is seven times greater than that for the refuges, and funding per acre for the larger National Forest System is four times greater than that for NWRS. The budget for operating and maintaining the largest system in the world of lands and waterways set aside specifically for wildlife is ridiculously low. Some refuges have begun to charge an admission fee to cover basic maintenance, and a national fee system is possible in the future. It is a good idea to check on the fee situation before visiting a refuge. These certainly are changing times for public lands.

Despite financial hardships, a great moment in the history of the NWRS occurred in 1997. Debate about the purposes of the refuges had been ongoing since the beginning of the refuge system. Some people felt that the refuges should be for the protection of wildlife and habitat, while others wanted to bring their jet skis, snowmobiles, and off-road vehicles. This group of users, and especially the industries that make these machines, advocated and lobbied for the refuges to be motorized recreation sites as much as they were areas for hunting and fishing. Energy and mining companies continue to apply political pressure to have oil, gas, and mineral extraction allowed on refuges.

Fortunately, in 1997 Congress passed the NWRS Improvement Act, which mandates that wildlife conservation is the singular mission of the refuge system, and human activities must be consistent with that mission. At the same time the act gives priority to certain wildlife-dependent recreational uses on national wildlife refuges—hunting, fishing, wildlife observation and photography, and environmental education and interpretation. The controversy continues, and some activities still need to be eliminated on some refuges. However, in the history of the national wildlife refuges the goals and purposes for the 95-million acre system have never been clearer: it is wildlife conservation, first and foremost.

The National Wildlife Refuge Association is a private nonprofit organization dedicated to protecting, enhancing, and expanding the NWRS. Individual memberships help support the association's work (www.refugenet.org). Also, a coalition of 20 organizations called C.A.R.E. (Cooperative Alliance for Refuge Enhancement) have banded together to advocate for the NWRS. They are another excellent source of information about advocacy for the national wildlife refuges and can be contacted through the National Wildlife Refuge Association.

GREAT GANGS OF GULLS

Ask any kid to name a bird that lives at the beach and the answer will be sea gulls, for gulls are the most conspicuous wildlife along almost any stretch of coastline in North America. In our region "sea gull" is one of the first birds young children learn to identify, right along with duck and owl. It's kind of ironic then that no bird has the official common name *sea gull*. This always comes as a surprise whenever I mention it in birdwatching classes or programs. How can I say there is no such thing as a sea gull? What do I mean by official common name?

Bird watchers are lucky because ornithologists have established a system whereby every bird in North America has one official common name in English that everybody uses. This is not the case with other animals and plants, where there is often lots of confusion over common names. To be accurate and consistent with other living things, scientists and amateur naturalists are forced to use the mumbo jumbo of scientific names, something that turns off a lot of people. But with birds the situation is wonderful. The A.O.U. (American Ornithologists Union) establishes the common names and then books, birders, and naturalists, professional or amateur, use them. This way it is always clear what people are talking about. Sometimes the names are changed, such as oldsquaw to long-tailed duck or rock dove to rock pigeon, but overall, the system makes learning and using bird names easy.

So, if they aren't sea gulls, what are they? Well, they are gulls—lots of different kinds of gulls with different names like western gull or mew gull, but all gulls. Gulls are found throughout the world in coastal areas, rivers and lakes, and marshes. Sea gull is a misleading name because few gulls spend much time in the open ocean, and many live inland in freshwater habitats. Some gulls never even see an ocean in their life. But they are definitely waterbirds and are well adapted for swimming with webbed feet, as are ducks. Gulls do not swim underwater as many waterbirds do and only very rarely dive into the water like their close relatives the terns. Gulls swim on the surface and either pick food off the surface or poke their head underwater to grab it. They also spend lots of time walking on the shores of oceans, rivers, and lakes eating whatever they can find that has been washed ashore.

Gulls are omnivorous and will eat almost anything, including carrion.

Their importance as scavengers has long been recognized by complete legal protection. They are often called the garbage men of the beach. Like many other omnivores, gulls are quite intelligent and adaptable and are famous for some of their feeding behaviors. Gulls will fly over rocks with mollusks (mussels, clams) and drop the mollusks on the rocks to crack them open. Some gulls have even learned to leave hard-shelled animals scattered over parking lots where cars will run over them and crack them open. If you have ever picnicked on the beach, you know that gulls can quickly determine if people have food and will move in for handouts or the chance to snatch a morsel from the inattentive picnicker. Some people enjoy launching crackers or slices of bread like Frisbees and watching the gulls' skill at snatching them out of the air. This is not, however, a healthy diet for gulls.

Gulls are one of the most gregarious of birds and are always in flocks, even when nesting. Sometimes they form huge flocks numbering in the thousands with several species intermixed. You may see different species side-by-side, allowing you to compare their field marks.

As birders know, gulls present identification problems. Most of the many different species are similar in appearance. Even worse, each has a breeding plumage that is different from its non-breeding (or winter) plumage. Plus, gulls take two, three, or even four years to get their adult plumage. Immature gulls are really a bird identification nightmare: don't even think about trying to identify immature gulls until you've got a good handle on the adults. Gull identification usually centers on the color of the mantle (the top of the wings and back), contrast between the mantle and the wing tips, bill color and markings, and leg color.

The Pacific Northwest, with its coastline and freshwater habitats, is great gull country. Thirteen species of gulls, almost a third of the world's total species, are regularly seen in our region, although some are much more common than others. There are also a few rarities that only show up occasionally. Winter is the best time to see gulls because many breed north of us or in the interior and spend the winter along our coast. During the winter there is plenty of gull movement and many are also seen along interior rivers and unfrozen lakes, and in urban areas where there is food. However, the best gull action is on the coast.

Two gulls breed along our coastline and are common there all year, the western gull and the glaucous-winged gull. Glaucous-winged are more common as you go north; the opposite is true for western gulls—they are more common the farther south you go. The two interbreed regularly where they occur together, and some question whether they are really separate species. The other common, year-round gulls in our region are the ring-billed and California gulls, which are common breeders in the interior and spend a lot of time on the coast. Six gulls breed north of us and pass through during migration or spend the winter here: Bonaparte's, mew, herring, Thayer's, and glaucous gulls and the black-legged kittiwake. Of these six, the glaucous gull (not to be confused with the glaucous-winged) is really a bird of the far north and is the rarest of the gulls seen regularly. Three other gulls occur in small numbers in winter. Sabine's gulls are seen regularly during migration but are usually well off shore, so they are normally seen on pelagic birding boat trips. Franklin's and Heermann's gulls are summer visitors who stay into the fall but are usually not around all winter.

During the winter you can find gulls near almost any large body of unfrozen water. They are particularly numerous on the edges of estuaries and bays and in wet pastures and fields along the coast. They are common at garbage dumps and sewage treatment ponds—not the most scenic spots for birding, but often productive. At city park ponds where ducks are fed they'll be there for a handout. They often congregate in large numbers around a good food supply; for example, at places such as fish cleaning tables on a wharf. Unless regularly harassed, they show almost no fear of people and are usually easy to approach.

▶ GREAT GANGS OF GULLS BEST BETS OREGON

Westmoreland Park, in the Sellwood-Moreland neighborhood of Southeast Portland, has many different species of gulls in a small area, making it a good place to practice your identification skills. Portland birdwatchers will often stop there when going between Crystal Springs Park and Oaks Bottom Wildlife Refuge. These three Portland city parks make for an awesome trio of urban wetlands, sometimes resulting in a dozen different species of ducks alone. Westmoreland Park is the spot for the gulls because many well-intentioned but misguided people go there to feed the birds bread. Head east on Bybee Blvd from its intersection with SE Milwaukie in the Westmoreland district and turn right on SE 22nd Ave. Drive south on 22nd until you can see the lake in the park, and then park on the street. Check out the area on the west side of the lake and along the outlet stream that flows south.

Unless they have gone to feed on smelt in the Columbia River, you should be able to find plenty of gulls: glaucous-winged, herring, Thayer's, California, ring-billed, mew, and occasionally Bonaparte's.

▶ GREAT GANGS OF GULLS BEST BETS WASHINGTON

Ediz Hook, the large spit that shelters Port Angeles harbor, provides some great birding, including gulls. It is considered one of the better spots in the state to find large rare gulls, such as the glaucous gull, and is a good place to work on separating herring from Thayer's gulls. Ediz Hook also has a nice variety of shorebirds, wintering waterfowl, and sea birds, including long-tailed and harlequin ducks. In the town of Port Angeles, get on Front St (one of the main east–west streets near the waterfront) and take it west until it turns into Marine Dr. Continue on Marine Dr, driving through the middle of the huge Daishowa paper plant (which will seem a bit odd). Just keep going, watch for the stop sign and go slow, and follow any Coast Guard and Ediz Hook signs you see. The public road ends at the gate and parking area for

the Coast Guard station. You cannot go into the Coast Guard area, but you can stop anywhere along the spit between the paper plant and the Coast Guard station. Most birds will be inside the harbor, but it's worth checking the other side a few times. The big rafts of logs often attract shorebirds and gulls, as well as other birds.

Grays Harbor, one of the largest estuaries on the west coast, is one of the state's most famous birding spots. The southern end of the Ocean Shores peninsula has several well-known birding areas—Point Brown, Damon Point, and Oyhut WA—that are good for gulls, shorebirds, waterfowl, and seabirds. This area is described in August (Fall Shorebird Migration).

▶ GREAT GANGS OF GULLS BEST BETS BRITISH COLUMBIA

The farm fields of the Delta-Ladner area, between Boundary Bay and Hwy 99, are great for gulls, as they are for raptors and waterfowl. This area is described in January (Wintering Raptors), and the time to go is during the highest tides.

Just a few miles to the northwest of Delta is another of British Columbia's hottest birding spots, Iona Island, which consists of a large sewage treatment plant and Iona Beach RP. Drive the road to its end in the regional park at the parking area with restrooms. The pond, just east of the parking area, was established

for birds and is usually the best pond on the island for waterfowl, grebes, coots, and gulls. The dune grass and bushes around the beach may have birds such as wintering sparrows (white-crowned, golden-crowned, white-throated, Harris's) or northern shrike. A walk or bike ride on the 2.5-mile jetty, which contains the waste water effluent pipe and heads southwest into the Strait of Georgia, may reveal seabirds and waterfowl. In addition, the rocks of the jetty itself are good for rock-loving shorebirds, such as tattlers, turnstones, and surfbirds. But if you're looking for gulls, search the areas around the ponds, mudflats, and shores. Iona is also known for a good variety of wintering raptors—keep your eyes open for short-eared owls, merlins, peregrine falcons, and maybe even a gyrfalcon. Wow!

A popular attraction on Vancouver Island is the drive along the southeastern coast of Victoria from Beacon Hill Park, near the Parliament Buildings, toward the University of Victoria. This is sometimes referred to as the scenic marine drive or Victoria breakwater. To start head west on Dallas Rd until you get to the turnout at Clover Point Park. This is a great place to study gulls, but also check the shoreline for rock-loving shorebirds and, of course, check the water. From here continue west on Dallas Rd, which goes through a confusing series of road name changes and ends up as Beach Dr. Just stay on the main road and don't worry about the name changes. Continue on Beach Dr as it winds around the tip of Vancouver Island and heads north past Oak Bay, finally arriving at Cattle Point. This is another park where you can explore the different habitats for gulls, shorebirds, harlequin ducks, alcids, cormorants, and so on. In the spring the oak woodland part of the park on the other side of Beach Dr can be full of wildflowers and songbirds.

The fall salmon run in Goldstream Park is a major "gull event" worth knowing about. In November large numbers of gulls show up in the park to eat salmon eggs and spawned-out carcasses along the Goldstream River (also see October).

FEBRUARY'S NATURE NUGGETS

GREAT BACKYARD BIRD COUNT The Christmas Bird Count is well known because it's been going on for over 100 years and involves thousands of people. Now there's a new count in the neighborhood. The first Great Backyard Bird Count was in February 1998 and participation is growing. Registration and reporting is online. The results, which pour in from all over North America, show up on the Web site almost immediately. This four-day count is another way to get an idea of the trends in bird populations over the years.

IMBOLC In some ways the ancient Celtic calendar made more sense than our system today. The first days of the seasons were not on the equinoxes and solstices, but on the days halfway between them. The longest day of the year was in the middle of summer, not at the beginning, the shortest day of the year in the middle of winter, and so on. The first day of spring was Imbolc, which corresponds to one of the first days of February. In the Northwest this rings true because we see many early signs of spring in February, at least west of the Cascades. The first trees are blooming: red alder, filbert, and Indian-plum. Pacific chorus frogs (treefrogs) are calling, and by the end of the month the first migrating birds, tree swallows and turkey vultures, return. By the spring equinox, spring is really in gear—not just starting. Interestingly, the Celtic first day of spring lives on today in another holiday.

The early Catholic Church turned Imbolc into the Christian holy day Candlemas. The day of Candlemas, February 2, came to be seen as a harbinger of spring. The weather on that day would predict the end of winter. With the Protestant Reformation the celebration of Candlemas almost died out, but German farmers had developed a tradition of watching hedgehogs at this time of year to predict the weather. If the hedgehog saw his shadow on Candlemas, more harsh winter weather was ahead. Is this starting to sound familiar? When German farmers immigrated to Pennsylvania they couldn't find any hedgehogs (there are none in the New World) so they picked a common native animal, a type of marmot that we now call the groundhog or woodchuck. Some guys in the town of Punxsutawney, Pennsylvania, decided to make a special day out of this tradition: Groundhog Day was born.

WINTER SPARROWS Seeds are a major and available food source during winter, so the seed-eating sparrows are among our most common wintering songbirds. Song, fox, and white-crowned sparrows are present year round and are abundant in winter, as are dark-eyed juncos, down from their breeding grounds in the mountains. Lincoln's and savannah sparrows are primarily summer residents but are also present in small numbers during the winter, mainly on the warmer west side. Winter brings thousands of golden-crowned sparrows to the Northwest from their northern breeding range (which starts at the northern edge of our region). The real excitement comes from a small group of sparrow species that show up almost every winter, though unpredictably and in small numbers. They are often seen flocking with other sparrows, making it worth a careful check of sparrow flocks during the winter in the hope of seeing these rare winter visitors. White-throated and Harris's sparrows are usually seen flocking with their relatives—the other "crowned" sparrows. Tree sparrows and snow buntings are usually seen only on the east side. Swamp sparrows and Lapland longspurs are most commonly encountered near the coast. Good places to look are in brambles near fields. Often the best sites are fence rows along dirt roads in farmland. Your non-birder friends will think you've really flipped when you say you're headed out into cold winter weather to search for sparrows in blackberry thickets. Happy sparrow hunting!

EAST SIDE, WEST SIDE: A CLOSER LOOK

The Pacific Northwest has the greatest coniferous forests in the world (in terms of tree size and diversity) and the highest rainfall in the contiguous United States. People familiar with the region know, however, that most of Oregon and Washington are actually arid to semi-arid lands and are commonly called high desert. The Pacific Northwest has a wide range of climates and habitats that are intermingled somewhat, but it's easy to divide the region into two main parts: the wet part and the dry part.

The Cascade Range essentially makes a north-to-south running barrier that divides the region into roughly one third wet (west) and two thirds dry (east). The terms *east side* or *west side* refer to the appropriate side of the crest of the Cascade Range. In British Columbia "the wall" is not as straight and gets closer to the coast, but British Columbia's Coast Mountains function as an extension of the Cascades, as far as rainfall is concerned.

The two sides of the Pacific Northwest have different communities of plants and animals. Of the many factors that determine what types of plants and animals will occur in a particular spot, climate is usually the most important. So what causes the Pacific Northwest to have the type of climate it has?

Latitude certainly plays a big role, but other local factors can easily override its influence. For example, the Pacific Northwest has a much milder climate than Newfoundland, another coastal area at the same latitude. Three factors interact to determine the climate in the Pacific Northwest: the Pacific Ocean, the region's mountains, and the westerly winds. How do they interact to give us our weather?

All bodies of water act as heat reservoirs, gaining and releasing heat slowly and thereby moderating temperature changes on nearby land. The bigger the body of water, the stronger the moderating effect. The Pacific Ocean, the largest body of water on Earth, has a strong maritime effect on our region. Surface temperatures in the ocean off our coast are usually about 50°F and typically vary less than 5 degrees during a year. The maritime influence is so strong that it affects the climate as far away as the eastern borders of Oregon and Washington.

Temperature differences between the east and west sides can be striking. Temperatures change much less on the west side, both daily and annually. For example, the two Washington cities of Aberdeen and Yakima are close to the same latitude but 160 miles apart. Aberdeen is on Grays Harbor, just

15 miles inland from the coast, while Yakima is about 40 miles east of the Cascade crest. The average minimum temperature for January is a chilly 16°F in Yakima but a mild 34°F in Aberdeen. Come summertime, Yakima heats up with an average maximum for July of 88°F while Aberdeen is again more temperate at 70°F. The range between average minimum and maximum temperatures is 72°F in Yakima but only half that, 36°, in Aberdeen.

Oregon shows the same pattern. The average annual Fahrenheit temperature range in Ontario, in eastern Oregon, is over 80 degrees while Brookings, on the southwest coast, is only 40 degrees, again about half the range. Daily temperature range shows the same pattern. The average daily temperature range in July is 40 degrees Fahrenheit in Summer Lake but only about 16 degrees in Brookings. Brookings is so much warmer than the rest of Oregon during much of the winter that weather reporters often call it "the banana belt."

The weather in our region can be seen as a battle between two forces—the moist and mild maritime climate versus the dry and temperature extreme continental climate. The battle line is the Cascades which more or less separates the two and maintains the typical weather on each side. But exciting changes can occur when high and low pressure areas shift and either force invades the other. Such a shift brings storms and can bring unseasonably extreme temperatures to the west side or carry abnormal amounts of precipitation to the east side. The Columbia River Gorge, the big gap where the weather of the two sides is constantly mixing, is almost constantly very windy and prone to storms.

The mountains of the Northwest have a profound influence on precipitation. All mountains have some effect on their local weather, but when you have a major mountain range like the Cascades running the entire length of both states, north to south, the effect is dramatic indeed. The prevailing winds cause this strong effect. Semi-permanent high and low pressure cells over the North Pacific Ocean result in westerly winds blowing steadily from the ocean eastward over the land. Loaded with moisture from the ocean, these winds interact with the mountains to give us our noted precipitation.

The warmer that air is, the more water vapor it can hold. As winds blow over the ocean at about 50°F the air becomes saturated with water. These moist winds come off the ocean and blow over the land. The colder that air is, the less moisture it can hold. If the temperature over the land is colder than the temperature over the ocean (a common situation for much of the year) condensation occurs, resulting in fog or precipitation. As the air moves farther east, hits the mountains, and starts to rise, it gets colder, about 5 degrees Fahrenheit for every 1000 feet in elevation. As the air gets colder more water vapor condenses and falls as precipitation. Hence, the west or windward sides of the mountains get soaked. By the time the air has moved over mountains as high as the Cascades, it has lost most of its moisture. As the air descends on the east side the opposite process occurs. Falling air warms up and absorbs more moisture, actually drying out the land on the east side of the mountains. The resulting lower precipitation on the leeward side of the mountains is called a rain shadow.

The same process occurs when air travels over other mountains. The Coast Ranges, the Olympic Mountains, and the Vancouver Island Ranges intercept a lot of moisture from the wet westerlies before they hit the Cascades. East of the Cascades, interior ranges like the Blue Mountains and the Selkirks show the same, though less dramatic, rain shadow effect. Because most of the mountains in the Northwest run north and south, and the winds bring the moisture from the west, a map of the region color-coded for precipitation shows a series of north and south running bands, paralleling the mountains—latitude has little to do with precipitation patterns here.

A check of the precipitation records for Yakima and Aberdeen demonstrates how dramatic this rain shadow effect can be. Yakima receives only 8 inches of precipitation a year while Aberdeen averages 85 inches, 10 times as much.

Another striking example occurs on the two sides of the Olympic Mountains. The Hoh Rainforest averages 135 inches of rain a year while the town of Sequim, just 40 miles to the northeast, receives only 15 inches. Of course, between the two are the 7000-foot Olympics, which collect most of the moisture and have some of the highest snowfall levels in the lower 48.

Many factors interact to determine which communities of plants and animals are found in a particular location. Topography, soil, and interactions between living things play a big part but the most important factor is climate. Once you understand the basic climates of the Northwest, the distributions of different plants and animals fall into logical patterns.

MARCH

GRAY WHALE MIGRATION

The change in public attitude toward whales is one of the fastest and most dramatic turnarounds I have ever seen. In just a decade from the 1960s to the 1970s, public opinion about whales went from indifference or exploitation to concern and reverence. What were once seen as monsters by many and as sources of oil and fertilizer by a few became widely respected and highly admired for their intelligence, beauty, and exquisite adaptation to their marine environment. This change in human attitudes and behavior, brought about by an incredibly small but highly dedicated group of activists, is one of the most encouraging examples of what we can do to help our planet and its wildlife.

Whales are the largest animals that have ever lived on Earth. Any animal that can reach 100 feet in length and weigh 220 tons is going to get some attention, even if it does live in a different world than ours. Prehistoric people started hunting whales for food at least 6000 years ago in what is now Korea and Japan. Whale hunting spread to different countries and increased slowly over the centuries, then increased tremendously with new technology in the last 200 years. As with many other animals, whales were overhunted until many species were on the brink of extinction by the 1900s. Fortunately, early conservationists and the Save the Whales campaigns of the 1970s changed global public opinion. In 1982 the International Whaling Commission voted for a moratorium on commercial whaling, which took effect in 1985–1986. However, not every country abides by the moratorium; some whales continue to be killed, mainly by Japan and Norway. The recent increase in the number of whales killed remains a political issue.

Fortunately, the more people learned about whales, the more concerned they became about their survival. New knowledge made it clear that whales

A pair of great blue herons settles in for the nesting season.

are intelligent animals with social organization and complex communication. Thousands of people were enchanted listening to recordings of the eerie and hauntingly beautiful songs made by whales. Some musicians, most notably Paul Winter, were inspired to write music based on whale sounds and to even play music to, and with, whales. To some, whales became mystical beings with a spirituality and intelligence beyond our understanding. Whale watching, from shore and by boat, has become an extremely popular activity and a major type of ecotourism. What a difference for an animal that used to be systematically slaughtered for corset stays and oil.

Whales are mammals, not fish, which they superficially resemble. Like mammals they breathe air with lungs, are endotherms (warm blooded), and nurse their young. Whales evolved from ancient ancestors that were land animals. This evolution, with many adaptations for a totally aquatic life, has fascinated scientists for decades. The term *whales* refers to the order or group of mammals named *cetaceans*, which includes whales, porpoises, and dolphins. The cetaceans are divided into two large groups, the baleen whales and the toothed whales, which includes porpoises and dolphins.

The gray whale is a medium-large baleen whale 35 to 50 feet long and weighing 20 to 40 tons. They are gray in color—but very blotchy with light and dark gray spots, patches of barnacles and white scars where barnacles have been. Instead of a dorsal fin, they have a series of bumps on the rear of their back. Gray whales are unique in that they are the only living member of their family and fossils are unknown. They undertake the longest migration of any mammal, swimming 8000 to 14,000 miles round trip every year between their summer range in the North Pacific and their winter range in Baja California. They are the most coastal of the baleen whales, rarely venturing far out to sea.

Like all baleen whales, gray whales do not have teeth but have sheets of baleen or whalebone that hang down from their upper jaw. Baleen is made of the same material as our fingernails and looks and feels like plastic. The sheets of baleen have fringed edges, making an effective filter or sieve. These animals feed by filtering vast quantities of small animals out of the water. It seems paradoxical that the world's largest animals feed on such small prey, but it is the incredible numbers and reliable occurrence of small prey, such as crustaceans, that have allowed the great whales to evolve to their huge size. Gray whales are the only bottom-feeding whales, feeding primarily by sucking up and filtering soft bottom sediments.

Because gray whales regularly swim close to shore during their migrations, they were probably one of the first whales known to humans, and thus one of the first to be exploited. Aboriginal hunters in Asia and North America killed limited numbers for centuries, probably with little environmental impact, but modern whaling between 1845 and 1930 quickly decimated the population. Fortunately the United States, Mexico, and the International Whaling Commission passed various laws and regulations in the 1930s and 1940s, which resulted in complete protection by 1946. The result is one of the happiest stories of wildlife conservation. The recovery of the gray whale has been the fastest of any whale. It is believed that the approximately 20,000–24,000 now living is close to the population centuries ago. In 1994 the gray whale was removed from the endangered species list, the first marine animal ever delisted.

The gray whale's amazing recovery, their habits, and their range make them one of the best known of all whales. Because they migrate very close to the Pacific Coast of the United States every year, millions of people have seen them from shore and, increasingly, from boats and even small airplanes. Whale-watching boat tours have become a major business in many coastal towns, and some fear the whales might get harassed by the boat loads of their admirers. Of particular concern are the shallow bays in Baja where the calves are born during the winter and where whale-watching tours have increased dramatically. Governmental agencies and concerned organizations have produced various guidelines and laws governing whale-watching activities and reputable tour companies will follow these procedures.

Gray whales pass our coast during two periods. The majority of gray whales spend the summer feeding in the Bering and Chukchi seas. In October, the pregnant females are the first to leave for the southern wintering and calving lagoons, followed over the next two months by the males, juveniles, and non-pregnant females. Peak numbers occur off our coast in December with most animals making it to Baja by the end of January, although stragglers pass by for months. On their southward journey the whales tend to move faster and farther from shore than on their return in spring.

During December in the calving lagoons of Baja the females give birth to their single young, which grow quickly on their mother's rich milk, gaining as much as 60 pounds a day. By mid-February the first whales have already started back north, but the moms and their new calves won't leave until May or even June. Peak numbers of north-bound whales occur from mid-March to mid-April. The whales, particularly the mothers and new calves, move slower and closer to shore during their spring migration, making this the best time for observation. Several hundred gray whales actually skip the long journey back to the Arctic and hang out along our coastline all summer, joining the main population when it passes through the next winter. With all the early starters, stragglers, and dawdlers, it is now possible to see gray whales off our coast any time of year, but the prime time is during the peak of spring migration.

To see whales from land, get as far out into the ocean as you can, such as on a point or headland. Being elevated is also a huge advantage. You find whales by looking for their spouts ("thar she blows"), so the calmer the water, the better. This means early mornings are usually better than afternoons, when winds often pick up and make whitecaps. Overcast skies are best but that is usually not a problem in the Pacific Northwest. Watch the water about an inch below the horizon. Gray whales usually make 3 to 5 blows, 30 to 50 seconds apart, before they make a dive for 5 to 10 minutes. They usually travel in small groups, so where you see one blow, you'll usually see others. Once you get used to their pattern of diving and blowing, you'll be able to find them more easily with binoculars and spotting scope for closer looks. If you are lucky you may see them breach—a spectacular jump almost out of the water.

Seeing whales by boat can be a great family outing, but take care to dress much more warmly than you would think. It is amazing how windy and cold it can be standing around on a moving boat. I recommend taking motion sickness medication in advance of the trip (my favorite is meclizine). Ask the chamber of commerce or visitor information center in coastal towns for information on tour operators.

▶ GRAY WHALE MIGRATION BEST BETS OREGON

Oregon is awesome for gray whale watching because it has the most public access to the coast and the Whale Watching Spoken Here program. This is a cooperative program between Oregon state parks and the Sea Grant Program at the Hatfield Marine Science Center, part of the Oregon State University Extension Service, in Newport. For decades, this amazing program has had 200 trained volunteers at 28 whale-watching sites on the Oregon coast for two weeks to help tens of thousands of folks see and learn about the migrating gray whales. One week is the week of school vacation after Christmas; the second week is spring break, usually the last full week in March. Isn't it nice that the whales migrate during school vacations? Volunteers are at all 28 sites for several hours every day during a Whale Watching Week. Signs that read "Whale Watching Spoken Here" are posted on the highway at each site. The winter week catches the whales headed south and the spring week is right at the peak of the migration north—the best time to see the most whales. Most tour boat operators do not run tours during the winter migration but wait until March and April because of weather and sea conditions.

The best places to look for gray whales in the summer are Boiler Bay, Depoe Bay, and Yaquina Head. I had my closest encounter ever with gray whales, mom and calf, right offshore from the tidepool area at Yaquina Head. Another Whale Watching Week with volunteers at these three sites occurs the week before Labor Day. A story about the event appears in major newspapers in the state usually the week before each Whale Watching Week. Here are eight of the 28 best sites recommended by staff at the Marine Science Center:

- Ecola SP, just north of Cannon Beach, has several easy trails that lead to good observation sites.

- Some turnouts along US Hwy 101, as it traverses Neahkahnie Mountain in Oswald West SP, provide breathtaking views of the coast from Tillamook Head to Cape Lookout. You'll find volunteers at the largest turnout, the site of a historical marker.

- For excellent views, from the parking lot at Cape Meares SP walk about 0.25 mile on a paved trail to the lighthouse on the tip of the cape. Watch for the unique population of gray jays that live on the cape and check out the Octopus Tree.

- The 2.5-mile hike from the trailhead at Cape Lookout SP to the end of the cape is one of the best spots in the Northwest to see gray whales. The cape sticks so far out into the ocean that the whales "hug the point" as they pass and sometimes you are almost looking straight down on them as if you were in a helicopter. The trail to the end of Cape Lookout is spectacular by itself with dramatic views of Cape Meares to the north and Cape Kiwanda to the south. It's a three-capes grand slam. The trail has magnificent sections of old-growth Sitka spruce and western hemlock forest with a rich understory of flowers. It's a wonderful day's adventure even without the added bonus of whale spotting.

- Boiler Bay SP is right on US 101, about halfway between Lincoln City and Newport, and is one of the most convenient sites.

- Yaquina Head, just north of Newport, also has easy access as well as excellent viewing of not only whales but also birds, seals, and tidepools.

- The turnout on US Hwy 101 between Heceta Head and Sea Lion Caves, just north of Florence, is another convenient spot.

- Cape Ferrelo, near Brookings, is one of the better spots to see gray whales during the summer.

▶ GRAY WHALE MIGRATION BEST BETS WASHINGTON

Washington does not have the number of rocky headlands so characteristic of the Oregon coast and public access to the shore is much more limited. The best gray whale–watching spots are in the coastal section of Olympic NP. At Cape Alava, the most westerly point of land in the lower 48 states, you might see not only gray whales but tidepools, seals and sea lions, many birds, and even the possibility of some of the few sea otters reintroduced along the Washington coast. Cape Alava is fairly isolated, being a 3.3-mile hike from the Ozette Ranger Station in the far northwestern corner of the park.

A closer area is near the town of La Push. Just north of the town of Forks take the La Push road toward La Push, but follow signs for Mora and eventually Rialto Beach in Olympic NP. Whales will sometimes enter the estuary of the Quileute River and be quite close. The easiest access and viewing of gray whales in Washington is along the stretch of US 101 that hugs the coast from Ruby Beach to Queets. Any of the turnouts or parking areas on the cliffs will give you access to views of the water.

The most popular way to see gray whales in Washington is by boat out of the busy seaport town of Westport at the mouth of Grays Harbor. Sometimes during spring high tides whales actually enter the harbor, coming very close to the waterfront of the town. The municipal fishing pier, rock jetties, seawall, and inner harbor provide interesting sights and opportunities to see a variety of coastal birds, from loons to shorebirds. Contact the Westport-Grayland Chamber of Commerce (www.westportgrayland-chamber.org) to get a list of charter boat companies running whale-watching trips. Trips are two to three hours long and usually available March through May.

▶ GRAY WHALE MIGRATION BEST BETS BRITISH COLUMBIA

Although some gray whales occasionally wander into the Strait of Juan de Fuca, most migrate off the west coast of Vancouver Island, which has limited access. The place in British Columbia for gray whale watching is the Long Beach Unit of Pacific Rim NP and the nearby towns of Ucluelet and Tofino. The two towns and the park have joined together each spring since 1987 to produce the Pacific Rim Whale Festival, a nine-day, event-packed community festival that includes field trips, exhibits, kid's activities, art, food, and music. The dates change a bit year to year but are in the middle of March, the same time as the public school spring break.

To reach Pacific Rim NP by car, drive west on Hwy 4 from Port Alberni. When you reach the area, stop at the Wickaninnish Center in the park to get maps and information. From Port Alberni, you'll reach a major junction where you can turn left (south) to Ucluelet or right (north) to the park and Tofino. Just over 3 miles from the junction is the road to Wickaninnish. The center has some excellent displays, movies, outdoor observation areas, an amazingly great little restaurant (plan a meal here) and park staff that can answer your questions. Wickaninnish Center is a great place to visit if it's raining, a likely possibility, because this area has the highest rainfall in British Columbia. The center is closed during winter; hours vary other times of year.

The best spots in the park to see whales from land are at Wickaninnish Center, Wya

Point, and Box Island, the eastern headland to Schooner Cove. The last two spots require hikes of about 2 miles round trip. The best spot from land, however, is at the coast guard station and lighthouse on Amphitrite Point, less than one mile south of Ucluelet. Drive through Ucluelet on the main road and just south of town turn right onto Coast Guard Rd. A small sign reads "Lighthouse." Drive a short distance to the end of the road and park in the parking lot. Look in the carport for the sign to the viewpoint and follow it to a wonderful view off the point. Whales often pass close to the point and bald eagles are commonly seen.

Several charter companies in both Tofino and Ucluelet run whale-watching boat trips; ask at Wickaninnish Center for a list or check the festival Web site. Tofino and Ucluelet both offer a wide range of accommodations and restaurants, and although they are only 25 miles apart, each has its own character and style. Pacific Rim NP has excellent examples of ancient forests and is also well known for its tidepools.

EARLY BLOOMERS

Winter is short in the Northwest at low elevations on the west side. The time from when the last leaves fall to when the first plants are blooming may be only a couple of months. The first flowers I notice every year are the long greenish-yellow catkins hanging down on the western hazel (wild filbert) in late January. These are soon followed by the reddish catkins of the red alder. The extended catkins give the tops of the alders that fuzzy orange look at the peak of their bloom, in late February or early March. These inconspicuous catkins are certainly not what most people think of when they think of wildflowers—many will miss this subtle sign of spring.

The next, and much more noticeable, tree to show some action is Indian plum or osoberry. In February the flower clusters hang down from the tips of the branches, but it is the new leaves that come out at the same time that attract attention. These new leaves are a bright green, almost chartreuse, and stand straight up on the branches. The trees look like some kind of strange candelabra with bright green flames. In the otherwise bare, gray woods they really stand out. About this same time we get the first real splash of color from the large, bright yellow spathes of skunk cabbage. Skunk cabbage likes it really wet, actually growing in standing water, so its distribution is spotty. It's particularly common in flooded pastures near the coast where it sometimes makes large displays.

After these earliest bloomers the wildflower season gets underway with one of the showiest and most beloved Northwest flowers, the western trillium. These spectacular flowers have three large, bright-white petals that fade to pink or purple as they age, fooling many into thinking there are two differ-ent species in the same place. (There actually are two other, quite distinctive, species of trillium in the Northwest, but they are uncommon.) Once the tril-lium are out, the blooming season is really underway, and one can keep busy botanizing; that is, looking for wildflowers until the end of summer by going to different habitats and elevations. Some of our most common early wild-flowers in west-side forests are wood violet, coltsfoot, wild ginger, bittercress, salmonberry, slender toothwort, red-flowering currant, candy flower, and Oregon grape. These are closely followed by fairybells, bleeding heart, camas, buttercups, large-leaved geum, star flower, vanilla leaf, mitrewort, youth-on-age, fringecup, and foam flower.

As with animals, each species of plant has a preferred habitat, which is often a helpful clue in location and identification. Some, like Douglas-fir, are generalists and grow in a variety of conditions while others, like the cobra lily, are very restricted. Plant guides usually include some description of each plant's habitat.

Scattered throughout our coniferous forests are areas with lower rainfall or with shallow and often rocky soil where conifers do not do well. This results in meadows or open woodlands with Oregon white (or Garry) oak and madrone, often mixed with Douglas-fir, as the dominant trees. Many early wildflowers are found here because these areas get more sunlight and dry out faster. Some conspicuous flowers of these habitats are blue-eyed grass, yellow bells, grass widows, fawn lilies, prairie stars, some buttercups, shooting stars, some saxifrages, and the confusing desert parsleys.

Exactly when a particular plant blooms can vary greatly from place to place and year to year. Such factors as elevation, slope, exposure, and weather will affect the particular micro-habitat of each plant. In general, the blooming season is later east of the Cascades because of higher elevations and longer, colder winters. Blooming is also later and the season shorter at higher eleva-tions, so alpine areas aren't in bloom until July or August. The key to successful wildflower hunting it to start early in the season and get out as much as pos-sible as the season progresses. Plan to revisit these areas as different flowers come into bloom throughout the spring.

The network of amateur botanists and naturalists in your area can also help.

These groups will usually be a native plant society or an Audubon chapter in the States and a natural history society or the Federation of BC Naturalists in Canada. Botanical gardens, natural history museums, and occasionally garden clubs can also be good sources of information about wildflowers. Community colleges and park departments may also have wildflower classes and trips.

Good books are the other important resource for flower identification; you'll find my recommendations in the bibliography.

▶ EARLY BLOOMERS BEST BETS OREGON

The Klamath Mountains create a rain shadow in the valleys of the Rogue River and its tributaries, making the southwestern corner of Oregon just a bit sunnier and drier than the rest of western Oregon. Here you'll find animals that are much more common in California but are rarely found in our region: black phoebe, oak titmouse, blue-gray gnatcatcher, California towhee, two types of kingsnakes, ringtail, and California kangaroo rat. The plants also show strong California affinities with forests and woodlands that are a mix of black oak as well as Oregon white oak, madrone, Douglas-fir, ponderosa pine, sugar pine, tanoak, and incense cedar. Extensive stands of various species of ceanothus, manzanita, and other chaparral species lends a distinct California feel to the landscape. Southwestern Oregon is a great mixing area, with plants from the Cascades, the Sierra Nevada, and the Northern California Coast Range all intermingled.

Upper Table Rock and Lower Table Rock are two conspicuous mesas in the Rogue Valley that have open sunny grasslands with vernal pools on top. They have a fabulous display of California and Northwest wildflowers in the spring. Both Table Rocks are a mixture of private land and BLM-managed public land, with The Nature Conservancy a third owner of Lower Table Rock. The BLM designated the Table Rocks an Area of Critical Environmental Concern to protect the special plant and animal species, geology, scenic values, and educational opportunities. Both Table Rocks now have a paved parking lot with a well-established trail going to the top of the mesa. Lower Table Rock also has an easier, more accessible loop trail with interpretive panels about the oak savannah community so common in this part of Oregon.

The Table Rocks trails are among the most popular in southwestern Oregon, and the potential environmental impact from visitors is a concern. Please stay on the trails or roads, and avoid disturbing the vegetation and wildlife. Dogs are not allowed on either of the Table Rocks as part of this resource protection. Also be aware that at times you may be on private land so be a good guest.

The Medford District of the BLM has a full-time education coordinator for the Table Rocks, in collaboration with The Nature Conservancy. Every weekend in April and May, naturalists lead public hikes in the region specializing in a variety of topics. By the way, the words *upper* and *lower* have nothing to do with the elevation of the mesas; Upper Table Rock is upstream on the Rogue River from the downstream Lower Table Rock.

To reach either Table Rock, take the Central Point exit (Exit 32) from Interstate 5 north of Medford. Head east about one mile on Pine

St (which becomes Biddle Rd), then turn left and go north on Table Rock Rd. After 5 miles you'll reach the intersection with Modoc Rd. To get to Upper Table Rock, turn right onto Modoc and drive 1.5 miles to the parking area on your left. To get to Lower Table Rock from the intersection of Table Rock Rd and Modoc, continue past Modoc on Table Rock Rd for 2.5 miles, and then turn left onto Wheeler and go 0.75 mile to the parking area, also on your left. From the parking area it is a gradual uphill hike 1.5 miles to the top of Upper Table Rock and 1.75 miles to the top of Lower Table Rock. Most folks feel that Lower Table Rock, where the more accessible interpretive trail is located, is a bit wilder.

Take plenty of water and sun protection—this area can be hot and dry during sunny weather. Also be aware of three pests—poison oak, ticks, and rattlesnakes. What fun. Poison oak and rattlesnakes (which are rare) can easily be avoided, but ticks are harder to detect. Your best protection from the three is to stay on the trails, but I still spray my arms and legs with insect repellent in tick country.

Two other BLM-managed areas—Eight Dollar Mountain and Rough and Ready Botanical Wayside, have recently installed new wheelchair-accessible trails and viewing decks. To reach the Eight Dollar Mountain interpretive trail, head south on Hwy 199 from Grants Pass. After 24 miles turn right onto Eight Dollar Mountain Rd and drive 0.8 mile to the trailhead and small parking area. The elevated boardwalk is 700-feet long and has two viewing platforms. This is a good spot to see California pitcher plants. News flash! Just as this book heads to production there is great news. Oregon State Parks has just (2008) bought Eight Dollar Mountain for a new state natural area. This should protect the area and its fabulous plant diversity and mean more public access in the future.

You can look for more flowers by continuing on Eight Dollar Mountain Rd into the Siskiyou National Forest. About 2.5 miles from Hwy 199, Eight Dollar Mountain Rd will split off to the right, and the main road you are on will become FR 4201. Stay on FR 4201, which will curve to the left and cross over the Illinois River. There are no established trails or parking areas from here on, so this is open-ended exploring. Stop in any area that looks interesting and park safely along the road. Stay on FR 4201 as it starts climbing. In about 2 miles from the bridge over the Illinois River, the road will make a sharp, hairpin turn to the right. Park at this turn and a few hundred yards to the south you will find a huge patch of the wonderfully weird carnivorous California pitcher plants. FR 4201 continues uphill to the border of the Kalmiopsis Wilderness Area, named for the rare *Kalmiopsis leachiana*, an azalea-like shrub endemic to this part of the Siskiyou Mountains.

Rough and Ready Botanical Wayside is south of Eight Dollar Mountain on Hwy 199. From Cave Junction drive south for 5.2 miles, and then turn right into the parking area. The trail is an old mining road that heads west. Just 0.2 mile from the start, a short spur trail goes left to an overlook of Rough and Ready Creek. Take the spur trail to the overlook and explore that area, then return to the old road and continue west another 0.5 mile.

Common flowers of the western forested lowlands grow in almost any good chunk of native forest, but four places in Portland and one in Eugene offer a variety of flowers, convenient access with some visitor services, and guided walks and other programs about wildflowers. The Audubon Society of Portland's wildlife sanctuary has an excellent stand of second growth forest and several trails. The sanctuary is also the site of the society's book and nature store, meeting rooms, and offices. In Audubon

House you can get trail maps and information from the friendly staff and volunteers.

Close to Portland Audubon is Hoyt Arboretum. Much of the arboretum has plantings of trees and shrubs from around the world, but there are plenty of native plants as well. Self-guided trail maps are available at the visitor center. Guided walks are usually held on weekend afternoons from April to October. Children's programs as well as wildflower and other natural history classes are offered.

The Arboretum and the Audubon Society are part of a greater Forest Park system that stretches 9 miles from Washington Park to Newberry Rd. Linking the natural areas in this system is the 30-mile Wildwood Trail. Forest Park, with about 5000 acres of undeveloped land, is one of the largest city parks in the United States and has a total of 50 miles of trails. That's a lot of good habitat for wildflowers and in the fall, mushrooms. The Arboretum Visitor Center and Audubon House are both good sources for Forest Park information.

Tryon Creek State Natural Area straddles the boundary between Portland and Lake Oswego and is generally the same habitat as the Arboretum–Forest Park–Audubon ecosystem. Tryon Creek has a visitor center and, with the help of the Friends of Tryon Creek SP, offers a variety of natural history programs, guided hikes, activities, and a yearly native plant sale. For over 30 years, Tryon Creek has celebrated the abundant trillium with their annual Trillium Festival during the first weekend in April.

Leach Botanical Garden is unique among gardens. While the Leaches were living in this lovely southeast Portland estate, Lilla Leach collected and transplanted plants from all over Oregon and developed a living collection of native plants, now a city park. Yes, this is the Lilla Leach that discovered *Kalmiopsis leachiana*, the rare endemic shrub of the Siskiyou Mountains named for her. Though not in their natural plant communities, dozens of wildflowers await amateur naturalists at the botanical garden. Leach also has tours and programs and a plant sale that features some native plants.

The Mount Pisgah Arboretum is just east of Eugene and south of Springfield and occupies 209 acres within the Howard Buford Area, shown on more detailed maps. Seven miles of trails wind through a variety of plants native to the Willamette Valley and some from outside the state. Here you will find wildflowers typical of oak woodlands and the southern part of Oregon. The arboretum has a full range of programs and activities including a Spring Wildflower Festival in May and a Fall Mushroom Show at the end of October. In addition to being a great spot for botanizing, Mount Pisgah is an excellent birding spot for migrating songbirds. From I-5 take the 30th Ave (Exit 189). From the east end of 30th, turn left onto Franklin and head north. Follow the signs to the arboretum and you'll end up going east on Seavey Loop Rd. In a couple of miles you'll enter the Buford Recreation Area and turn onto Frank Parrish Rd, continuing to follow signs to the arboretum.

▶ EARLY BLOOMERS BEST BETS WASHINGTON

The most famous and popular wildflower area in the Northwest is the Columbia River Gorge. The Gorge has a wide range of habitats and is a mixing area of species from the west side, species from the east side, glacial relicts from colder times, southern species left from warmer periods, and a number of endemics. At least 800 different species of flowering plants have been found in the Gorge. Such a botanical treasure deserves, and gets, its own book—*Wildflowers of the Columbia Gorge* by Russ Jolley.

The Washington side of the Gorge, with its south-facing slopes, greens up and blooms earlier than the shadier, wetter Oregon side. In addition, the east end of the Gorge blooms earlier than the west end, so the best action in March is almost all in the pine-oak woodlands and the shrub-grasslands east of Hood River on the Washington side.

The Lewis and Clark Highway, State Hwy 14, winds its way along the Washington side of the Columbia River. Some of the best areas for early wildflowers in the region are off the stretch of Hwy 14 between Bingen and Columbia Hills SP, in the Columbia River Gorge National Scenic Area. You may find flowers anywhere along this section of the highway, but the traffic makes stopping a risk. Fortunately, there is a stretch of about 6 miles where Hwy 14 is paralleled by the "Old Highway," officially named County Road 1230. An outstanding area on this stretch of the old highway is Catherine Creek, which has a new wheelchair-accessible trail.

Heading east on Hwy 14 from Bingen, turn left onto Road 1230 just before you come to milepost 71 at Rowland Lake. After 1.5 miles you'll see a small parking area in front of a green gate. This is the entrance to the Catherine Creek area—check for information posted on a sign by the fence. The two areas here have different types of trails and scenery. If you go south and cross the county road toward the river, you'll reach the new 1.25-mile paved, universally accessible loop trail. This trail winds through a beautiful, open area with great views up and down the Columbia River. This is one of the best nature trails I've seen for folks with walking difficulties or in a wheelchair.

The going is much rougher north of the old highway. Go through the fence and then veer off to the right heading downhill toward the creek. You'll come to a dirt road that heads up Catherine Creek canyon. Soon the road forks and the right branch crosses the creek and heads up to some old corrals. The left fork winds up to the top of the western ridge. You can explore the different branches of the road and the different microhabitats in the canyon. Because of the wider diversity of habitats, you will see a larger variety of flowers in the canyon area north of the old highway than on the south side. Stay on the roads and established trails as much as possible to minimize impact on the area and to avoid the poison oak and ticks which are common here. Catherine Creek will have a progression of flowers from March through May.

Seven miles to the east of Catherine Creek is an area that has been well known for its early spring wildflowers for years. Horsethief Lake SP has been a Washington state park since the early 1960s, but in 1992 the state bought the Dalles Mountain Ranch, added part of that land to the park, and renamed the combined area Columbia Hills SP. The Department of Natural Resources manages the other portion not in the park, which is now the Columbia Hills Natural Area Preserve. The former ranch headquarters is now the visitor center and park headquarters—the place to stop for information about the park and preserve. There has been a burst of new activities and programs in the new park, and Dalles Mountain Ranch is a great addition to the state park system.

One mile east on Hwy 14 from its junction with US Hwy 197, Dalles Mountain Rd heads northeast into the Columbia Hills. About 3 miles from Hwy 14 you'll reach the old ranch buildings where you can get current information. A steep dirt road heads up a hill by the buildings. You can drive a short way, park, and continue up the road by walking or you can explore other areas. Continuing uphill on Dalles Mountain Rd from the old ranch buildings, drive to the top of Dalles Mountain for fantastic views on a clear day. Along the road you may come upon good displays of early wildflowers, such as grass widows, draba, shooting star, desert parsleys, and the endemic Dalles Mountain buttercup. You'll also have a good chance of seeing east-side birds, such as magpie, chukar, prairie falcon, lark sparrows, and vesper sparrows.

Washington's Olympic Mountains, with elevations around 7000 feet, create a significant rain shadow to their northeast. This difference is impressive with some areas in the rain shadow getting less than 20 inches of rain a year. This lower-than-average precipitation, combined with the thin soils left by glaciation, has resulted in some plant communities much more like the Rogue Valley or eastern Washington than the rest of the Salish Sea area. When you see Rocky Mountain juniper and prickly pear cactus growing here, you know something's different. Included in this rain shadow is the northeastern corner of the Olympic Peninsula, the San Juan Islands, Fidalgo, most of Whidbey and the Gulf islands, and the Saanich Peninsula (Victoria region). There are many open grasslands and rocky outcrops and woodlands of Oregon white (Garry) oak, madrone (arbutus), and Douglas-fir. The grasslands and rocky outcrops, in particular, start blooming early, in some years creating quite a display in March, although peak times are usually a bit later.

Any of the parks on the San Juan Islands are good for botanizing: Mount Constitution in Moran SP on Orcas, Iceberg Point on Lopez, and Cattle Point on the southern tip of San Juan Island. Both British and American Camp, part of the National Historical Park, are good for flowers and excellent for spring songbirds. The most famous island for flowers is spectacular Yellow Island, a Nature Conservancy Preserve. Access is only by boat; check with the Conservancy before planning a visit.

Washington Park in Anacortes and Deception Pass SP both give you a taste of the San Juans without the boat trip. To get to Washington Park head west on State Hwy 20 through Anacortes and, before you get to the ferry terminal, stay to the left and go onto Sunset Ave, following signs to Washington Park. When you enter the park, you can turn either right or left. A right turn takes you to the pebble beach, with views of Rosario Strait and waterbirds in season. But to see flowers, take a left turn onto the scenic Loop Rd, which goes around Fidalgo Head. You can pull off at a number of places to explore the roadside and trails. On the south-facing slopes are the unique open woodlands of Douglas-fir, madrone, and Rocky Mountain juniper. Deception Pass SP, Washington's most popular state park, straddles both sides of Deception Pass between Fidalgo and Whidbey Island. Many consider the trails on Goose Rock to be the best for flowers.

▶ EARLY BLOOMERS BEST BETS BRITISH COLUMBIA

The southeastern tip of Vancouver Island, the Saanich Peninsula, is similar in appearance to the San Juan Islands. However, scrub jays and poison oak are absent from the oak woodland habitat on Vancouver Island. I miss the jays, but not having to worry about poison oak, or ticks (which are very rare), is a blessing. The out-of-print *Naturalist's Guide to the Victoria*

Region by Weston and Stirling has an excellent section on botanizing the area, if you are lucky enough to find a used copy.

Some of the choice areas near Victoria for the oak woodland flowers are Mill Hill and Thetis Lake regional parks and Uplands Park (Cattle Point) in Victoria. In Mill Hill take the Summit trail up to the top and loop back down on the Calypso Trail. At Thetis Lake also make a counterclockwise loop: start at the sign showing wildflowers of the park and head easterly on the Lewis Clark Trail, take it to the Seymour Hill Trail, and then come back near the lake. Wander the trails through the oak woodland portion of Uplands Park that is on the other side of Beach Dr from the Cattle Point parking area in Victoria.

The most awesome floral display I've seen on Vancouver Island was at Lone Tree Hill, a smaller and not as well-known regional park. Lone Tree Hill RP is just a few miles north of Thetis Lake and Mill Hill parks. From Trans-Canada Highway 1, 2 miles west of Thetis Lake, head north on Millstream Rd. After 3.3 miles, veer to the left to stay on Millstream Rd and don't follow what seems to be the main road to the right which is Millstream *Lake* Rd. In just under 1.5 miles, on your right you'll see a sign and small parking area. It's a steep (but only a mile) hike to the top. For more information, contact the Capital Regional District Parks Department.

SPRING WATERFOWL MIGRATION

Say the word *migration* and most people think of V-shaped strings of geese flying over fields in autumn. Although the majority of the birds in the Northwest are migratory species, the huge flocks of waterfowl have become the symbol of migration for most North Americans. Indeed, the majority of waterfowl found in our region are migratory. Most waterfowl migrate long distances and round trips of several thousand miles are common. Waterfowl fly at an average speed of 50 mph when migrating; some fly for as long as 40 hours or 2000 miles without stopping, some even longer.

Birds that migrate through our region in the fall will pass through again in the spring on their return to their breeding grounds. However, most folks are much more aware of the fall migration than they are of spring migration, for a couple of reasons. First, fall migration is more spread out than spring migration, creating a longer period during which the birds are seen coming and going as they pass through. In spring birds are anxious to get back to their breeding grounds, and they don't stop and hang out much along the way. Unless something like bad weather holds them up, most migrating birds zip through in the spring, many at night, so it's easy to miss them. Also, when an animal that hasn't been around for months suddenly starts arriving in large, noisy flocks, it is much more noticeable than when ones spending the winter start slipping away until one day you realize they are gone. If you catch spring migration at the right time, however, it is as impressive as the biggest fall migration, and the birds are in their peak breeding plumage.

In February (Wintering Waterfowl) we looked at the most common waterfowl that spend the winter in the Northwest. Here we'll focus on the more transient waterfowl, the ones that pass through in fall and spring. During spring migration you can see them all—winter visitors, migrants, and summer breeders like cinnamon teal. The time of waterfowl migration varies with the weather and from one location to another, but the peak time for most species is between mid-March and mid-April, although all of March and April are potentially good.

SPRING WATERFOWL MIGRATION BEST BETS

Any major wintering area for waterfowl will be excellent for observing spring migration. You'll see the birds that have spent the winter as well as migrants passing through. All the Best Bets for Wintering Waterfowl (February) are applicable to this chapter. Most NWRs were established primarily for wintering and migrating waterfowl, and Oregon and Washington have 25 that are excellent for waterfowl. Hunting will be finished at all refuges by spring migration.

West of the Cascades birds are spread out over large areas because there is abundant waterfowl habitat. On the drier east side, where wetlands are much more limited and scattered, more spectacular concentrations of waterfowl stop in these critical areas on their journey north—a good example of what is sometimes called the oasis effect. The following Best Bets focus on these east-side locations.

▶ SPRING WATERFOWL MIGRATION BEST BETS OREGON

One of the West's largest inland marsh systems is in the Harney Basin, which includes Malheur NWR, one of our most famous birding areas. Burns is the largest town in the basin and host to the annual John Scharff Migratory Bird Festival and Art Show. Business people, service clubs, agency personnel, and folks from throughout the basin have joined together to develop what is one of the best examples of ecotourism that I know of in the West. The festival increases understanding and apprecia-

tion of local wildlife resources, provides some excellent wildlife viewing (especially for novices) without disturbing the animals, and adds to the local economy. The festival is held the first full weekend in April every year. Contact information is in Resources.

Malheur NWR has good birding, but the best action is usually just south of Burns in the pastures and fields that are normally flooded this time of year. Maps of the best areas around Burns are available at the festival, and the chamber of commerce can probably mail them to you in advance. Contact Malheur refuge directly to get their maps and checklist.

The best birding area is roughly bordered by US Hwys 20 and 395 on the west, Monroe St and State Hwy 78 (north), State Hwy 205 (east), and Greenhouse Ln (south). You can see almost everything from your car as you slowly drive along Egan, Hotchkiss, Greenhouse, and Hwy 205 in this area. Be sure to watch for traffic, and pull over as far as you can when you stop. Go west on Hotchkiss Ln to the sewage ponds, which are usually loaded and best seen from the roadside on their north side. Continue on this road as it turns south and goes between the sewage ponds and the huge wooden shed of the former lumber mill. The fields along this section of road are usually flooded and packed with birds. Sora and Virginia rails have been heard frequently (and seen rarely) at the bend in the road just before it turns, goes over the railroad tracks, and dead ends in the mill. You can turn around at the road's end, but do not park on mill property (west of the tracks).

You can get the latest birding information —especially for snow and Ross's geese—at the Bird Central Booth at festival headquarters in the high school. If the geese are roosting in a particular field, get there before sunset and you may be lucky to have 5000 to 10,000 white geese swirling and calling around you as they come to land and settle for the night. It's a transcendent experience. You'll also see thousands of Canada and hundreds of white-fronted geese, as well as lots of ducks. Some of the more conspicuous shorebirds will be American avocet, black-necked stilt, willet, long-billed curlew, and snipe, which should be winnowing over the fields late in the day. The biggest thrill for many is the sandhill cranes. Some will be stopping on their way through and others will be arriving to nest. You might even see some cranes starting to do their spectacular courtship dance. This also is the best time of year to see the sage-grouse strutting on their lek or display grounds; consider taking one of the early morning grouse tours. All in all, this is a fabulous time to visit a fabulous area. Make your motel reservations as soon as you can because the town will fill up for the festival. If you don't go for the festival itself, you can see the same birds a week or two on either side of the dates.

Two other spectacular areas for spring waterfowl migration in eastern Oregon are Summer Lake and the Klamath Basin, particularly Lower Klamath and Tule Lake NWRs, covered in January (Swans) and February (Bald Eagles).

▶ SPRING WATERFOWL MIGRATION BEST BETS WASHINGTON

Turnbull NWR and the Potholes Reservoir and Columbia NWR areas in eastern Washington are the counterparts to the Harney and Klamath basins in Oregon. The two areas are about a hundred miles apart and both are near Interstate 90, making it possible to visit both in a couple of big days of birdwatching.

Turnbull is different from most national wildlife refuges in that no hunting occurs on the refuge. The habitat, forested with scattered small lakes and marshes, also varies from that of most refuges. Turnbull has almost 10 miles of hiking trails set in a mixture of ponderosa pines, aspen groves, rocky scablands, grasslands, and the various wetland habitats. In addition to its animal life, Turnbull is noted for its spring wildflower display in early May. The refuge is easy to find and visitor areas are

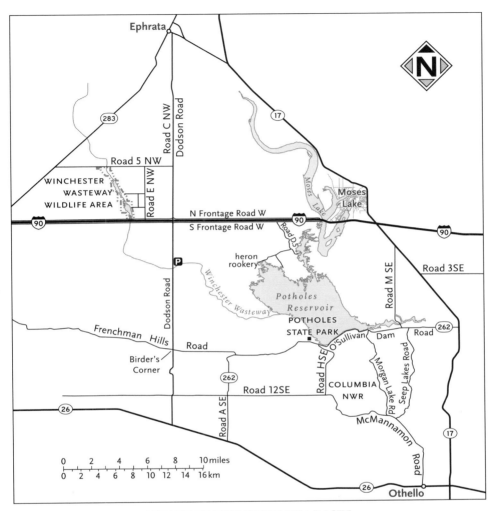

HEART OF THE COLUMBIA BASIN

well marked. The college town of Cheney is about 12 miles southwest of Spokane. From 1st St (State Hwy 904) near the southern end of town, turn onto Cheney Plaza Rd where you see a brown sign directing you to the refuge. Go 4.5 miles on Cheney Plaza, and then turn left onto Smith Rd and drive into the visitor area where you can get maps and checklists and pay the small daily use fee. Drive the auto tour route, and perhaps hike some of the trails in the Middle Pine Lake area.

For a longer auto loop that goes around the refuge and through some good grasslands that are excellent for grassland sparrows, meadowlarks, eastern kingbirds, and other open country birds, go back to Cheney Plaza Rd and head south (left turn). Stay on Cheney Plaza as it turns and heads east, then turn left (west) onto

Pine Grove Rd. Pine Grove ends at Wells Rd, where you again turn left and head north until Wells turns into Cheney Spangle Rd, which takes you back to Cheney. Considering making this trip for the wildflowers in May.

The Columbia Basin area around the towns of Moses Lake and Othello has excellent habitat for a wide range of wildlife, especially waterbirds, but it's a confusing mosaic of federal, state, and private lands. The best source about birding this area is the chapter by Mike Denny and Andy Stepniewski in *A Birder's Guide to Washington* by Hal Opperman. I am indebted to them for lots of new information and refer you to that book for more details on this rich area.

For a general loop around the area, let's start in the town of Moses Lake. Our first stop is the state's largest wading bird colony, with hundreds of nests of great blue herons, great egrets, black-crowned night-herons, and double-crested cormorants. Just west of Moses Lake SP is Exit 174 from I-90. You can use this exit to get on the South Frontage Rd that parallels I-90 or at the southern edge of Moses Lake SP get on West Sage Rd and head west until it turns into the S. Frontage Rd. Go west on S. Frontage Rd 2.5 miles (from Exit 174) to a dirt road on your left that may be signed "Road D 5 NE" or have a sign indicating public fishing and hunting. Turn left and head down this road through the sandy, brushy habitat. You will probably pass a "Potholes WA" sign. This sounds a bit mysterious, doesn't it? (Some of the signage might be ambiguous, and it's difficult to know which signs will be there and which ones might not be there anymore.)

After about 2 miles you will reach forks in the road; always go right—your goal is to curve around to the west. Soon you will begin to see a line of trees with nests to the northwest. Eventually you will drive to the edge of the lake and then be driving on a dike through some good wetland habitat. Park when the road turns off to the left. From here you can walk toward the nests, getting your best views without disturbing the birds. Stop now and then to watch the birds. If they appear to be getting nervous, back off. Drive out the way you came in, back to the S. Frontage Rd, then turn left and head west 8 miles to Dodson Rd.

When you reach Dodson Rd (also known as Road C NW) you can turn either north or south. You can make a relatively quick side trip north to the Winchester Wasteway WA if you have the time. This small area can have a surprising variety of waterfowl at times and if you have several days in this area it is worth checking, especially if you are driving by on I-90 at any time. Go north 4 miles on Dodson Rd to Road 5 NW, and then turn left and go west. In 2 miles turn left again to go south on Road E NW. From E NW you can go west on both Road 3 NW and 2 NW to the edge of the wasteway to look over the open water and search the tickets of willows and other shrubs along the shoreline. The wasteway is a low area that collects irrigation runoff from the surrounding fields, indeed the source of most of the water in the Potholes region. The water level varies greatly so this area is best in winter and early spring.

From Winchester Wasteway head south on Dodson Rd. Cruise slowly so you can look in the mosaic of ponds mixed with sagebrush. You will see a few parking places and a short road on your left where you can stop and explore—just be sure to pull completely off the road before stopping. In addition to spotting ducks and other waterbirds, you can see birds of the shrub-steppe, such as sage thrashers and lark, sage, and even grasshopper sparrows.

Frenchman Hills Rd is 3.75 miles from the frontage road. This intersection has come to be known as Birder's Corner, with good reason. You can drive in either direction on Frenchman Hills Rd, exploring little side roads and stopping to scan various ponds and marshy areas. If you continue south on Dodson and then work your way east toward Othello (Road 12 SE is good) you will travel through an area frequented by migrating sandhill cranes. To continue our present tour route, head east on Frenchman Hills Rd.

About 5 miles east of Dodson Rd, Frenchman Hills Rd ends where it intersects State Hwy 262, also called O'Sullivan Dam Rd. Continue east on this road. Dirt roads heading off into the bush may have signs indicating public fishing and hunting. These public access roads go to the edges of the wasteways, little rivers with marshy areas—explore any that look interesting. Stop only in pullouts. You will drive along the top of O'Sullivan Dam, longest earthen dam in the United States. At the eastern end of the dam is the access road for Columbia NWR.

The loop through Columbia NWR and the adjacent state wildlife area land takes you by many small lakes and riparian areas scattered among the sagebrush and rocky areas, making for great scenery, a mix of habitats, and a fabulous mix of water and land birds. Watch for burrowing owls and mammals, such as coyote, muskrat, beaver, mule deer, bobcat, and badger. Numerous small roads head to lakes and primitive campsites on state land. Rattlesnakes are also here; use caution if the weather is warm enough for them to be active. You can ask about rattlesnake activity at refuge headquarters.

At the very eastern end of O'Sullivan Dam turn south on Morgan Lake Rd, a dirt road across O'Sullivan Dam Rd from a big boat ramp. This road should be signed Morgan Lake Road, but it could also read Columbia NWR, Soda Lake C.G. 1 mi., or Road K.2 SE, or any combination of these. Wander south following signs to Othello. Stop anywhere that looks interesting. In about 6 miles you'll hit pavement and then reach McMannamon Rd. Turn left on McMannamon toward Othello, but in 0.5 mile turn left again onto Seep Lakes Rd (hard-to-see sign) and take it north. This rough road takes you back to O'Sullivan Dam Rd. Along this road you'll again be able to explore as you work your way north. When you get to O'Sullivan Dam Rd you can turn right, drive 2.5 miles, and then turn left and head north on Road M SE to State Hwy 17 and back to Moses Lake. The thousands of sandhill cranes in the area can often be seen along State Hwy 26 west of Othello.

NESTING GREAT BLUE HERONS

Portland is Heron Town. Although great blue herons (GBHs) are very common across North America, Portland was the first city to adopt this species as its official city bird. Various types of artwork and logos depicting this handsome bird grace publications and signs not only from the city government, but also from a variety of local businesses and organizations, including the Audubon Society of Portland. The city's largest golf course has been renamed Heron Lakes in honor of the adjacent heron nesting colony. We even have Blue Heron Ale, a popular local microbrew. In late May or early June every year, Great Blue Heron Week honors our city's mascot. Why the fuss about a common bird? It's because GBHs are big beautiful birds that nest right in the city, symbolizing nature in the urban landscape which Portlanders value as part of our quality of life.

GBHs are conspicuous, reaching a height of 4 feet with a wingspan just over 6 feet. They often feed in open areas, making them easier to observe than many animals. Many people regularly see GBHs feeding but don't see them nesting because the birds tend to find isolated, undisturbed areas for their nesting colonies. Sometimes, however, a heron colony will be accessible for easy viewing, giving an unusual opportunity to witness some very interesting behavior. The large size of the herons and the presence of many nests together makes for entertaining birdwatching, often suitable for children and others who like their nature observation on the lively side. A heron nesting colony is also called a heronry and sometimes a rookery. Although rookery is not technically correct for herons, it is commonly used these days for groups of nesting herons as well as for many other animals.

Wherever possible, GBHs nest in trees and an established colony may be used for decades. Preferred sites for colonies are islands or frequently flooded land to reduce the risk from ground predators like raccoons. But like all things in nature, colonies do change and even long-established heronries, like the famous one on Ross Island in downtown Portland, may be abandoned and new ones established. A heronry is a dynamic place with changes taking place from year to year. Each bird does not necessarily use the same nest each year and not every nest in the colony will be used. Some pairs will build new nests while other nests finally fall apart. In some colonies other birds such as cormorants and other herons will nest alongside the great blues, and the accumulated droppings may eventually kill the trees. The young have an interesting defense against predators—they will lean over the edge of their nest and regurgitate onto the unwelcome and unfortunate intruder, humans included. Yeeech.

The herons start returning to the nests and pairing up as early as February, but March is when they start becoming really active with nest building, territorial displays, courtship displays, and mating. The action in the heronry continues to build as the first young hatch in April and stays busy through June. Unfortunately, here in the Pacific Northwest GBHs usually nest in cottonwoods and it becomes very difficult to see what's going on once the trees leaf out. Viewing in late February and the first half of March is usually the best compromise between visibility and activity. Starting in February, watch the cottonwoods in your area carefully and begin your heronry viewing as soon as the trees show the first signs of new growth. This will vary some from year to year and with different locations.

GBHs have been well studied, and they have many intriguing and easily-seen displays. The three volumes of *A Guide to Bird Behavior* in the Stokes Nature Guides series are great books for understanding bird behavior. Some of the more interesting behaviors seen at the nest and described in the Stokes book are the Head-Down, Swaying, and the Stretch. In the Head-Down, the heron stands in the nest, sticks its neck and head out very straight, angled down on the outside of the nest, and snaps its bill. Often it raises the feathers on its head and neck at the same time. This is a territorial display that signals others to stay away. What's really fun is when both members of a pair display at the same time, crossing necks and clacking away with their beaks.

You might call Swaying kissing heron-style. The pair locks bill tips and moves their heads back and forth together. In the Stretch, the bird points its beak and head straight up into the air, then lowers its head toward its back while making a sound described as crooning or howling. This is sometimes done after the male brings the female a gift of a nice stick to add to the nest, which is a common practice. The male usually brings sticks to the female, who actually does the building of a new nest or the remodeling of an established one. Both birds take turns incubating the three to five eggs, which hatch in about a month, and care for the young. Three months after hatching, the young will be fully grown and independent.

It's easy to see GBHs feeding in almost any kind of wetland throughout the year. Herons are wading birds and will stand in shallow water and spear or grab just about any animal they can get, although fish make up about two-thirds of their diet. Sometimes you will see them feeding in fields, and people often wonder what they're getting on dry land. Their main upland prey are voles, also known as meadow mice, and also large insects, frogs, or snakes. It can be quite entertaining to watch a heron trying to subdue and swallow a good-sized garter snake.

GBHs are common throughout our region anywhere near water, from mudflats in salt water bays to freshwater marshes in the desert. They are year-round residents, with some seasonal movements east of the Cascades when water begins to freeze. Although generally considered shy and sensitive to disturbance, GBHs have shown themselves to be quite adaptable and some can be found in disturbed areas and places with significant human activity. The most common location for colonies in our region is in the cottonwoods in riparian woodlands. Look for colonies during the winter when the trees are bare, and then come back and check for activity in late February or early March. It's easy to spot the colonies because you will clearly see lots of big stick nests near the tops of the trees—herons and cormorants are the only birds in the Northwest that do this. Remember to observe from a distance and avoid disturbing the birds. A scope is really necessary to see the birds' behavior without disturbing them.

▶ NESTING GREAT BLUE HERONS BEST BETS OREGON

For the best view I've ever had into a heron colony, check out the one on Goat Island. This small island is in the Willamette River at its confluence with the Clackamas River, where the towns of Gladstone, Oregon City, and West Linn meet. From a bluff in Meldrum Bar Park in Gladstone you can look 0.25 mile across the Willamette right into the nests. Morning is the best time to avoid looking into the afternoon sun. If you take Exit 9 from Interstate 205 and head north 0.5 mile on State Hwy 99E (McLoughlin Blvd), you'll cross the Clackamas River and reach the intersection with River Rd in Gladstone. Turn left and drive 0.3 mile northeast on River Rd to Meldrum Bar Park Rd. Turn left into the park (large sign), drive 0.25 mile, and then turn left at the small sign for Dahl Beach. Drive another 0.25 mile to the covered picnic tables on the bluff overlooking the Willamette River. Park here and walk to the bluff. Look across the Willamette into the tops of the trees that are near the middle of Goat Island. This area is also interesting in the winter for gulls and waterfowl, but don't get confused by the strange mongrel ducks that are the results of hybridizing between the mallards and various domestic breeds of ducks released here.

▶ NESTING GREAT BLUE HERONS BEST BETS WASHINGTON

Across the mighty Columbia River from Portland is one of the largest heron colonies I have ever seen. Located across the road from the main parking lot for Vancouver Lake Park in Vancouver, Washington, this colony has had over 200 active nests and can easily be seen from a reasonable distance without disturbing the birds. From Interstate 5 in Vancouver take the Fourth Plain Blvd exit and head west on Fourth Plain, which becomes River Rd and is also Hwy 501. In about 5 miles you'll reach Lower River Rd (State Hwy 501) where it makes a turn to the left. Go straight toward the entrance to Vancouver Lake Park, and you'll now be on Erwin Rieger Memorial Highway. Park in the parking area near the entrance. There may be an entrance fee; this varies seasonally. Walk back out the entrance road to a safe place where you can stand on the side of the road and search the trees across the road from the parking area. After you have located the colony, you can decide where to go to get the best look. During this time of year traffic on Rieger Highway is minimal, but be very careful when near the road. Exactly which groups of trees and nests are used for nesting varies a bit from year to year. You might drive back south to Lower River Rd, and then take it north to look for good vantage points if the views from Rieger Highway are not the greatest.

The largest heron colony in Seattle is in Kiwanis Ravine, just east of Discovery Park in the Magnolia neighborhood, south of the Lake Washington Ship Canal. In 2006 there were at least 50 nests in the maple and alder trees growing in the protected natural area. For the best views of the nests, take the "secret passage" on a hidden pedestrian bridge. West of the south end of the Chittenden (Ballard) Locks is Commodore Park; there's a parking lot in the park off Commodore Way. Starting in the lot, walk east about a block along Commodore Way until you see the street sign for 33rd Ave and Harley on the south side of Commodore. Cross Commodore, walk up Harley, and then walk another block uphill on 33rd. Look for the alley on your right that goes to the pedestrian and bike-route bridge over the railroad tracks. Follow any Bike Route signs you see. This path eventually ends at the intersection of Gay and 32nd avenues. Don't go that far but stop at the north end of the bridge after it crosses the railroad tracks, and you'll see a forested ravine. Search through the trees to the southwest, in the direction of Discovery Park. The exact location of the nests changes a bit from year to year, but because you are there before the trees have leafed out (right?), you should be able to find the big nests. You'll need binoculars or, better, a spotting scope to be able to watch the herons' behavior. These herons are fortunate to have their own volun-

teer organization looking after their welfare, and Seattle has passed building regulations to protect the birds from disturbance during their nesting season. To find out more about these birds and their human friends check out the Heron Habitat Helpers at www.heronhelpers.org.

The largest colony in King, Snohomish, and Pierce counties is Renton's Black River GBH colony with 130 active nests. You'll be impressed at how tough these herons are when you see how their colony is hemmed in by some pretty dense development, with I-5 and Interstate 405 on two sides. The future of the colony is looking good because a series of fundraising efforts over the years has resulted in the permanent protection of 93 acres as open space. Herons Forever is the nonprofit group that formed to protect these birds and their nesting colony. The Black River Riparian Forest is usually well marked on Seattle or Renton maps. To see this colony, from Seattle head south on I-5, and then take Exit 157 to get on Martin Luther King Jr. Way, which is also State Hwy 900. Just before you have gone 3 miles you will come to the stoplight for 68th Ave South. Turn right onto 68th Ave and take it down the hill to where its name changes to SW Oakesdale. After you cross the railroad tracks, drive about 3 blocks and turn left into the small parking area. From the parking area walk north on a grassy path down the short hill. From the base of the hill take the trail to the right for another 150 yards. The main nests are in the tall cottonwood trees on the opposite side of the water to the northeast.

In the Potholes WA near the town of Moses Lake is the largest wading bird colony in Washington. It's in the northwestern corner of Potholes Reservoir about 6 miles west of the city of Moses Lake and is described in Spring Waterfowl Migration.

▶ NESTING GREAT BLUE HERONS BEST BETS BRITISH COLUMBIA

This is the easiest one yet. GBHs have been nesting in Stanley Park, in downtown Vancouver, since at least 1920 and certainly for centuries before it was Stanley Park. Different sites have been used over the years but in 2001 the adaptable birds settled on a site near the Park Board office and tennis courts, near the intersection of Beach Ave and Park Ln. The 2005 nesting season report by the Stanley Park Ecological Society reported 176 active nests that year. This is now one of the largest colonies ever recorded in the city. As one would expect, the herons have become local media stars and are lauded as a symbol of the city's quality of life—as if the 25 pairs of bald eagles nesting in town weren't enough of a symbol. Just think, you can go to Stanley Park in February and into March and see thousands of wintering waterfowl and other waterbirds, a dozen bald eagles, and get to watch the herons start their nesting season. Vancouver, Boundary Bay, and the Fraser River delta make this part of Canada one of the best winter birding areas in North America.

MARCH'S NATURE NUGGETS

WORM PILES Ever notice those funny little piles of dead leaves on bare soil at the edge of a lawn or under a tree? Carefully lift up the whole pile, and you'll see a hole in the ground about as big around as a pencil. This is the burrow of a night crawler, and it made the little pile by reaching its head end out of the hole, grabbing the leaves with its mouth, and pulling them back into, or around the entrance of, the hole. They do this at night when it's raining or very damp, and if you're sneaky enough you can catch them in the act. Charles Darwin did, and he wrote a great description of this back in 1881. The amount of earthworm activity varies with temperature and moisture, so more piles will appear at certain times of the year. In areas where the top layer of soil freezes, the earthworms hibernate together in little dens below the frost line. When the soil finally thaws completely, earthworm activity suddenly reappears. In New England this usually happens in March, and some Native Americans in that region called the full moon of March the Worm Moon. Is there a Worm Moon where you live?

PACIFIC HERRING SPAWNING The herring family contains some of the world's most important fishes used as human food and includes sardines, alewife, menhaden, and shad. Herrings are extremely important in marine food chains. Pacific herring spawn in shallow coastal waters, and the greatest concentration of spawning herring in our region is along the eastern coast of Vancouver Island, between Ladysmith and Comox. This gathering of hundreds of thousands of tasty fish and their eggs attracts a massive assemblage of mammalian and avian predators. One day during the peak of the spawn, in a one-half-mile stretch of coastline, wildlife biologist Neal Dawe estimated that he saw 50,000 gulls, 10,000 scoters, 5000 brant, 3200 long-tailed ducks, 3000 red-breasted mergansers, 1000 harlequin ducks, 10,000 other assorted diving ducks, 10,000 dabbling ducks, dozens of bald eagles, and scores of northern and California sea lions and harbor seals. What a feast. Some of the best places to witness this feeding frenzy are on Denman and Hornby islands, accessible by ferry from Buckley Bay, about 12 miles south of Comox and Courtenay. Boyle Point and Fillongley provincial parks on Denman Island and Halliwell PP on Hornby Island have fabulous views of the channels, bays, shorelines, the Strait of Georgia, and distant scenery. Both islands have numerous bed and breakfasts, as well as camping, making them very attractive for an early spring wildlife-watching getaway. There is also good viewing along the shore of Vancouver Island itself, especially between Deep Bay and Union Bay. Highway 19A has some turnoffs, and you can find other small roads that get closer to the shoreline. Kim Goldberg's wildlife-watching guide for the island is very helpful for this area.

OTHELLO SANDHILL CRANE FESTIVAL The Othello Sandhill Crane Festival, started in 1998, is an example of community-developed eco-tourism. This event involves the Greater Othello Chamber of Commerce, the Columbia NWR, the Othello School District, Othello citizens, as well as residents from neighboring Ephrata, Moses Lake, and Royal City. The festival is a three-day event, Friday through Sunday, at the end of March. It has many tours for crane viewing and other birding, Bretz Flood tours, a Columbia NWR tour, plus the festivities in Othello. This time of year 10,000 lesser sandhill cranes stop in this region on their migration north to their breeding grounds. To go out on your own, drive west on State Hwy 26 from Othello in Columbia NWR and explore the roads that head south from the highway. Folks at the headquarters, Othello High School, can give you good information. This is as homemade and genuine as they come.

OWLING: A CLOSER LOOK

Owls have always fascinated people. Being nocturnal, they have been associated with dark, mysterious, and spooky things. But they have also been considered symbols of wisdom, an odd image because owls are not very intelligent compared to other birds. How did they come to be a symbol for intelligence? Owls are unique among birds in that their eyes are close together on the front of their head, just like human eyes. Owls are the only birds with faces that are remotely human-like, and perhaps this is why we think they are smart—like us. Another factor may be that owls are nocturnal and secretive, thereby making them mysterious, and mysterious things are often thought to have special powers. To be realistic, however, we should have cartoons of crows with mortarboards on their heads at high school graduation instead of the owls.

Although they might not be the Einsteins of the bird world or have magical powers, owls do have amazing adaptations for their way of life. The positioning of their eyes gives owls excellent binocular vision—the ability to judge depth and distance. This is important for a predator that has to drop from the sky and hit its prey dead-on. Although owls are not unique in having binocular vision, they have the best by far among all birds.

The owl's huge eyes are extremely sensitive to light, allowing it to hunt by moonlight and starlight. However, even an owl can't see well enough to hunt when it is really dark. That's when its equally acute hearing comes in. Owls have among the most sensitive ears in the world. Their stereoscopic hearing can pinpoint the source of a sound better than any other animal. The two ear openings in their skull are shaped and located differently from each other to exaggerate the stereo effect. To help collect sound waves and direct them into the ear openings, owls have a circular pattern of feathers around their eyes called facial disks, which are a distinctive part of an owl's unique appearance.

Owls have specially built feathers that result in silent flight. It's a startling experience when a large owl flies soundlessly right over your head. This silent flight means that their prey can't hear them coming. Owls, then, are the "stealth" birds of prey. Instead of using high speed and diving on their prey like falcons or hawks, owls sneak up on their prey, silently flying low and slow over the ground and then suddenly dropping out of the night sky onto their prey.

Owls are one of the two orders or groups of birds that comprise an informal category called birds of prey or raptors. The other order of raptors includes the hawklike birds—hawks, eagles, falcons, accipiters, and others (discussed in January). Other predatory birds, such as kingfishers or shrikes, are sometimes mistakenly called birds of prey, but to be a raptor a bird must be a member of either the owl or hawk order. All raptors have certain characteristics in common, such as talons and meat-tearing beaks, and it's logical to think they are related. Surprisingly, owls and hawks are not closely related and provide an excellent example of convergent evolution. Both groups of birds have the same tools because they have the same job, not because they are related.

Owl sightings are among the most sought after by birders and are very exciting to more casual nature observers as well. I've known birders who rate the success of an outing by the number of owls they see. However, finding an owl is tough work. They are nocturnal and do their best to hide during the day. Owls are notoriously elusive and this behavior, coupled with their silent flight, camouflage, and keen senses makes owling one of the more challenging tests of observational skill and patience. Fortunately, some naturalists have become quite expert at this and share their experience through field trips, classes, and books.

The Pacific Northwest's diversity of owls reflects the extent of forest and woodland habitats, the preferred habitats of most owls. We have 10 owls that can be found year-round in the right habitat: great horned owl, western screech-owl, common barn owl, short-eared owl, northern pygmy-owl, northern saw-whet owl, spotted owl, great gray owl, long-eared owl, and barred owl.

The flammulated owl is migratory and here for only the summer breeding season when it is actually quite common, although almost never seen, in pine forests. The declining burrowing owl, also migratory, is here mainly in the summer with a few wintering west of the Cascades. Two more owls are northern species that sometimes come this far south from their normal range during severe winter weather: the snowy owl and the very rare Northern hawk owl. There is evidence that the boreal owl is a year-round resident and breeder in a few limited areas, but little is known about its status.

The easiest way to find owls is not to look for them but to listen. Most owling, including some census work, is done by sound. During the breeding season most owls become quite vocal, calling off and on all night, but especially just after dusk and just before dawn. March is an excellent month for owling because our resident owls will be in breeding season by then and should be calling. Calling will continue into June for some owls. To find owls by sound, first find an area of good habitat. Listen carefully and be as quiet as possible, which usually means going by yourself or with one other person. Wear clothes that don't make noise when you walk, and avoid movements, such as putting your hands in your pockets. Calm, clear nights are best, and the more moonlight the better. Temperature seems to have little effect on the owls but can sure affect the owlers, so dress warmly.

To pick good owling spots, read about the preferences of the owls in your area and ask local birders for tips. Most owls like to inhabit the edges of forests and woodlands that are adjacent to open fields or meadows where they can hunt. The less human disturbance the better, although some owls, like the barn owl, are fairly adaptable to the presence of people. Go just before sunset and plan to be out a couple of hours, or start two hours before sunrise if you are really gung ho. It is wonderful if you can go with a knowledgeable owler who can identify the different calls for you to learn. The next best thing is to listen to recordings of owl calls before you go out.

At your selected area, decide on a route and walk it slowly, stopping frequently to listen and look carefully. Check possible perches on the tops of trees or poles. When you hear an owl try to locate it and move closer, being as silent as possible. If you actually see an owl, slowly sink to the ground or move behind a bush or tree to hide yourself as much as possible. Watch the owl carefully; its behavior will tell you whether it knows you're there and is alarmed or if it is relaxed. Remain still and hidden, and you may be able to see some common behaviors, such as hunting. Seeing an owl, of course, depends on having enough light. Carry a strong flashlight for safety, and in case you get close enough to it to toss a beam on it. Some owls do not seem to be bothered by flashlights. Most of the time, however, you'll have to be satisfied just to hear the owls.

It is also possible to owl by car. Slowly drive roads through good habitat sticking your head out the window as a dog would and listening. (Needless to say, the quieter your car, the better.) Stop frequently and listen for several minutes while looking carefully at possible perching sites. Patricia and Clay

Sutton, in their book, *How to Spot an Owl*, suggest bicycling as an excellent way to cover a lot of territory quietly.

A well-established but controversial technique for finding and seeing owls is either to copy their calls with your voice or to play recordings of their calls. Several owls are very responsive to this technique—great horned, screech, pygmy, saw-whet, and barred—and will answer when you make the calls. Some may even fly over to check you out, allowing for some incredible sightings. Unfortunately, some birders have overused tapes and have disturbed the birds' normal breeding behavior. Many birders and biologists recommend that people not play tapes or make calls of owls during their breeding season. Fortunately, this is when the owls are calling the most any way and they usually don't need extra coaxing. Outside of the breeding season, from July through January, you can use tapes sparingly to try to get owls calling or to lure them in for a closer look. I have always felt that trying to copy owl calls with my voice instead of using recordings was somehow less intrusive and more fair, as well as more fun and a lot more convenient. Trying to copy owl calls is also a great technique for learning to identify them. If you decide to dabble in playing recordings, check on local restrictions. It is illegal to play tapes in NPs, in some NWRs, and in some special areas of NFs. It is also illegal to ever play tapes of spotted owls because they are an endangered species. Play tapes at moderate volume—louder isn't better—and don't overdo it. You should play calls for three to five minutes, then stop and listen for at least five minutes. I wouldn't play a tape any more than two or three times in one place. Once you get a good response, stop playing the tape.

You can also look for owls during the day. Short-eared owls, pygmy owls, and burrowing owls are often active during the day, especially in the early morning or late afternoon. You may also be able to find owls perched and snoozing by noticing clues such as whitewash (droppings) or pellets on the ground. However, to really get into the owl's world it's more fun to go out at night. Of course, when you're out looking for owls during the magic hours around dawn or dusk, your chances for seeing other wildlife are also good.

A MILLION SHOREBIRDS

Shorebirds are a striking example of the tremendous advantages that flight provides birds. Because of their fabulous flying abilities, shorebirds are able to utilize two different and greatly separated habitats that are both rich in food resources. The typical shorebird spends the majority of the year along seacoasts in the mid to low latitudes then migrates long distances to breed in very high latitude tundra, marsh, or prairie. The question is, of course, why? If the west coast of Mexico is a great habitat for 10 months of the year, why risk the dangers of flying 4000 miles to the Alaskan tundra, for only a month or two, to nest? The main reasons are the two most important factors affecting the survival of almost every animal—food and predators.

The northern nesting grounds are frozen and covered with snow most of the year, which make them inhospitable. Only a few animals live there on a year-round basis. However, as bleak as these regions can be, the brief Arctic summer brings an explosion of life. Hundreds of Arctic plants and invertebrates (mainly insects) come out of dormancy, growing and reproducing with amazing speed and intensity. For the animals that can get there, food is abundant for the energy-intensive process of reproducing and feeding the babies when they arrive. Nesting areas also are plentiful, if nesting on the ground isn't a problem.

At the same time, predators are scarce. Not many of them can survive on the slim pickings during the winter in the Arctic. The logical question is, Why don't a bunch of predators also bop on up to the Arctic and eat all those birds that flew up there? Well, some predators do, but the only ones that can really make such a journey are other birds. The predatory skuas, jaegers, gulls, hawks, and owls take their toll, but it's nothing like the predation these birds

Chocolate lilies on Vancouver Island

would experience in regions with warmer climates and a host of predators on the ground, in the trees, and in the water. This is especially important because shorebirds are ground nesters.

Nesting in the Arctic (and near-Arctic) has huge benefits that birds can take advantage of because they can fly. Shorebirds are fast, strong flyers and most of them fly thousands of miles a year. Some of the small sandpipers that weigh only a couple of ounces can nevertheless zip on down to Argentina from Alaska—and back. When not on their nesting grounds, shorebirds feed in other habitats that are also incredibly rich with life. The intertidal areas of seashores and estuaries are home to a huge variety of invertebrates. The mud flats in estuaries, in particular, are some of the most productive habitats in the world in terms of total biomass. Mud flats, much more than sandy beaches or rocky shores, are the feeding grounds with the largest variety and largest numbers of shorebirds.

As a group, shorebirds are easy to recognize. They have long legs and long narrow bills, and most spend their time wading in water or walking near the edge of water, in fresh- and saltwater habitats. It's no mystery how they got the name *shorebirds*. In Europe this group is commonly called waders, while in the United States they are sometimes called the small waders to distinguish them from the herons or long-legged waders.

All shorebirds have basically the same diet, which is any animal they can catch. Each species, however, has adapted to eating a particular type of prey. The most obvious evidence of this specialization is seen in the variety of bill sizes and shapes we see on different shorebirds. Some, like the plovers, run and pick little critters off the surface of the sand. Many sandpipers probe the mud for prey, probing at different depths depending on the length of their bill. Oystercatchers have chisel-like beaks for whacking and prying limpets and mussels off the rocks, while avocets use their unique bill for filtering crustaceans out of the water. And those long, curved curlew bills fit perfectly into the burrows of marine worms and crabs. Because of the variety of bills and feeding styles, many different shorebird species can feed in the same general area without being in direct competition. This is a great example of one of the basic laws of ecology: no two species can compete directly for the exact same resource; they will specialize so each has its niche.

Most of the 35 or so species of shorebirds seen regularly in the Pacific Northwest are primarily migrants; we see them as they pass through in spring and fall. A dozen common species winter in significant numbers: black-bellied and semi-palmated plover, killdeer, black oystercatcher, black turnstone, surfbird, sanderling, western and least sandpipers, dunlin, long-billed dowitcher, and Wilson's snipe. Roughly the same numbers of species are the only regular breeders in our region: snowy plover, killdeer, black oystercatcher, black-necked stilt, American avocet, willet, spotted sandpiper, long-billed curlew, Wilson's snipe, and Wilson's phalarope.

The spring and fall migrations of shorebirds differ. In spring the birds are adults in breeding plumage, making identification a lot easier than at any other time. However, the period of migration is short, the birds move through quickly, and it's easy to miss the main movement, although if you're in the right place at the right time, the numbers can be astronomical because they travel in much larger groups in spring. In general, the peak of spring migration for shorebirds is from mid-April to mid-May. While large numbers of individual species occur in spring, the variety of different species is lower than in the fall. Red knots and ruddy turnstones are the only shorebirds that are more commonly seen during the spring migration than in the fall.

▶ A MILLION SHOREBIRDS BEST BETS OREGON

Although we usually think of shorebirds migrating up and down the coast, most of our regular migrants can be found on both sides of the Cascades. Oregon's best shorebird places in the fall are west of the Cascades (see August for Fall Shorebird Migration). Eastern Oregon, however, is different. Seven shorebird species breed in eastern Oregon so they are more common on the east side than on the coast. They're also easier to see in eastern Oregon in the spring because they aren't just passing through—once they arrive, they stay and nest.

In addition, because wetlands are less common in the drier east side, the shorebirds are more concentrated around the best habitat. Five species that are common and widespread nesters in eastern Oregon are black-necked stilt, American avocet, willet, long-billed curlew, and Wilson's phalarope. The snowy plover and upland sandpiper are difficult to see because they have small localized populations. The three best areas for seeing eastern Oregon's nesting shorebirds are Malheur NWR, Summer Lake WA, and the Klamath Basin NWRs.

▶ A MILLION SHOREBIRDS BEST BETS WASHINGTON

The most famous shorebird spot in the Northwest is Bowerman Basin in Grays Harbor. Over 1 million shorebirds stop here on their way north in the spring, making this the largest concentration of shorebirds on the West Coast south of Alaska. The majority are western sandpipers; the other most common species are dunlin, short-billed and long-billed dowitcher, and semi-palmated plover. An additional dozen shorebird species occur regularly in smaller numbers. This is a particularly good spot to see red knots. The establishment of Grays Harbor NWR in 1988 saved this critical area from potential development. Bowerman Basin has been featured in magazines and on TV. Starting in 1996 the Grays Harbor Audubon Society, Grays Harbor NWR, and the City of Hoquiam have held the Grays Harbor Shorebird Festival every year at the end of April.

The peak time at Bowerman Basin is between April 15 and May 15 with some yearly variation. Timing your visit to the tides is critical because the birds concentrate in Bowerman Basin for a period of about an hour or two on either side of the high tide. Bowerman Basin is one of the last places in Grays Harbor to be covered by the tide and the first to be exposed as the tide begins to ebb. This concentrates all the birds in the only place they can feed when the tide is near its highest point. Fortunately for us, that puts them in a close spot for viewing, with the light at our backs. Once the tide has dropped enough, the birds have acres and acres of mudflats to feed on throughout Grays Harbor.

During the Shorebird Festival, visitors to Bowerman are asked to park at Hoquiam High School and ride a shuttle bus to the viewing area. The shuttle bus runs continuously during the best viewing times on Saturday and Sunday. If you want to avoid the crowds, pick a weekday when you can arrive for the high tide in the morning or consider coming in early May, when there are still thousands of birds.

The new Hoquiam High School is just west of the town of Hoquiam on State Hwy 109 (do not go to the old Hoquiam High School building in the middle of town). If you're coming when the shuttle bus isn't running, turn left onto Paulson Rd off Hwy 109, just west of the high school, following signs to the airport. Turn right at the T intersection and drive toward Lana's Hanger Cafe (great for lunch). Park across from Lana's and walk west through a gate. Continue west on the blacktop road until it ends at the trailhead for the Sandpiper Trail. For years dedicated birders had to wade through wet grass, mud, and water in their rubber boots, but now there is a boardwalk and trail. From the trailhead to the shorebird viewing area is about 0.5 mile; the round trip from Lana's, out to the end and back, is 2 miles. Just enough to justify that pie at Lana's. While watching the shorebirds, look for raptors—peregrine falcons and merlins regularly hunt here during migration. If the limited parking near Lana's is full, turn around and drive 250 yards back to the east and park at the F.A.A. building.

▶ A MILLION SHOREBIRDS BEST BETS BRITISH COLUMBIA

One spot that has great shorebirding in spring and a lot of bird action in general is known

as Brunswick Point, although this is not an official name on maps. In the town of Ladner (on the south shore of the Fraser River) take Ladner Trunk Rd west until it becomes 47th A Ave. In just a few blocks 47th A Ave turns into River Rd; continue west on River Rd. In a bit under 2 miles you will pass the turn off to George C. Reifel Migratory Bird Sanctuary which is well signed and which we will visit in October. Take River Rd to its end and park there, being careful to follow parking signs and not block any gates. Continue to head west, walking on the top of the dike. In about one mile you will come to the end of the point where the dike turns and heads southeast toward Roberts Bank Superport. Watch for any falcons that may be hunting shorebirds or ducks, although this would be more likely in the winter. All five falcons have been seen here in one day, and I saw my first gyrfalcon here. The Vancouver Natural History Society's birding guide recommends walking Brunswick Point when the high tide is expected to be between about 10 and 12 feet.

BOTANIZING TO THE MAX

April and May are the peak months of the blooming season almost everywhere in our region below about 3000 feet, so this is the best time to get out and botanize. Botanize? Is that a word? You bet it is. It's in the dictionary but is rarely used, unlike "birding," which is so common. Birders are the largest identifiable group of nature hobbyists, but my impression is that "wildflower watchers" are the next most numerous group. But what do you call people who go out looking for wildflowers? Are they botanists? Botanizers? Wildflower watchers? Flower people? I think this is one reason that looking for wildflowers is not recognized as the popular activity it is. Without a good name, this large group of people just doesn't have much of a public identity.

Botanizing has actually had much more attention during the last 15 years. Celebrating Wildflowers is a cooperative program of the US Forest Service, Bureau of Land Management, National Park Service, and the US Fish and Wildlife Service. Starting with the Forest Service in 1991, personnel in many offices of these agencies have been developing guided hikes, brochures, self-guided trails, displays, and other activities highlighting native plants in the lands they manage. In addition, groups like garden clubs, botanical gardens, native plant society chapters, nurseries, universities, and public schools actively participate in Celebrating Wildflowers. These agencies and partners are working together to promote wildflower programs on about 20% of the nation's landmass. That gives botanizing almost as much recognition as birdwatching.

Celebrating Wildflowers is still a developing program that depends on volunteer time so what is offered at any particular national park, national forest, or BLM district will vary from year to year. In addition to checking the national Web site, contact the individual forests in which you are most interested, beginning in March. In recent years every national park and just about every national forest and grassland in the Northwest has had some programs.

Another sign of the interest in botanizing is the local wildflower show or festival. Oregon seems to be the hotbed for small-town wildflower festivals, which often raise money for a community service. A wildflower show will have samples of the local blooming plants displayed and identified at the festival's headquarters. In addition, there are often guided walks, presentations, and sometimes native plant sales. This is really a fun and effective way to get to know your flowers. Sometimes other cultural or social events take place in conjunction with the wildflower festival. Most of these events are in small towns and have plenty of local character. Whether you go botanizing at a wildflower show, on a guided hike, or by yourself, the most important thing is to get out there and do it, for spring is over all too soon.

Wildflower Shows and Festivals

DARRINGTON WILDFLOWER FESTIVAL Darrington School, Darrington, Washington. Washington's only wildflower festival does not have picked flowers on display but has guided walks, slide shows, and displays. This is really a general community event with arts and crafts, music, food, and kids' activities. Held the third weekend in June. Contact the Darrington City Hall, PO Box 14, Darrington, WA, 98241; (360) 436-1131.

GLIDE WILDFLOWER FESTIVAL Glide Community Building, Glide, Oregon, 17 miles east of Roseburg on State Hwy 138, the North Umpqua Highway. Food is available and the building is wheelchair accessible, but to preserve the plants it's not heated, so bundle up. In 2006 the community of Glide celebrated its 40th annual Wildflower Festival. Blooming flowers as well as many other plants of southwestern Oregon are on display. This claims to be the largest display of native plants in the Pacific Northwest. Held the last full weekend in April. Contact the Glide Wildflower Show, PO Box 332, Glide, OR, 97443; www.glidewildflowershow.org.

MOSIER WILDFLOWER SHOW Mosier School, Mosier, OR. Mosier School is obvious as you drive into the tiny town from Exit 69 off Interstate 84, about 5 miles east of Hood River. This show displays a large collection of blooming flowers from the Columbia River Gorge. You can do some serious botany here, maybe even try to distinguish the many species of *Lomatium* (desert parsley). In Mosier you're just west of one of the Columbia River Gorge's premier flower spots, the Rowena Plateau and the Tom McCall Preserve, so allow plenty of time to see the show and spend some time in the field. Held the same day as the Mosier Volunteer Fire Department's annual Fireman's Smorgie fundraising feast, usually on one of the last two Sundays in April; 10 a.m. to 4 p.m. For the exact date call the Mosier Volunteer Fire Department (541) 478-3391, in March or early April.

MOUNT PISGAH SPRING WILDFLOWER FESTIVAL AND PLANT SALE Mount Pisgah Arboretum, 6 miles southeast of Eugene, Oregon. This is a big wingding with displays, hikes, plant sale, nature store, and food. Held the Sunday after Mother's Day. Contact Mount Pisgah Arboretum, www.efn.org/~mtpisgah, (541) 747-3817. They also have a big mushroom festival at the end of October.

SHADY COVE WILDFLOWER SHOW Shady Cove School on Cleveland St in Shady Cove, Oregon, about 20 miles north of Medford on State Hwy 62 (the route to Crater Lake). Food available; wheelchair accessible. About 200 species of wildflowers and weeds from within a 12-mile radius of Shady Cove are on display. There is a lot more going on at this down-home community event besides the flower show. Held the first weekend in May. Contact Shady Cove City Hall, www.shadycove.net, (541) 878-2225, Tuesday–Thursday, or the Wildflower Association of Shady Cove, PO Box 978, Shady Cove, OR 97539.

SILVER FALLS MOTHER'S DAY WEEKEND WILDFLOWER SHOW South Falls Lodge, Silver Falls SP, 20 miles east of Salem on State Hwy 214. Park entrance fee. About 150 native wildflowers on display; cultivated varieties are for sale. This is a great resource if you're interested in landscaping with native plants. There are also guided hikes, programs, and a barbecue dinner. Held on Mother's Day weekend. Contact Silver Falls SP, www.oregonstateparks.org, (503) 873-8681.

TRYON CREEK TRILLIUM FESTIVAL Nature Center in Tryon Creek State Natural Area, 11321 SW Terwilliger Blvd, Portland, Oregon. This is not a display of picked flower specimens; flowers are seen blooming along park trails. There are guided hikes, a native plant sale, indoor programs, kids' activities, and music. Held the first weekend in April, unless Easter falls on the Sunday, then the festival is the last weekend in March. Contact the Friends of Tryon Creek, www.tryonfriends.org, (503) 636-4398.

▶ BOTANIZING TO THE MAX BEST BETS OREGON

The Nature Conservancy has a small preserve that is like another world plopped down in the midst of the Portland metropolitan area. Camassia Natural Area actually was created, or drastically modified, by forces from afar. When the Bretz Floods swept over the Portland region, it washed away everything growing on the top of this bluff along with the topsoil. Since then only a thin, rocky soil has developed, just like the many other scablands caused by the floods. This has created excellent habitat for an Oregon white oak and madrone woodland, a rare plant community these days in the northern Willamette Valley. There are also perched wetlands, low points atop the bluff that have thin soil but hold water because the basalt underneath is impermeable. The result is a beautiful, sunny oak-madrone woodland with small scattered wetland prairies, a habitat more common farther south, such as in the Rogue Valley. The mid- to late April explosion of blooming camas, sea blush, blue-eyed Mary, and saxifrages is breathtaking and rare in the Portland region.

This is a fragile environment. The Nature Conservancy asks visitors to be careful and stay on the trails. As in all Conservancy preserves, dogs are not allowed and obviously neither is picking flowers. The preserve, in West Linn, is a bit tricky to find. Drive south on State Hwy 43 (SW Macadam) from Portland or drive south on Interstate 205 and take the West Linn exit (Exit 8) and then turn left onto Highway 43 at the end of the off ramp. Either way, you'll drive south on Hwy 43 and drive under I-205. After you drive under I-205 turn right before the gas station to go uphill onto Willamette Falls Dr. Drive one block, and then make a sharp left turn to stay on Willamette Falls Dr. Drive just 0.25 mile on Willamette Falls Dr, and then veer right onto Sunset Ave. Sunset goes uphill and over I-205. The first street you come to after crossing over I-205 is Walnut. Turn right onto Walnut St and drive to its end. Park carefully in the area at the end of the road. Please do not block any of the local residents' driveways. The trailhead is signed. I like to take the left fork of the trail to head up to the top of the bluff. Watch out for poison oak here; it's very common. You will work your way uphill on the trail and then emerge at the top in another world.

The Columbia River Gorge is one of the premier wildflower spots of the West and the Washington places described in March (Early Bloomers) will continue to be interesting to the end of May. But as spring progresses the action shifts from the drier Washington side to the shady, moister Oregon side and moves up in elevation. You really can't go wrong hiking on any of the Gorge trails in spring. The heart of the west Gorge is the section of the old Historic Columbia River Highway (also called the Scenic Highway) between Corbett (Exit 22) and Dodson/Ainsworth SP (Exit 35). This section is almost all public land and has the main waterfalls, lots of trails, and a variety of plants blooming from March through July. Other favorite areas a little farther to the east include the trail to Elowah Falls and Upper McCord Creek Falls and the trail to Wahclella Falls, also called Tanner Falls.

The trail for Elowah and McCord Creek falls starts at the parking area in Yeon SP, just before the Columbia River Highway rejoins Interstate 84 at Exit 37. Wahclella Falls is another 3 miles to the east. From I-84 take the Bonneville Dam exit (Exit 40) and find the paved parking area just south of the exit. From the parking area a trail starts as a gravel road, then becomes the trail to Wahclella Falls. This trail makes a 2-mile loop to the falls and back in a narrow canyon with a huge plunge bowl.

About 35 miles farther east in the oak woodland belt of the Gorge is one of the area's most popular botanizing spots—Rowena Plateau. The plateau is a mixture of state park land and the Tom McCall Preserve of The Nature Conservancy. From I-84 take the Rowena exit (Exit 76), and then head west on the Mosier–The Dalles Highway (State Hwy 30) following signs to Rowena Crest Viewpoint. In about 3.5 miles you'll come to the parking area for the viewpoint, and the view is indeed awesome. The preserve is across the highway where a large sign has a map of the area and other information. Please stay on the trails and don't bring dogs. Information is on The Nature Conservancy's Web site. After walking around the area you can continue driving west for a beautiful drive to Mosier, which has a complete interchange with I-84.

As the season progresses into June and July more plants are blooming at higher elevations, so start exploring places such as Larch Mountain, Wahtum Lake, and Rainy Lake. Be sure to get the latest edition of Columbia River Gorge National Scenic Area, a Forest Service map.

▶ BOTANIZING TO THE MAX BEST BETS WASHINGTON

Because we are in the heart of the Gorge, let's jump the state line to the other side of the Columbia in Washington. Both Dog Mountain and Hamilton Mountain are known for their wildflowers and for giving hikers a good workout. Dog Mountain is 12 miles east and Hamilton Mountain is 7 miles west of the Bridge of the Gods at Cascade Locks. Both trails go through several different habitats with a variety of flowers and provide scenic views of the Gorge. Because both can involve a 2000-foot elevation gain, you'll pass through a range of blooming seasons as you go up. The Gorge is famous for its strong winds, and the wind gets worse the higher you go. So if it's very windy consider taking a shorter hike.

Olympic NP ranges from sea level to almost 8000 feet, with flowers blooming somewhere in the park for half the year. Park Ranger Rod Norvell suggests five easy-to-moderate hikes in the northern part of the park that give an excellent representation of typical west-side forest flowers. Maps and information about these hikes and areas are available at park visitor centers:

ALDWELL NATURE TRAIL The main visitor center in Port Angeles. An easy trail with a nice sample of flowers.
HEART OF THE FOREST TRAIL Five miles up the road to Hurricane Ridge (excellent for alpine flowers).

SPRUCE RAILROAD TRAIL The north shore of Lake Crescent. Goes through more open, rocky areas for a little variety. Calypso orchids and chocolate lilies are favorites on this trail. A level trail, great for beginners; also used by mountain bikes.

MARYMERE FALLS TRAIL The south shore of Lake Crescent. Heavily used but passes through some excellent old growth forest.

SOL DUC VALLEY You can make a 6-mile loop by using the Sol Duc Falls and Lovers Lane Trails.

Just south of Olympia, in the prairies of Mima Mounds Natural Area Preserve, is a different type of habitat from the Olympics. About 10 miles south of Olympia take Exit 95 from Interstate 5 and go west on Maytown Rd (State Hwy 121). In 3 miles you'll reach Littlerock School where Maytown Rd turns into 128th Ave SW. Keep going straight (west) another 0.8 mile and 128th will end at Waddell Creek Rd. There is a small sign for the preserve here. Turn right onto Waddell Creek Rd, drive north about 0.5 mile, and then turn left at the signs. Mima Mounds Preserve is full of unusual mounds of soil. Interpretive signs explain the mounds and theories as to how they got there. Although debate has continued for decades, no one knows how these strange mounds were formed. Perhaps you will be the one to solve this mystery. The preserve has lots of flowers during spring, but the two peaks are in mid-April and mid-June. Where there are flowers, there are also insects; Mima Mounds is also one of our Best Bets for Butterflies and Moths (June).

Different wildflower species occur east of the Cascades although these are usually close relatives of the common flowers on the west side. If you are familiar with the west-side plants you will recognize the many buckwheats, daisies, larkspurs, paintbrushes, lupines, penste-

mons, and desert parsleys. Other common east-side flowers are locoweeds, balsamroots, sandworts, phlox, evening primroses, and mariposa lilies. Often the wildflower displays on the arid east side are more spectacular than on the wetter west side because blooming is compressed into a shorter period of time, and the flowers stand out in bold contrast to the normally more barren landscape.

Springtime visits to the Turnbull and Columbia national wildlife refuges in eastern Washington are great for wildflowers, as well as productive for observing wildlife. Because east-side weather and blooming times can vary quite a bit from year to year, contact the refuges for information about blooming activity before making a long trip to either spot. The spring waterfowl action will be tapering off as the wildflower blooming gets underway, so you will never see the peak of both at the same time. April and into May are the best times for an overall nature adventure with both birds and blooms.

If you're heading east on Interstate 90 from the west side to either of these refuges, a section of I-90 has a scenic alternative that is known for wildflowers. The Vantage Highway goes from Ellensburg to Vantage on the Columbia River, just north of I-90, and on most maps is rightfully keyed as a scenic route. All along the highway can be good for flowers but the interpretive trail for Ginkgo Petrified Forest SP, 2 miles west of Vantage, is a good place to get out and hike around. As you drive along Vantage Highway keep your eyes out for badger burrows in the dirt mounds by the side of the road. Immediately north of the highway and the town of Vantage, on the Columbia, is the interpretive center for the park—a good source for tips on the best wildflower areas and times. Unfortunately, the center's hours fluctuate with its budget so call for information (509) 856-2700.

Two other eastern Washington state parks noted for their wildflowers are Steamboat Rock and Fields Spring state parks. Steamboat Rock is at the north end of Banks Lake and the best area is the top of the rock itself which can be reached by a steep, one-mile trail that starts at the entrance to the northern campground. Across State Hwy 155 from the main park is Northrup Canyon, excellent for flowers and songbirds. Fields Spring SP is in the far southeastern corner of the state in the Blue Mountains. This is probably Washington's most remote state park, perfect if you want to get away from it all and still have a developed campsite. This park is worth a visit if you are in the Blue Mountains or Hells Canyon area. Trails through the open forest to Puffer Butte have lots of flowers, and the view from the top of the butte is spectacular.

Much of eastern Washington is BLM land, and the agency's Wenatchee office has produced *Watchable Wildflowers: A Columbia Basin Guide*. This booklet and the accompanying brochures with plant checklists cover 10 sites in an area that is basically the southeastern quadrant of Washington. These sites are fairly remote places, off the beaten path for the adventurous botanist.

▶ BOTANIZING TO THE MAX BEST BETS BRITISH COLUMBIA

Just north of the US border, east of White Rock, is Campbell Valley RP. This large regional park is in an out-of-the-way location and not close to the population centers of the region, so it's not heavily used. The park has a good variety of habitats with meadows, marsh, forests, and woodlands resulting in a variety of flowers. The two main access points are the North and South Valley entrances. The South Valley entrance is the most developed with a butterfly and wildlife garden and many facilities, while the North Valley entrance has parking, picnic tables, and restrooms. The Little River Loop Trail, from the north entrance, is a good introduction to the habitats of the park and is an easy 1.5 miles long.

To get to Campbell Valley RP take the White Rock and 8th Ave East exit (Exit 2) from Hwy 99 and go 4.75 miles east on 8th Ave to the south entrance. To get to the north entrance, take 200th St north from 8th Ave to 16th Ave and go east about 0.5 mile to the parking area. There are lots of signs to the park and maps are usually available at the south entrance or from the Vancouver Regional Parks office. This park is also very good for migrating and breeding songbirds in the spring.

Three favorite spots on Vancouver Island for April and May flowers are Honeymoon Bay Ecological Reserve, Francis/King regional parks, and Goldstream PP. Don't forget to also go back to the places described in March (Early Bloomers) because the show continues through the spring.

Honeymoon Bay Ecological Reserve is a small preserve established primarily to protect the pink fawn-lily, uncommon on the island and very rare elsewhere in BC. In addition to the fawn-lily, for which it is famous, Honeymoon Bay reserve has many common west-side forest flowers: trillium, wood violet, bleeding heart, vanilla leaf, wild ginger, candy flower, false lily-of-the-valley, fringecups, fairy lanterns, foam flower, both species of false Solomon's seal, and star flower, among others. This is an obscure place, so don't worry when you get the "This can't be it" vibes. As of 2006 the only indication that there is something here is a small sign up high on a telephone pole on the left side of the road, followed by an old dirt driveway blocked with boulders. But don't worry; here are the best (and only) directions to this place you will ever find.

Honeymoon Bay Ecological Reserve is near the south shore of Cowichan Lake about 24 miles west of Duncan. As you head west on South Shore Rd from the town of Cowichan Lake, you will drive through the small village of Honeymoon Bay. Mark the store near the fire hall as zero and continue another mile to where South Shore Rd turns left. Turn left instead of going straight to Gordon Bay PP. Pass the golf course (nice snack bar) and go another 0.6 mile to where you see the dirt driveway blocked by the large rocks. Pull over on the right side of the road and park safely off the road. Cross the road and walk in the driveway and into the clearing in the woods. You'll know you are in the right place when you see the large sign with the paintings of common wildflowers. You'll see trails heading off in different directions; explore wherever you want. There is very little traffic here, so don't worry about your parked car on the side of the road. While botanizing, watch for the common Hammond's flycatcher, which nests here.

Goldstream PP, just 11 miles northwest of Victoria, has several different habitats with a good variety of flowers. The park is also famous for its fall salmon run. The main parking area is just off Trans-Canada Highway 1 in the northern part of the park. From here trails lead through wet forest habitat to the Goldstream Nature House which has displays and a bookstore, as well as helpful naturalists. If the center is closed, the trails to the center and into the marsh are worth taking for the flowers and birds of those habitats.

The uncommon and exotic-sounding black lily can be found in the marsh area north of the nature house.

To experience the drier madrone–Douglas-fir–oak forest habitat, drive to the park campground off Sooke Lake Rd in the southern end of the park. Across from campsite 40 is a parking area at the trailhead for the Arbutus Ridge Trail. You can make a loop by taking this trail to the Arbutus Loop Trail and then back to your car. A park trail map is a good idea. This trail has the bizarre candystick, numerous coralroot, including the uncommon albino form, and several other orchids, making it a bit of an "oddball flowers" trail. While looking for spring flowers in Goldstream, you'll hear plenty of bird song. Winter wren, Pacific slope flycatcher, and Townsend's and orange-crowned warblers are particularly abundant.

Francis/King, one of the Capital Regional District Parks west of Victoria, is near several other regional parks that are good for flowers. It has more moist forest habitat than other parks and flowers very similar to those mentioned for Honeymoon Bay. An outstanding feature of the park is the Elsie King Trail, a universally accessible boardwalk trail that is the longest and nicest I have ever seen for those with limited mobility. To get to Francis/King RP from Victoria, head west on the Trans-Canada Highway 1 to the Helmcken Rd exit (the exit for Victoria General Hospital). Turn right and go north on Helmcken less than 0.5 mile to West Burnside and turn left. In less than one mile, turn right off W. Burnside onto Prospect Lake Rd (there is a small sign for the park here). Soon you'll see signs for the park showing you where to turn off Prospect onto Munn Rd and into the park's parking area.

SAGE-GROUSE STRUT THEIR STUFF

We could hear the weird popping-gurgling sound coming out of the dark around us. We were three graduate students in a tiny wildlife blind stuck in the middle of a high sagebrush plain in northern Colorado. It was March and we were at about 6000 feet. I had on every stitch of winter clothing I owned and still felt like an endotherm going torpid. But I had never seen sage-grouse displaying, or doing anything else, for that matter, and I couldn't pass up the opportunity. I had just become an active birder and started serious pursuit of what would become my career as a naturalist, and this trip to see sage-grouse was one of my earliest and most memorable wildlife adventures.

As the first rays of dawn brought some faint light to the scene we started seeing flashes of white accompanying the noise. With more light we could see that these were the bright white breast feathers of the bird and that there were bizarre yellow air sacks in the feathers. The yellow sacks were being inflated and deflated by the birds, making the unique sound and highlighting the white feathers. While they made the pop and flash display, the birds held their wings down stiffly at an odd angle and held their tail feathers straight up, keeping them erect and fanned-out evenly. To top it off, they had bright yellow eyebrows which they seemed to arch and lower as if they were saying, "Hey bay-bee, hey bay-bee."

Well, this was worth it—I had never seen anything like it before. Since then I have taken people to see sage-grouse displaying on other leks, and many have considered it one of the most fascinating wildlife experiences they have had. Unfortunately, it is a sight that is getting harder and harder to see.

Sage-grouse are truly an animal of the American West. As John Terres says in his *Encyclopedia of North American Birds*, the sage-grouse is "as western as a Stetson hat and sagebrush." Actually, you could take the Stetson hat out of the West but you couldn't take the sage-grouse out of the sagebrush. Sage-grouse are an excellent example of an animal that is highly specialized for a very specific habitat. Sagebrush is almost 100% of the grouse's diet in winter and 75% from late spring to early fall. During the warm growing season, the birds will add to their diet whatever shoots, buds, blossoms, and succulent new leaves become available. They also eat insects, a critical food source to the chicks. All other members of the sage-grouse's group, the order of chicken-like or gallinaceous birds, are known for their large, very muscular gizzards adapted for grinding seeds. But the sage-grouse has a soft, thin-walled gizzard, just right for a diet of soft sage leaves. In addition to food, sagebrush provides cover for nesting, shelter from the weather, and protection from predators.

To be accurate and up-to-date, there are two species of sage-grouse, now spelled with a hyphen. Ornithologists decided that a small, isolated population of sage-grouse in southwestern Colorado is a separate species that has been named Gunnison sage-grouse. The rest of the sage-grouse in the world, including ours, are now called greater sage-grouse. To keep things simple, I have used "sage-grouse" for what is now officially the "greater sage-grouse."

Sage-grouse are large birds; the larger males tip the scales at over six pounds. Like many gallinaceous birds, sage-grouse were an important and favored food of western settlers. They are still legally hunted today in many states where they occur. Although overhunting was clearly responsible for decreasing the number of sage-grouse in the past, habitat destruction is now their biggest threat.

The range of sage-grouse and their numbers have decreased dramatically because of the systematic destruction of sagebrush. Although it is the dominant plant of one of the main natural habitats in the West, sagebrush has basically been treated as if it were a weed that had to be eliminated. Why? Well, the European cows and sheep we like to eat don't like to eat sagebrush. So the sagebrush is removed using fire, chains, and bulldozers, or herbicides, encouraging more grasses to grow naturally or followed by seeding of the area, usually with nonnative grasses. This manipulation is termed range improvement or rehabilitation, but it's really the destruction of a natural habitat and its native wildlife for the benefit of a few nonnative, domestic animals that are very poorly adapted to the environment. Ironically, overgrazing by domestic sheep and cattle is one of the main causes for the increased proportion of sagebrush over grasses in many areas.

Because of habitat loss, sage-grouse have been extirpated from British Columbia and are just barely hanging on in Washington. As with their close associate, the pronghorn, southeastern Oregon is the place to see this resident of the Great Basin sagebrush steppe. There is still a limited hunting season on sage-grouse in Oregon even though they are listed as sensitive in some parts of their range and are a candidate for listing under the Federal Endangered Species Act.

Sage-grouse are viewable any time of the year in the right habitat, but they are unpredictable and difficult to find when not on their display grounds or leks. One way to increase your chances is to be near a body of water where they come to drink early in the morning or late in the afternoon. If you're lucky enough to be near their route from the water to the sagebrush, you might catch them going from one to the other. However, the ultimate sage-grouse experience is to see them displaying on their lek. Leks and territories are discussed in A Closer Look at the end of this month.

Locating a lek would seem relatively easy because leks are used for decades and become well known to wildlife managers. Unfortunately, sage-grouse leks are a good example of a dilemma faced by wildlife managers and authors of books like this one. Although you want people to have outstanding and unique wildlife experiences, such as seeing a sage-grouse lek, you realize that too many people can negatively impact the wildlife being observed. Some areas simply can't be visited by the public and survive. Other sites can be visited by people who practice proper wildlife-watching etiquette. With sage-grouse this is especially important. All those who visit a lek must follow the single most important rule for lek watching: do not get out of your car.

▶ **SAGE-GROUSE STRUT THEIR STUFF BEST BETS** OREGON

The lek on Foster Flats Rd near Malheur NWR is one well-known sage-grouse lek in southeastern Oregon that BLM wildlife biologists feel can withstand its current visitation. Staying at the Malheur Field Station gives you the shortest drive to the lek in the early morning hours. Get to the lek while it is still dark, at least half an hour before sunrise. Foster Flats Rd heads west from State Hwy 205, south of milepost 3 and about 11 miles south of the turnoff to refuge headquarters. After you turn onto Foster Flats Rd, drive 8.3 miles and pull over on the side of the road as far as you can and park. You'll probably see other cars there which will help you find the spot. Many people feel it is better to note the 8.3 mile spot, and then slowly drive past it a bit to where you can turn around and drive back to the spot and park. This way when you leave you can just go forward out of the area. This avoids disturbing the birds as you might if you made the turn and then drove back through the lek after the sun is up. Foster Flats Rd is sometimes very muddy and can be impassable, so call refuge headquarters or the BLM's Hines office for road conditions and any other information pertinent to visiting the lek.

After you have parked at the lek site, you'll just have to sit there in the dark and wait until it starts to get light enough to see the birds. Leave your engine and lights off, and be as quiet as possible. It will probably be very cold, so dress warmly. At some point you will want to lower a window to better hear and appreciate the sounds the birds are making. Just make sure everyone remains silent during listening time. Photographers will also want to take pictures; get set up in advance. Most importantly: never open a door or get out of your car. If someone gets out of a car (usually an overzealous photographer) the birds immediately fly away, and that's it for the day. Such thoughtless behavior will make instant enemies of other grouse watchers present and could eventually result in the area being closed.

When you're ready to leave, start your car and creep out of the area as quietly as possible. Avoid driving into the area during the day if you are unable to get to the lek before light. The grouse may start displaying as early as late February and a few may persist until early May but March and April are the best times. Another way to see this lek is to go on one of the organized grouse-viewing field trips offered as part of the annual Migratory Bird Festival held in Burns.

▶ SAGE-GROUSE STRUT THEIR STUFF BEST BETS WASHINGTON

The Yakima Training Center (Department of the Army) is now the only place in Washington where people can regularly see sage-grouse at leks. Access is limited and normally the only way you can visit these leks is as part of an organized sage-grouse trip with the Yakima Valley Audubon Society or the Seattle Audubon Society. Begin to check with them in February.

BRANT MIGRATION

During September and October virtually the entire Pacific population of brant, about 140,000 birds, gathers in Izembek Lagoon near the tip of the Alaska Peninsula to get ready for their mass migration south. Then, almost overnight—they're gone, on a 3000-mile, 60-hour nonstop flight to Mexico. An impressive flight for a little goose barely larger than a mallard.

Brant are a small, dark sea goose, one of the world's smallest geese and one of the few that spend their entire life in or right near saltwater. They breed in the tidal wetlands of the Arctic, farther north than any other goose. In the Arctic they eat a variety of plants and invertebrates, but in the bays and estuaries of their wintering grounds, brant feed almost exclusively on eelgrass. Eelgrass is one of the few flowering plants that grow in salt water. Eelgrass spreads by seeds and by rhizomes, so once it gets established in the right environment, it can quickly spread to form huge beds, or eelgrass meadows, that are an ecosystem unto themselves with many associated animals.

The brant's dependency on eelgrass proved disastrous during the early

1930s when disease killed most of the eelgrass along the Atlantic coast. The Atlantic brant population (considered for many years a separate species) crashed and many folks feared their extinction, but the birds adapted and switched to other aquatic plants. Eelgrass along the Pacific Coast has not suffered similar epidemics, and in the West the association between eelgrass and brant is still very strong. Their next favorite food is an alga appropriately named sea lettuce, which you have probably seen in tidepools, and thought looked a lot like lettuce. I love names like that. Along our coast, stop-off spots for brant have either rich eelgrass beds, lots of sea lettuce, or a bit of both, and maybe a few other items, making a sea salad.

Historically, many brant spent the winter along the coasts of Washington, Oregon, and California. But starting in the late 1950s more and more skipped these states entirely, flying straight to Mexico. California, for example, went from being a major wintering area to having almost no wintering brant at all. What happened? The birds just couldn't take the disturbance from the boaters, anglers, water-skiers, and shoreline developments in the bays they had favored.

Fortunately, plenty of unsettled wintering habitat in Baja and some on the west coast of mainland Mexico still exists. The brant adapted by shifting their wintering grounds farther south to Mexico and just skipping most of the crowded West Coast of the United States. A small but significant population of brant that have wintered in the waters of the Salish Sea, from Padilla Bay north to the Strait of Georgia, has been growing recently. The total population of brant has fluctuated over the decades, but the Pacific population as a whole has declined enough in the last decade to cause concern. The recent, rapid population growth on the eastern coast of Vancouver Island may be pushing brant out of some choice habitat.

Here's the good news. Vancouver Island's well-established Brant Wildlife Festival, a Best Bet, seems to be helping the birds. In 1993, partly as a result of the festival, 17 kilometers of intertidal foreshore were declared The Parksville-Qualicum Beach Wildlife Management Area. Then in 2000, about 800 square kilometers of land encompassing these two communities and about 400 square kilometers of marine area were designated Canada's 10th biosphere reserve under the Man and Biosphere Program of UNESCO. For

American readers not familiar with square kilometers, that's almost 300,000 acres or a total of about 463 square miles. Wow! This area is now called the Mount Arrowsmith Biosphere Reserve.

Most brant may pass us by in the fall as they head south, but in the spring it's a different story. Instead of migrating far offshore and making the trip in a few days, brant returning to their breeding grounds in the spring hug the shoreline and make frequent stops to eat. As they travel north the brant stop for days at a time, eating almost constantly to put on weight so they arrive at their breeding grounds in peak condition. While feeding in large flocks, they keep up an almost constant chatter of a honking and croaking sound that has led some to call them the talking goose.

Brant follow the typical breeding behaviors of other swans and geese: they mate for life. The female does the incubating while the male stands guard, and both parents defend their nest site and rear the young. The Arctic summer is short, and young brant must grow quickly. They can walk and swim within a day of hatching, dive underwater in two days, and fly in six weeks. The family group stays together until just before the migration south.

From November through April, you may find brant in any bay or estuary along the Pacific Coast. You'll see the most along the east coast of Vancouver Island between Nanaimo and Comox. Just think, for some residents in this area the arrival of the "talking goose" is a sign of spring.

▶ **BRANT MIGRATION BEST BETS** OREGON

Oregon has the fewest brant, but they are still fairly regular from November through April. The estuaries that most consistently have brant are Tillamook, Netarts, Yaquina, and Coos Bays. Of these Yaquina has the most extensive eelgrass beds, so it's the best of the four. A map of the area is in February (Wintering Waterfowl). Tillamook Bay, covered in August (Fall Shorebird migration), is also a good spot. In Coos Bay the best spot for finding brant is from the boat basin in the town of Charleston, reached by Newmark Rd and the Cape Arago Highway from US Hwy 101. The eastern shore of Netarts Bay is hugged by a road with changing names—Cape Lookout Rd, Whiskey Creek Rd, or Netarts Bay Dr at different sections. This road provides good views into the bay and places where you can safely park on the side and scope the bay.

▶ BRANT MIGRATION BEST BETS WASHINGTON

The largest population of wintering brant north of Mexico is in the part of the Salish Sea around the international border between Washington and British Columbia. Most of these wintering birds are in Washington, especially in Padilla, Samish, Bellingham, and Birch bays. During the spring migration thousands more join this population of about 15,000. Any place in the Salish Sea that has wintering waterfowl also is a good bet for brant migration, but the Best Bet is Padilla Bay.

Most of Padilla Bay is included in the 11,000-acre Padilla Bay National Estuarine Research Reserve, one of the 27 reserves in the little-known National Estuarine Research Reserve System managed by state agencies in conjunction with the National Oceanic and Atmospheric Administration (NOAA). Padilla Bay is one of only five reserves on the west coast and was selected because it has the largest known eelgrass meadow in the Pacific Northwest. "Ah-ha," you say, "Eelgrass means brant," and right you are. Brant are regularly seen in Padilla Bay during the winter; during April tens of thousands are sometimes seen.

Access to Padilla Bay is along Bayview-Edison Rd, which goes up the eastern shore of the bay. Bayview-Edison Rd intersects State Hwy 20 at a major intersection with a signal, roughly halfway between Anacortes and Exit 230 on Interstate 5. From Hwy 20, go north on Bayview-Edison Rd 3.5 miles and you'll come to Bayview SP where you can park right on the shore and look over the bay. About another mile north is the excellent Breazeale Interpretive Center which has exhibits, including aquaria of bay life, and is your resource for information about the bay. Another good place to overlook the bay for brant and other birds is from the Shore Trail, parking for which is just south of Bayview SP. Ask for a map at the interpretive center. Between October and April, look for other waterfowl as well as for raptors in the nearby Skagit and Samish flats. You can easily spend a couple of days birding western Skagit County between November and April, and a lot of birdwatching groups do just that.

Another major stop for migrating brant is Willapa Bay, the largest estuary in Washington. Willapa NWR consists of five different units that include several thousands of acres of tidelands, with eelgrass, as well as some upland habitats. It is an excellent spot for wintering and migrating waterfowl and migrating shorebirds, as well as the brant. Unfortunately, viewing of the bay is somewhat limited or involves long hikes. Refuge headquarters, on US Hwy 101 about 4 miles west of its junction with State Hwy 4, has maps, checklists, and current information.

The best all-around birding spot in the Willapa area is the Leadbetter Point Unit of the refuge at the tip of the Long Beach Peninsula. Take State Hwy 103 north on the Long Beach Peninsula from its junction with US 101 and follow signs for Leadbetter Point SP. Highway 103 ends at the park, where there is a parking area with a large interpretive sign. Follow the very short trail that goes due east from this spot to the shoreline and scan the bay. Then get back in your car and drive the short distance to the final end of the road and the parking area for the trail heading northeast into the refuge.

Rubber boots are a good idea—the ground gets muddy and you may have to walk in some shallow water. As you look out over the bay and shoreline along this trail, you should see plenty of brant and other waterfowl, gulls, herons, some loons and grebes, and flocks of shorebirds. If you are lucky and hit it just right, you will be flabbergasted by the number and variety of birds. A large sign at the trailhead indicates which part of the point is closed from April through August to protect nesting snowy plovers.

As with most tidal areas in the Northwest, the birding is best at high tide or as high tide is receding. At Leadbetter Point, however, the highest tides will limit where you can walk so don't go at the peak of a spring tide. Find the times for the tides in local newspapers, at sporting goods stores, at visitor information centers, or in advance from the Internet. In the Willapa Bay area, tides are usually given for the Columbia River at Ilwaco. The tides are two hours later than Ilwaco at Nahcotta,

inside the bay, so use this as your adjustment for Leadbetter Point or the southern end of the bay.

Willapa Bay is home to one of the largest oyster fisheries on the West Coast. In Nahcotta visit the Willapa Bay Interpretive Center (hours irregular) that tells the story of the Willapa Bay oyster industry. Turn onto 273rd St from Hwy 103 at the Jolly Roger Seafood sign in Nahcotta. The Long Beach Peninsula is a major tourist area and you can get information at the visitor center at the intersection of US Hwy 101 and Hwy 103. Jake the Alligator Man of Marsh's Free Museum in Long Beach is a Northwest legend among fans of vintage roadside attractions.

▶ BRANT MIGRATION BEST BETS BRITISH COLUMBIA

This is it—20,000 or so brant migrate north through the Strait of Georgia and stop along the east coast of Vancouver Island to eat and rest. The two beach resort communities of Parksville and Qualicum Beach have held a Brant Wildlife Festival every April since 1991 to celebrate the arrival of the geese and to focus attention on the importance of protecting the coastal wetlands. Activities include birding competitions, exhibits and workshops on wildlife art and photography, field trips for wildlife viewing, and various feasts.

Four areas on the east coast of Vancouver Island provide excellent views of brant and the many other waterbirds present in April: Rathtrevor Beach PP, Qualicum Beach, Deep Bay, and Comox Harbor.

Rathtrevor Beach PP in Parksville is the easiest site to find because there are signs for brant viewing that lead you right to the best spot (near parking lot 1). Again, it is important to go at high tide or just as high tide is reced-

ing. Sometimes brant are just offshore from Rathtrevor but are hard to see from the park. Another site nearby may give a better view.

As you leave Rathtrevor Park go northwest a short distance on the Island Highway (19A) and turn right onto Plummer Rd. Stay on Plummer until it turns into Shorewood Dr and take Shorewood until it intersects Mariner Way. At this T intersection, you can go left onto Mariner or right to continue on Shorewood. Three unpaved sections of public road take you less than one block from Mariner and Shorewood to the shore. All are posted with a "no camping or overnight parking" sign. You can park on the road and walk to the shore for good views into the Strait of Georgia near Rathtrevor and toward the mouth of the Englishman River. Stay on the roads and respect private property.

Qualicum Beach is the second place to view brant. The Island Highway hugs the shoreline for about one mile in Qualicum Beach, with

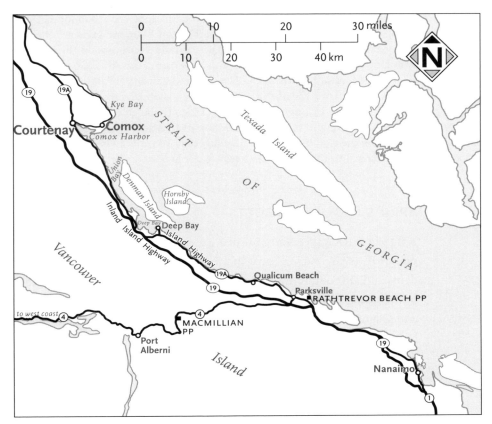

EAST VANCOUVER ISLAND

several pullover areas including a roadside rest with a brant viewing area sign.

The third area is the stretch of coast between Qualicum Beach and Courtenay. One excellent spot here is Deep Bay, just off the Island Highway, a bit over 2 miles north of Bowser. Heading north, turn right onto Gainsburg Rd following the sign to Deep Bay. Stay on Gainsburg, going left at the train tracks, then turn right onto Burne Rd and then left onto Deep Bay Dr. Where Deep Bay Dr curves left, park in the area where you can see the Chrome Island Lighthouse. Get out here and check the shore and water carefully. Then drive to the end of

Deep Bay Dr, park, and sneak out to the end of the point on a short trail to search the shoreline and channel. Check the charming little harbor itself on your way back out to the highway, where you should see ducks galore, brant, scads of western grebes, some loons, gulls, herons, cormorants, and shorebirds.

Continuing north on the Island Highway, the road runs along the shore in the stretch between Fanny Bay and Union Bay. There is an official roadside rest that provides a great view across Baynes Sound toward Denman Island.

Comox Harbor, noted for its large population of wintering trumpeter swans and great for waterfowl in general, is also a good spot for brant. The swans will be gone by the time the brant migration starts, but you may see one when you're looking for the other. Goose Spit RP is on the neck of Goose Spit which sticks out into Comox Harbor from the north shore. To get onto the spit, go through the center of Comox on Comox Rd and turn left onto Pritchard, following the sign for Goose Spit. Continue on Pritchard to the first stop sign and turn right onto Balmoral. Drive a few blocks and Balmoral ends at a stop sign on Lazo Rd but continues on the other side with a new name, Hawkins. Go straight onto Hawkins and stay on it until you drive out onto the spit. Park along the road and scan the area. You can't go to the end of the spit, which is a military installation. I once watched 80 brant feeding only 20 yards away on large clumps of sea lettuce here.

APRIL'S NATURE NUGGETS

ANIMAL BABIES Harbor seals are the most abundant and familiar of the pinnipeds (seals and sea lions) in the Northwest. They are year-round residents and are commonly seen resting on beaches, mudflats, and low rocks. In the spring the females seek shallow, protected waters to have their pups, and the mother will sometimes leave her baby parked on a beach while she hunts for food nearby. This usually begins to happen in April and continues into May. People occasionally see these baby seals lying by themselves on the beach and sometimes assume that they are abandoned and need help, when in fact Mom is waiting nearby for the people to leave. They pick up the baby seal and then try to find somewhere to take it to be cared for. They may try the police, a Humane Society, an Audubon Society, or a zoo. Some of these "kidnapped" babies end up at a proper wildlife rehabilitation center and eventually are released, but they would be much better off if they were just left alone.

The same thing sometimes happens to fawns and some other mammals, but the largest number of animal kidnappings are the thousands of baby birds picked up by people during the nesting season. In almost every case of a so-called abandoned baby bird, the parents or mother is nearby and will return to take care of the youngster once people leave. This tendency of many people to want to do something for these young animals is a wonderful indication of care and concern, but the best rule is, leave them alone.

NIGHTTIME MAMMAL MOVEMENT The spring breeding season is also a time when many mammals start roaming about more than usual in search of mates. Because most mammals are nocturnal this means a large increase in mammal traffic across roads at night. We all know the tragic end for some of these critters when we see their carcasses on the road. The most common victim west of the Cascades is either North America's only marsupial, the Virginia opossum, or the raccoon. (Outside of cities and east of the mountains, skunks may be the most common.) The frequent encounters between people and the unattractive remains of deceased opossums on roads may contribute to the generally negative attitude most people have toward these benign and helpless creatures. As sad as these deaths are, they sometimes provide opportunities for examining animals you might not otherwise see. I've seen mountain beaver (also known as boomer) and long-tailed weasels on the road at Portland Audubon that I didn't know lived in the area. Your parents were right; do not handle dead mammals because they can carry diseases. Whenever possible I will move dead animals off the road and into a place where they can decompose with dignity instead of being smeared on the pavement.

TERRITORIES AND LEKS: A CLOSER LOOK

Bushtits may be buddy-buddy most of the year, but when it comes time to breed, even these highly social birds are driven by their raging hormones to seek their own space. Territoriality, a common and widespread phenomenon among animals, is one of the main causes of the patterns of animal distribution in an area. Because birds are so conspicuous, noisy, and easy to study, their territorial behavior is the best known. Some animals, like mountain lions and eagles, maintain territories all year, but the majority of animals maintain territories for a limited period of time and for a specific purpose.

The word *territory* has a definite meaning in animal behavior and biology and should not be confused with *home range* or *range*. An animal's home range is the area within which that animal is usually found and which it rarely, if ever, leaves. Thus, an animal's home range would have to provide all the necessities for life. Range refers to the entire geographic area where that animal can be found and usually includes the area where a whole species occurs. Terms like *winter range* or *breeding range* often are used to describe different parts of an animal's total range. In contrast, an animal's territory is specifically the area that it will actively defend against others, usually of its own species, and is usually much smaller than the animal's total range, although it may sometimes be close in size to the home range.

Some territories are single purpose, such as a feeding territory. For example, the feeding territory of a rufous hummingbird might be an area of blooming flowers that one rufous hummingbird will aggressively defend against other rufous hummers. Sometimes individuals will keep out members of other species as well as their own. Clearly, this type of territory would change greatly over time with changes in the flowers that were blooming. Sometimes a group of animals with defend an area against other groups of the same species. This is common among chickadees and some rats and mice.

The most common type of territory is the all-purpose breeding territory that a breeding pair of animals establishes to raise their young, where the defended territory provides food, water, shelter, and space for displays and other activities. A classic example is the nesting territory for a pair of breeding songbirds. The male typically establishes and defends the territory. When birds sing in the spring they are saying, "Keep out—this is my space, reserved for my family alone." If a male bird does not yet have a mate, his singing also functions to advertise for one.

Why do animals set up territories? Territories somewhat evenly divide up or partition the limited resources, such as food, in an area so that each animal, or group of animals, gets enough. By establishing an exclusive foraging area for himself and his family, a male robin increases the chances that his offspring will survive. Besides providing a stable food source, the territorial system reduces predation because nests are dispersed and harder to find. Also, the territory system greatly reduces sexual hanky-panky with outsiders which could disrupt the business of raising a family.

This sounds great, but doesn't establishing and maintaining a territory require a tremendous amount of time and energy? Can the pay-off really be large enough? Actually, the return on the investment saves time and energy. If an animal had to constantly fight with outsiders over food, nesting sites, space, and mates, it would use up much more energy and be at risk of injury. Once territories are established, the boundaries are amazingly well respected and require relatively little energy to maintain. Actual fights are almost completely eliminated.

Animal territories have interesting variations that are adaptations for the particular challenges each species faces. One of the most interesting, and particularly fascinating to people, is the lek system. A lek is a special area where the males of a particular species traditionally gather every year during the breeding season to strut their stuff for the females who come to the lek and select a mate for breeding. Ten quite different bird families around the world have some species that show lek behavior, but one of the most famous, and the classic example for North America, is the sage-grouse.

In the lek, also called an arena or strutting ground, each male has a very small individual territory around him that he defends against other males. Sometimes fights over territories can get bloody. The cocks put on elaborate displays involving visual elements, behaviors, and sounds. All this is to keep other males out of the way and to attract the hens. Unlike the majority of birds, male and female sage-grouse form no pair bond for breeding and raising young. The hens saunter on over to the lek and cruise through the males who are displaying their lives away in the hopes that one of the seemingly indifferent females will pick them for mating. The female picks the cock of her choice and enters his territory, where the two copulate. Then the female leaves and goes off to nest, incubate, and raise the young by herself. The cock continues his display, hoping to attract another hen.

The territories in the center of the lek are the most valued because the males that occupy these territories will mate with a large majority of the females. The most dominant male sage-grouse, or master cock, in the center of the lek may mate with 80 to 90% of the hens that visit that lek. Some master cocks have been recorded mating with twenty hens in a morning. Once the territories are well established, the males will spend several hours every day, morning and evening, for as long as two months, doing their best displays. Males have less time to eat and rest, and some biologists believe that these spring mating rituals are a major factor in the mortality of male sage-grouse.

MAY

SPRING ON THE OREGON COAST

In the 100 miles between Yachats and Bandon lies one of the most outstanding chunks of coastline in the United States for both scenery and wildlife. During spring the major natural attractions available along the central Oregon coast are gray whale migration; shorebird, waterfowl, and songbird migrations; the state's best tidepools; the beginning of nesting by breeding seabirds; ancient forests; breeding newts; wildflowers; and two plant specialties. In addition to the natural wonders, you'll find many tourist attractions and accommodations in the towns, three of which are some of the most charming on the Northwest coast—Yachats, Florence, and Bandon. Public access is almost unlimited, and about fifty miles of beach are included in the Oregon Coast Trail.

One reason to go to the central coast in May is to see the rhodies. The Pacific rhododendron ranges from northern California to just inside southern British Columbia and is common in many areas west of the Sierra-Cascades crest. This showy rhody really flourishes and reaches peak densities in the understory of the transition coniferous forests that dominate the sand dune area of the coast from Coos Bay to a bit north of Florence. US Hwy 101 goes right through the heart of the rhododendrons. Heceta Beach Rd, just north of Florence, usually has a spectacular display. South of Florence, trails in Honeyman SP and in the Siltcoos and Tahkenitch Lake areas of Oregon Dunes NRA provide opportunities for hiking among the rhodies. For over 100 years, Florence has celebrated this spectacle with an annual Rhododendron Festival the third weekend in May, complete with floral parade, carnival, arts and crafts booths, sock hop, Rhody Run, and other events. This is

Its name says it all: Pacific giant salamander

a homespun event and not swarmed with large crowds, but if you go make your lodging arrangements well in advance.

Near Florence you can also see one of the most unique and bizarre plants in the West—the cobra lily or California pitcher plant. One look at this strange plant, and you know something is weird about it and, sure enough, you're right. It eats bugs. Most folks know that some plants catch insects for food, but the idea of a carnivorous plant still amazes and fascinates many, including me. The California pitcher plant is so unusual that it has its own genus, in a family with other pitcher plants. It is the only member of its family in the West and grows only in very limited parts of northern California and southern Oregon.

Like other pitcher plants, the cobra lily catches insects passively by forming a pitfall trap with its leaves. The highly modified leaf forms a hollow tube, up to 2-feet long, with an enlarged, bulbous hood at the end. On the underside of the hood is the small opening into the hollow leaf, and projecting downward from this opening is a forked, petal-like appendage that looks kind of like a giant snake's tongue. The leaves usually grow straight up from the base of the plant, although some may lie along the ground. All the leaves twist 180° as they grow, ending up facing to the outside of the plant, presumably because this is better for catching insects. The leaves range from green to yellow to red, changing from the base to the top and with age. These features make the plant look much like some kind of stylized cobra rising up and flaring its hood—hence the name cobra lily. When the tall leaves with their hoods and tongues sway in a breeze, it makes them look more snakelike and menacing.

Why would any insect be foolhardy enough to enter the rather small hole on the underside of the hood? The cobra lily uses that age-old plant lure, nectar; only this time it's not for pollination but for a one-way trip to the bottom of the pit. Nectar glands on the tongue and lip of the opening attract insects who regularly venture further inside the hood seeking more goodies. Once inside, they may start to slip on the waxy inside surface and then try to crawl or fly back out the opening. However, distributed about the hood are spots where the leaf tissue has lost almost all of its usual insides (chlorophyll and such) and has formed translucent spots. These thin "windows" look like openings, and the confused insects keep trying to fly out these spots until they fall exhausted into the bottom of the leaf. Those that try to crawl out have a little surprise also. The inside top of the leaf is covered with a slick, waxy secretion that makes footing practically impossible. As the hapless insect slides farther down the leaf, it encounters a myriad of tiny, sharp, downward-pointing hairs. These hairs make progress down the tube of the leaf easy but escape upward impossible. Bit by bit the victim sinks lower and lower into the tube of doom until it finally falls into the water contained in the bottom of the leaf.

Once in the water, the insect drowns. Unlike some carnivorous plants, such as sundews and Venus flytraps, the cobra lily does not produce digestive enzymes to digest its prey. Instead, the bugs just rot, and as bacteria go about their usual business of breaking down the bodies into simpler compounds, the useful nutrients are absorbed by the plant. Like almost all carnivorous plants, the California pitcher plant grows in boggy soil, which is very low in nitrogen, so it has adapted by getting its nitrogen the way animals do, from the protein in animal flesh. From an evolutionary standpoint, carnivorous plants are doubly fascinating because several different types in unrelated families have developed different methods for eating bugs, all to solve the same basic problem of low nitrogen in the soil.

A healthy stand of cobra lilies grows in the Darlingtonia State Natural Site, just 5 miles north of Florence off US Hwy 101. Heading north from Florence, watch for the signs and turn right onto Mercer Lake Rd. The trail to the plants is short and level; restrooms are available at the parking lot.

Another unique natural attraction near Florence is America's largest sea cave, home to the only permanent colony of Steller, or northern, sea lions on the mainland of North America. Steller sea lions are the largest members of the eared seal family, and males can reach 2000 pounds. Ten miles north of Florence is Sea Lion Caves, a private wildlife sanctuary and tourist attraction that has operated continuously since 1932. The 208-foot elevator descent into the grotto provides a unique experience and an opportunity to see these marine mammals up close.

The largest number of sea lions is inside the cave during fall and winter. By May the sea lions have begun to spend most of their non-swimming time at the rookery on the rocky ledges just outside the cave entrance. Near the top of the cliffs is an observation deck where you can view the rookery (take your binoculars). Other marine mammals you might see are harbor seals,

California sea lions, gray whales and, rarely, orca. In spring and summer a number of seabirds nest in and about the cave. Gulls, cormorants, and pigeon guillemots are the most common. The outside viewing decks are excellent for seeing migrating gray whales earlier in the spring and have a great view of the Heceta Head Lighthouse, one of the most scenic on the West Coast.

Here is a summary, from north to south, of the main natural (and a few human-made) attractions in this amazing hundred miles of coast:

YACHATS Tidepools.

CAPE PERPETUA SCENIC AREA IN SIUSLAW NF Tidepools, ancient forest, giant Sitka spruce, gray whales, scenic overlook, visitor center.

NEPTUNE SP Tidepools, harbor seals at Strawberry Hill.

DEVIL'S ELBOW SP AND HECETA HEAD Tidepools, seabirds, gray whales, lighthouse.

SEA LION CAVES. Sea lions, whales, seabirds.

DARLINGTONIA STATE NATURAL SITE Cobra lilies.

FLORENCE. Siuslaw estuary and south jetty for seabirds, waterfowl, shorebirds.

HONEYMAN SP Rough-skinned newts breed in Cleawox Lake.

OREGON DUNES NATIONAL RECREATION AREA Florence to Coos Bay: Spectacular rhododendron display. Siltcoos Lagoon has freshwater wetlands, beaver, waterfowl, herons, and osprey. Plenty of good hiking trails; a hiking guide is available from Siuslaw NF.

COOS BAY Shorebirds at Pony Slough in North Bend.

CAPE ARAGO Chain of three great state parks: Sunset Bay, Shore Acres, Cape Arago. Tidepools; seals and sea lions, including possibly elephant seals; seabirds.

SOUTH SLOUGH NATIONAL ESTUARINE RESERVE Outstanding wetland and upland habitats in 4400 acres; best seen by canoe.

BANDON Nesting seabirds (including puffins) on offshore rocks; Bandon Marsh NWR.

MALHEUR IN MAY

The most famous birding spot in the Northwest is Malheur NWR in south-eastern Oregon. Roger Tory Peterson chose it as one of the Dozen Birding Hot Spots in the nation. The 187,000-acre national wildlife refuge is the second largest in the Northwest and contains one of the West's largest freshwater marsh systems. What makes Malheur even more dramatic is that this huge wetlands system is surrounded by the arid and rugged country of the northern Great Basin. This oasis-in-the-desert setting has a major effect on diversity. Within a relatively small area you can find wildlife from many different habitats. Malheur also "sucks in" traveling birds from a wide area that are seeking the water and vegetation so scarce in the surrounding hundreds of square miles. Malheur regularly produces many of the most unusual bird sightings in the region, and many Oregon birders consider no year complete without at least one trip to this legendary hot spot.

Late May is the birder's favorite time to visit Malheur. May has the greatest diversity of species, and most of the more unusual bird sightings occur in this month. In spring you also have the advantage of seeing birds in their finest breeding plumage and hearing them sing, both extremely helpful for identification. In a two- or three-day visit an experienced birder can expect to see about 125 species in 35 different families.

The northern part of Malheur NWR is about 25 miles south of the town of Burns, Oregon. The long T-shaped refuge then stretches for another 40 miles south, more or less paralleling State Hwy 205, to the tiny town of Frenchglen. Most visitors get to the refuge from Burns and proceed from north to south, so we'll do the same. Take State Hwy 78 east from Burns almost 2 miles to the intersection with Hwy 205. Turn right and head south on Hwy 205. En route to the refuge you will drive through hayfields that when flooded provide excellent birding. These fields south of Burns are an outstanding birding area in their own right, especially during spring waterfowl migration (see March).

About 10 miles south of Hwy 78 is an interesting geological formation called Wright's Point, a tongue of basalt that is a cast of an ancient river canyon. Just before coming to the top, as you drive up the northern side of Wright's Point, you'll see a small, rough turnout on your right. This turnout

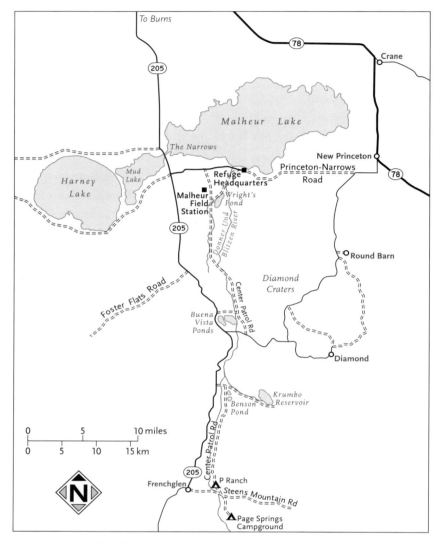

MALHEUR NATIONAL WILDLIFE REFUGE

is in a jumble of collapsed rimrock and chokecherries that for many years has been a good location for finding both rock and canyon wren, ash-throated flycatcher, and sometimes sage thrasher. Look for yellow-bellied marmots, which love the rimrock in this part of the country. From this spot you'll also have a great view north to Burns and the Strawberry Mountains.

Ten miles south of Wright's Point you'll find yourself driving on a causeway. This is The Narrows, the point where the road separates Malheur Lake on the east from Mud and Harney lakes on the west. The amount of water in these lakes has varied phenomenally since the 1980s—you may be driving in the middle of a lake or over dry and cracked mud. What birds are there will depend on the amount of water present, but The Narrows usually produces some interesting waterbirds and shorebirds.

Just south of The Narrows, turn left at the gas station onto Princeton-Narrows Rd going east to the refuge headquarters (HQ). Here you can pick up maps and checklists, visit the excellent museum with mounted specimens of birds of the area, use the nicest public restroom for many miles, and bird one of Oregon's most famous hot spots.

A variety of native and exotic trees have been planted around HQ over the years, and this artificial oasis in the Great Basin desert pulls in birds like a magnet. Some rarities seen over the years include yellow-billed cuckoo, gray catbird, veery, black-and-white warbler, northern parula, Cape May warbler, scarlet tanager, indigo bunting, and rose-breasted grosbeak. You can always count on finding a few great horned owls hanging out in the larger cottonwoods, usually young ones in the cute "ball o' fluff" stage. Ask other birders what they've seen and what's around, or check the bird sighting records in the office and museum where birders record their noteworthy finds. The best time to bird HQ is early in the morning. The refuge office and museum hours may change seasonally, so check before you go.

After spending time at refuge headquarters, drive south through the refuge on the dirt Center Patrol Rd, which locals and regular Malheur birders call the CPR. The CPR's upper or northern section goes from near HQ to the Buena Vista area. At Buena Vista the CPR ends and you have to drive west to get back on Hwy 205 and continue south. About 8.5 miles south of Buena Vista, off the Krumbo Reservoir Rd, the CPR starts again and heads south to P Ranch—the lower or southern CPR. You may want to drive just one section if your time is limited and you have recent bird news indicating one section is livelier than the other.

For a basic tour, leave HQ and drive southwest through the Wright's Pond area until you come to the CPR. The road coming in from your right is the road from Malheur Field Station. This area, at the head of the CPR near

Wright's Pond, is one of the most reliable places in the state to see short-eared owls. Look for their unusual butterfly-like flight in the morning and in late afternoon. This is also an excellent spot to see American bitterns. Proceed south on the CPR keeping a sharp lookout. As usual it's best to stay in your car and use it as a blind, but some spots will be so tempting that you'll want to get out to scan the marsh and enjoy the scenery. The list of possible birds is enormous; just about any freshwater bird found in the Northwest could show up. As the surrounding land gets drier you can pick up your pace a bit until you get to Buena Vista.

In about 12 miles you'll come to a sign for Buena Vista, State Hwy 205. Turn right and head west on the road that is the northern border of the Buena Vista Ponds. This area is usually an excellent place for soras and Virginia rails. These birds are notoriously difficult to see but can often be heard calling. There has been much debate about the ethics of using recorded bird songs to attract birds. You will have to use your judgment and develop your own guidelines for using tapes. If you decide to play rail calls at Buena Vista, you will almost surely get some response with one or two calls. If you do get a good response, stop playing the recordings. The soras here in particular are usually pretty noisy without much encouragement.

Other birds to look for in the fields north of the road are sandhill cranes, Wilson's snipe, and a variety of blackbirds. At Buena Vista ponds, south of the road, look for the resident trumpeter swans, numerous other waterfowl, grebes, black terns, and common freshwater marsh birds, such as the marsh wren and common yellowthroat. Seeing a marsh wren can be almost as difficult as seeing a rail. Choose a place where you can hear several of them making their incessant, fussy songs, and then just watch and wait. Sooner or later one will pop into view on the top of a reed, vibrate like mad while giving a song, then hop back into the marsh. You've got to be quick to get your binoculars on this one.

Just before the Buena Vista road intersects Hwy 205, a short road goes south to a scenic overlook. This is well worth the few minutes it takes to get to the top of the rimrock and get a fantastic view east across the marsh to the Diamond Craters area. If it is warm and sunny, the rocks around the scenic overlook are usually alive with side-blotched lizards, one of the most common reptiles in the area.

After exploring Buena Vista, get on Hwy 205 and head south toward Frenchglen. For most of this drive you'll have wetlands on your left (east) side and rimrock and sagebrush on your right (west) side. The rimrock is excellent for raptors. On a section of the road between mileposts 42 and 46, the rimrock rises around you on both sides of the road. I call this Eagle Alley because it's the most reliable place I know to see golden eagles. Sometimes if I don't spot one from the car I'll just stop and get out and wait. Usually within 15 minutes, I'll sight an eagle although it may be far away. I've also seen red-tailed hawks, prairie falcons, northern harriers, turkey vultures, American kestrels, and short-eared owls. On the rimrock just after milepost 44, red-tailed hawks and great horned owls have nested and you can sometimes find their nests and young. When you're not watching raptors, keep your eyes on the marshes and ponds as you drive along and you may see trumpeter swans. There will be a myriad of waterfowl, herons, gulls and terns, white-faced ibis, and probably shorebirds. This stretch of road is also good for seeing mule deer and an occasional coyote.

Eight-and-a-half miles south of Buena Vista, a dirt road heads east to Krumbo Reservoir. Krumbo's deep water sometimes attracts diving birds—loons, grebes, and diving ducks—that you may not see elsewhere on the refuge. If you decide not to go all the way to Krumbo Reservoir, be sure to go the short distance to a pond by the road that is great for ducks. Krumbo Duck Pond, as it is informally called, is 1.3 miles east of Hwy 205 and has a rough pullout where you can park. Scan this pond carefully; on some trips I've seen the greatest number of duck species in one place at this spot. From Krumbo Duck Pond drive about 4 more miles to Krumbo Reservoir for a quick look, or turn around and head back toward Hwy 205.

As you drive west back toward Hwy 205 on the Krumbo road, watch for the beginning of the southern CPR. It's the dirt road heading south just east of the Blitzen River, which you crossed coming from Hwy 205. From here the CPR heads south toward the P Ranch, Frenchglen, and Page Springs. Depending on your time, and the latest bird sighting news, you may not want to drive the entire length of the southern CPR. You can get to Frenchglen and Page Springs much faster if you need to by driving back out to Hwy 205 and going south that way. However, one nearby stop is worth checking even if you don't take the CPR the entire way.

Just off the CPR, a mile south of the Krumbo road, is Benson Pond. On the northern edge of Benson Pond is a road that goes east to a large grove of cottonwood and willow trees. This road has been closed for autos and is now a walk-in area. From this road you'll have good views of Benson Pond where you will occasionally see the resident trumpeter swans. Park at the beginning of the road as signed, and walk the road into the trees where you'll see a small, abandoned stone building. Often this grove of trees at Benson is like birding around HQ with lots of migrants swarming through the treetops. You'll probably find great horned owls and maybe porcupines in the cottonwoods. Benson is best in the early morning but always seems to end up in the middle of a day's itinerary. Regardless, Benson is a lovely spot, a good place to stretch your legs, and always has some interesting wildlife sightings. It is a good place to find western racer, gopher, and garter snakes. From Benson drive back out to the CPR and turn left (south), or go right to backtrack to Krumbo road and Hwy 205 and then head south.

The tiny town of Frenchglen is historic, quaint, and has the Frenchglen Hotel, an Oregon State Park that is a functioning hotel and restaurant and a great place to stay to be in the heart of the birding action. Frenchglen is also a migrant trap because of the many planted trees. Sometimes it will produce bird sightings as exciting as those at HQ. Check the cottonwoods nearest the hotel (good for sapsuckers and orioles) and the willows around the little stream and outhouse. This is another good place to meet other birders and get the latest birding gossip.

Many people's favorite place at Malheur is actually just outside the refuge on BLM land. Page Springs Campground has tables, water, and outhouses located in a small valley where the Blitzen River comes rolling off the base of Steens Mountain. With open meadows, streamside thickets, and juniper woodlands, it's one of the nicest places to have a picnic lunch if the weather is good. It's also the best "Bird Camp" you'll ever find. Because it's at the base of Steens Mountain and has junipers, you'll see birds that are not always in the refuge: Townsend's solitaire, house wren, ash-throated flycatcher, mountain bluebird, and sometimes Cassin's finch. The open grassy fields sometimes have lesser goldfinch and lark sparrow.

From the campground a trail follows the river up the canyon. In sunny weather this is a beautiful hike and leads to excellent spots to see yellow-breasted chat and lazuli bunting, or you can just lie in the grass and soak up some sun. Along the swiftly flowing river you might see spotted sandpiper, common merganser, belted kingfisher, and occasionally osprey. This is also a great place to find snakes. Garter snakes are by far the most common, but gopher snakes and racers are also regularly seen. So is the western rattle-snake, although this unfortunate snake has been so relentlessly persecuted by humans that its numbers are quite low. Its presence, however, does mean that hikers should exercise the normal cautions of traveling in rattlesnake country.

I've just given you the essential Malheur tour. Other areas in the refuge, however, are just as productive for wildlife and very scenic. One is the Diamond area. Diamond Ln (paved) goes east from Hwy 205 just south of Buena Vista. At 6.8 miles is Diamond Junction. If you drive straight ahead (unpaved), you'll arrive at the Diamond Hotel and store (gas, food, and lodging) after driving through usually lush fields commonly loaded with white-faced ibis. If you turn left at Diamond Junction and head north, you'll drive through some fields that often provide some exceptional birding. There are usually plenty of ibis as well as some sandhill cranes and herons, including an occa-sional American bittern or cattle egret. These fields are one of the better sites in Oregon for seeing the bobolink, a very rare bird for the West. They are usu-ally west of the road about 0.5 mile north of Diamond Junction (before you reach the farmhouse).

After you drive through the fields north of Diamond Junction, you begin to rise onto higher, drier land. At 3.2 miles north of Diamond Junction, near a small, red cinder cone, an inconspicuous dirt road heads west into the Dia-mond Craters Outstanding Natural Area (BLM). Turn onto this road, stay to the left, and drive to the first crater. Sit on the crater's edge and, after soaking in the magnificent views, search the crater walls opposite you for baby great horned owls. They are usually there but hard to see. This crater is a good place to find rock wren, canyon wren, and Say's phoebe. If it is warm enough, side-blotched and western fence lizards are probably active on the rocks. The rest of the Diamond Craters Outstanding Natural Area offers interesting geology, birds, and reptiles. The BLM office in Burns has a self-guided tour brochure available for the area.

From Diamond Craters you can make a long loop trip back to refuge HQ by returning to the paved road and going north to the historic and unique Round Barn, then continuing north to the Princeton-Narrows Rd (paved), and then taking the Princeton-Narrows Rd west to HQ (unpaved). Some of the dry grasslands near Round Barn are excellent for loggerhead shrike, horned lark, and vesper and lark sparrows. As you near Princeton, you'll begin to enter a rich area for raptors. The first few miles of the road from Princeton to HQ, through irrigated fields often swarming with ground squirrels, can be awesome. It's possible to see golden eagle, turkey vulture, red-tailed, ferruginous and Swainson's hawks, northern harrier, prairie falcon, and American kestrel in one drive down this road. About 6 miles from Princeton, begin watching carefully for burrowing owls; there have been some sightings near the dirt piles by the road. In addition to the birds, this loop often provides some good views of pronghorn. The Harney County Chamber of Commerce in Burns is a good resource for information about the region, including lodging nearest the refuge.

SONGBIRD MIGRATION

The return of migrating songbirds to their breeding grounds in the north has captured the attention and romantic spirit of people since ancient times. And no wonder. After the quiet, drab winter, color and song are suddenly everywhere. Songbirds flying north to breed are in their full breeding plumage and singing their hearts out. At no other time are birds more conspicuous.

Spring is in many ways the zenith of the natural year, and naturalists are dying to be outside every possible moment. It is the time when birders do wild things like Birdathons and Big Days, trying to find as many species as possible in a single day. Not only are there new arrivals from the tropics, but the year-round residents have also been swept away by hormones and are acting like different birds than they did just months ago.

Spring songbird migration starts with the return of tree swallows in February and proceeds species by species until late May or even early June for the last arrivals. The peak is between mid-April and mid-May at low elevations. Spring follows the melting snow as it retreats up the mountains to higher elevations.

Songbirds can concentrate in areas often called migrant traps—islands of choice habitat in the midst of mediocre habitat. Migrant traps can take different forms:

OASES These are areas with water, and therefore plenty of vegetation, in an otherwise arid and sparsely vegetated region. Urban wetlands function the same way; only in this case, the wasteland is the urban area, not a desert.

FORESTED HILLS IN URBAN AREAS Good examples are city parks with mixed woodlands or forests and with openings and edges. As with oases, they are also habitat islands. Migrating birds congregate on the hilltops so if the habitat is good and has good access, you've got a birding hot spot.

HEADLANDS Headlands are isolated clumps of trees and large shrubs on a point of land sticking out into the ocean. They are often called landfalls because it's where birds flying over the water first reach land.

Look for places that meet these conditions and you may discover your own migrant trap. What really excites birders is when a migrant trap is so good that it attracts the few migrating birds in the area that are really lost and totally out of their normal range. These lost birds are called vagrants and nothing gets a serious birder drooling like a good vagrant trap.

In spring birds become active and start singing very early in the morning, so birding is better the earlier you can get going. In some cases, access to an area like a state or city park may be closed until 6 a.m. or 7 a.m. The eager and early birder should verify opening time before trying to get into a park at, or before, dawn.

► SONGBIRD MIGRATION BEST BETS OREGON

The most famous migrant traps in the Northwest are two oases in southeastern Oregon that are 75 miles apart. The headquarters of Malheur NWR is described in Malheur in May. Like the Malheur NWR headquarters, the tiny settlement of Fields, 75 miles south, is included by most birders in any spring trip to Malheur. From Frenchglen (another birding oasis) head south on State Hwy 205 and stay on the main road (Catlow Valley Rd) following the signs to Fields or Denio, Nevada. When you get to Fields consider getting one of the famous milkshakes at the cafe before doing any birding. You might even hear some bird news in the cafe. Fields also has a small store, gas station, and limited lodging.

Bird around the Fields Cafe, and then cross the street to the large clump of trees just to the east known as the Fields Oasis. Explore every nook and cranny of this little microhabitat. Many of the rarest sightings in Oregon and the entire Northwest have occurred in this small clump of trees and bushes. It is most famous for spring vagrants—mainly eastern songbirds that are really lost: least flycatcher, blue jay, gray catbird, black-and-white and Cape May warblers, wood and gray-cheeked thrushes, summer tanager, and rose-breasted grosbeak. Great horned owls nest here every spring; expect to see baby owls in the trees in May. From Fields you can head out on a longer adventure by driving north through the Alvord Basin to Mann Lake, and then to State Hwy 78 and back to Burns.

In the southwestern corner of the state are birds that are much more common in nearby California. These birds, the "California specialties," are the California towhee, blue-gray gnatcatcher, oak titmouse, ash-throated flycatcher, and black phoebe. Every Oregon birder has to make at least one trip to the area to add these birds to his or her state list. Several good places in the Rogue River Valley near Medford are easy to find with a good map or John Rakestraw's Birding Oregon. Among these are Lower Table Rock, Tou Velle SP, Agate Lake County Park, and Prescott Park, which includes Roxy Ann Peak. Another little-known, but great spot is Salt Creek Rd.

Salt Creek Rd is about 20 miles northeast of Medford and near the above-mentioned sites, making for good birding in a relatively small area. Driving north on State Hwy 62, turn right and head east on the Lake of the Woods Highway. In 12.3 miles turn left onto Salt Creek Rd. This road goes through private property for the first 3 miles where you can stop and bird from the road, until you enter BLM land with public access. In the next few miles you travel through a great sample of different habitats.

On the southern Oregon coast, Cape Blanco SP provides an example of a headland vagrant trap. The park is 4 miles north of Port Orford and 5 miles west of US Hwy 101. The area around the lighthouse at the tip of the cape has produced a few outrageous sightings of eastern warblers, but it's not in the same league as the Malheur area.

Portland and Eugene both have some well-known urban hilltops for spring migrants. The Pittock Mansion, an interesting historical building atop one of Portland's West Hills, is surrounded by a small park. From Powell's Books in downtown Portland (where you can buy extra copies of this book for your friends) head west on Burnside St. Watch closely on the right for green signs to the mansion, and in about 2 miles turn right and keep following signs up Pittock Ave. After parking in the lot, a left turn as you reach the mansion, begin checking the trees surrounding the area. Walk around the mansion, looking down on the hillsides as well as in the trees. By the time you get back to the parking lot, you'll probably notice new birds in the trees.

Sometimes the first part of the Wildwood Trail heading north is very productive. Pick up the trail in the northwest corner of the parking lot and within the first 0.2 mile you'll come to some great spots for looking into the tops of trees without having to crank your neck way back. Hillside trails like this can give you a great vantage point for looking into tree tops without getting "warbler neck." In addition when you're on this section of the Wildwood Trail, the sun at your back lights the tree tops beautifully.

For exercise and time in the forest, you can walk downhill from here to the Audubon Society of Portland's wildlife sanctuaries, a little over a mile. Singing winter wrens are as guaranteed as wild animals can be on this stretch of the Wildwood Trail. On the uphill return you could cover some new ground by ascending on the Upper Macleay Trail which splits off from the Wildwood for awhile. A cautionary note, city maps may show the main part of the Audubon Wildlife Sanctuary as the Pittock Bird Sanctuary. People frequently confuse this with the Pittock Mansion. They are not part of the same place and are not connected by an easy driving route, although they are connected by the Wildwood Trail.

Another favorite migration stop in Portland, east of the Willamette River, is Mount Tabor Park. From the Willamette River, take Belmont St east until it ends at 69th Ave, and then turn right and drive south into the park. Go left when you get to the fork, drive around the east side of the mountain for about 0.25 mile, and then make a hairpin turn to your right and head to the top. In 0.2 mile you'll come to a small parking area with roads on either side blocked by locked gates. Park here and saunter up the road to the top or take the large stairway. Both are to the east or your left as you sit in your parked car facing the hill. The paved road that circles the top is closed to

cars. You can make the circuit looking down into a variety of shrubby habitats as well as up into the trees. Remember to maneuver so you have the sun at your back. You can explore any other parts of the park that look inviting. The entire park is closed to motorized vehicles on Wednesdays so plan to do more walking if you go then.

In Eugene a similar situation exists on Skinner Butte Park, on the Willamette River just north of downtown. Take High St north and curve to the left as it enters the park and becomes Skinner Butte Loop. Before reaching the playground, turn left onto a small, paved road and drive to the parking lot on top. Another excellent spot for songbirds is Mount Pisgah Arboretum just southeast of Eugene.

Fern Ridge Reservoir, just west of Eugene, is one of the best all-around birding areas in the Willamette Valley. The three parks at the north end of the reservoir—Richardson, Kirk, and Orchard Point—are good for migrants and are reached by going west on Clear Lake Rd from State Hwy 99 northwest of Eugene. Fernridge is also great for fall shorebirds and wintering waterfowl and raptors.

▶ SONGBIRD MIGRATION BEST BETS WASHINGTON

Washington doesn't have the famous migrant traps as those of southeastern Oregon, but there are places that have a great variety of the regular migrants and the resident species. The Blue Mountains in the southeastern corner of the state, east of Walla Walla, has numerous wildlife and scenery and is lightly visited except during elk hunting season. This is woodpecker heaven because all the woodpecker species of Washington can be found here. Some sought-after breeding birds include mountain quail, green-tailed towhee, broadtailed hummingbird, and turkey. Local birders

favor Coppei Creek in the western foothills of the Blues.

From Walla Walla, head northeast on State Hwy 12 and in 8 miles pass through the town of Dixie. Two more miles from Dixie, turn right onto Lewis Peak Rd just after milepost 350. Cross the old railroad bed, and when the road forks turn left onto Walker Rd. In just 1.4 miles Walker ends at South Fork Coppei Creek Rd. Carefully park on the side of the road near this intersection and do a "birder's walk" in either direction on South Fork Coppei Creek Rd. A birder's walk is where you quietly creep along listening like an owl and watching like a hawk, taking a couple of hours to walk a mile. This, of course, drives people who are out to hike completely nuts. Be realistic when choosing your birding companions.

To try another area get in your car and drive downstream on South Fork Coppei Creek Rd, which would be by turning left when you came in on Walker. In just 0.8 mile you'll reach North Fork Coppei Creek Rd; turn right. After 3.2 miles and past a bridge, park on the side of the road and then continue walking uphill, birding from the road. Leave the way you came in.

Little Pend Oreille NWR is in the northeast corner of the state, just 35 miles south of the Canadian border. Little Pend Oreille (pronounced: pon-do-RAY) is the only mountainous, mixed-conifer forest refuge in the National Wildlife Refuge System outside of Alaska but is not well known except locally. The best access is from the small town of Colville, 70 miles north of Spokane on State Hwy 395. In Colville head east on 3rd St (State Hwy 20). In 6 miles, just past White Mud Lake, turn right on Artman-Gibson Rd. Travel 1.7 miles south on Artman-Gibson Rd to its intersection with Kitt-Narcisse Rd. Turn left onto Kitt-Narcisse Rd and drive 2.2 miles to a fork in the road and take the right hand fork onto Bear Creek Rd. Drive 3.3 miles southeast on Bear Creek Rd (I hope you see a bear) until you reach headquarters at the bottom of a fairly steep hill. All of these intersections do have signs to the refuge. Because getting around on the refuge is a bit complicated, you might want to ask for the refuge's map, *Birding Hot Spots: Spring and Summer*, which shows good birding locations or print the map from the Web site before you go.

Many of the best areas are along the main wildlife-viewing route that includes Bear Creek Rd and the area around McDowell Lake. Four primitive camping areas (no drinking water) are open from April 14 to December 31. Because of various hunting seasons, the best time to visit the refuge for wildlife viewing is from May 16 to August 31. Almost 200 bird species can be seen in the refuge over the year and June is the month for peak songbird activity. McDowell Lake is well known for nesting red-necked grebes. Other noteworthy nesting birds include turkey, eastern kingbird, veery, gray catbird, red-eyed vireo, and American redstart. Little Pond Oreille is also home to 50 different species of mammals and is an excellent place to see beaver, muskrat, coyote, black bear, deer, elk, and moose. Yes, moose in Washington!

Many spring migrants stop to nest in northern Washington, and Okanogan County has the highest number of nesting species of any county in Washington. Good habitat is widespread, however, and you'll need *A Birder's Guide to Washington* if you really want to cover the region. A great place for sampling the mid-elevation birds is Loup Loup Campground off Hwy 20, about halfway between Twist and Okanogan. This is a well-developed campground that usually opens in May. Camping here makes it possible to be in the right place at sunrise to catch the dawn chorus and other early-morning bird action. This campground has a good assortment of owls and excellent birding in May and June.

Across the state on the southern coast are two points of land that represent the headland phenomenon, Leadbetter Point in Willapa Bay and Ocean Shores in Grays Harbor. When you are looking for songbirds in these places, also check out the mudflats for migrating shorebirds.

Summer on the San Juan Islands can be extremely crowded and hectic, so plan to visit off season when, among other benefits, you'll find some great bargains in lodging. Wildlife watching and nature appreciation on the islands are best outside of the summer months, with the exception of orca watching. San Juan Island has the best birdwatching with the largest variety of habitats in the archipelago. Some think the island could become known as a good migrant trap if more birders regularly visited. San Juan Island National Historical Park has two units, American Camp and British Camp, with a visitor center in Friday Harbor. Both are great for birding.

British Camp is known for its very tame wild turkeys, making this one of the easiest places in the state to see these huge birds and hear them gobbling in spring. I think some people feel a little guilty checking these turkeys off their state or life list because it can seem a bit like walking by someone's barnyard. But they are wild birds, descendants of introduced wild turkeys. British Camp is also known for the trail to the top of Young Hill. The trail is a steep 0.8 mile from the visitor center to the top and offers a fabulous view of San Juan Island and beyond on a clear day.

American Camp has extensive grasslands and some classic clumps of conifers on a headland, a landfall for migrants. A small colony of the Eurasian skylark used to nest here, descendants of the established population of these introduced European birds on southern Vancouver Island. These skylarks were famous because American Camp was the only place in the United States where you could see this species, but they appear to have all been eaten by feral cats and introduced foxes. During migration the grasslands and sand dunes can have horned lark, American pipit, western meadowlark, vesper and savannah sparrows, Lapland longspurs, and snow buntings.

Large parks in urban areas often act as an island, attracting many more birds than would normally be found in an area their size. One such urban oasis is Discovery Park in Seattle, an Emerald City birder favorite. An oft-quoted fact is that half of the bird species found in the state have been seen at least once in the park. The visitor center is just inside the east entrance to the park on West Government Way, off 36th Ave West. The best area for migrating songbirds is near the north parking lot, reached by a short road from the east entrance and visitor center. Park in the north lot and walk the road (usually closed to cars) to the Daybreak Star Indian Cultural Center. From here walk back toward the parking lot on the trails that go around the ponds (the north pond is largest), eventually hooking up with the Wolf Tree Nature Trail, a 0.5-mile, self-guided interpretive trail. Other trails in other parts of the park reach the shoreline, which is a good spot for sea birds, waterfowl, and gulls during fall migration and into the winter.

▶ **SONGBIRD MIGRATION BEST BETS** BRITISH COLUMBIA

Victoria and Vancouver have classic urban hilltop migrant traps. Queen Elizabeth Park is south of downtown Vancouver, between Main and Cambie streets at 33rd Ave. The weather greatly affects the birding here. Under thick, low clouds on a cool day, the park can be packed with migrants waiting for the weather to clear. But when it's a warm, still, sunny day the park can be very quiet, at least for birds. To get to the park from Granville St (Hwy 99) go east on 33rd Ave which goes right into the park. You can drive through the park and pick areas that look best to you, but the eastern side of the park has more varied habitat. In the park is the Bloedel Conservatory, a huge greenhouse with a tropical rain forest and many tropical birds inside. Pretend you're in Mexico for awhile.

Stanley Park, one of the largest urban parks in North America, is an excellent spot for birds. It is birded mainly during the winter when waterfowl and sea birds are abundant, but during spring migration the many native trees and shrubs will be as lively with songbirds as any similar habitat within the metropolitan area. You can also easily see the nesting bald eagles and great blue herons in the park.

In Victoria check out Mount Tolmie and Mount Douglas Park. Mount Tolmie is near the University of Victoria. Go east on Cedar Hill Cross Rd from its intersection with Shelbourne St. Be aware that there is a Cedar Hill Rd and a Cedar Hill Cross Rd. In about five irregular blocks turn right onto Mayfair Dr, where there is a large sign for Mount Tolmie Park. You'll be driving up the northeast slope of the hill to the top. At the top, check out the birds and the view. The best habitat, however, is the oak woodland that you drive through on the northeast side. As you descend, park in any of the parking areas along this stretch and hike any trails that look inviting.

Mount Douglas Park, about 2.5 miles north of Mount Tolmie, is higher, much larger, and more forested. Drive north on Shelbourne, turn left into the park on Churchill Dr, drive up to the top, and park. On either side of the parking area are two small peaks, and you get a slightly different view from each. Look and listen down the slopes from each peak. You can take somewhat roundabout routes back from the tops of the peaks to the parking area looking in probable areas. After checking out the area around the top, walk back down the road a ways. You'll find a different group of birds by parking in one of the lower parking areas near the entrance and hiking through the lush forest below. Both parks are very good places to see wildflowers in May, making trips to these two little mounts rewarding.

NEWTS

The rough-skinned newt could certainly be considered for mascot of the moist forests of Cascadia. It is common and widespread from the Coast Range near San Francisco through our entire region west of the Cascades all the way into southeastern Alaska. It's the most conspicuous salamander in the Pacific Northwest and in some areas is the most familiar of all amphibians and reptiles. Rough-skinned newts are more commonly seen than other amphibians because they are the only ones that are regularly active out in the open, above ground, during the day. They are also found in huge populations, as high as 5000 in one lake, making them pretty hard to miss when they are present.

Although common, newts suffer from the confusion about reptiles and amphibians in general. Many people think newts are lizards and I've often heard people discussing whether they are newts or salamanders. Newts are simply a kind of a salamander the same way a mallard is a kind of a duck. The easiest way to tell salamanders from lizards is to look at their skin. Like all reptiles, lizards are covered with scales, while salamanders have the smooth, wet skin of amphibians. Rough-skinned newts, however, do look a lot more like lizards than other salamanders because when on land they actually have fairly dry, granular skin which can appear scaly.

Naturalists assume that the newts must be able to crawl around in the open during the day because of their highly poisonous skin. Many amphibians have poison glands in their skin, but our newts are among the most toxic animals in the world. The poison in their skin is tetrodotoxin, the poison made famous by puffer fishes eaten in Japan as sashimi fugu. This toxin is reputed to be used in voodoo to make zombies. Any animal that eats a rough-skinned newt, including an adult human, will die quickly. The only known exceptions are some types of garter snakes which can eat newts and toxic toads without any harm. Many people are stunned to hear this because they have caught and handled newts many times with no ill effects. Teachers who have had newts as classroom pets are especially distraught to discover the potential danger from newts, widely believed to be totally harmless.

The danger of newt poisoning is actually very slim because the animals can control the release of the poison and apparently save it for critical uses, much the way rattlesnakes do. More importantly, the toxin cannot penetrate skin—it has to be eaten to have any effect—and when people catch newts, they are probably inadvertently washing toxin off their hands in water. However, some people (including myself) have been mildly poisoned by handling newts and then eating without washing their hands, thereby transferring some poison onto their food. Newts can be handled safely. Make sure the handlers have no cuts or sores on their hands, wash their hands afterward, and keep fingers out of mouths, noses, and eyes. Doesn't sound like a good preschool activity, does it? Given the number of kids handling newts in the Northwest, it's astounding that there aren't more cases of poisonings and that newt toxicity isn't well known.

Like many other poisonous animals, our rough-skinned newts have a warning color that stands out and lets predators know that they are nasty to eat. The entire underside is a bright orange and when disturbed they often make an unusual defensive posture, arching their head and tail up and toward each other to show more orange color.

Newts are amphibious amphibians and have distinct terrestrial and aquatic periods each year. The adults spend most of the year on land living in leaf litter, rotten logs, and soil of moist forests. When the breeding season starts, they migrate to traditional breeding sites in ponds, small lakes, and the slow backwaters of streams. Newt migrations can be large, and there is a road near Berkeley, California, with a "Newt Xing" sign. There have even been temporary road closures to alleviate the slaughter of thousands of amorous newts by cars. The males arrive at the breeding sites first and undergo a remarkable transformation into an aquatic stage characterized by smooth, slimy skin; a vertically flattened tail for swimming; and a swollen area around the cloaca. The cloaca is the common opening of the urinary, digestive, and reproductive systems that is found in all vertebrates except mammals.

When the females arrive at the breeding ponds they are often overwhelmed by a number of waiting males resulting in the "ball of newts" sometimes seen in early spring. Eventually, one male and one female pair up and go through a courtship routine that includes the male rubbing the female's head with his chin, which has a gland that produces secretions. The secretions induce appropriate mating behaviors by the female. Fertilization takes place in a rather unique way that is different from the "squirting gametes" style of external fertilization characteristic of frogs. After holding and rubbing the female, the male releases her and does a special walk in front of her on the bottom of the pond. She follows him closely. The male deposits a small bag of sperm, called a spermatophore, on the bottom of the pond, and the female moves over it and picks it up with her cloaca. She stores the sperm inside her reproductive track and uses it to fertilize the eggs internally before she lays them.

Newts start their migration to the breeding ponds sometime between February and July. This is a wide range for breeding dates but these adaptable salamanders range from sea level to just about timberline, over more than 20° of latitude, creating a lot of variation between populations. During the winter and early spring you may come upon newts if you are hiking in forests during or just after it rains. At lower elevations, newt activity in ponds begins to pick up in April, with May and June being very lively. In the mountains, newts are common in shallow lakes in June and July, assuming, of course, that snow and ice have melted. Toward the end of the summer the adults and the recently metamorphed young migrate onto land. In mountain lakes the young have such a short growing season that they stay in the lakes and change into adults the next summer.

▶ NEWTS BEST BETS OREGON

Rough-skinned newts are so widespread that it is hard to name specific places as Best Bets. Any shallow, quiet, permanent body of freshwater, in or near forests and woodlands (and sometimes in grasslands), west of the Cascade crest is a good possibility. The pond in the wildlife sanctuary of the Audubon Society of Portland is a sure bet for newts and a great place to visit in general. Maps to the sanctuary trails are available in Audubon House—a multipurpose visitor center, meeting hall, and natural history bookstore. In northwest Portland head west on Lovejoy St and after crossing NW 25th Ave, follow the curve to the right. You will then be on Cornell Rd (there is a sign to Bird Sanctuary and Macleay Park). Stay on Cornell Rd as it weaves its way into the West Hills. Turn right at the stop sign, go through two tunnels, and Audubon will be on your right. Some maps have the antiquated name Pittock Bird Sanctuary for Portland Audubon's location. The location is correct, but don't get Pittock Sanctuary mixed up with Pittock Mansion.

Many lakes in the Mount Hood NF, near Portland, have good populations of rough-skinned newts. Mirror, Lost, Trillium, and both Twin Lakes are some of the most well known. On the way to Mount Hood, the BLM's Wildwood Recreation Site has some good examples of newts using slow-moving side channels and meanders (of the Salmon River) for breeding, and they can be seen from the Wetlands Trail.

▶ NEWTS BEST BETS WASHINGTON

McLane Creek Nature Trail is a few miles west of Olympia in the Capitol State Forest managed by the Washington Department of Natural Resources and is one of this agency's few interpretive trails. A loop trail circles several beaver ponds while winding in and out of mixed coniferous-deciduous forest habitat with some open grassland areas. The trail and viewing decks provide excellent access to a mix of habitats, home to many typical west-side plants and animals. This is a great place to visit through the seasons and watch the dramatic changes taking place. The ponds are loaded with newts as well as Pacific chorus frogs and many other wetland species. Head north on US Hwy 101 from its intersection with Interstate 5 and in 1.5 miles take the Black Lake Blvd exit and head southeast on Black Lake Blvd. After 3.5 miles Black Lake Blvd makes a turn to the west and becomes 62nd Ave, which you take just 0.5 mile to Delphi Rd. Turn right on Delphi, and then drive 0.8 mile to the entrance of McLane Creek and turn left. Drive to the end of the road, and when you start on the trail take the left fork to go clockwise around the ponds. This takes you directly to the observation decks with the best views into the water. While you are here I recommend a stop at Mima Mounds Natural Area Preserve, only 10 miles from McLane; see June (Butterflies and Moths).

MAY'S NATURE NUGGETS

SPITTLEBUGS "Eewww, what's that spit on the grass?" These words are often heard on May school field trips as we walk by the stems of reed-canary grass. "Who knows what this is?" asks the park naturalist. Usually some student will know, "spit bugs, spit bugs." "Yeah, that's right," I say, "but have any of you seen what's inside the spit?" So begins one of my favorite discussions with second graders. I will carefully wipe some blobs of the white foam off on my finger and reveal the little insect that is inside. It's a little green, sometimes yellow, immature insect called a spittlebug or often just spit bug. The most fun comes when I tell them that the foam is not spit but actually the insect's pee. You can imagine the response. The little spittlebug holds onto the grass and sucks sap out of the stem. This means that it gets a lot of water so it pees a lot. The both gross and fascinating thing is that the little bug whips its pee into the foam with its legs and abdomen, creating a little foam nest to live in. "Why would this insect build a little pee-foam nest to live in?" I ask. Usually after a moment's thought the students are coming up with various ideas involving protection from predators, making for a very successful exploration. The insect we call the spittlebug eventually matures into the insect called froghopper as an adult. The tiny, jumping froghoppers, however, rarely get any attention.

CYANIDE MILLIPEDES In May you may be walking on a trail in a forest and see several, sometimes dozens, of flat, black millipedes with yellow or orange spots down their sides. They are easy to catch and pick up, and if you do and smell them you will notice a peculiar smell that most people find a bit unpleasant. You have just smelled cyanide gas. Yes, these millipedes have cyanide in them and will release a bit of cyanide gas when they are attacked or disturbed. It is easy to guess why they do this because they sure appear to be easy prey. If a bird eats one it usually will not die, but it will get very sick and will probably never eat one again. In case any predators forget how nasty they are, these millipedes have the bright orange spots for easy recognition and release the gas for an olfactory reminder. You will see congregations of cyanide millipedes in certain places in May where they are gathering to mate.

Folks often confuse millipedes and centipedes. They both have lots of legs, but centipedes never have 100 legs and millipedes never have 1000, despite their names. These two groups of arthropods are similar but with a few big differences. On each segment of their long bodies centipedes have one pair of legs. Millipedes, in contrast, have two pairs (yes, four) legs on each segment. This is fine and dandy if you catch them and examine them closely, but I have an easier, instant way to tell them apart. If you can catch it easily, it's a millipede. Centipedes are fast and wiggly and much harder to catch than millipedes. This characteristic is the result of the other big difference between the two creatures. All centipedes are predators with poison fangs for killing their prey. They are fast runners, just like little cheetahs. Millipedes eat dead plant material and don't have to be fast to run down a dead leaf. All millipedes are harmless decomposers that never bite people, which works out nicely for bug-catching kids because they are so easy to pick up. Some centipedes in other parts of the United States are large enough to bite people, but not in the Northwest. Both are important members of a healthy ecosystem, including your home garden.

KABOOM Okay, this may be cheating, but May will always be remembered in the Northwest as the month Mount St. Helens blew its top. May 18, 1980, was the day when more Americans became aware of the reality of volcanoes than ever before. Several million people could actually see, feel, and even hear the effects of the blast that day, and many more were dealing with the effects within days. With great wisdom the Mount St. Helens National Volcanic Monument was created, and now you can visit the site of this amazing catastrophic event. The interpretive displays at the Johnson Ridge Observatory help to create an appreciation for what happened that day as well as an understanding of what is happening on the mountain now. Go on a clear weekday when the mountain is covered in snow. Drive up State Hwy 504 to the top at Johnson Ridge without stopping and check it out first, then wind your way back down. Be sure to see the audio-video presentation—it will blow your socks off.

BIRD SONGS: A CLOSER LOOK

Bird songs are probably the most complex, musical, and downright pleasant natural sounds that humans have ever heard. I'll bet a case could be made for bird song being the original inspiration for human music. The two have a lot in common structurally, and some of the intervals and harmonies we find so innately pleasing in our music are present in bird song. The sound of the clarinet, for example, has a harmonic structure very similar to the songs of thrushes.

Bird sounds have been one of the most conspicuous components of the ambient sound of life on Earth because birds evolved at least 100 million years ago. Only in fairly recent times have large numbers of people become isolated from this experience. But it doesn't have to be that way. Even someone living in our urban centers will be exposed to at least 30 different bird sounds during a year if they spend any significant time outdoors. An experienced birder on a prime day in spring might be able to identify upwards of 100 birds by sound. Tuning in to bird sounds is a great way to tune in to nature and its seasonal changes.

Why do birds sing? The most common answer to this question is "Because they are happy." They may be happy and I wouldn't rule out that birds sometimes sing just for fun, but we can never really know how they feel when they are singing. Most people, however, realize that the reason birds sing is to communicate with each other.

If birds are talking to each other, what are they talking about? Let's distinguish between songs and calls, even though the distinction is not always easy. In general, song refers to the complex, melodic, species-specific vocalizations that birds primarily make during the breeding season. Songs are characterized by patterns of notes grouped into phrases which are repeated and are mostly made by male birds to defend a territory, identify themselves, and attract a mate.

All other vocalizations made by birds are referred to as calls, a catch-all term. Different types of calls may be made by birds of different ages or different sexes and are certainly made in different contexts.

The calls baby birds make when begging to be fed by their parents are specific and are made for a very short time. For baby birds born in large colonies, their little peeps are their identification badges, allowing their parents to pick them out of the hundreds of others the same age. Some begging calls can be distinctive and fairly loud. The flat, nasal caws of young crows begging for food is easy to hear in July any place where crows are common.

Another common type of bird call or vocalization is the companion call. These are usually short, quiet, wispy sounds that are made by birds when they are flocking or by a pair when they are feeding near each other. These calls serve to touch base with the others in the group—keeping the flock together or letting your partner know that everything is okay. The perfect example is a bushtit flock. These cute, tiny birds live their whole lives (except when nesting) in large flocks, moving about in search for insects. Flocks of 30 to 40 keep together through the constant lisping twitter that usually announces their appearance before you see them.

Alarm calls are made to announce danger to other birds in the area. Sometimes other members of the species making the alarm will pick it up and repeat it, thereby sending the alarm out in concentric circles. Birds vocalize to communicate with their own species and for the most part ignore the sounds made by other kinds of birds. Alarm calls are often an exception to this general rule and can serve as an international language understood and even passed on by different species. A classic example in the Northwest is the Steller's jay, the "sentinel of the forest." These common jays may respond to alarm calls by another bird, such as a winter wren or song sparrow, and give their own raucous alarm call. The jay's loud calls let the whole forest know something is going on and even mammals have learned to respond to these calls. You have to watch out for those clever jays—sometimes they will make false alarms just to scare other birds away from a feeder so they can get more food. Humans can learn to use the alarm calls of birds to know when a predator or disturbance is in the woods. Jon Young explains this skill in recordings available from Wilderness Awareness School in Duvall, Washington.

Birds have a unique structure called the syrinx which produces the sounds we call songs or calls. One of the earliest discoveries in bird vocalization no doubt happened years ago when our ancestors noticed that chickens and ducks occasionally continued to cluck and quack even after their heads were chopped off. Not a very precise procedure, but clear enough to demonstrate that the source of bird sounds was somewhere in the body, not the head (or neck).

The syrinx, or song box as it is sometimes called to distinguish it from the mammalian voice box, is located where the trachea joins the two bronchi at the lungs. Membranes in the syrinx vibrate with passing air and can be controlled with sets of muscles, giving different pitches and timbre. Amazingly, in some birds the syrinx actually has two halves, with each bronchial tube having its own set of vocal cords that operates independently. This means that some birds sing two different songs at the same time which blend to make some of the most complex and beautiful sounds in nature.

Do birds learn their song or are they born with it? The answer seems to be yes, they do both. Some birds seem to have their songs hard-wired in them from birth and will sing the correct song upon maturity, even if raised in total isolation from any bird songs their whole life. Other birds have to hear their song and practice it until they sound like their parents. Others seem to be in between. Some birds are very flexible in their songs and mimic other birds as well as some other sounds occasionally. The most famous mimics are parrots, starlings (including the myna), and mockingbirds. Mimics do not copy the songs of other birds to fool them; they are just getting new material to add to their elaborate and changing repertoire.

Bird vocalizations are an invaluable aid to bird watchers who want to identify the singer. Most birders find that as they gain experience, they increasingly rely on sound for identification. Some birds are much easier to hear than to see, and some are much easier to identify by their sounds than their appearance (flycatchers, for example). Bird sounds should be given equal status with field marks as a tool for identification but are, unfortunately, often neglected in birdwatching classes or on field trips.

Unfortunately, most people seem to have a much harder time learning bird sounds than learning what birds look like. Maybe this is because we are visual animals and learn so much by seeing. One handicap to learning bird songs is that most birds sing only during the breeding season. A migrant bird may sing for only a month while it's passing through in the spring. This gives you plenty of time to forget what you just learned, and I find that every spring I have to relearn some songs I knew the previous spring. Don't worry; those will get fewer and fewer with each year.

Technology also contributes to the difficulty of learning and remembering bird songs. While an illustration or photograph of a bird in a field guide is readily available, it's much harder to represent sounds in print or to store and access recordings. CD-ROMs and digital players may be more helpful for learning bird songs than the records and tapes that preceded them. One useful media resource is *Birding By Ear*, a CD set in the Peterson Field Guide series. These CDs are a tutorial on how to tell similar bird sounds apart. Songs are compared one-on-one, with plenty of tips for differentiating the sound-a-likes.

What is the best way to learn bird sounds? Regardless of whatever technological wizardry comes along, nothing comes close to the experience of seeing and hearing the real bird singing in its natural habitat. When you hear real birds singing you don't hear them in isolation and out of context. You hear the bird while you see the bird and its habitat, feel the weather, smell the air, and hear other sounds. The bird's sounds fit into a big picture, and the other parts of that picture go along with the sound to tell you who that bird is. When I hear a new bird sound I try to find the bird and watch it sing. I try to establish a link between the sound and the visual image in my brain. I'll close my eyes and listen and try to imagine the bird I just saw, and then I'll open my eyes to confirm and reinforce my associated image. As in learning anything else, it takes time and practice. So be patient and just get out in the field and listen as much as you can. You will find that you are almost never without bird sounds around you.

NESTING SEABIRDS

"Hey, do you guys know about the penguins at Cannon Beach?" "I was at the coast this weekend and there were dead penguins all over the beach." These were some of the common phone calls to the Audubon Society of Portland every summer when I worked there. People from the Portland area had seen, for the first time, a common bird along the Oregon coast—the common murre (pronounced: mur as in murmur). They had no idea what it was, so they had given it the name of the only thing they knew that looked like the strange new beast. Birders and knowledgeable nature folk laugh at an idea as wacky as penguins in Oregon, but these untrained observers had actually done a great job of matching an unknown object with the next closest thing.

Alcids or auks are a family of birds that are unknown to most Americans. Alcids are pelagic birds, birds that spend their whole life in the ocean except when coming to land to breed. They are rarely seen except by avid birdwatchers and those that spend a lot of time at sea. Alcids are a good example of just how much a bird can adapt to swimming and diving and still be able to fly. In their extreme adaptation for life at sea and for diving, the alcids have only one rival among birds—the penguins. What is fascinating is that these two unrelated orders or groups of birds, penguins and alcids, are similar in many ways and have divided up the planet, so to speak, into exclusive fishing grounds. The well-known penguins inhabit the Southern Hemisphere and the alcids inhabit the Northern.

Both families of birds have webbed feet, thick layers of fat, strong rib cages to withstand pressure when diving, large salt glands, short and narrow flipper-like wings, countershading, and legs far back on the body. As with owls and

The Northern Hemisphere's version of penguins— the common murre hawks, penguins and auks are an excellent example of convergent evolution. Both groups have the same set of adaptations because they do the same thing. What they do best, among all birds, is dive deep and swim fast by "flying" through the water. Most swimming birds swim with their webbed or lobed feet—rarely, if ever, using their wings for propulsion. Auks and penguins, however, swim under water by flapping their wings, using their webbed feet only as rudders or for paddling about on the surface. This method of swimming allows these birds to dive deep in pursuit of prey. The common murre can dive over 500 feet; the emperor penguin can reach almost 800. Among foot swimmers, only loons can compete in this league.

How come alcids fly and penguins do not? It's an evolutionary tradeoff—loss of flight for deeper diving. A larger and heavier bird can dive deeper, but it's more difficult to fly with the small, flipper-like wings required for deep diving. The common murre and the little blue penguin are the largest alcid and the smallest penguin and are almost the same size. The little blue penguin, however, is a bit larger than the murre and can't fly, while the slightly smaller murre can (just barely). The murre is apparently the maximum size possible for a bird that swims and dives like it does and is also able to fly. The little blue penguin is just over the limit in weight and can't fly. These two birds are in a kind of transition zone of evolution toward the ultimate diving bird.

What advantage could explain selection for diving ability over the power of flight? Auks and penguins mainly live in a band around the earth about 20° to 50° latitude away from the North and South Poles, respectfully. That part of the Southern Hemisphere is 90% ocean, while the same part of the Northern Hemisphere is about 80% land. Because they live in such a watery world, being great swimmers has been very advantageous for penguins. However, it appears that flight is necessary when faced with the variety of land predators that the auks face in the Northern Hemisphere. Flight probably would have helped the one auk that did not fly, the now extinct great auk, when faced with that cleverest and most ruthless of predators, humans.

All alcids live in salt water, coming to land only to breed. They can be sighted from shore, but the best way to see them is either by boat or by watching them at nesting sites that are close to land. In our region the common murre, the pigeon guillemot, and the tufted puffin nest on islands and offshore rocks, and on a few cliff faces, where they can easily be seen.

Three other alcids also nest here but are much harder to see. Rhinoceros and Cassin's auklets are primarily nocturnal, coming and going from their nesting burrows at night. The endangered marbled murrelet is another local breeder but nests high in old growth trees and is so hard to see nesting that it was the last bird in North American to have its nesting site discovered, not until 1974. These three alcids may be hard to see nesting, but they are regularly seen at sea most of the year on pelagic birding trips. Rhinoceros auklets are common during summer near some of their nesting islands in Washington waters and are regularly seen from ferries in the Salish Sea.

Nesting in the same areas as these alcids are other seabirds that contribute to making the nesting colonies lively, interesting places, with birds numbering in the tens of thousands at some sites. *Seabird* doesn't have an official definition but generally refers to any swimming bird that spends most of its life in salt water. This includes the pelagic birds: alcids, tubenoses, and a few others. Usually included as well are cormorants, pelicans, gulls, and terns—several groups that are primarily coastal. In addition some groups that winter in salt water, such as loons, grebes, and some waterfowl, are sometimes called seabirds.

The seabirds that nest with the alcids along our coasts are double-crested, Brant's, and pelagic cormorants; western and glaucous-winged gulls; and Leach's and fork-tailed storm-petrels. The cormorants and gulls are easy to see, being among the most common and conspicuous residents of the coast. The storm-petrels, on the other hand, are present only in small numbers in scattered locations and are nocturnal, making them among the hardest birds to find.

Some islands may have as many as half a dozen different species nesting together. How can they all compete for the same limited nesting sites? When competing for limited resources, each species specializes for slightly different nesting niches. The gulls like flat ground, guillemots prefer rock crevices, pelagic cormorants seem to hang on impossible cliff ledges, while puffins and rhinoceros auklets dig burrows in soil. In that regard, here is an important tip for finding puffins. Look for offshore rocks that have grass growing on them and look in the grass for puffins. Because puffins dig burrows up to 6-feet long they need lots of soil and if there is enough soil for puffin burrows, there is usually grass growing on it.

The breeding season is April through August, with June and early July being the peak of activity at the nesting colonies. Seabird colonies are sensitive to disturbance and are strictly protected by federal and state laws. In Oregon and Washington, 2807 islands, offshore rocks, and reefs are protected as national wildlife refuges and human entry is prohibited.

▶ NESTING SEABIRDS BEST BETS OREGON

Oregon is the best place to see nesting seabirds on the West Coast. It has more seabirds nesting in its coastal waters than California and Washington together, plus incredible public access to the coast. Except for occasional great luck, you'll need a spotting scope to get satisfying views because these birds will always be far away. However, once you become familiar with the different species, you'll often be able to identify them with good binoculars. Viewing is best in the morning with the sun at your back.

Haystack Rock at Cannon Beach is an important nesting site for western gulls, pelagic cormorants, pigeon guillemots, and tufted puffins, which usually steal the show. The puffins nest in the grassy area on the north side of the rock. Look for them at a low tide, the lower the better, so you can get as close as possible to the rock. If you are visiting on a day when the Haystack Rock Awareness Program is in action, someone with the program may know where to find the puffins. If not, you might find one right away by looking in the grass, or you may have to wait awhile until one pops out of a burrow or comes flying in. I usually spot them flying to the rock, watch where they land, and then try to find them in my scope. They will often hang out for awhile where they land before going into their burrow. Spotting a flying puffin is pretty easy because they stand out from the other birds. Look for a black football with a red tip flying through the air with tiny wings flapping like crazy. That's what a flying puffin looks like.

From Cape Meares, which is about 10 miles west of Tillamook, you can see two offshore rocks that are loaded with nesting seabirds. In downtown Tillamook take Third St west from US Hwy 101 and follow signs for Cape Meares SP, Three Capes Scenic Loop, or the Octopus Tree. Third St turns into the Netarts Highway. Cross over the Tillamook River, and then turn right onto Bayocean Rd. Stay on Bayocean until you see the sign for Cape Meares SP. Turn left and head uphill. On your right, just before you enter the park, are great views of Tillamook Bay and the coast north to Neahkahnie Mountain. Cape Meares NWR surrounds Cape Meares SP. Drive into the park; the road will end at a circular parking area. Nearby are observation platforms, a picnic table, a drinking fountain, restrooms, and interpretive panels.

North of the parking lot is a viewing platform on the edge of the cliff that has an outstanding view of the two large offshore rocks, the small rocks below, and the nearby cliffs to either side. Sometimes the top of the closest, largest rock will be covered with thousands of common murres. They may all leave at one time to go fishing, or they may disappear because one of the nearby peregrine falcons has just made a strike. You'll also see cormorants, gulls, guillemots, and usually black oystercatchers on the rocky base of the cliffs. On the cliff to your right is a small colony of pelagic cormorants, which is where I've had the best views ever of this smaller cormorant. Tufted puffins have nested here in small and varying numbers for many years. You may be lucky and get a good look at one on the cliffs or swimming in the water below. The big thrill for many here is not a seabird; it's the nesting peregrine falcons. They can be difficult to find or they may fly up right in front of your face. You may see them catch and eat a murre. The nest site has moved around a bit, but for many years it has been on the distant cliff to your right as you face north. There is an interpretive sign about the falcons on the platform. Often other birdwatchers there will know exactly where the birds are—don't hesitate to ask. This is one of the best spots on the coast to pick up the latest birding news from other birders because many folks will stop here to check out the falcons as they work their way up or down the coast.

Two other viewing platforms are positioned along the trail that goes to the lighthouse. From the parking lot a paved trail goes slightly downhill for just 0.2 mile to the end of the cape and the historic Cape Meares Lighthouse, first lit in 1890. Watch on your right for the two other lookout points on the edge of the cliffs. Scan the same areas for birds, but take advantage of the different angle to look carefully at the cliffs that you could not see before. Once again, you may first spot a puffin when you see the "flying black football."

The short hike to the tip of the cape gives you some great views up and down the coast, and the forest along the trail can be quite lively with birds such as chickadees, nuthatches, creepers, juncos, white-crowned and song sparrows, wrentits, winter wrens, and warblers. Occasionally you may see gray jays. Most people are flabbergasted to see gray jays anywhere else except high in the mountains, but a small population lives in this part of the Coast Range. You may have some views of birds from the tip of the cape by the lighthouse, but they are usually pretty far away. The cape is a great place to see migrating gray whales and once I saw a huge sunfish floating just offshore.

Just south of Cape Meares is Three Arch Rocks NWR, the first national wildlife refuge in the western United States and home to the largest murre colony south of Alaska. You can see the rocks from Cape Meares but you are too far away to see wildlife. To experience huge swarms of birds (instead of looking at individual ones), leave the cape and head south for 2 miles on the Three Capes Scenic Loop to the tiny town of Oceanside (watch for a right turn into town). Drive through town and park at Oceanside Beach State Wayside. You can scope the rocks and water from the parking area or walk down onto the beach to get a bit closer. In addition to seeing a couple of hundred thousand birds, you will usually see some Steller's sea lions hauled out on the lower rocks. Rosanna's Restaurant in Oceanside is the best within many miles.

Yaquina Head Outstanding Natural Area, just north of Newport, has the closest view of nesting seabirds I have ever seen. Just offshore from the lighthouse is Colony Rock with a nice viewing deck with interpretive signs so close to the birds that this is one place where binoculars are fine and dandy. You'll see western gulls, common murres, and Brandt's and pelagic cormorants, pigeon guillemots, and a few puffins. The puffin's nests are out of sight on the back side of Colony Rock so you will see them flying or possibly swimming. While you are there taking in the seabird colony, keep an eye out for whales. This is the best spot on the Oregon coast to see gray whales year-round.

Near Bandon is a chain of over a dozen offshore rocks with interesting shapes, names, and stories. The most striking is Face Rock, which looks so much like the face of a giant looking up out of the sea that it can give you the willies. Although a trip to Face Rock Wayside is worth it to see the face, the best place to look for seabirds is from Coquille Point, the mainland viewing area for the Oregon Islands NWR. Half a mile south on US 101 from the Old Town Bandon sign turn to go west on 11th St until it crosses Scenic Beach Loop Dr and enters the parking area for Coquille Point. The nearby paved loop trail gives you views of the different offshore rocks as well as a stairway down to the beach. All of Oregon's regularly nesting seabirds are here, but you'll probably see common murre, tufted puffin, western gull, Brandt's and pelagic cormorants, and pigeon guillemot.

▶ NESTING SEABIRDS BEST BETS WASHINGTON AND BRITISH COLUMBIA

Unfortunately for wildlife watchers there are no seabird nesting colonies in Washington or British Columbia where people can get as close as they can in Oregon. The nesting colonies in the Salish Sea are on rocks and small islands that are closed to public entry. Boats can get near these protected seabird sites, but they must remain at least 200 yards away.

The Port Townsend Marine Science Center offers cruises to the waters surrounding Protection Island with center naturalists. Protection Island is home to an astounding 70% of the nesting seabirds of the Salish Sea south of the Gulf Islands. These cruises follow all regulations, of course, and take extra measures to not disturb the birds.

Ferries are an easy way to see seabirds any time of year. Smaller ferries, which lie closer to the water, provide a better opportunity to see swimming birds than their larger counterparts. Traveling between Port Townsend and Whidbey Island, The Keystone ferry is best for summer seabirds because it's the closest to Protection Island, and some of the birds nesting there fly through Admiralty Inlet. Who knows, you might be lucky and also see some interesting marine mammals.

HERPS

Herps is a slang term commonly used by naturalists and biologists for reptiles and amphibians. It is derived from herpetology, the study of reptiles and amphibians, which is in turn derived from herpeton, Greek for "creeping thing." That there is one term for the study of two distinctly different groups of vertebrates is a historical accident that adds to the confusion about these two groups of animals. Amphibians really have as much in common with fish as they do with reptiles, and reptiles have more in common with birds than they do with amphibians. Regardless, the words herpetology and herp are here to stay. The word herptile has even slipped into print but is scorned by most biologists.

Herps have certainly been among the most unpopular animals in human history. Even today in highly educated societies they remain mysterious and the amount of confusion, misinformation, and mythology circulating about them is astounding. Some herps are more acceptable to people than others. Frogs and turtles are generally considered cute and harmless, and lizards, as long as they're small, seem to be more or less tolerated. Salamanders, though, are borderline—maybe a bit cute, but often considered yucky. Several crocodiles and alligators are clearly dangerous to humans so their unpopularity is understandable. Nothing, however, approaches the worldwide fear and loathing of snakes.

The fear of snakes has a logical basis; after all, a small but significant minority of them are venomous, and in some parts of the world thousands of people die from snake bites annually. In North America, however, we have very few venomous snakes, and most of them are of moderate size and do not have highly toxic venom. Most modern Canadians and Americans see snakes of any kind only occasionally and rarely encounter venomous snakes. In our two countries combined, fewer than 10 people a year die from snake bites, compared to about 90 who die getting struck by lightning. Yet fear and hatred of snakes is still widely felt. In every survey of people's attitudes toward animals I have seen, snakes are the most disliked and usually the most feared animals. Snake phobia is so strong and persistent that some biologists have argued that it's an innate part of our primate heritage.

Fortunately, we have very little to worry about in our region. In the whole northwestern quadrant of North America there is only one venomous reptile, the western rattlesnake. Western rattlesnakes are of modest size, rarely over 3 feet long, and not very aggressive. On average, only a dozen people are hospitalized for rattlesnake bites each year in the Northwest, and only one person dies from a bite here every 15 years. All one has to do is exercise reasonable caution when in rattlesnake habitat during the half of the year, April through October, when they are active. Watch where you step, don't put hands under logs or in cracks in rocks, and don't try to handle any snake that you can't identify. The western rattlesnake tends to like rocky areas and open sunny habitats with scattered brush or trees. They are widespread east of the Cascades, from Oregon north to interior British Columbia, but on the west side are usually found only in the Willamette Valley and the valleys of southwestern Oregon.

Although it is one of the most interesting herps in the Northwest, the western rattlesnake is only one of about 65 different species of native reptiles and amphibians found in our region. Despite the number of different kinds, most of our herps are not common and are rarely seen. The best time to see them is in the spring as they emerge from hibernation and start breeding. At this time reptiles are active on sunny days, some amphibians are in their breeding ponds, and frogs are calling at night.

Amphibians prefer cool, moist habitats, especially forests, so it's no surprise that the Northwest has a good complement of salamanders and frogs, most only on the wetter west side. Reptiles, on the other hand, tend toward warmer, drier habitats resulting in a relatively small number of species in our region, with a heavy bias for the east side; another example of the basic wet side–dry side split in our region. The Northwest has 12 endemic species of salamanders and is one of the world's centers of salamander diversity. Our reptiles, on the other hand, are generally common western species that reach the northern limit of their range here.

Awesome Amphibians

Everybody recognizes a frog as a frog (toads are included here), but far fewer know what a salamander is or that the two are related and in a group called amphibians. One reason for the confusion is the existence of the adjective *amphibious*, which can refer to anything that lives in water and on land. Hence, many animals that are not amphibians, such as alligators, turtles, and beaver, are sometimes called amphibians because they are amphibious. Another problem is that salamanders look much like lizards, so they are frequently mistaken for reptiles (See Newts in May).

Go into almost any freshwater wetland on a warm night in early spring and what do you hear? Chances are good you'll hear the familiar "rib-bit" or "kreck-ek" calls of Pacific chorus frogs. The Pacific chorus frog, until recently called the Pacific treefrog, is our most widespread and conspicuous frog, amphibian, and herp. These small frogs, just under 2 inches long, are widespread throughout our region from sea level almost to timberline. You have heard their songs your whole life because they are just about the only frog sound you ever hear in movies or TV shows. This is because they live near Hollywood and are easy to record in large choruses. Although usually green, these cute little frogs can be gray or brown so look for the dark mask over their eyes and their little toe pads to confirm their identity.

The other frog commonly seen is the bullfrog, conspicuous by its huge size. You may have heard them if you thought you heard a cow drowning in a pond. Hence the name bull-frog. Unfortunately, when you see bullfrogs you usually won't see any other frogs because the bullfrogs have eaten them. The intentional introduction of bullfrogs, native to the eastern United States, into many parts of the West has been disastrous. Bullfrogs eat any creature they can swallow with their huge mouth, including fish, snakes, baby turtles, ducklings, and other frogs. They have clearly played the major role in the disappearance of the Oregon spotted frog from western Oregon and Washington and are suspected to be a major factor in the dramatic decline of our native frogs, as well as the western pond turtle. Never transport bullfrogs or their tadpoles from one location to another, and never release them into the wild.

The only other amphibian that is common and conspicuous in our area is the rough-skinned newt, which is so noticeable it has its own chapter. The Pacific Northwest has 21 other species of salamanders, but they are so secretive and many have such limited ranges that most people never see them. If you look for them, or if you are moving old, rotten logs around in your garden, you may someday find a long-toed salamander, a western red-backed salamander, or an ensatina. If you spend a lot of time hiking in the woods on rainy days (or better yet on warm, rainy nights) you may be lucky enough to find a Pacific giant salamander, largest land salamander in the world and one of our claims to amphibian fame. The others are hard to find without damaging their habitat.

A peculiar and unique amphibian of the Northwest is the tailed frog, the only frog in the world with a tail. It's actually not a tail but a copulatory organ, making this unusual frog the only frog in the world with internal fertilization. Internal fertilization is an adaptation to mating in the fast-flowing streams that are the frog's habitat. Sperm would be washed away with the typical external fertilization characteristic of other frogs.

Righteous Reptiles

Because the Northwest is reptile poor, few are a conspicuous part of our wild-life. The most commonly encountered reptiles are the garter snakes. Variation in coloring between the four species (and numerous named subspecies) of garter snakes in the Northwest makes them difficult to tell apart. All but a few garter snakes, however, will have a light stripe down their spine; a dead giveaway that it is a garter snake of some kind. If you see a snake with a stripe down its back west of the Rocky Mountains—it's a garter snake. Garter snakes have many local, unofficial names such as red racer, water snake, and ribbon snake, in addition to many variations of garter such as "gartner," "garden," and "gardener." Having lots of names like this is usually a sign that an animal is common and widespread. Garter snakes were named after the striped garters that held up socks, an article of clothing once common but now so out-of-date that many people, especially kids, haven't a clue what the word means.

As with all snakes, garter snakes are predators and eat insects, worms, fish, frogs, and (gardeners take note) slugs. Almost all snakes are beneficial from our standpoint because they often eat animals we consider pests. Garter snakes are harmless and are frequently caught by interested humans, but they will sometimes try to bite. The weak, harmless bite is usually an ineffective defense, so garter snakes usually let go with their extra stinky feces in a more successful attempt to be set free.

You may also encounter the gopher snake and the racer, sometimes called the yellow-bellied racer. Both are widespread and common east of the Cascades and are found locally west of the Cascades in Oregon, but are rare on the west side in Washington and British Columbia. They prefer open, sunny habitats and are fairly tolerant of human presence. They are often found around farms, pastures, and sources of water that attract their prey.

Although widely recognized as beneficial rodent eaters by farmers and ranchers, gopher snakes are sometimes killed because they perform a great rattlesnake impersonation. They will sometimes coil and strike (with mouth closed), hiss like crazy, and may even vibrate their tail in dry leaves to sound like a rattle. This impressive trick may have been an effective defense for several million years but has certainly served them poorly since the arrival of humans, who seem to have a powerful urge to kill anything resembling a rattle-snake. The gopher snake, also called bull snake, is the largest snake in western North America, and in the Northwest it can reach lengths of over six feet. Although they may appear intimidating because of their size, gopher snakes are usually pretty mellow snakes and can often be handled. This is in sharp contrast to racers. Racers, as the name suggests, move fast and are generally high-strung and aggressive. If you try to catch one, assume you'll be bitten several times by a strenuously thrashing snake.

As someone who grew up catching lizards in the Sonoran desert, I consider the Northwest's lack of lizards one of the region's major drawbacks. Lizards like open, sunny areas, so few are found in the typical forested habitats west of the Cascades. The most common and often the only lizards found on the west side are the alligator lizards. These aggressive lizards are distinctive and easy to recognize although the two species are difficult to tell apart. The northern alligator lizard is adapted to cooler temperatures and lives farther north than any other lizard in North America. One of its amazing adaptations to the shorter, cooler summers is that it gives birth to live young, an extremely rare occurrence in lizards.

In much of Oregon and parts of eastern Washington you can find western fence lizards and western skinks in the right habitat. Fence lizards are sometimes called blue-bellies because of their blue bellies. Young western skinks have bright electric-blue tails that in some places earn them the name blue-tailed lizards. These are certainly two unofficial common names that make sense.

A common name that does not make sense is "horny toad." These animals are neither toads nor amphibians, going back to that confusion over reptile and amphibian. The proper name is horned lizard; therefore, they are a reptile. Most folks are shocked to hear that we have horned lizards in the Northwest but we actually have two species. The desert horned lizard is restricted to southeastern Oregon and is not common. Like the Northern alligator lizard, the short-horned lizard is one of the few lizards that ranges into British Columbia and like the alligator lizard, it also has live birth. Tiny newborn horned lizards are as cute as a reptile gets.

Southeastern Oregon is the northern limit of the Great Basin, and four lizards that are common in the Great Basin range into this part of the state but are not found anywhere else in the Northwest. In addition to the already-mentioned desert horned lizard these Great Basin lizards are the Mojave black-collared lizard, long-nosed leopard lizard, and the western whiptail.

It's hard to write about turtles and not use the word venerable. They live longer and have been on the planet longer than any other terrestrial vertebrate. The Northwest is quite turtle poor with just two native turtles, although various others occasionally show up that were pets and somehow got liberated. The western painted turtle occurs in Oregon, Washington, and British Columbia, but its population is stable only in Washington. This sensitive species is being monitored carefully in British Columbia and especially Oregon, where its population has declined dramatically. The western pond turtle has fared worse. It does not occur in British Columbia, is a state Endangered Species in Washington, and is listed as Sensitive in Oregon. As with most vanishing wildlife, the greatest threat to these turtles is habitat change by humans, although predation of the young by bullfrogs is a significant factor. I hope that the current effort being spent on these reptiles will result in some stable populations.

Although generally ignored by most folks, many herps have been severely impacted by collecting for the pet trade, biological supply companies, and gung-ho herp collectors. For many species in the Southwest, illegal collecting for a thriving black market has become the greatest threat to their survival. Wildlife laws have been changing recently to provide more protection for reptiles and amphibians in much of the West. In most states it's illegal to keep native reptiles and amphibians in captivity without a permit from the state or provincial wildlife agency.

It is unfortunate that it has become necessary to enact such strict protection of reptiles and amphibians. One great thing about herps, unlike other vertebrates, is that many of them can be safely caught and examined closely and then released without harming them. Some can also be humanely kept in captivity for a period of observation and study and then returned to their original home. Many of today's adult naturalists caught frogs, lizards, or snakes as a kid. However, carefully catching animals, admiring them, photographing them, and then releasing them unharmed back into their home is allowed.

▶ HERPS BEST BETS

Except for rough-skinned newts, discussed in May, we have few specific locations to go to for herpetological Best Bets. It is in the nature of herps that they are not often concentrated in the way that migrating birds, wintering mammals, or spawning fish are. Those that are easy to find are widespread throughout the proper habitat and those that are difficult to find are too sensitive to disturbance to have specifics listed here. One exception to this generalization is when amphibians gather in breeding ponds.

Pacific chorus frogs can be heard calling in just about any still freshwater from February to May. They are even common in flooded roadside ditches in rural areas. Bullfrogs are, unfortunately, also widespread and can be found in many ponds and small lakes. Occasionally you may come upon a pond in the mountains where western toads have bred and see thousands of toadlets (the actual official term) emerging from the water and lining the edge of the pond in staggering numbers. Salamanders can sometimes be found out and about by hiking through dense, moist forests on warm, rainy, nights in early spring with a flashlight or headlamp. You can see the challenge.

Reptiles are also hard to pin down to specific sites. Look for garter snakes in grass along the edges of thick bushes or forests on sunny spring mornings. They are also common around freshwater. Other reptiles are pretty much a "see them when you see them" deal but always be on the alert for snakes in sunny areas near water and lizards in rock piles when east of the Cascades.

Smith and Bybee Wetlands Natural Area in Portland—where I've worked since 1998—is one place where seeing western pond turtles is just about guaranteed. Smith and Bybee is managed by Metro Regional Parks and Greenspace. On any bright, sunny day from April through June, walk down the trail to what is generally called Turtle Turnout and look at the floating logs that are in the sun. Any time after about 10 a.m. you'll see the plate-sized turtles basking in the sun, unless something has just frightened them. The turtles are usually 30 to 60 feet away and blend in with the color of the logs and water so you'll need to look closely to see them. With binoculars or a spotting scope you can really see why they are called painted. Come on a guided turtle walk in April, May, or June with a Metro naturalist and you'll get great scope views, if it's not a cloudy day. To find out when the turtle walks are, visit the Metro Parks Web site.

Southern Oregon has the best assortment of reptiles in the region. The Table Rocks near Medford, famous for their spring wildflowers, are also known for their nice complement of reptiles, reflecting the California affinities of these two mesas.

By far the richest reptile area in the Northwest is the southeastern corner of Oregon near Malheur NWR. Grassy areas near water, particularly around Benson Pond and along the trail up the Blitzen River from Page Springs Campground, are prime spots at Malheur for garter snakes, gopher snakes, and racers. You'll find lizards in many rocky areas on or near the refuge, such as at the Buena Vista Overlook or in the Diamond Craters area. But the ultimate lizard adventure in the Northwest is to the Alvord Desert, on the east side of Steens Mountain. This is where you'll find the Great Basin lizard specialties—desert horned, Mojave black-collard, long-nosed leopard, and western whiptail—along with the more widespread western fence, sagebrush, and side-blotched lizards.

The dirt road that runs up the east side of Steens Mountain from Fields to State Hwy 78 could well be called Lizard Lane but is instead unimaginatively named the Fields-Denio Rd or State Hwy 201. Several small, dirt roads head east from this road and driving and walking any of these could be productive, but Oregon reptile man Alan St. John recommends the road to Mickey Hot Springs.

About 30 miles north of Fields, or 2 miles north of the Alvord Ranch, the Fields-Denio Rd makes a right-angle turn to the east, goes one mile, and then makes another 90° turn, this one a left turn headed north. At this turn, by a lone tree, an unsigned dirt road heads southeast and then eventually heads more directly east toward Mickey Hot Springs. You can see this clearly on page 74 in the Oregon Delorme Atlas. Take this road and drive slowly, getting out to hike around any place where you spot some lizard action or that looks inter-esting. In 6 miles you'll reach Mickey Hot Springs, identified by a sign and small parking area. The spring is too hot for bathing, but there is a mini-geyser that erupts occasionally and other thermal features. This is a sensitive area—a portion is a BLM Wilderness Study Area and an Area of Critical Ecological Concern (ACEC)—so any off-road driving is illegal. Be sure to keep out of any posted areas. No-trace primitive camping is permitted but not near the thermal areas. You can continue to explore on roads to the northeast and southeast from the spring. Contact the Burns BLM office for road conditions and any other information before heading out into this remote area. Be sure to take along plenty of water and gasoline, a spare tire, first aid kit, food, and so on. It's an adventure.

MOUNTAIN BIRDS

Because spring comes later at higher elevations, peak times for most natural events are different in the mountains than in the lowlands. Spring songbird migration and the onset of the nesting season are delayed a bit, making June an excellent month for birding in the mountains. Some of the birds seen in the mountains during the breeding season are year-round residents there, while others are long-distance migrants or birds commonly seen in different areas of the Northwest during other seasons.

Many birds that commonly breed in the mountains move down the slopes into the foothills or valleys for winter. How low they go will depend on the weather and food supply, some years they may be very common in a particular area but during another year, with a mild winter, they may be pretty scarce. This altitudinal migration, common in the Northwest, is typical for dark-eyed junco, varied thrush, evening grosbeak, pine siskin, mountain bluebird, and Townsend's solitaire. As the snow melts and more food becomes available, these birds move back up into the mountains for breeding season.

Some of our other mountain birds are neotropical migrants and fly long distances to breed in our mountains. Examples are flammulated owl; calliope hummingbird; Hammond's, dusky, and olive-sided flycatchers; most ruby-crowned kinglets; green-tailed towhees; hermit warblers; and western tanagers. Then there are the real mountain birds, the ones who tough it out and spend the whole year, including the winter, high in the mountains. Examples of these are blue grouse, mountain chickadee, several woodpeckers, pine grosbeak, rosy finch, raven, and those two bold marauders of the high country—gray jay and Clark's nutcracker. The gray jay, nutcracker, and raven are the most noticeable mountain birds because they act like most members of the corvid family—smart, noisy, and bold. The gray jay and nutcracker are common companions of lunching cross-country skiers. Ravens scavenge after humans also, but usually after the people are out of sight.

The Pacific Northwest is known for its coniferous forests and where there are lots of trees you can expect woodpeckers. About 60% of North American woodpecker species live in the Northwest. Three of our woodpeckers have a fairly limited range in the western United States and are not common, making them much sought after by birders. White-headed woodpeckers can actually be easy to see in some locations. Look for them in ponderosa pine forests on the east slope of the Cascades. The two woodpeckers with three toes, the black-backed and the three-toed woodpeckers, live almost exclusively in lodgepole pine forests and are not common. Look for tree trunks with bare patches where these two woodpeckers have flicked off the bark.

Woodpeckers are important members of any forest community. It's common knowledge that woodpeckers peck holes in trees for their nests, but what most folks don't realize is that the excavating woodpeckers will usually use their hole only once, and then it's up for grabs by other forest creatures. Woodpeckers will sometimes even drill a hole that they never use, creating even more holes to go around. Many other animals use these abandoned woodpecker holes for nesting, and sometimes shelter. One study in eastern Oregon found 60 species of birds and mammals that utilized old woodpecker cavities.

Much of the forested mountain habitat in the Northwest is similar from one place to another, so any of your summer travels in our mountains are potentially good birdwatching trips. Be on the lookout for good habitat and listen carefully. Check probable places early and late in the day; many of the most productive areas are along edges where one habitat meets another. In the mountains this usually means openings in the forest cover around meadows and areas near water.

▶ MOUNTAIN BIRDS BEST BETS OREGON

One of the most predictable and easiest places to see Clark's nutcrackers must be in the parking lot of the visitor center at Rim Village in Crater Lake NP. The nutcrackers are always here because people continue to feed them despite pleas by the park staff. Please resist the urge to toss a few potato chips at them. Gray jays will sometimes hang around the village and also scavenge human food. Some people feel that seeing these beggars in the parking lot is not a satisfying wildlife experience and will seek them out in their natural habitat. Mount Scott Trail and Garfield Peak Trail, two of the highest trails in the park, are good not only for mountain birds but also for wildflowers and marmots.

About 50 miles north of Crater Lake is an area with over a dozen lakes within only 40 miles, all accessible by road. These lakes are along the Cascades Lakes Highway, officially FR 46, starting as Century Dr in Bend and eventually joining State Hwy 58 near Odell Lake. Crane Prairie Reservoir and Davis Lake also have good mountain birding. Crane Prairie Reservoir is famous for its large number of nesting osprey, while Davis Lake has a variety of Cascade mountain birds plus some nesting waterbirds from the east side such as eared grebe, western grebe, Forster's tern, and black tern. Osprey are also common at Davis Lake, as they are at almost all high Cascade Lakes. The north and south ends are considered the best birding areas. The Deschutes NF map

will help you explore this area, which makes an excellent three- to five-day camping trip.

Cold Springs and Indian Ford NF campgrounds, near the town of Sisters, have good ponderosa pine forests that are known for nuthatches and woodpeckers. At both of these places I have seen all three western nuthatches—red-breasted, white-breasted, and pygmy—in the same tree at once. You can also see white-headed, hairy, and downy woodpeckers, northern flickers, red-breasted sapsuckers, and red-naped sapsuckers. Even a few vagrants show up now and then. Cold Springs Campground is 4 miles west of Sisters on State Hwy 242. The actual springs are to the west of the parking area and are a must, but be sure to check all the habitats. Indian Ford Campground is also west of Sisters, but 5.5 miles on US Hwy 20. Both of these highways are part of the McKenzie-Santiam Pass Scenic Byway. Heading west from Sisters turn right onto Indian Ford Rd, and then immediately turn right again into the campground. You'll see similar birds at each campground, but you'll always see something at one that you don't see at the other. The unpaved Cold Springs Cutoff Rd, or FR 1012, goes from US 20 to Hwy 242, connects the two campgrounds. You can use this road to drive a triangle route from Sisters, to both campgrounds, and then back to Sisters.

▶ MOUNTAIN BIRDS BEST BETS WASHINGTON

Mount Rainier NP is one of the best places in the Northwest for seeing wildlife and flowers in summer. Two popular visitor areas give easy access to trails near timberline where the high mountain birds can be relatively easy to see because trees are few and short. Both Paradise and Sunrise have lots of visitor services and are centers for activity in the park; both are quite crowded in the summer. Sunrise has significantly fewer visitors, so it's a better destination for nature watchers. The area around the Sunrise Visitor Center can be lively with smaller birds like chickadees, nuthatches, and kinglets. Two birds sought in the park are white-tailed ptarmigan and rosy finches, sometimes seen on either the Mount Fremont Lookout or the Burroughs Mountain trails west of Sunrise. You may also see marmots, pikas, mountain goats, and wildflowers. Oh yes, and some of the most spectacular mountain scenery in the Northwest.

West of and between Yakima and Ellensburg, in the eastern foothills of the Cascades, is Wenas Valley, a popular east-side birding spot. The Washington Audubon chapters have held a big campout every Memorial Day weekend at the Wenas Campground (Boise Cascade Park) for over 30 years. The campground is primitive with no piped water or toilets, so be well-provisioned if you plan to stay here. It can be a popular area in spring and summer, so it is wise to go on a weekday. There is a wide range of habitats along Wenas Creek, and the number of species of breeding birds, blooming flowers, and butterflies can be amazing from mid-May through June.

You can reach Wenas Campground from either Ellensburg using Umtanum Rd or from Selah (near Yakima) using North Wenas Rd. Either way is a bit of an adventure, and a high-clearance car is advantageous on the upper part of the road. The route from Selah is more direct with more paved road, so let's go that way. From Exit 30 on Interstate 82 go north on State Hwy 823 or 1st St. In downtown Selah turn right onto Naches Ave to stay on Hwy 823, and then in one block angle left onto North Wenas Rd. Drive northeast on North Wenas Rd to where it forks and Hwy 823 (Harrison Rd) goes to the right. Go to the left so you stay on North Wenas Rd. From here on stay on North Wenas Rd as it winds its way up the Wenas Valley. You'll see a variety of vegetation from aspen and cottonwood along Wenas Creek to ponderosa pine and sagebrush on the slopes. Check out any area that looks interesting. In 22 miles you'll reach a three-way intersection where there is a large stump. To the right is the Wenas-Ellensburg Rd; to the left is Maloy Rd. Continue going straight, following Wenas Creek, on the road alternately named Audubon Rd or North Wenas Rd. Go north for about 2.5 miles, and then turn left to take the wooden bridge over Wenas Creek to the campground. You can explore many areas by foot using the campground as a base.

State Hwy 20 is the North Cascades State Scenic Byway. This 140-mile transect of the North Cascades from Sedro-Woolley to Twisp goes through many different habitats on its way up and over Washington Pass (5477 feet) and provides access to the high mountain regions. From the outdoor observation deck at the North Cascades NP Visitor Center on Hwy 20 in Newhalem, you can look for one of the park's specialties near the cliffs towering above you to the north, on the other side of the highway. This is the most reliable spot in Washington to spot black swifts, a very difficult bird to find in the Northwest. The visitor center is a great source for information about the park and about recent wildlife sightings along Hwy 20. The area around the center, the campground, and the town of Newhalem has a variety of forest birds.

Farther east on Hwy 20 is an area with several trails leading into high country that has mountain birds, pikas, and marmots. Rainy Pass has a major parking and picnic area with two trailheads. One trail goes south to several spots making it easy to take as long or as short a hike as you'd like. The one-mile paved and level trail to Rainy Lake is easy and universally accessible. Successively farther and harder are Lake Ann, Heather Pass, and then Maple Pass. A loop can then be made back down to the Rainy Lake Trail—a total of almost 8 miles and an ambitious day hike. To Lake Ann and

back is about 5 miles. On the other side of Hwy 20 the Pacific Crest Trail heads north for 4 miles to Cutthroat Pass at 6820 feet. Mountain goats are sometimes seen along this trail. You also can reach the Cutthroat Pass and Cutthroat Lake areas from another trailhead at the end of a spur road that leaves Hwy 20 farther east near milepost 167.

The highest road in Washington, and probably the most dramatic, goes to Hart's Pass and Slate Peak, to the north of Rainy Pass and on the edge of the Pasaytan Wilderness Area. This area is probably the only place in Washington where you could possibly see such North Woods birds as spruce grouse, three-toed woodpecker, boreal chickadee, pine grosbeak, white-winged crossbill, and just maybe even white-tailed ptarmigan all in one day.

▶ MOUNTAIN BIRDS BEST BETS BRITISH COLUMBIA

Manning PP is like Mount Rainier NP in that it has it all for summer in the mountains and it shows up repeatedly in this book. The subalpine area near Blackwall Peak offers great access to extensive subalpine meadows. For real alpine habitat and the best chance to see white-tailed ptarmigan and rosy finches, it's backpacking up to Mount Frosty, highest point in the park and a 14-mile round trip. Strawberry Flats and Beaver Pond both have an excellent variety of mid-elevation mountain birds. The park is a good place to see pine grosbeak, three-toed woodpecker, and boreal chickadee.

The large provincial parks just north of Vancouver help to make this one of the most attractive cities in the Americas. Cypress and Mount Seymour provincial parks have large areas of mountain hemlock forest and many desirable mountain birds like three-toed woodpecker, red and white-winged crossbills, pine grosbeak, black swift, and the regular guys like gray jay and blue grouse. The best areas in Mount Seymour are Goldie Lake Loop, with numerous wetland habitat, and Mystery Lake Trail, which also goes around Mystery peak. Both leave from the same main parking lot at the end of the road. The favorite trails in Cypress are Yew Lake and Black Mount Loop.

BUTTERFLIES AND MOTHS

While hiking on the Elkhorn Crest National Recreation Trail, we found ourselves on a mountain ridge at 7000 feet surrounded by a column of thousands of butterflies flying around us as they followed the ridge north. It was summer

2006, one of the years when there was a population explosion of tortoise-shell butterflies. Fortunately for us, standing on top of the world as we were with black and orange butterflies around us in the sunlight, it was more like ascending into heaven.

Insects are usually not well-liked, often called bugs, with a shudder. Butterflies, however, have always been popular. Think of the classic image of a nature nerd running around with a butterfly net. The scene is different now after the publication of several major butterfly identification books in the early 2000s. Butterfly watching (butterflying?) is now having a boom in popularity similar to birding in the 1980s. Many new butterfly watchers are birders who have found another group of animals to figure out. This makes perfect sense because both birds and butterflies are colorful, active, diurnal, harmless, and they have many common species that are easy to see. As with birds, familiarity with butterflies connects you with habitats and seasons.

As everyone knows, butterflies do not start life as a butterfly. All members of the insect order Lepidoptera (butterflies and moths) start as eggs and undergo a radical metamorphosis from larva to pupa to adult. The larva of a butterfly or moth is called a caterpillar and all a caterpillar does is eat, poop, and grow. Unfortunately, some caterpillars, as well as some other insect larvae, are called worms, as in cutworm or inchworm, which is confusing and is as accurate as calling a tadpole a fish. Worms are worms and are always worms—they don't change into something else. Caterpillars, like all larvae, eventually turn into adult animals that usually look very different from the larvae.

Once a larva has eaten enough it turns into a pupa, a stage when nothing seems to be happening but, in fact, the animal is undergoing a radical transformation into the adult form. The pupa of butterflies is called a chrysalis and butterfly larvae do not spin cocoons. Most moth larvae burrow into the ground and turn into a pupa, but some stay above ground and spin a cocoon that surrounds the pupa for extra protection. Think of a cocoon as a fancy, extra silk coat that some moths have over their pupa. The pupal stage can last days or months depending on the species and its life cycle. Many insects spend the winter in the pupal stage. Eventually, the adult butterfly or moth emerges from the pupa or cocoon and pumps its folded wings until they are fully-spread, dry, and ready for flight. Then off they fly to mate.

The adult stage is the reproductive stage, and mating and egg laying are the main activities. Some adults do not even have functional mouth parts and cannot eat. The bold, colorful patterns on their wings, which we find so beautiful, serve several functions. They proclaim the identity of the butterfly and are important in courtship and territorial displays. The colors may also identify the animal as poisonous, as in the case of the monarch, or attempt to frighten predators with patterns that resemble eyes. And for many, wing coloration serves as camouflage, so predators cannot see the well-hidden moth or butterfly.

Adult lepidopterans have a long, thin tube for sipping nectar instead of the munching jaws of the larvae, and that's why you'll find butterflies where there are flowers. Butterflies like sunshine and do not fly in the wind and rain, so you never have to brave the bad weather to see them. From April through September, any place that has flowers will have some butterflies on a calm, warm, and sunny day. How nice for humans who want to see them.

Most butterflies, with some notable exceptions, die within a few weeks of emerging. Many members of the brush-footed butterfly family (also called nymphs) can hibernate and overwinter as adults, living from early fall until early the next spring. Best known of these is the mourning cloak, which you might see flying about on warm days in the middle of winter. Other relatives include some tortoiseshells, anglewings, painted ladies, and checkerspots. Some species in this family will migrate to survive the winter, but the champion insect migrator is the famous monarch, which is known to migrate up to 1000 miles.

With only about 200 species of butterflies in our region, the Pacific Northwest is not very rich in butterflies. Insect diversity increases dramatically the closer you get to the tropics and the cool, wet Northwest just isn't butterfly paradise.

The one butterfly everyone has heard of is the monarch, the rock star of butterflies, famous for its long migrations. Monarchs are rare in the Northwest, but because of their notoriety many people think they have seen them, identifying any butterflies colored orange and black, such as the fritillaries, as monarchs. More monarchs existed west of the Cascades before human development reduced the number of milkweed plants, the only plant that the larvae eat.

The lower elevations west of the Cascades are a mix of forests and wood-lands and the land that has been converted into agricultural and urban uses. Because this is where the vast majority of the Northwest's people live, but-terflies that are adaptable and can live in and around west-side cities, suburbs, and farms are some of the best known and most widely distributed. Swal-lowtails are the largest butterflies in North America and, with their bright-colored wings, they are also the most familiar. The two most common kinds of swallowtails are the western tiger swallowtail and the pale swallowtail.

Many members of the brush-footed butterfly family are common in west-ern valleys, including the mourning cloak, painted lady, and Lorquin's admi-ral. The mourning cloak is easy to identify on the fly with light outer edges on its dark wings. Because it is a hibernator that sometimes comes out on warm winter or early spring days, it is sometimes the only butterfly around. The cosmopolitan painted lady is famous for being the most widespread but-terfly in the world, found on every continent except Antarctica.

The family of sulphurs and whites is large and widespread. Among the first butterflies to emerge in spring are the cabbage white and the distinctive Sara's orange tip. The cabbage white, an introduced butterfly from Europe, is one of the few butterflies whose larva is a major agricultural pest. Cabbage whites are adaptable and abundant in most of North America, sort of the starlings of the butterfly world. The easiest sulphur to identify is the alfalfa butterfly or orange sulphur, another widespread and common relative that is also an agricultural pest.

Another large and particularly confusing family contains the blues, cop-pers, and hairstreaks. There is at least one species of each type of these small butterflies just about anywhere, but they can be hard to see and are difficult to tell apart. Blues are the most noticeable and the echo blue or spring azure is a fairly common early spring butterfly. Skippers are another large and confusing group and many look a lot like moths. The peppy little woodland skipper is common in grassy areas but telling different skipper species apart is tough.

Because butterflies favor open, sunny areas they are not common in the thick coniferous forests west of the Cascades except around openings and edges. As you begin to climb in elevation in the Coast Range or on the west-ern slope of the Cascades, you begin to get some mountain butterflies that are found at mid-elevations. Common are the anise swallowtail and their close relatives, the Parnassians. Parnassians are noted for the unusual "chastity belt" that forms on the female after mating, presumably to keep out additional sperm from other males. Fritillaries are common in moist meadows and riparian areas. The great spangled fritillary is the most well known of this group, probably because it has such a cool name.

Above about 5000 feet into the subalpine and alpine meadows, you'll see a new set of high-mountain butterflies. The anise swallowtail and phoebus parnassian will continue to be common as will several fritillaries.

California and Milbert's tortoiseshells are great wanderers that can show up almost anywhere but are usually seen in mountains. These are the butterflies we experienced for days in the Elkhorn Mountains, as described at the beginning of this chapter. The California tortoiseshell is famous for its occasional population explosions that result in mass movements of millions of butterflies. Driving through these swarms can be hazardous as windshields become coated and roads turn slick with the smashed bodies. These two tortoiseshells are hard to tell apart and can be confused with their relative the painted lady, which also has occasional mass migrations.

Many common, familiar butterflies from the west side are also on the east side: anise swallowtail, mourning cloak, painted lady, and cabbage white. As you go farther east, the Oregon swallowtail joins the anise swallowtail and several more whites, especially western white, are common. The small ochre ringlet is widespread but most common on the east side as are the wood nymphs. There are several checkerspots that are hard to tell apart. They are similar to fritillaries but lack the silver spots on the underside of the hindwings that are usually noticeable on fritillaries.

Moths do not usually have colorful markings because most are active at night. There are 10 times as many species of moths as there are butterflies, but they get little attention because most are small, gray, and nocturnal. Most identification books on butterflies leave out the moths altogether. However, many moth larvae are serious agricultural pests: cutworm, codling moth, corn earworm, gypsy moth, armyworm, fruitworm, this-worm and that-worm. Remember, these are not worms, they are larvae.

The giant silk moths are the most spectacular moths but unfortunately are represented by only a few species in the West. Occasionally people find the huge polyphemus moth west of the Cascades, and if you are ever so lucky you'll never forget it. On the east side the equally-spectacular ceanothus silk moth is more common. The Pandora moth is smaller and plainer than most of its relatives but makes up for its looks with its numbers. These moths have a two-year life cycle and often show extreme population fluctuations. In July of the odd years between 1989 and 1995 huge outbreaks of Pandora moths occurred near Bend. These populations eventually crash and then the moths are much less common. Twenty to 30 years later, another population explosion may occur with hundreds of thousands of adults appearing every two years.

The tiger moths are another family of good-sized and colorful moths. Many kinds of tiger moths have bright patches of white, red, orange, or yellow on their wings, especially the hind wings which often are hidden when the moths are perched. This family includes one moth whose caterpillar is much better known than the adult moth and is one of the most familiar insects in America—the woolly bear caterpillar. Woolly bears, famous for the myth of their weather-forecasting abilities, turn into a medium large, orangish-colored moth called the Isabella moth.

Sphinx moths are large, very active moths also called hawk moths. They are noticeable because they often feed during twilight, hovering over flowers as they feed and making a humming noise with their wings that you can hear as they swoop past. We called them hummingbird moths when I was a kid. Many of the larvae are large, plump, green caterpillars with a little horn-shaped projection at the end of their body, giving them the name hornworm.

Unfortunately, one reason for increased interest in butterflies is the increased concern that many species of butterflies are showing dramatic population declines as their habitats are altered. About 20 species of US butterflies are now on the endangered species list and many others are of concern. The Xerces Society was started in 1972 by butterfly expert and author Robert Michael Pyle to promote the conservation of invertebrates and their habitats. It is named after the Xerces blue, the first butterfly in North America known to become extinct because of human actions. Portland bugsters are proud to have the Xerces Society headquarters located here.

BUTTERFLIES AND MOTHS BEST BETS

To find butterflies, go where there are lots of flowers on a warm, calm, sunny day. All of the places described in this book for wildflowers are Best Bets for butterflies, especially during the summer. The east side of the Cascades, with more open, sunny habitats, is significantly better than the west side. Particularly good are riparian zones in canyons, places where there is moisture and a variety of plants. Open woodlands are much better than dense forests. As summer progresses, the action moves up into the mountain meadows, just as it does with wildflowers.

▶ BUTTERFLIES AND MOTHS BEST BETS OREGON

All of the eastern Oregon mountain ranges (Ochoco, Strawberry, Blue, and Wallowa) are productive where dry, open forests meet moist meadows. Big Summit Prairie, about 40 miles east of Prineville has been a favorite of butterfly watchers, birders, botanizers, and fans of gorgeous western scenery for decades. This high mountain prairie (4500 feet) is a giant collecting basin for the headwaters of the Wild and Scenic North Fork of the Crooked River and stays wet well into the summer. The prairie itself is privately owned and has been managed by ranchers since the 1880s but it is surrounded by public land.

Big Summit Prairie is almost bordered by four US Forest Service roads. Going clockwise from the north: FR 22 is the northern boundary, FR 3010 the eastern, FR 42 goes along the southern edge, and FR 4210 is the western road that connects roads 22 and 42. The roads are public and except for some small areas along the southern edge they are on public land, so it's okay to pull over safely and get out to wander around. The side roads that lead away from the prairie are in the national forest; they are good for parking or exploring.

You should have the latest Ochoco National Forest map, which clearly shows which land is public and which is private, from the Forest Service for this trip. Walton Lake Campground is a very nice Forest Service campground

about 5 miles from the prairie; it makes a great headquarters for exploring the area. The lake is great for a swim if the weather is hot enough, and Cooper's hawks were nesting in the campground the last time I was there. To get to Walton Lake head east on US Hwy 26 from Prineville, last stop for provisions. Go 16.5 miles then turn right onto County Rd 123 and head northeast, following signs for Ochoco Ranger Station or Walton Lake. At some point the road becomes FR 42, and 9 miles from US 26 you'll reach the Ochoco Ranger Station. The ranger station has been closed for several years, but it may be reopened when you are there. Just after the ranger station turn left to go north on FR 22 and in 7 miles you'll reach Walton Lake. The campground sites have picnic tables, and piped water and outhouses are nearby. For an awesome view, and maybe some higher-altitude butterflies, drive to the old lookout at the top of Mount Pisgah (this is not the one near Eugene).

Warner Canyon and Camas Creek, along State Hwy 140 between the town of Lakeview and Hart Mountain National Antelope Refuge, are good areas as are the shores of nearby Crump Lake. North of Hwy 140 is Bull Prairie and Drake Peak, reached by FR 3615 and 019. Heading west from Lakeview to Klamath Falls, Hwy 140 goes over Bly Mountain Pass, about halfway between the little towns of Dairy and Beatty. A number of little roads heading in different directions from near the pass are worth exploring if flowers are blooming.

Open meadows and riparian zones in the Sisters area are representative for the east slope of the Cascades ponderosa pine forest. Check for mountain birds and butterflies along the Metolius River from Camp Sherman downstream, and along Three Creeks Meadow about 5 miles south of Sisters on FR 16.

▶ **BUTTERFLIES AND MOTHS BEST BETS** WASHINGTON

Bellevue has a great system of parks, greenbelts, nature trails, and wetlands. Next to the ranger station in Lake Hills Greenbelt Park is a demonstration butterfly garden and a hummingbird garden. Heading east from Mercer Island on Interstate 90, take the 148th Ave exit and head north on 148th Ave to SE 16th St. Turn right to head east on 16th St to its intersection with 156th Ave. The ranger station is on the northeast corner at 15416 SE 16th St.

Seattle also has a city park with a butterfly garden. Bradner Gardens Park was developed as a gardening education center through a partnership of several organizations and the city. Bradner Gardens is also a pesticide-free park, which makes it especially butterfly friendly. The park is not far from downtown and the stadiums, but if you don't know Seattle well this can be a tricky area for driving. First get onto Rainier Ave heading south under I-90. If you're heading south on I-5 from downtown, take the Dearborn St exit (Exit 164). Take Dearborn east about 0.5 mile, and then turn right onto Rainier Ave South. After you go under I-90 turn left at a traffic signal onto South Massachusetts St. Head east about 8 blocks to 29th Ave South, turn right, and the gardens will be on your right. You will enjoy the artwork, old windmill, and landscaping in addition to the gardens and the beautiful bugs. Thanks to the authors of *Nature in the City: Seattle* for the directions to this one. It's tricky to explain, and they nailed it.

April (Botanizing to the Max) described the Best Bets for spring wildflowers, which will continue to attract butterflies as long as the blooms last into the summer. Mima Mounds Natural Area Preserve has a long bloom, and in June the blooming composites, such as sunflowers, asters, and daisies will also attract the butterflies.

Washington has several high-elevation natural areas, accessible by car, that are good mountain butterfly areas. These are some of the same areas where you would go for mountain flowers in two incredible national parks—Olympic and Mount Rainier. The highest road in Washington is Hart's Pass Rd covered in September (Raptor Migration). The drive up is a little scary, but the views are unbelievable. This is an excellent starting point for trails into the Pasaytan Wilderness Area and provides instant access to high mountain meadows for viewing wildflowers and their attendant butterflies, as well as the cute marmots and pikas.

The riparian areas in the canyons near Leavenworth and Yakima are favorites of Washington butterfly watchers. Icicle Creek is a main tributary of the Wenatchee River and joins it in the unique Bavarian theme town of Leavenworth. Upstream on the Wenatchee River is Tumwater Canyon, a great place to see spawning salmon in the fall and good spot for a mix of butterflies because of the plant diversity.

Icicle Canyon, upstream from the Leavenworth National Fish Hatchery, has the same habitat as Tumwater Canyon but with less traffic and lots of small campgrounds. Be sure to stop at the fish hatchery in the summer when there should be lots of fish to view.

Oak Creek WA, northwest of Yakima, is described in December (Elk). The road up Oak Creek Canyon itself starts just south of the elk feeding station on State Hwy 12. Just under 5 miles further southwest on Hwy 12 is the start of the Bear Canyon Rd, which eventually connects with the Oak Creek Rd. Both are good dirt roads that wind through some great oak woodland habitat with riparian vegetation along the creeks. This is an all-around great place for wildflowers and wildlife. It's also one of the few places in Washington to see the western gray squirrel, a threatened species in the state. Spring and early summer are best for flowers in Oak Creek because things get pretty hot and dry up soon most years. Be sure to come back in winter to see elk and bighorn. Other good canyons nearby are the Yakima River Canyon and the upper parts of two tributaries of the Yakima River—Wenas and Umtanum creeks.

▶ BUTTERFLIES AND MOTHS BEST BETS BRITISH COLUMBIA

Campbell Valley RP has a nice butterfly garden, with native and ornamental plants, at the South Valley Entrance, reached by way of 8th Ave. The park is also a good spot for native wildflowers and spring songbird migration, making it an ideal destination for a June outing.

Manning PP will be coming up next month for mountain flowers, but the lowest meadows in the park will be blooming away in June and into July. A popular hike is the trail to Strawberry Flats, which begins at the end of the park road that goes west from the lodge area. Strawberry Flats is known for its great floral diversity, a result of the overlapping ranges of many coastal, interior, and alpine plants.

JUNE'S NATURE NUGGETS

SALMONFLIES An awesome display of insect abundance is the giant stonefly hatch on the Deschutes and Yakima rivers. *Pteronarcys californica* is one of the largest stoneflies in the world and throughout the West is usually called a salmonfly, especially by anglers. Stoneflies spend most of their life as aquatic nymphs in streams with rocky bottoms. At breeding time, the nymphs climb out onto plants or rocks at night, their backs split open, and the winged adults emerge. The adults live only long enough to mate and lay eggs; most don't even eat and die within days. A salmonfly hatch creates a feeding frenzy of animals that eat insects, from magpies to trout. Northwest anglers dream of being on the Deschutes during the salmonfly hatch.

These giant stoneflies are over 2 inches long and have a distinctive retro-prehistoric look. They are slow, run more than fly, and are completely harmless because they can never sting or bite—not with their useless little mouths. So these are the perfect bug to catch and watch up close. You can easily catch a bunch, put them on your shirt, and have large, cool, scary-looking bugs crawling all over you. What could be better? The peak on the Yakima is between May 15 and the end of the month; the Deschutes is usually best between June 10 and 15. You can ask at the local fly-fishing stores to find when the best time is for other rivers.

The Yakima River is easy to access from the Yakima Greenway Path in Yakima, or you can see the bugs by driving up the Yakima River Canyon on State Hwy 821. An easy place to see them on the Deschutes River is from Mecca Flat, a primitive camping, parking, raft-launching area near Warm Springs. To get to Mecca Flat take Mecca Rd, the dirt road in Warm Springs that starts just east of the bridge over the Deschutes River and goes between the river and the gas station. Drive about 1.5 miles and park in the Mecca Flat area where you can pick up the trail that goes along the east bank of the Deschutes River. Good bugging.

AMERICAN SHAD American shad are native to the Atlantic and were introduced from the East Coast to California in 1871. They quickly spread and soon became established in the Columbia and many other rivers of the Northwest, increasing dramatically with the building of the dams. Ironically, the slow water of the reservoirs that contributed to the demise of Columbia River salmon benefited the shad, originally adapted to the slower rivers of the Atlantic Coast. Once The Dalles Dam submerged Celilo Falls in 1957, the upper river became shad country and their population exploded. Runs in the Columbia have averaged around 2 million but have been twice that in peak years. Although a tasty and hard-fighting game fish, sometimes called the aristocrat of the herrings, shad are considered "under fished" in the Northwest. Shad are anadromous, like salmon, and during the peak of their run upstream, in late June, 60,000 may go through the Bonneville fish ladders each day. You can witness this "chrome tide" at the Bonneville Dam fish viewing rooms on both sides of the Columbia.

MORE WILDFLOWERS June is bustin' out all over and the wildflower Best Bets described in March and April will continue to bloom through May and June, although the peak may be over. In June the largest flowering activity moves up in elevation so head for the hills for continued botanizing. Three modest peaks in Oregon are famous for their June blooms.

At 5455 feet Iron Mountain is a perfect mid-elevation mountain for Oregon, just about in the middle of the lowest and highest point in the state. Because of its latitude, distance from the ocean, range of elevations, and geologic history, Iron Mountain and its immediate surroundings provides an excellent sample and representation of the flowers of the western Cascades from southern British Columbia to the California border. Over 300 species of flowering plants, not counting grasslike plants, grow here. From the town of Sweet Home drive east 32 miles on US Hwy 20 to FR 035. This dirt road is not obvious and will be on your left a couple of miles before you get to the Tombstone Pass parking area. From US 20 drive 2.6 miles on FR 035 to the parking area for the Iron Mountain Trail. Part of the trail is open and sunny (and full of flowers) so take plenty of water. The view from the old lookout on top is spectacular. Reach out and touch the Three Sisters.

Saddle Mountain State Natural Area is 12 miles east of Seaside as the raven flies and they do because they nest on the mountain. Reach the trailhead at the end of the park road from US Hwy 26. It is 2.5 miles to the top of the mountain and its 1600-foot gain is steep in parts. You pass through several different habitats before reaching the open, sunny (I hope) top. The constant singing of white-crowned sparrows will serenade you, and the ravens flying overhead will be checking you out.

Humbug Mountain SP is 6 miles south of Port Orford off US Hwy 101, which goes through the park. Located on the ocean in the southwest corner of the state, this park has some of the mildest weather in Oregon, creating lush vegetation and a long blooming season. The 3-mile trail of the 1748-foot mountain is steep, but the top provides incredible views on a clear day. The hike goes through one of the last uncut old-growth groves of Port Orford cedar, a tree with one of the smallest ranges in North America.

SONGBIRD NESTING: A CLOSER LOOK

Reproduction is the major activity of spring and we have already discussed some of the behaviors associated with breeding birds—singing and establishing territories. All this is leading up to the main event: laying eggs and raising young. Because birds lay eggs they all face the same major problem: they have to find a safe place to incubate them. For most birds the solution is to build a special structure specifically for holding and protecting the eggs and, in most cases, the baby birds. This is, of course, a nest.

Strictly speaking, a nest is a structure built by an animal only for the purpose of raising its young. Nests are not used for anything else except breeding and are, therefore, not used most of the year. Unfortunately, people commonly use the word *nest* and *nesting* in different ways and most think of a nest as the equivalent to a house.

Birds aren't the only animals that make nests. Members of all vertebrate groups and many invertebrates make them. We are all familiar with wasp nests which really are a true nest, used for nothing except raising the young. Honeybees, on the other hand, live in a hive which is not only a nest but a food warehouse and shelter used all year, for many years. Of all the nest builders in the world, however, birds are the champs. They build the largest and most complex nests in the widest variety of locations and with the greatest diversity of styles.

Rather than build nests, some birds—many sea birds, shorebirds, and some raptors—just lay their eggs on the ground. Almost all other birds, however, make nests of some kind even though they may be very simple. The master nest builders are the song or perching birds, the passerines.

A nest performs several functions. It holds the eggs and young and protects them from predators and bad weather, and to some extent protects the parent bird from the same dangers. It can also act as insulation, helping keep the eggs at the proper temperature. With their powers of flight birds can put their nests in an amazing variety of places and their main technique for keeping their nest away from predators is to build it where predators can't get it. This isn't always possible so birds also use camouflage. In other parts of the world birds use some neat tricks to protect their nests. Some build their nests near a larger predatory bird that isn't able to catch them but that can catch other predators. Some birds build their nests near, or even in, wasp nests.

The variety of materials used is pretty dazzling, especially when one considers that many birds have started to incorporate human-made items. I remember an oriole nest at Malheur that lasted several years and attracted a lot of attention with its orange, blue, and green plastic strings incorporated into the design. Probably one of the most unusual nests in our region is that of the Vaux's swift. This fragile shelf is made of nothing but little sticks and dried saliva, which glues the sticks together and attaches it to the inside of a hollow tree or chimney. The largest nests in our area are the bald eagle nests which can weigh one ton.

Each bird builds a specific type of nest in a particular type of site, and nest-building behavior is innate. Birds will adapt, however, and can use innovative materials or locations when the need arises. There is usually competition for choice nest sites among each species and laying claim to a good site is one of the main functions of bird songs and other territorial behavior. With polygynous birds like grouse, the female alone may select the nest site. In many species, site selection is an important part of courtship, and the male and female select the site together. In many of our migratory songbirds the male arrives first and establishes his territory around a choice nesting site or sites. House wren males even start building the nest before the females have even arrived. What optimists.

Female grouse and most female ducks are single parents from the moment they mate, building the nest and incubating by themselves. For most songbirds, both male and female select the nest site and then build the nest. After the nest is finished the female will start laying eggs, usually one a day, until the clutch is complete. The number of eggs for a clutch is genetically determined, although sometimes birds will lay more eggs if food is abundant. The female usually does the incubating with the male often feeding her in the nest so she can keep the eggs at a constant temperature. This pattern varies, however, with many songbird parents working in shifts. Incubation for most songbirds is just under two weeks; larger birds have longer incubation periods.

Once the eggs hatch, the babies will grow to adult size in about two weeks. That means lots of food given pretty much nonstop during daylight hours. While the young are in the nest they are called nestlings, and when they leave the nest they are called fledglings. The parents will continue to feed and take care of their young after they leave the nest, anywhere from a week or two to a whole year for some larger birds. Once the young have left the nest, the nest is history. Most birds will never reuse a nest, and as soon as the young fledge they will have nothing to do with it. However, some large birds of prey will use and modify the same nest for years, and some cavity nesting birds may use a cavity again. A bird's nest is not like a house; the birds don't want to be near it any more than is necessary because being there puts them at a greater risk of predation.

Much confusion exists about the nestling and fledgling stages in a bird's life. Every spring, people "rescue" thousands of fledglings that are found on the ground. There are a few wildlife rehabilitation centers in the Northwest that will care for these birds, the largest being the Wildlife Care Center at the Audubon Society of Portland. Most people, however, will not find any help for the fledgling, which is sad because the bird didn't need to be rescued in the first place. Young birds commonly leave their nest just before they are able to fly, and many of them end up on the ground for a few days. Their parents will find them and feed them wherever they are if they are left alone. A common misconception is that once a baby bird is out of its nest, its parents won't (or can't) take care of it and it is doomed. When people pick up these fledglings they are not rescuing them, they are kidnapping them.

Of course, people who see a helpless fledgling on the ground want to help it, and most people correctly realize that the bird faces a high risk of being killed by cats or dogs, which are abundant wherever there are people. Birds do suffer the greatest mortality during this period, and many fledglings die every spring. If you find a fledgling and feel you must take action, try to get the bird off the ground as near as possible to where it fell. Sometimes you can put the bird back in the nest, if you are sure it's the right one and you can get to it. Some people mount a small box or empty margarine tub in a tree and put the bird in that. Sometimes you can find a crotch in the branches that you can set the bird in. The parents will find it and feed it. Do not put the bird where is will be in the sun. The idea is to leave them where they are, but away from Fido and Puffy.

Now you're thinking, "If I touch the baby bird with my hand, its parents will smell my scent and won't take care of it." This is one of the most widespread, persistent myths in America. Some people even believe that the parents will kill the baby if it has been touched. However, as far as we can tell, most birds have no sense of smell, so they cannot tell if you've touched their baby or not. Birds will sometimes abandon their nest or young if there is too much disturbance. But this will happen because of what the birds see and hear, not what they smell. So your touching the baby bird once for a short time will not have any influence on the parent's care of their young.

Another difficult situation between nesting birds and people is when birds build a nest where people don't want one. Barn swallows commonly build their mud nests on buildings, and Vaux's swifts seem to be increasingly building their nest in chimneys. This is a temporary situation. The birds are going to be using that nest for only about a month, and once they are gone you can remove the nest. If you can wait it out, it will be over soon.

The preventative approach is best. As soon as you see birds starting to nest in an inappropriate place, start shooing them away without hurting them. They'll try to find another location. Once the eggs are in the nest, you either have to wait it out or have the deaths of baby birds on your conscience. Try putting up nesting boxes or similar structures to attract the birds to areas where you would like them to be. Remind yourself that every swallow that nests in your yard will eat tens of thousands of mosquitoes.

JULY

MOUNTAIN WILDFLOWERS

Northwesterners have been heading up into the mountains in the summer for thousands of years. Native Americans moved up the slopes following game or other food resources such as the many delicious berries with which the Northwest is blessed. Modern Americans and Canadians head for the hills in droves for recreation—backpacking, fishing, climbing, camping, hiking, hunting, boating or just loafing around the lodge or cabin. We go, of course, because we can. Areas that were life-threatening tests of winter survival skills become sublime alpine paradise offering escape from lowland heat and every-day life. Many backpackers live for the summer when mountain wilderness becomes accessible and just plain pleasant.

You can enjoy many wonders and activities high in our dramatic mountains during our three-month window of the warmest and driest weather, July through September. In a region of scenic superlatives the display of mountain wildflowers is near the top of the list. I use "mountain wildflowers" to refer to flowers that grow from about 5000 feet on up in the zones or regions formally called montane, subalpine, and alpine. These terms describe the different habitats found around timberline, the region where we go from the continuous, thick, closed montane forest to the completely treeless alpine tundra of higher elevations. None of these terms can be precise because they all deal with a transition zone where there are no clean borders. What these terms define is the result of the continuously more difficult conditions for life as one goes up in elevation—the slope is steeper, the soil is thinner, and the weather is more extreme.

The areas that most appeal to botanizers are the meadows interspersed

Previous page: Naturalists prefer "sea star" to "starfish" because this sure isn't any kind of fish!

with small clumps of trees in the subalpine zone and the alpine meadows just above timberline. It is in these open, sunny habitats where we see the explosion of flowers typical of plants that live where the growing season is very short. Just when any particular area reaches peak bloom varies of course, but the first plants will start blooming as the snow retreats. Some plants will even send their flower stalks right through the last thin layer of snow. In most of our region mid-July to mid-August is usually the best time for mountain flowers. If you are planning a botanizing trip to a specific area, call the local district ranger stations or lodging businesses to get accurate and timely information about current conditions.

It's impossible to mention here all the common flowers you will probably see but here are the most widespread and conspicuous ones to look for. Among the most common white flowers are the spectacular avalanche lily, beargrass, Sitka valerian, partridge foot, yarrow, pearly everlasting, western pasqueflower (also called tow-headed baby because of the conspicuous seed heads), and American bistort.

The most common though sometimes difficult to tell apart yellow members of the sunflower family are arnicas, groundsels, goldenrods, and mountain-dandelions. There are so many confusing members of this family that some botanizers use the term DYC for "damn yellow composite." Other common yellow flowers are sulphur flower and other buckwheats, desert parsleys (an identification challenge), stonecrops, monkeyflowers, and buttercups.

The red-to-pink flowers really stand out, and the various types of paintbrushes are usually the most prominent. Others include fireweed, spreading phlox (which actually varies in color to blues and white also), Lewis's or pink monkey flower, and various louseworts and penstemons, another confusing group.

Lupines probably dominate the blue-to-purple group. Others in this color range include monkshood, larkspur, Jacob's ladder, asters and fleabanes, gentians, bluebells, and more penstemons. There is one very conspicuous and distinctive plant with green flowers—corn lily or false-hellebore. You can probably see all of these in a couple of visits to one of our Best Bets at the right time.

▶ MOUNTAIN WILDFLOWERS BEST BETS OREGON

The most famous wildflower trails in Crater Lake NP are in the southwest quadrant of the park, near Rim Village and park headquarters. Castle Crest Wildflower Trail is a short, easy hike with many labeled plants, making this an ideal beginning wildflower walk. Discovery Point Trail is an easy 2.6-mile round trip to the west along the crater rim. The Garfield Peak Trail heads east and climbs 1000 feet to fabulous views and higher-elevation flowers at 8000 feet. The elevation gain makes this 3-mile round trip more strenuous. Other amateur botanist favorites are Annie Creek Canyon Trail at Mazama campground and the short hike up to The Watchman. Summer activities include ranger talks and guided hikes about plants. Many National Park rangers are very knowledgeable naturalists, and the helpful staff at the visitor center are usually delighted to talk to someone about something other than where the bathrooms are.

At the other end of the state is Oregon's highest mountain, Mount Hood, in the Mount Hood NF. You'll need a Northwest Forest Pass to park at any of the trailheads. The Timberline Trail, about 75% of which is in the Mount Hood Wilderness Area, circles the peak at about timberline. The entire trail has flowers because it winds in and out of subalpine meadows and forests, but two areas are ideal. Cloud Cap Campground is on the northeast side of the mountain and on the Timberline Trail (#600), providing easy access to the timberline region. Drive to the campground and head west on the Timberline Trail (#600) toward Elk Cove. It's about 5 miles to Elk Cove, but it doesn't matter how far you go because you'll begin to see plenty of wildflowers almost immediately.

To get to Cloud Cap from the town of Hood River, head south on State Hwy 35. Thirteen miles south of Hood River is the Hood River Ranger District office, a good source for maps and information. After 21.5 miles turn right onto FR 3510 and follow the signs for Cooper Spur. Head north, then west for 2.5 miles until you reach the Inn at Cooper Spur, and then turn left onto FR 3512. Continue to follow signs to Cooper Spur and to Cloud Cap. At the next two forks keep to the right and follow the signs for Cloud Cap. The dirt road gets narrow and rough for about the last mile but a regular car can make it just fine if you take it easy. The parking area and sign for Trail #600 are easy to find.

Almost directly opposite Cloud Cap on the other side of the peak is Paradise Park, which is most easily reached by hiking 5 miles west on the Timberline Trail (#600) from Timberline Lodge. This is a popular backpacking destination and gets a lot more traffic than the northern side of the mountain.

Top Spur Trail (#785) offers a quick route up to good flowers and some awesome views. This is the quickest way I know to get from Portland to a trail with mountain flowers. The Lolo Pass Rd leaves US Hwy 26 right across the highway from the Zig Zag Ranger Station. Take Lolo Pass Rd 4 miles and go right onto FR 1825, the road to Old Maid Flats and Ramona Falls. Go just 0.5 mile on FR 1825 and before you drive over the Sandy River turn left onto FR 1828. This is an easy turn to miss. Take FR 1828 northeast and soon it will start climbing. Continue for 6.5 miles to the fork in the road where FR 1828 continues to the left and FR 1828-118 goes right. Turn right and take FR 1828-118 (some signs may say 118) about 1.5 miles until you see the sign for the trailhead. Park head-in on the road, opposite the trailhead. The roads and trail are well signed.

Take the Top Spur Trail up a mile until you meet the Pacific Crest Trail (#2000). Turn right and continue to the confusing junction of the Pacific Crest Trail, the Timberline Trail, and the Bald Mountain Trail. You want to take the Pacific Crest Trail south toward Ramona Falls. At the Mount Hood Wilderness Area sign, walk through the forest for awhile, and then come out into the open on the south slope of Bald Mountain. Wait until you see the view of Mount Hood as you continue on the trail! The trail here cuts across the big bald on Bald Mountain and here you'll see a whole different plant community than what you saw in the shady woods. After exploring Bald Mountain, return the way you came. As with any wildflower walk it's not about how far you go; it's about what you see along the way.

▶ MOUNTAIN WILDFLOWERS BEST BETS WASHINGTON

Bird Creek Meadows, on the southeastern slope of Mount Adams, in Tract D of the Yakama Nation, is where I have seen the most awesome display of mountain flowers in my life. Trails into the area originate at Bird Lake, which has a camping area managed by the Yakamas (their spelling for their people and nation). For decades there has been a $5 per vehicle day use fee and a $10 per day camping fee at Bird Lake. Come prepared—the fee could go up, Yakama rangers do not always have change, and they accept only cash. If you do not see a Yakama ranger when you arrive or before you head out on your hike, don't worry; one will probably find you when you return.

Getting to Bird Lake and knowing where to go once you get there are a bit tricky so get the best map available, in addition to the one in this book. The Yakama rangers will usually have a map to give you. The Forest Service's Mount Adams Ranger District map, published in 2003, is very good. The last few miles to Bird Lake are on a very rough dirt road. The Yakamas did some serious grading of the road in the early 2000s and it is much better than it had been, but prepare yourself for tough driving.

To get to Bird Lake from the town of Trout Lake, head north on the Mount Adams Recreation Area Rd, the main road out of town. In about a mile the road curves to the right where it intersects FR 23 to Randle. Don't go toward Randle; stay on the main road as it curves. In 0.5 mile turn right again onto FR 82; don't go straight on FR 80. You can always follow signs to the Sno-Parks because you will drive past all of them. In a couple of miles you will enter Gifford Pinchot NF. Stay on FR 82 following any signs for Bird Creek Meadows. In 10 miles FR 82 becomes FR 8290 and you enter Track D. Now the fun driving begins. About 3.5 miles after entering Yakama land you'll reach Mirror Lake. Turn left and head west just over 0.5 mile to Bird Lake.

From the southwest end of Bird Lake is the trailhead for the Crooked Creek Falls Trail which goes north to meet the Round the Mountain Trail. From this junction there are wonderful wildflower meadows to the east or west on the Round the Mountain Trail for a couple of miles. Bird Creek Meadows proper is to the east. If you hike west you'll enter the Mount Adams Wilderness Area (Gifford Pinchot NF), where backpack camping is permitted. The Yakamas do not want people camping on reservation land outside of their developed campgrounds. You can take a slightly shorter hike by going to the northwestern corner of Bird Lake and taking the trail to Bluff Lake and then heading northwest into the heart of the meadows. Combining these two makes a great loop. Bird Creek Meadows is not usually open until July 1 and is usually at its best at the end of July or early August. A forest fire swept through this area in the summer of 2008. Check conditions at the Mount Adams ranger station in Trout Lake before you come.

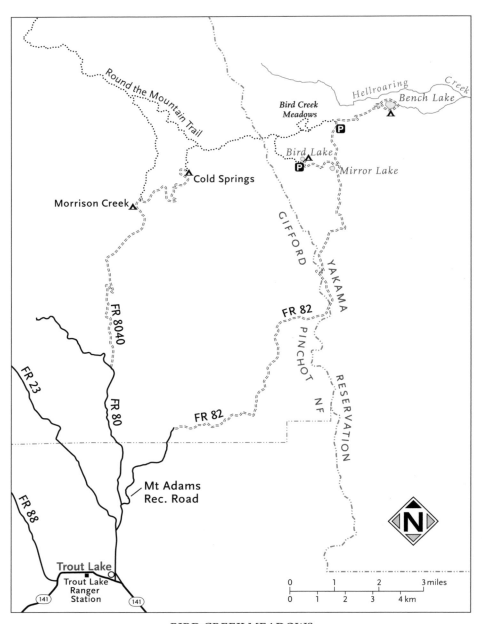

BIRD CREEK MEADOWS

Washington's two well-known national parks, Olympic and Mount Rainier, are both famous for mountain wildflowers. Mount Rainier NP has two areas that are very accessible, too accessible, actually, for the welfare of the plants. Paradise and Sunrise are both major visitor sites with visitor centers and services and both have suffered from being "loved to death." Fortunately, visitor awareness of the problem is increasing significantly, and some volunteer groups have been heavily involved in revegetating some areas. It is very important in high-use areas like these to stay on established trails and follow other regulations. Between the two areas, Paradise gets significantly heavier use. Mount Rainier gets lots of weekend use from the Puget Sound metropolitan area which makes midweek trips much more desirable. Both areas are easy to find with a park map and have rangers to ask for suggestions of the best current flower spots.

Hurricane Ridge on the northern end of Olympic NP offers great wildflowers as well as good looks at Olympic marmot and deer. Hurricane Ridge is a major tourist attraction 17 miles south of Port Angeles. On a clear day views from the road and the top of the ridge are spectacular. There are daily interpretive programs in summer, some highlighting wildflowers, as well as some exhibits and services such as the snack bar. *Guide to Hurricane Ridge* by Charles Stewart, for sale in the gift shop, is a nice little guide to the area featuring the most common plants and animals.

▶ MOUNTAIN WILDFLOWERS BEST BETS BRITISH COLUMBIA

The primo mountain flower spot on the mainland of southwestern British Columbia is Manning PP, 135 miles east of Vancouver. Highway 3 runs through the park, and the two other roads in the park head in different directions from the visitor center and lodge area. Both roads go to fabulous wildflower areas. A paved road goes from Hwy 3 to Cascade Lookout, and from there a gravel road continues to Blackwall Peak. From the Blackwall Peak parking area trails wander north through a subalpine meadow area, sometimes called Blackwall Meadows, that's almost 50 square miles. There is the self-guided Paintbrush Nature Trail, as well as guided walks from the Naturalist's Hut. These are the most accessible and some of the most extensive subalpine meadows in southern British Columbia.

Just across Hwy 3 from the road to Blackwall Peak is the road to Strawberry Flats. The road ends at the Strawberry Flats parking area and from here a trail winds through the flats and up to the Three Falls Trail. Strawberry Flats, lower and lusher than Blackwall Meadows, is famous for its diversity. About 150 different species of wildflowers have been found in the twelve acre area. Peak blooming time for both areas is mid-July into August, with Strawberry Flats being a bit earlier than Blackwall. But don't worry, any time in this period you'll have more than enough to keep busy if you start trying to identify all you see.

Garibaldi PP is closer to Vancouver and also has outstanding mountain meadows, but they require considerably more effort to see. The area is ideal, however, for backpacking and botanizing. The Black Tusk is a 7600-foot rock "fang" sticking up over Garibaldi Lake. Around its southern base are extensive meadows that are well known for their dazzling display of mountain wildflowers toward the end of July. The trail to Black Tusk starts at the Rubble Creek parking area. The short road to this parking area is 22 miles north of Squamish on Hwy 99. The trail is a fairly steep climb for about 3.5 miles to a trail junction. The left fork leads to Taylor Meadows camping area in another mile, which is the closest camping to the meadows. The right fork goes to the camping area on the shore of Garibaldi Lake in just under 2 miles. From here another trail heads north into the meadows but it is a bit farther than from Taylor Meadows. At both camping areas there are a few shelters and outhouses. The view at Garibaldi Lake is beautiful and sublime. You could do this hike in one long 10-mile day, but wouldn't you really rather wake up in the meadows or at the lake and have a whole day to explore? The Black Tusk is a popular climb with incredible views and it's a nontechnical challenge. However, the view from the ridge at the base of the tusk is spectacular enough to satisfy most folks and from there you can't see Whistler, making you think you are at the edge of civilization.

Strathcona PP is BC's first provincial park and the largest one on Vancouver Island. Most of the park is wilderness without any trails, a hard concept for those of us from the States to grasp. With just over 800 square miles of mostly mountain terrain, the range of possibilities at Strathcona is pretty overwhelming. Three areas have the best reputations as wildflower havens. Flower Ridge Trail is accessible from Butte Lake Rd near its southern end. The trail climbs steeply for 3.5 miles into the alpine zone, and then continues for another 3.5 miles. Marble Meadows is another hike up out of the central valley dominated by Buttle Lake. Unfortunately, the trailhead for the Marble Meadows Trail is in the Phillips Creek marine campground, which is across Buttle Lake from the park road. So if you don't have a boat you'll need to arrange for a water taxi to take you across and pick you up. With this type of access, most backpackers have Marble Meadows to themselves.

Then there is Forbidden Plateau. Aren't you just dying to go to a place called Forbidden Plateau? Especially because it is the home of Paradise Meadows. This area is accessed from outside of the park by the road that goes from Courtenay to the Mount Washington Ski Area. Head northwest on the Inland Island Hwy 19 out of Courtenay, and then take the Strathcona Parkway exit (Exit 130). Follow signs to Mount Washington ski area. The parking area for the Paradise Meadows trailhead is near the Nordic ski lodge. You could spend many days wandering around up here in the alpine meadows with all the scattered lakes. Of course, there will be mosquitoes so come prepared. It's a shorter drive to get to Forbidden Plateau than it is to get into the center of the park, and you start out hiking up high, where you want to be. Not so forbidding, eh?

TIDEPOOLS

Peering into a tidepool is like looking through a window into another world. There are strange animals that look like plants, plants that don't look like anything on land, and weird things—who knows what they are—that look like aliens. It really is another world for us terrestrial humans who have very little direct experience with life in the vast oceans. One place where we can come into contact with the marine world is where the oceans meet the land—the seashore. When the tide goes out, this fringe of contact between land and ocean reveals a wondrous sample of marine life that is easily accessible to us land dwellers.

This is the intertidal zone, the land between the tides. Although it is in many ways one of the harshest environments on Earth, the intertidal zone is packed with an astounding variety of plant and animal life that has adapted to the daily changes in temperature, moisture, oxygen, food availability, and predation. It is dominated by invertebrates and algae, life forms unfamiliar to most humans, accustomed as we are to the large, conspicuous vertebrates and flowering plants on land. But many cultures throughout the world and throughout history have relied on this ecosystem for food and special materials. Exploring the intertidal zone can be a very rewarding and a fun outing for people of all ages, even if they aren't planning to eat their discoveries.

Tides are caused by the pull of the moon's and the sun's gravitational fields on our planet and its oceans. Because the earth rotates while the moon orbits the earth, a point on earth will experience two high tides and two low tides every 24 hours and 50 minutes. This difference of 50 minutes between the tidal cycle and the daily cycle is the reason that the tides are not at the same time every day.

An important characteristic of tidal cycles is the difference between spring tides and neap tides. When the earth, moon, and sun are arranged in a straight line with each other (at the new and full moons), the difference between high and low tides is at its greatest—high tides are the highest and low tides the lowest. These tides, both high and low, are called spring tides (from the verb for jumping) and happen every month, not just in the spring. When the moon is at right angles to a line between the sun and the earth there is less difference between low and high tides, and these tides are called the neap tides. It is during the spring tides that you want to go looking for life in the intertidal zone.

Tides vary greatly from place to place. On our Pacific Coast we usually have clearly defined sets of tides—two unequal high tides and two unequal low tides every day (approximately) and two sets each of spring tides and neap tides each month. During part of every pair of spring tides, one of the two low tides each day will be a minus tide, below the average low tide level. These minus tides provide the golden opportunities for finding the greatest variety of intertidal life because the greatest area is exposed. During the winter half of the year, most minus tides are at night. (Walking over wet rocks at night in the winter is not a good idea.) Minus tides during daylight hours, and most of the lowest tides of the year, occur from April through September.

To plan when to go tidepooling get a tide table for the area in which you're interested. In past years many sporting goods stores, charter boat companies, motels, and chambers of commerce in coastal areas would have tide tables for their local area printed for free distribution. Nowadays the trend is to go to Web sites for tidal information.

Get the tide forecast table for the place and the months you are interested in and look for the days with minus tides occurring at convenient times. Some tide tables highlight the minus tides, making it easy to find the best days and times for exploring the intertidal zone. Canadian tide tables use a different datum or zero point that is 2.5 feet lower than what we use in the United States. On a Canadian tide table, any tides below +2.5 feet are the same as minus tides in the States. A Canadian low tide of 0.0 will be awesome.

Rocky shores—ledges, boulders, vertical rock faces, and crevices—provide the best opportunities for viewing intertidal life. Among the first things people notice in a rocky intertidal area during a minus tide are the bands or layers (called zonation) of different living things at different heights. This zonation can be divided into three parts: upper intertidal zone, middle intertidal zone, and lower intertidal zone. Each zone has characteristic animals and plants. Once you know which zone you are in, you will know what organisms to expect.

Let's take a quick look at some of the most obvious animals found in each zone. These animals are common and conspicuous in most rocky intertidal areas that get some direct wave action. This is just a general guide, of course. Protected waters, such as in the Salish Sea, will vary considerably and some organisms will not be present. There are many good books to aid you in your intertidal journey of discovery, and you'll find my favorites in the bibliography.

The highest parts of the intertidal zone receive only occasional water. Of the few marine animals that can survive there, the most conspicuous are the small acorn barnacles which often cover large areas of rock by the thousands in tightly packed "mats." When out of the water they appear quite dead, but you may see them in a pool of water extending their feathery feet out of their shell and sweeping them through the water to gather food. Although they have shells and look like mollusks, they are actually crustaceans like their relatives, the shrimp. A barnacle starts life as a free-swimming "shrimpy" larva, but then finds a suitable place and attaches itself by its head using the original super glue. The barnacle then starts growing the plates of shell that will protect it for the rest of its life.

Of course, predators are never far away. Among the acorn barnacles might lurk their main predator—dogwinkles or rock whelks of several species. Rock whelks have an elongated shell, about an inch long, usually with distinct striping. These snails drill a hole in a barnacle's shell, squirt digestive juices inside, and then suck out the contents. They are known for their characteristic eggs, called sea oats, and for their high incidence of cannibalism. Also found in this highest zone are different kinds of limpets, another mollusk with a very different lifestyle. Limpets have one shell that looks like a little volcano and they are very slow-moving vegetarians, more like the snails we find in our gardens than the predaceous rock whelks.

The small shore crabs become quite abundant below the preceding animals, and range from the upper to the middle intertidal zones. During low tides in the day the shore crabs remain hidden in nooks and crannies or among mussels and may be hard to see at first. Sometimes you'll see them scurry for cover as you approach a tidepool. At night they are active on exposed rocks and in the water nibbling on seaweed and playing an important role as scavengers. Another small crab, the porcelain crab, can normally be found by looking carefully under rocks. This distinctive crab is recognized by its uniquely flattened body and large claws.

The black turban snail is usually the most common and conspicuous snail in the upper intertidal zone in areas with significant wave action. The shell is dark black when wet, dingy gray when dry. We would expect turban snails to be as slow as limpets because they are also vegetarians that scrape algae off rocks. But these snails often wander into lower zones where sea stars try to eat them and apparently they can move very fast, for a snail, when escaping from this predator.

Both the California mussel and the goose (or gooseneck) barnacle must have wave action and are not found in more protected waters. They dominate and define the animal community in the middle intertidal zone, often making the most distinct band in the intertidal area. In good habitat the California mussel forms huge clusters, called mussel beds, covering large areas of rock. The goose barnacle is usually scattered irregularly through the mussel beds in smaller clumps. Both animals are sedentary filter feeders but use quite different techniques.

Like other bivalve mollusks, mussels draw water into their body through their siphon. The water passes over the gills which remove oxygen from the water but which also are covered with a layer of sticky mucus. Particles of food in the water become stuck in the mucus layer which slowly moves across the gills and into the mussel's mouth. The used water is sent out the exit siphon. Instead of bringing the water into their body like mussels, barnacles (a crustacean) stick their highly modified legs, called cirri, out of their shell and wave them through the water, catching the same types of small food particles which are then scraped off the feathery cirri into the mouth. Barnacles have no gills so it is assumed that oxygen is absorbed by the cirri. Both animals have the same adaptation for being left high and dry by the low tide—close up your shell and wait it out.

Mussel beds provide a huge food resource for animals that can get inside the shells of mussels and barnacles. Humans have consumed mussels for millennia, and the California mussel is prized for its taste. The mussels' worst nightmares, however, are the sea stars or starfish (they are no more a fish than we are). Sea stars are uniquely adapted to eating bivalves with their amazing hydraulic system of tube feet and their bizarre technique of extruding their stomach out of their bodies and into the pulled-open shells of their prey, where most digestion takes place. The most conspicuous sea star is the ochre or common sea star. Don't be fooled by the different colors of this fairly large, up to a foot in diameter, sea star. They come in orange, purple, and brownish tones, but they are all the same species, just different color variations. These stars range into different tidal zones but are usually concentrated at the lower edge of the mussel beds. Indeed, they cause the lower edge of the mussel bed, similar to the browse lines made by cows on trees.

The middle intertidal zone is loaded with a variety of mollusks including different kinds of snails, limpets, and chitons. Check snail shells carefully; some will contain hermit crabs instead of the original owners. Chitons are fairly flat and oval-shaped and have eight interlocking plates for their shell instead of the much more common one or two. The chitons' protective coloration and hiding habits make them hard to find. The easiest to spot is the large black chiton (also known as the leather chiton or black Katy). This bold chiton is out in the open more than others and is easy to identify because its girdle (the soft stuff) covers all of its plates except for a row of roughly diamond-shaped patches in the middle of its back.

The next distinct band of animals, and the border with the lower intertidal zone, consists of two sea anemones, relatives of jellyfish and coral. The aggregating anemone is about an inch in diameter and lives in huge groups, all clones, which sometime completely cover a rock. When closed up during low tide, sand and shell fragments are usually stuck to them making them easy to overlook. Once you recognize them you'll be astounded at their numbers. When open, they have pink in their tentacles.

Found lower in the lower intertidal zone than the aggregating anemone is the handsome green anemone, one of the world's largest. Large specimens can reach a foot across, but half that is the norm. These are often seen completely opened up in tidepools and can be fed small crabs, snails, or mussels which the tentacles push into the digestive cavity in the middle of the beast. They digest the good stuff and spit out the shells. If you gently rub your fingers on the tentacles you will feel a strange stickiness caused by the stinging cells firing into your skin, which is fortunately tough enough to stop their penetration. The green color actually comes from algae living inside the anemone's body, a relationship of mutual benefit.

Found with or below the green anemones in some areas are two sea urchins, the purple and the red. The uncommon red sea urchin is really an animal from below the tidal zone. The purple urchin, in contrast, can be very abundant and can completely line the sides of some tidepools. These mellow algae grazers will actually carve out little depressions in the rock in which many generations may live. Sometimes a small urchin will enter one of these pits and then grow too large to get out the opening, trapping itself forever. But no problem; as long as it gets enough food it's as happy as, well, as happy as a sea urchin in a sea urchin pit.

Animals in the lower intertidal zone may require some luck to find. The most famous are the gumboot chiton and the nudibranchs. A foot in length, the gumboot or giant Pacific chiton is the largest chiton in the world. This behemoth's plates are covered by its bumpy, dark orange girdle. Nudibranchs, or sea slugs, are the jewels of the tidepools—delicate, often brightly colored, and hard to find. The most commonly seen is also the most common in appearance, the sea lemon. This bright yellow fellow, a couple of inches long, looks just like a piece of its namesake.

Intertidal Etiquette

Intertidal habitats may well be the most sensitive areas visited in this book, and naturalists, resource managers, and marine biologists throughout our region are extremely concerned about the impact on these areas. Please observe proper intertidal etiquette when you visit:

- Avoid stepping on any plants or animals. Step on bare rock or sand.
- Do not collect any living things. Enjoy them where they are, in their natural habitat.
- If you do gently pick up something, put it back exactly where you got it as soon as possible.
- Do not pull off animals attached to the rocks. A few animals, such as hermit crabs and snails, can be picked up gently from the bottom of pools, but if you have to use any force don't do it; you can damage the animal.
- If you lift and look carefully under seaweed or rocks, return them gently to their original condition.
- Please remove any litter whenever possible.

Some biologists and resource managers feel that people visiting intertidal areas should not touch anything or disturb rocks in any way. Others feel that careful and aware tidepoolers can explore these areas without harming them. Some areas such as marine gardens and national parks are legally protected from disturbance.

In addition, take safety precautions. Wear shoes with grippy soles. Avoid stepping on seaweed; it's as slippery as mucus. Pay attention to the waves and incoming water.

▶ TIDEPOOLS BEST BETS OREGON

Because of the geology of the Oregon coast and the terrific public access to many intertidal areas, Oregon provides the best opportunities in our region for tidepooling. The Oregon State Parks brochure *Oregon's Rocky Intertidal Areas* lists 25 good tidepool spots on the Oregon coast.

Cannon Beach is one of the most heavily visited tourist towns in the Pacific Northwest, and right in the middle of the beach, at the edge of the ocean, is Haystack Rock. This giant monolith of basalt and the surrounding reefs and smaller rocks provide some of the best tidepooling in the Northwest. Over the years, the increasing impact of thousands of tourists, many collecting animals for no reason, threatened to destroy this wonderful area despite its legally protected status. People climbing the rock also disturbed the nesting sites of many seabirds. Wildlife managers debated what to do. Build a huge fence around it? Post guards? Arrest people? Then a wonderful thing happened.

A group of concerned residents started the Haystack Rock Awareness Program (HARP), a public education program designed to protect the rock. Seasonal paid staff and many volunteers provide a range of programs, the most exciting and effective taking place at the rock itself during the lowest tides of the summer. Friendly guides show visitors around the rock, and the demonstration tanks with sample animals and plants, telescopes for watching the birds, and interpretive signs are engaging and informative.

These types of activities allow everyone to see the neat stuff living about the rock without causing harm. They learn what the organisms are and what they do. People contacted through the program have a greater understanding of the importance of the Haystack Rock environment and treat it properly. A significant number have become very protective and actually tell other people to leave the animals alone during times when the program is not active. Word has spread and the negative impact has been reduced. Plan a trip to Cannon Beach during a minus tide, and visit Haystack Rock when the program is going.

Inspired by HARP, a group of volunteers in the Pacific City area formed KELP—Kiwanda Environmental Learning Program. Cape Kiwanda State Natural Area is a mile north of the main part of Pacific City on the Three Capes Scenic Route. On the south side of the cape across from Pacific City's Haystack Rock is a large parking area (no fee). Yes, there are two Haystack Rocks in Oregon. The south side of the cape has the good intertidal area, and KELP volunteers are usually there during the minus tides on summer weekends.

The intertidal area at Yaquina Head has also suffered from heavy visitation over many years, but visitor awareness is improving and the tidepools are still excellent. Go north 2.5 miles from Newport on US Hwy 101 and turn west onto the well-marked road for Yaquina Head Outstanding Natural Area (ONA). You'll need to pay a fee at the entrance booth. You can go to the excellent interpretive center first or drive directly to the parking area at the end of Lighthouse Dr, where you can descend the stairs to the cobble beach and the tidepool area. This is also the closest parking to the lighthouse and the amazing view of Colony Rock, covered with nesting seabirds in summer. The BLM has developed Yaquina Head ONA into a wonderful educational site; the interpretive center is truly outstanding. In 1994 work was completed on the Quarry Cove tidepools, the world's first man-made, natural tidepool area. An old quarry was rehabilitated into rocky intertidal habitat with a system of universally accessible trails that are exposed during any zero or lower tide. Don't forget to also look for gray whales while you're at Yaquina Head.

South of Yachats for about 5 miles is an almost continuous, wide rocky ledge in the intertidal zone that provides many excellent opportunities for tidepooling. To reach Yachats State Recreation Area, on the north side of the mouth of the Yachats River, follow the sign in central Yachats and go west on 2nd until it ends in the park's parking lot. From the parking lot go down the stairs to the intertidal area, and work your way north to the best spots. To reach Yachats Ocean Rd State Natural Site,

south of the river, turn right on Yachats Ocean Rd just after crossing the bridge. Drive about 0.5 mile until you see informal parking areas overlooking the rocky area.

Just 2 miles south of Yachats is the Cape Perpetua Scenic Area managed by the US Forest Service. The Captain Cook trail leads from the interpretive center to the tidepool area. Bordering Cape Perpetua Scenic Area is Neptune SP, with its scenic stops with beach access along US 101. Strawberry Hill has excellent intertidal areas and is a great place to see harbor seals, especially babies in the summer. Please do not disturb the seals while you're exploring. Another mile south of Strawberry Hill is Bob Creek, another good access point to the rock ledge extending south from Cape Perpetua. A very large rocky area occurs south of the parking lot.

▶ TIDEPOOLS BEST BETS WASHINGTON

Not as many choice intertidal areas are accessible in Washington because of private land ownership and limited roads to the rocky sea coast. The areas that are accessible have three different types of exposure. Olympic NP represents maximum exposure to the open Pacific; Salt Creek represents the partially protected waters of the Strait of Juan de Fuca; and Rosario Beach represents the more protected waters of the San Juans and other islands in the Salish Sea.

Olympic NP includes 60 miles of beautiful, wilderness coastline. In the Kalaloch area Beach 4 is a popular tidepool spot, with guided ranger walks in July and August. Schedules for walks and tides are available at the Kalaloch Information Center. To go on your own, park in the Beach 4 parking area, take the trail to the beach, and head north for the rocks. Farther north in the park is Rialto Beach, near the Mora campground and ranger station and

reachable using La Push Rd from Forks. The road to Mora ends at Rialto Beach, where it is a 1.5-mile hike from the parking area to the tidepools near Hole-in-the-Wall. Plan to leave the Rialto Beach parking area an hour to an hour-and-a-half before low tide. The rangers schedule tidepool walks during July and August; the Mora Ranger Station has a schedule.

Salt Creek County Park of Clallam County, on the north shore of the Olympic Peninsula, is a great spot for camping and wildlife viewing. The offshore waters are part of the Tongue Point Marine Life Sanctuary. From Port Angeles head west on US Hwy 101 to the junction with State Hwy 112. Go west 7 miles on Hwy 112 to the well-signed turn off to Salt Creek and Camp Hayden Rd. After entering the park go straight, past the road to the WW II bunkers, and then head west (left turn) on any of the next roads driving as far as you can into the camping area toward the northwest corner of the park. There is a small parking area with an informational sign near stairs that lead down to the intertidal area. Two more nearby stairways lead to other rocky areas. In addition to intertidal critters you should have some excellent views of seabirds, although these are most numerous in the fall and winter.

Deception Pass SP is Washington's most popular state park and within the park is Rosario Beach, probably the state's most visited intertidal area. Like Yaquina Head in Oregon, Rosario is still an excellent tidepooling spot despite the heavy visitation. From State Hwy 20, south of Anacortes, take Hwy 20 Spur south to Whidbey Island. Follow the signs to Rosario Beach, about 5 miles from Hwy 20 and before the bridge to Whidbey Island.

▶ **TIDEPOOLS BEST BETS** BRITISH COLUMBIA

Most of the BC coast in our region is quite protected and not as rich as the west coast of Vancouver Island, which has direct exposure to the Pacific. Access by road is limited on the wild, west coast of Vancouver Island, so choice spots are limited. The two best places are Botanical Beach PP and the Long Beach Unit of Pacific Rim NP.

Botanical Beach PP may well be BC's most famous intertidal area. Botanical Beach is near Port Renfrew at the end of Hwy 14, about 65 miles west of Victoria. This is still a bit off the beaten path and lodging is limited, so if you plan to stay in Port Renfrew overnight you might want to make plans in advance. As you near the end of the highway in Port Renfrew, just before coming to the dock and the Port Renfrew Hotel, turn left (only way possible) onto Cerantes Rd. There is a sign for Botanical Beach and a street sign for Cerantes Rd. In about 2 miles you'll reach the parking area. From here one trail goes to Botanical Beach and another goes to Botany Bay. Outhouses are at the end of each trail near the beach.

Take the trail to Botanical Beach, the best tidepool area, and when you reach the shore, walk out onto the exposed rock and work your way to your right to the best areas. There are some amazing pools and other interesting formations carved in the easily eroded sandstone. This area is rich in mollusks with many limpets and chitons. Instead of returning the way you came, you can take the trail from Botanical Beach over to Botany Bay, and then take the trail back up to the parking area from there. This route is a triangular loop that travels through some nice forest habitat and adds about an hour to your trip.

Pacific Rim NP is the only national park in southwestern BC and has three separate units. The Long Beach Unit has visitor facilities and the easiest access; the other two units are mostly wilderness. The Long Beach Unit offers fantastic scenery; wonderful hikes in ancient forests, bogs, and beaches; and great viewing opportunities for birds, marine mammals, and intertidal life. The nearby towns of Tofino and Ucluelet offer a wide range of visitor services.

A visit to Wickaninnish Center is a must; it's a beautiful visitor center with great displays, restrooms, the South Beach Trail, and a surprisingly elegant little restaurant with great food. It's also a great place to hang out if it's raining, which is often. The best tidepool areas are on the South Beach Trail and at Box Island. The South Beach Trail starts at the center and within 0.25 mile goes past good rocky habitat. Pick one of the side trails that lead to a promising area, and start exploring.

Box Island is the largest of several offshore rocks in Schooner Cove. You can walk out to these rocks at low tide from the beach at Schooner Walk-in Campground. The parking area for Schooner is 9 miles north of Wickaninnish. From the parking area, the Schooner Campground trail descends through beautiful, lush ancient forest habitat to the walk-in campground and beach, a great place to camp. Whenever you are on the west coast of Vancouver Island, watch for whales.

MOUNTAIN GOATS

Ghostly white, shy enough to be mysterious, and living on the most rugged peaks, mountain goats are the spirits of the high mountains in the Pacific Northwest. These animals are superbly adapted for their extreme environment, easily scampering across rocky cliffs using the smallest ledges for footholds. Their legs are short for their size, giving them a low center of gravity. Their feet have tough inner pads that are rubbery and rough for traction, and hard outer hooves for gripping ice and rock. Their sense of balance is excellent. To survive the subfreezing temperatures and severe winds of winter in the high mountains, they have an impressive coat of shaggy, white fur. The outer coat consists of hollow guard hairs up to eight inches long, which are loaded with lanolin to repel water. Underneath is a three-inch layer of woolly underfur. Mountain goats are born to climb and kids instinctively start hours after birth.

Mountain goats are not closely related to our domesticated farm goats, although they are both in the large bovid family. The mountain goat's closest relatives are the chamois, serow, and takin, which have similar lives in the high mountains of Europe and Asia. Mountain goats are also from Asia, although they have been here for about 500,000 years. Mountain goats crossed into North America over the Bering Strait land bridge during the Pleistocene Epoch in the great ungulate invasion, which also included bighorn sheep, musk ox, elk, bison, and caribou. They were once much more widely distributed throughout the West when the climate was colder, as were many other subarctic animals. With the post-Pleistocene change to a warmer climate they have retreated to the mountains of Alaska and Canada, still ranging into the lower 48 in the Washington Cascades and the Northern Rockies of Idaho and Montana. In the last eighty years there have been introductions into other western states.

Confusion exists as to whether mountain goats are native wildlife in the Pacific Northwest, especially in Washington. I have heard some strange tales of mountain goat origins from folks in eastern Washington who were mixing up Pleistocene Epoch migrations and recent reintroductions. Mountain goats are considered native wildlife in Washington, although their numbers and distribution have varied greatly during the last 200 years. Washington currently has 6000 to 8000 mountain goats in about 100 scattered populations. Some populations are the result of reintroductions of goats into areas where they had originally occurred but had since disappeared. Mountain goats were introduced into the Olympic Mountains in the 1920s, and this population has been the center of much discussion and controversy. Despite claims otherwise, the scientific evidence is clear that mountain goats were never native to the Olympics and that they are having a negative impact on the alpine vegetation. Many goats have been live trapped in Olympic NP and released in other parts of the state. I suspect the source of much of the confusion about the goats' actual origins and status lies in the controversy over their introduction in the Olympics and the fact that many goats now living in other parts of Washington are the result of reintroductions.

British Columbia has always been the world's headquarters for mountain goats, with an estimated 50,000 to 60,000 in the province today. In Oregon debate continues about the original status of mountain goats. Some wildlife biologists believe mountain goats existed in northeastern Oregon prior to European contact, but more believe otherwise. Since 1950 the Wallowa and Elkhorn mountains have seen introductions of mountain goats, but these introductions have been controversial. Some biologists are concerned about the impact of the Elkhorn population on native vegetation.

Mountain goats are not easy to see because they live in remote, rugged mountainous terrain and are very wary of humans. They are rarely found below 5000 feet, even in Alaska. In Washington your chances of seeing them are good in a few spots, but your view will usually be from a distance. Binoculars or a scope are a must. Fortunately, their white fur makes mountain goats easy to spot unless they're on snow. In summer, look for rocky cliffs near timberline, and then search grassy ledges in the cliffs or the grassy areas between the base of the cliffs and the edge of the forest. I've seen them most frequently in this band of scattered trees and openings. They will sometimes be on the cliffs themselves. At higher elevations they may be out in the open on alpine tundra or rocky slopes. Be patient; you may have to wait hours before they wander into view from out of the trees or from rocks. They are most active early and late in the day and on overcast days. If they are in grassy areas or on the typically dark rock of the Cascades, they will stand out clearly with good light. Biologist Ron Warfield at Mount Rainier NP gave me a good hint: if you see a patch of snow get up and move, you've got yourself a goat.

At reasonable range, with binoculars or a scope, mountain goats are unmistakable. They are about the size of a small deer but much more compact and stocky, and they are completely white except for their black nose, eyes, hooves, and small, curved horns. Mountain goats have large humped shoulders and goatees that get longer with age. Males and females are very similar, though the males are slightly larger and have larger shoulders. The best way to tell them apart is by behavior. Nannies and their young live in small groups while adult males are usually solitary. The sure way to tell them apart is to watch them pee—nannies squat, while billies stretch.

Speaking of urinating, Dan Mathews makes an unusual suggestion in his excellent *Cascade-Olympic Natural History*. Mountain goats crave salt and will search for salty soil to eat—even traveling long distances to frequent salt licks. When hikers urinate on alpine turf, the goats will sometimes eat the anointed soil to get the salt, destroying the fragile vegetation in the process. Dan recommends that hikers urinate on rock or gravel when in mountain goat habitat.

Mountain goats are not picky and eat a wide range of plants. In winter, they use their extraordinary climbing ability to feed on steep slopes and cliffs where snow doesn't accumulate. As spring approaches they are often found feeding on south facing slopes, which are the first to green up with new plant growth. Their climbing ability also makes mountain goats fairly safe from predators. The main causes of death are extreme winter weather, food availability, and accidental falls. These factors are much greater for young goats.

▶ MOUNTAIN GOATS BEST BETS WASHINGTON

The best spots in our region for seeing mountain goats are in the southern Cascades near Mount Rainier and are all on our Mountain Goat Country map. In Mount Rainier NP itself, the Sunrise area in the northeast corner of the park has several spots the goats fre-

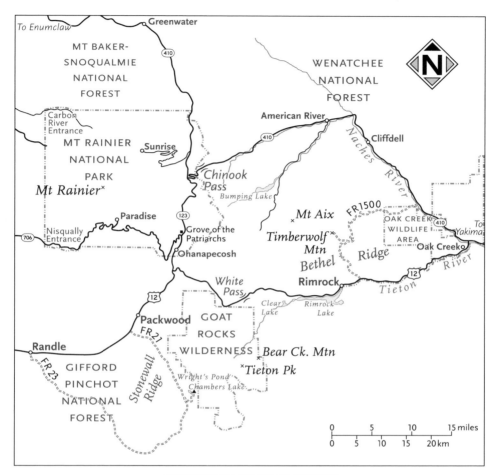

MOUNTAIN GOAT COUNTRY

quent. Sunrise also provides spectacular views, alpine wildflowers, marmots and pikas, and is a must see in the Northwest. There are also a ranger station, visitor center, and other services including a snack bar. The road up to Sunrise makes a sharp turn at Sunrise Point where you'll see a parking area and interpretive signs. Park here and go to the wall with the north view. Find the Cascade Range sign, and use it as a guide to locate Dege Peak and The Palisades. Carefully search the area between these points for goats, keeping in mind their preferred habitat. If the goats aren't in that area, search other suitable areas in view. Occasionally goats get quite close to the road here. For another spot, continue to Sunrise and go to the southern edge of the main parking lot. Scan the top of Goat Island Mountain, about 2 miles south on the other side of the White River canyon. This is a distant view, and you'll need a scope to see the dots in the distance.

You may see goats while hiking west from

Sunrise on the Sourdough Ridge Trail until it joins the Wonderland Trail. One and a half miles from Sunrise and just west of Frozen Lake you'll come to a four-way trail junction. From here you'll have views of Mount Fremont, Burroughs Mountain, and part of the Berkeley Park area. From this junction trails go to these three areas, which are all places where goats are sometimes seen. Ask the rangers at Sunrise where the latest sightings have been, or ask hikers if they have seen goats (or marmots and pikas). You may locate goats from the junction and be able to hike closer to them on one of the trails or you may have to hike on a trail awhile before getting any sightings. Or you may hike all day and never see one. Such are the risks of wildlife viewing, but hey, you're in one of the most beautiful places in the world, so why worry?

East of Mount Rainier NP and right on the eastern edge of the William O. Douglas Wilderness Area is one of the most reliable places to see mountain goats in the Northwest and one of the places where people get the closest to them. Timberwolf Mountain is as high as Sunrise (just over 6400 feet), and a Forest Service road goes right to the top. The breathtaking panorama rivals any in the state with great views of the Goat Rocks and Mounts Rainier and Adams (30 and 40 miles distant, respectively) towering above the surrounding Cascades.

For a trip to Timberwolf Mountain a Wenatchee NF map is handy, but not essential. Forest Road 1500, also called the Bethel Ridge Rd in places, travels about 30 miles from State Hwy 410 at Nile Rd, south to US Hwy 12 near Rimrock Lake. The road is paved for about the first 10 miles heading south from Hwy 410; the rest is a good dirt road with some washboard. The last spur road up to Timberwolf is one lane, steeper and rougher, but still passable in a regular passenger car if the road is dry. If you have any doubts about road conditions, check with the Naches District ranger station.

You can start at either end of FR 1500—the distance from Hwy 410 is almost twice as long, but easily twice as pretty, as the route from US 12. Let's take the pretty route. About 25 miles northwest of Yakima, turn onto Nile Rd from Hwy 410, the Chinook Pass Highway. In about a mile and a half, turn left onto FR 1500 following signs to US 12. You'll come to several intersections; all but one are well marked with signs to US 12. Just about 10 miles from your start at Hwy 410 is an unmarked fork in the road—turn right. At 10.8 miles is a scenic vista turnout with a name-that-peak sign to help you get oriented and a good view of Timberwolf Mountain.

From the turnout, FR 1500 goes up and over the ridge that includes Timberwolf. A small, poorly marked spur road, #190, goes from FR 1500 to the top of the mountain. At 18.3 miles you'll see a road going to the right. The last time I was there, the only sign was a small, yellow diamond, stuck up in a tree on the left, indicating an intersection. After you turn right onto this road you may see the small brown stake hidden in the vegetation with 190 on it, but you should definitely see the sign that indicates a narrow, rough road. Two-and-a-quarter miles up this road and you're at the top.

Enjoy the view and start looking around the mountain right below you. Move around to get different viewing angles, and search areas of good habitat on nearby peaks and slopes. Ask anyone else up there if they have seen any goats (or other wildlife). Most people you encounter on a place like Timberwolf are interested in wildlife and can sometimes be a good source of information. On the other hand, you may hear some pretty colorful tales of dubious authenticity. If you don't find goats right away, make yourself comfortable, get out some snacks, enjoy the view, and hang out for several hours. You may also spot elk, mule deer, ravens, red-tailed hawks, mountain bluebirds, gray jays, Townsend's solitaires, and other mountain birds.

If you don't want to backtrack, follow FR 1500 south in the other direction to US 12. To reach Timberwolf Mountain from US 12, turn onto Bethel Ridge Rd just west of Hause Creek Campground. Coming from the east on US 12 the road sign is a bit hard to see, so watch for Hause Creek and get ready to turn right after you pass the campground. Coming from the west, from Rimrock Lake, there is a sign for Bethel Ridge Rd, and the green road sign is much more visible. After you turn onto Bethel Ridge Rd you'll see a sign that reads 1500. Stay on FR 1500, following the signs for Hwy 410. Main intersections are signed, but there are some unsigned roads around five and six miles that go to your right. Continue straight ahead on FR 1500, which is clearly the main road. After going 10.2 miles from US 12 you'll reach the poorly marked spur road #190, already described.

Our last spot is near the Goat Rocks Wilderness Area, just south of Mount Rainier NP. Backpackers regularly see mountain goats in the wilderness area, especially near—where else?—Goat Lake. For those who want to see some goats without backpacking, head for Stonewall Ridge, a geological feature along Johnson Creek south of Packwood. Try this spot in the morning, when the light is best. Take FR 21, Johnson Creek Rd, south from Hwy 12, just 2.7 miles west of Packwood.

Using this as your zero point, drive 9 miles and turn left onto FR 2140, which is considerably rougher. FR 2140 is narrow, with little room to pull over, but you'll find a few wide spots in the road at just over 0.5 and at one mile up the road from FR 21. These points will give you great views of Stonewall Ridge, rising up before you on the other side of Johnson Creek. Search the band of good habitat along the base of the cliffs. If you don't find any goats you can wait for awhile or go to the next viewpoint and then come back later if you still haven't found them. You'll probably need to visit both of these viewpoints, because each gives different viewing angles and the goats may be visible from one but not the other.

The second viewpoint for Stonewall Ridge is a bit tricky to describe. Get back on FR 21 and drive another 0.7 mile south. Just after you pass a small sign for Wright Pond on your left, you'll see a small, overgrown road that goes to the right as the road you are on goes uphill and makes a turn to the left. The last time I was there, this road was marked #107 with a small, brown stake hidden in the bushes, but it's not on the Gifford Pinchot NF map. Where this road leaves FR 21 there is plenty of room to pull over and park. Walk back down FR 21 until you can get a good view of Stonewall through the trees. Again search carefully, especially at the edge of the trees below the cliffs. If you don't find goats at either place, I'd suggest that you go back and wait up on FR 2140, which is off the main road and more scenic.

SUMMER SALMON AND TROUT

If one animal was picked to symbolize the Pacific Northwest it would surely have to be salmon. Some have defined the Northwest as "where a salmon can swim to," and others have called salmon "the silver thread that weaves through the entire tapestry of the Northwest ecosystem" or the "soul of the Northwest." To the first Americans living in the Northwest, salmon were the abundant and dependable food source that permitted the development of the wealthiest native cultures north of Mexico. And today, in a region packed with anglers, where fishing is sometimes treated as a spiritual quest, salmon are revered as the ultimate fish.

Who are the Pacific salmon? A newcomer to the region will hear more names for salmon than for different types of rain. There are seven species of salmon that belong to the genus *Oncorhynchus* that live in the northern Pacific and spawn in the rivers and streams of western North America, from Alaska to California. The group has been split up into species a number of different ways and will probably be changed again as we learn more about their complex genetics. Any difficulty keeping them straight is compounded by the multiple names for most species.

Chinook salmon are the largest and least abundant of our salmon. Big chinooks can reach 4 feet and weigh 100 pounds so they deserve their other common name, king or tyee, which means big chief. Chinook are found in large streams and rivers and many spawn far inland. The Columbia River Basin was the world's greatest producer of chinook, which gave the Columbia its reputation as the great salmon river and started the canning boom. Because chinook travel far up the biggest rivers in the region, they have been heavily impacted by dams.

The other salmon that travels far inland is the sockeye, also known as blueback, red or Alaska salmon. These are the most colorful salmon, turning a bright red with a green head before spawning, and are often depicted in artwork. Sockeye differ from the others in that they spawn in lakes, where the young fish mature before leaving for the sea. Some sockeye have become land-locked and are called kokanee.

Coho and chum are similar in size and appearance, but the chum is more widespread and abundant than the coho. Both commonly use coastal streams for spawning. Coho are also called silver salmon, and chum are called dog salmon. Both can reach a length of 3 feet and a weight of around 30 pounds, but most weigh closer to 10 pounds. The most abundant and the smallest of the fish usually called salmon is the pink salmon, also called humpback or humpy. Pink salmon are known for their rigid two-year life cycle, and in our region they spawn in odd years. They rarely spawn far from the sea and are the least dependent on freshwater. Pinks are found in large numbers only north of the Columbia River.

Two fish that are usually called trout are now considered part of this group. A strain of rainbow trout that go to sea and return to spawn in freshwater, just like other salmon, are called steelhead. Some steelheads survive their first spawning and can spawn again after returning to the sea. Steelheads are about the size of chum and coho and are highly prized game fish. There is also a strain of cutthroat trout that spend some time at sea and can also survive their first spawning. These trout are often called coastal cutthroat or sea-run cutthroat and are the smallest of the Pacific salmon. Because these sea-going trout spend so much time in freshwater, both steelhead and coastal cutthroat are very sensitive to habitat disturbance, especially to loss of riparian vegetation and silting, and have therefore been heavily impacted by logging.

Everyone living in the Northwest knows the amazing life cycle of the salmon. Many actually know the term *anadromous*, which describes fish, such as salmon and shad, that are born in freshwater, migrate to the sea where they live for an extended period, and then return up rivers and streams to spawn. Salmon are famous for their ability to return to spawn in the exact location where they were born, after years roaming the Pacific. How they are able to do this is still not entirely understood, although it is currently believed that they use the earth's magnetic field to some extent for navigation and that they "smell" their way back to their home stream. In the Northwest, the annual cycles of the salmon have been one of the most important rhythms in nature since the Pleistocene. Many animals, in addition to humans, have depended on them, and their death after spawning returns needed nutrients to the land.

Here's how to see returning salmon and resident trout other than catching them or skin diving. The most aesthetically pleasing way is that rare setting where you can actually see the fish in their natural habitat. When looking for fish in the wild it helps to use fish glasses—inexpensive polarized glasses that improve your ability to see through the water. These are available at any store with fishing gear. (Also see October for Fall Salmon Runs.)

The easiest way to see fish is at fish hatcheries, where you can often see artificial spawning and other hatchery operations in season. Some hatcheries have fish ladders or holding ponds where you can see fish, but many people find hatcheries too artificial. However, they can provide some excellent opportunities to see fish up close and often have informative educational exhibits and materials.

Another place to see returning salmon is at the fish-viewing facilities at the fish ladders of some dams. This is a mixed experience because even though you may get some great views of fish swimming under the water, you are seeing them at the very dams that have been the main cause of their decline.

▶ SUMMER SALMON AND TROUT BEST BETS OREGON

The North Umpqua River is famous for its summer steelhead fishing (flies only) and for its scenery. Thirty-four miles are designated as a Wild and Scenic River, and the road that follows the river, State Hwy 138, is designated the North Umpqua Scenic Byway. The BLM's Deadline Falls Watchable Wildlife Site is near the beginning of the North Umpqua Trail at the Swiftwater Recreation Site. The North Umpqua Trail follows the river for 79 miles, all the way to the Pacific Crest Trail. Go 22 miles east of Roseburg on Hwy 138, and then turn right a mile after Idleyld Park to cross over the North Umpqua River on the Swiftwater Bridge. Turn left immediately after crossing the Swiftwater Bridge into the parking area for the North Umpqua Trailhead. The first 0.25-mile section of the trail provides easy access to the Deadline Falls viewing site and goes through beautiful old-growth forest. During the summer you can see chinook and steelhead jumping the falls very early or late in the day.

Winchester Fish Viewing Area, on the Umpqua River near Roseburg, is perhaps the viewing area with the closest freeway access. Coming from the north on Interstate 5, take the exit for Winchester (Exit 129), and then turn left at the first stop to head east. At State Hwy 99 turn right to head south just a bit, and then turn left into the fish viewing area parking lot. The fish are using a ladder to pass an old dam on the Umpqua. Fish, including steelhead or chinook and possibly coho, can be seen almost any time of year.

The large dams on the Columbia River between Oregon and Washington have fish ladders and fish viewing facilities that are well-marked and easy to find. Bonneville and McNary dams have the best viewing, available on both the Oregon and Washington sides. Different runs of different species pass through at different times—the best time is in the middle of the summer when there are runs of summer chinook, summer steelhead, and sockeye. Because each dam stops a percentage of the fish, Bonneville has more than upstream McNary. Bonneville also has a large fish hatchery with outdoor display ponds containing huge specimens of several species, which can be seen any time of year. The fish hatchery is reached from the Oregon side by the Bonneville exit from Interstate 84.

▶ SUMMER SALMON AND TROUT BEST BETS WASHINGTON

The Little White Salmon NFH is well developed for visitors; everything for the public is universally accessible. For those interested in hatchery operations, large viewing windows are available to watch the artificial spawning when it's taking place. Underwater windows in the adult holding tanks, unusual at a hatchery, provide views of huge, mature adults. Fish can also be seen jumping up the ladder and in the river. This is the oldest federal fish hatchery on the Columbia and celebrated its centennial in 1996.

Starting in Stevenson drive 12.5 miles west on State Hwy 14, and then turn left just before the bridge over the Little White Salmon River. Drive north about a mile along the river and through the lower part of the hatchery to the upper area. A run of spring chinook occurs from May through August, and spawning (artificial) takes place from mid-July into August. A good fall run of coho and fall chinook occurs from October to mid-November.

Leavenworth NFH opened in 1940 as the world's largest salmon hatchery to try to make up for the loss of salmon caused by Grand Coulee Dam, which completely blocks fish from going any farther up the Columbia. The hatchery now produces about 2,500,000 spring chinook and 100,000 steelhead each year and offers displays and an interpretive trail that describes the history and operations of the hatchery. The peak of the returning chinook is in July when adults can be seen in the holding tanks as well as in Icicle Creek from the interpretive trail bridge. Head west from Leavenworth on Hwy 2 and just outside of town turn south on Icicle Rd. Watch for the hatchery sign in 1.5 miles and turn left. To see wild salmon spawning in the Wenatchee River, come in October for the Salmon Festival.

Migrating salmon can be seen in Seattle at the Lake Washington Ship Canal fish ladder, part of the Chittenden Locks in the Ballard neighborhood. Chinook, coho, sockeye, steelhead, and coastal cutthroat pass through the ladder at various times of year, but the most action is from early July through September. The viewing area has interpretive displays and other information. The fish ladder can be reached from the north side of the canal, which has the main visitor facilities and botanical gardens, or from the south side for a more direct route.

To approach from the north get onto NW Market St in the Ballard neighborhood, heading west until you pass 28th Ave NW. Veer to the left onto 54th St, and then in 4 blocks turn left into the visitor parking area. This route is well signed. The southside approach, near Discovery Park, is much less crowded and hectic. Get on Commodore Way going west from Emerson St at Fisherman's Terminal, near the Ballard Bridge. Take Commodore Way to Commodore Park, park there, and walk to the fish ladder.

▶ SUMMER SALMON AND TROUT BEST BETS BRITISH COLUMBIA

If you really want to see salmon in British Columbia, you need to get the great little booklet *Where and When to See Salmon* from Fisheries and Oceans Canada. There are 54 sites listed for of British Columbia, 30 of them within our southwestern region.

Stamp Falls PP, on Vancouver Island, offers a chance to see wild fish jumping the falls in a dramatic setting. A run of sockeye move up the Stamp River from mid-July through August, followed by coho in August and September and chinook in September and October. Drive west on Hwy 4 through Port Alberni (a good stop on the way to Pacific Rim NP), and on the west side of town turn north on Beaver Creek Rd. After 7 miles watch for the park sign, and then turn to the left. Drive through the park to the locked gate, and then continue on foot down the road, which becomes the trail. At the end of the trail is an overlook of a large pool where the fish pile up waiting to go up the falls or up the ladder built to make the trip easier. There are good interpretive signs along the trail and a nice camping area in the park.

The Capilano Fish Hatchery, in Capilano River RP off Capilano Rd, provides a chance to see salmon right in North Vancouver. It's a major tourist attraction so try to come early or late in the day. Although this is an artificial hatchery setting, it has some great exhibits and fish are usually on view from July through October.

JULY'S NATURE NUGGETS

OSPREY Osprey are common summer residents along rivers and at many lakes in the Northwest. If you spend any time in the summer around rivers and lakes, you'll see osprey. The male and female arrive separately in March, unite with their former mate, and immediately begin establishing their territory and rebuilding their nest from previous years. The breeding season lasts until the end of August, with plenty of activity to see all summer. Most osprey have headed south by October.

Crane Prairie Reservoir, about 35 miles southeast of Bend, Oregon, is a major osprey nesting area because of the large number of snags. There are also a few nesting bald eagles. This mountain reservoir is on the Cascades Lakes Highway (FR 46) and can most quickly be reached from Bend by going 15 miles south on US Hwy 97 and then 21 miles west on FR 40, the road to Sunriver. Turn left from FR 40 onto FR 46 to go down the west side of the reservoir to Quinn River CG. Half a mile south of the campground is a wide spot in the road where you park for the Osprey Point Observation Trail (signed). Walk to the shore for great views of osprey and bald eagles as well as waterfowl. Rock Creek, Crane Prairie, and Cow Meadow campgrounds also have good wildlife viewing opportunities.

SUMMER WEEDS White Queen Anne's lace and blue chicory, two of our most abundant and heartiest wildflowers, grow along many roads that haven't been sprayed and in other disturbed areas on the west side. Both are European introductions and are commonly called weeds. However, weediness is in the eye of the beholder, and most folks find them a beautiful addition to the midsummer landscape, especially with their tendency to grow in trashed-out places that need some natural color. Queen Anne's lace is also known as wild carrot and is presumed to be the wild source of our domesticated carrot. It seems to have successfully immigrated to America on its own. However, chicory was brought here intentionally to be grown commercially as a coffee substitute (the roots are roasted) and escaped into the wild. The leaves have been a choice salad green since the time of the ancient Greeks and are still popular in parts of Europe.

CRANE FLIES Leave your windows or doors open and the lights on in your house this month, and you can be pretty sure of getting some crane flies as house guests. These impressive insects are often called mosquito hawks but, unfortunately, do not eat mosquitoes. Many people seeing them for the first time are horrified because they look like humongous mosquitoes and the thought of getting bitten by one of these big bruisers is pretty creepy. Not to fear, these gentile giants from the largest family of flies in the world are as harmless as can be; many of them don't even eat as adults. Those adults that do eat primarily sip nectar or nibble on rotten plants, although a few apparently do eat tiny insects. The larvae are tough-skinned maggots that live in decaying vegetation, moist soil, or streams. A few, called leather jackets, live in lawns and are considered a pest. Be careful as you escort them back outside, their legs are notorious for falling off easily.

GOING BATTY: A CLOSER LOOK

Figure this one out: the more ancient forests are cut down, the more people will be bitten by mosquitoes. What? How does that one work? The answer is a classic example of how everything in an ecosystem is interconnected. The important link in this relationship is bats. Bats eat mosquitoes. Not just a few mosquitoes, but as many as 1000 to 2000 per bat, every night, for some species. In the Pacific Northwest most bats roost (sleep or rest) in old trees and snags when they are not hibernating. Old trees and snags are the classic components of ancient forests, and bat populations are dropping as this type of habitat disappears. Fewer roosting sites mean fewer bats; fewer bats mean more mosquitoes.

Bats are undeserving of the bad time we've made for them. Any animal that eats insects, our main competitors on this planet for food, usually has a good reputation. But in some parts of the world, mainly America and temperate Europe, bats are one of the most feared, misunderstood, and persecuted animals. Bat populations, suffering from pesticides, loss of habitat, and other human disturbances, are dropping in many parts of the world. The greatest threat to bats in North America today is human disturbance to bats roosting in caves during hibernation and during the period when the females are raising the young.

Fortunately, public knowledge and attitude about bats has recently changed for the better, thanks to the efforts of Bat Conservation International, some Audubon societies, the National Wildlife Federation, the non-game programs of wildlife agencies, and other groups. We have even had postage stamps with bats. More people are becoming aware that bats are harmless and beneficial and are becoming concerned about declining bat populations. Some bat fanciers have responded by putting up bat houses to provide roosting habitat. A small industry has blossomed making and selling bat houses and bat house kits.

Bats deserve our respect and appreciation. They are, after all, the only mammal that has true flight. Bats are often mistaken for rodents and described as "flying mice," but they are not rodents. It would be more accurate to call them "flying shrews." Scientists now think they may be most closely related to us primates. One thing is clear—they have been very successful. Bats are an ancient type of mammal, and at present almost a quarter of all species of mammals in the world are bats. They dominate the nighttime sky and are the main predator of nocturnal flying insects.

It's downright scary to imagine what would happen if there were no bats. Studies have estimated that one huge colony of bats in Braken Cave, Texas, eats 250,000 pounds of insects every night. That's 45,625 tons of bugs a year. In just one part of Texas. I know, I know, it just doesn't seem possible that there are that many bugs, even in Texas, but the figures are entirely reasonable. Can you imagine what it would be like if there were no bats eating these bugs? Among the many insects bats eat are corn borer and cutworm moths, potato beetles, and grasshoppers, some of the worst agricultural pests. In the tropics bats are also extremely important as pollinators and seed dispersal agents.

Despite some improvement in bat public relations, many of the Euro-American myths about bats still prevail. Among the most common myths: they are aggressive and vicious, they get tangled in people's hair, they are blind, and most of them have rabies. All of these are far from the truth.

People who have worked with bats extensively know that they are not vicious or even ill-tempered, but instead are very gentle and unaggressive animals. And why would a bat want to get into someone's hair? Isn't it a bit absurd to think that an animal that can precisely determine the location and movement of a mosquito flying at night couldn't avoid flying into a human head? No one really knows the origin of this bats-in-hair fear, but it is possible, of course, that it has happened a few times over the centuries. But bats do not try to get into people's hair. Blind as a bat? Not quite. Bats have eyes, and most of them can probably see about as well as we can, except for color.

Like most mammals, bats can get rabies. However they are not infected at a rate any higher than other mammals, and most of the rabid bat stories in the news media are distorted or just plain not true. Everyone, children especially, should know not to touch wild animals except under well-known, safe circumstances, such as catching a garter snake or picking up an earthworm. Always be especially cautious if an animal is acting oddly, which for most wild animals means that they actually let you touch them. True, a few people have gotten rabies from bites by rabid bats (that they picked up), but the number is less than one person every two or three years in North America. You have a much greater chance of getting rabies from a dog or cat.

So who's who in our regional bat fauna? Here are some brief sketches of the most common and conspicuous bats in the Pacific Northwest:

LITTLE BROWN BAT These bats are just what the name says—small (9-inch wingspan) and brown. Little browns are the most common bat in the Northwest and are most commonly seen near water. They use a wide variety of places for summer roosts, including buildings, where they can form large colonies—placing them in conflict with humans. Little brown bats are often seen roosting and flying with large brown bats. Both are sometimes seen feeding around streetlights.

BIG BROWN BAT Another common and widely distributed bat. The hardy big brown bat is the only bat that overwinters in Canada. This is another great bat name—they are big (13 to 14 inches) and brown, with short, black ears. They are most common near forests and water, but are frequently seen in cities and towns. Big browns readily use buildings (sometimes all year) where, like their small cousin, they can form large colonies—also placing them in occasional conflict with people.

PALLID BAT One of our bigger bats (14 to 16 inches), the pallid bat has pale brown to tan fur and huge ears. They occur locally on the east side in rocky areas and canyons. Pallid bats are unusual in that they usually feed on the ground and their diet includes scorpions. These bats rely heavily on caves, so it's no surprise that they are on the Oregon Sensitive Species List.

WESTERN PIPISTRELLE This is the smallest bat in the United States and seems to be teamed up with the pallid bat as another pale bat of east-side river canyons. Although generally buffy, their contrasting black feet, face, and ears help to identify them in the unlikely case you ever got close to one. These bats come out earlier than most; you can see them flying over rivers in desert canyons before sunset.

HOARY BAT The largest bat in North America (up to 17 inches) is also the most widely distributed. Their brown fur is tipped with white (hence, the "hoary"), and they have an orange to yellow throat collar. Hoary bats are solitary and live in forests and woodlands, including wooded areas of towns, and roost in trees. They are unusual in almost always giving birth to twins. The huge drop in their population recently is probably a result of the loss of ancient forests.

Because bats are so sensitive to disturbance, biologists, resource managers, and responsible spelunkers do not reveal the locations of bat roosts. Instead of seeing bats by looking for their roost, find the places where they feed and you can watch them in action.

The strategy for finding a bat is to think like a bat: know the animal's needs, and pick the right habitat and the right time, which during summer is dusk—when lots of insects are flying around. Find a good spot just before sunset, settle in comfortably, and wait. Many bats start feeding during twilight, and you can watch them as long as the light lasts. Under these conditions you are basically watching silhouettes and can't see any markings or colors, making identification pretty tough. I've never had the opportunity to go out batting (?) with an expert, but I'm sure there are those who can identify some species flying in the twilight by their size, shape, and behavior.

To find the right habitat for bats, look for places that have an abundance of flying insects. Generally, over quiet bodies of water is excellent. On the west side small, quiet ponds with trees nearby are best although quiet stretches of rivers may be just as active in some areas. Small lakes and ponds are also good places to look in the mountains, and sometimes wet meadows will also have good concentrations. On the drier east side water plays an even bigger role in concentrating feeding bats and most rocky canyons with water flowing in them will have bats, mainly pallid bats and the western pipistrelle. People river rafting in the summer, especially in the warmer, dryer areas, will regularly see bats around sunset. Oh yes, don't forget to slather yourself with insect repellent before going bat watching.

People should not look for bats in caves; the biggest cause of the decline of bat populations is thought to be human disturbance of bats roosting and hibernating in caves. If you do happen upon roosting bats, try to leave the area immediately without disturbing the bats in any way. If you have problems with bats roosting in a building, seek advice from your state wildlife department or read *America's Neighborhood Bats*. The basic tactic is to wait till the bats leave, and then seal their entrance before they return.

AUGUST

ORCA

Quick, what's the most widely distributed mammal in the world, other than us humans? From the chapter title you probably guessed the killer whale or orca. There has been a fairly recent shift in this animal's name from killer whale to orca, but both are still in use. The switch to orca favors accuracy because orcas are technically not whales, but rather are the largest members of the dolphin family, but this is taxonomic nit-picking because both are cetaceans. The killer part of the name, however, is quite accurate because orcas are the top predator in the world's oceans. They have been known to eat just about everything, including fish, seals, porpoises, and even whales but not, interestingly enough, humans—which are their only predators.

Orcas are sometimes called wolves of the sea, because they live in family packs and cooperatively hunt. Orcas are very social mammals, living their entire lives in a matrilineal group that includes a female and her offspring, sometimes of several generations. The bond between a mother and her young is strong; it is believed that most orcas rarely leave their mother during their lives. Matrilineal groups may join together to form larger groups or pods.

In the Salish Sea there are two types of orca—residents and transients. The three southern resident pods, the best studied orcas in the world, are large (about 20 to 40 members), are very stable, and usually stay in the waters off the southern end of Vancouver from May to October. Transient pods are much smaller (2 to 6 members), travel long distances, and are much less predictable. Transient orcas primarily eat mammals while the resident orcas feed almost entirely on fish—especially salmon. The two types of orcas also have different types of vocalization—the clicking sounds used for echolocation and a variety of whistles and squeals used in communication with other

Fritillary butterflies are common in mountain meadows.

237

members of the pod. The resident pods are real chatterboxes, and each pod has its own distinctive dialect.

The history of the relationship between humans and orcas in the past is a strange story. Orcas used to be called killer whales and were regularly portrayed as the most fearsome, savage predators in the seas. For years fishermen shot them whenever they had the chance. Then in 1965 Namu became the first performing killer whale in captivity at the Seattle Aquarium. Ted Griffin, owner of the aquarium, had guessed right. Because killer whales are really dolphins, Griffin figured, they should be able to be tamed and trained as dolphins had been for years. Namu and his performing partner, Griffin, were a huge success until Namu died just under a year after being captured. But that was just the beginning of the captive killer whale era. Many more were captured from the waters around Washington and British Columbia, and 50 young killer whales were sold to marine theme parks throughout the world. They became superstars of the animal world, and attitudes about these animals seemed to change overnight. Many people became fascinated with these clearly intelligent, charismatic animals, scientists included, and the more that was discovered, the more people wanted to know.

More than a few people wanted to know just what the capture of these killer whales was doing to the killer whale population in Northwest waters. The general assumption had been that the captured animals were just some of the thousands of killer whales roaming the world's oceans that happened to come into our Northwest waters on their journeys. In 1971 Oceans and Fisheries Canada hired marine biologist Mike Bigg to do a census of killer whales in the waters around British Columbia. His first estimate was that there were only about 200–300 and that they were actually a resident population. Uh-oh, maybe a whole generation of young killer whales were being removed from this population.

The United States passed the Marine Mammal Protection Act in 1972. In 1976, under contract with the US National Marine Fisheries Service, Ken Balcomb started what has become the longest continuous study of cetaceans. Ken counted about 70 individual killer whales in the waters surrounding the San Juan Islands, and that year Washington State closed its waters to the capture of killer whales.

In the meantime, the killer whales in captivity played with their keepers, performed amazing stunts, displayed their intelligence, and totally charmed everyone who saw them. The savage killer of the sea had a total image change and got a new name. People no longer wanted the negative moniker killer whale. More and more people started using orca from the scientific name *Orcinus orca*, and now orca is a common word, at least in the Pacific Northwest. I've seen lots of kids, my daughter included, sleeping with their cuddly, stuffed toy orca. The gradual change in attitude toward orca and other whales is one of the most encouraging examples of knowledge bringing understanding and appreciation, and eventually respect and protection, for wildlife. The 1990s saga of Keiko, the orca in the movie *Free Willy*, showed the incredible human compassion for these marine mammals.

How ironic that our change in attitude may now be hurting our orcas as they get loved to death. As orcas became popular and the habits of the southern resident orcas became well known, a multi-million dollar whale-watching industry developed. In 2007 the Whale Museum estimated that every year 500,000 people go whale watching on commercial whale-watching boats in the waters around the San Juans Islands and southern Vancouver Island. Another 3000–8000 watch whales from their private boats. In the late 1990s there was a loss of 20 orcas from the southern resident population, the biggest loss since the period of captures. In 2005 the southern resident population of killer whales was listed as an Endangered Species by the US National Marine Fisheries Service. In 2008 a major controversy rages about the role of commercial whale watching in the decline of orcas. However, two other significant factors clearly play a part. One is the huge decline in the Salish Sea salmon population, the resident orca pods' main food, in the 1990s. Global oceanic pollution is also taking its toll on many marine organisms. Toxic pollution in Salish Sea waters specifically is affecting the health of orcas—the extent is just being discovered. One of the latest toxic threats to be identified to the surprise of many is flame retardant (polybrominated diphenyl ethers), which is expected to surpass PCBs as the leading contaminant in orcas. Who would have thought that so many tons of flame retardant end up in the Salish Sea?

Classification as endangered species in both Canada and the United States should bring funds for research and protection and hopefully will be one more force toward cleaning up marine waters. The Whale Museum and the

Whale Watch Operators Association Northwest are working on guidelines for whale-watching behavior and self-management. There are also groups advocating strong legal regulation of whale watching and boycotting of whale-watching boat trips.

▶ ORCA BEST BETS WASHINGTON

The first whale-watching park in the nation is still considered the best place anywhere to see orcas from land. Lime Kiln Point SP is on the west coast of San Juan Island, about 9 miles from Friday Harbor. The park has restrooms, trails to the beach, and picnic tables overlooking Haro Strait, an area used regularly during the summer by all three resident pods. Although the lighting is best in the morning, whales can be seen any time of day. This is a good test of patience; you might see orcas three times in an hour or once in two days, so go prepared to wait. Why not take a comfortable folding chaise lounge, snacks, your binoculars, and just hang out all day? It hasn't happened to me, but the word is that sometimes you can even hear the orcas blow when they come up for air. While watching for orcas, you'll also be able to see numerous marine birds and actually have a chance, although small, of spotting Dall's and harbor porpoises and minke whales. Unfortunately, the best time of year to see orcas is in the summer when the popular San Juans are overrun with visitors. Orcas are regularly seen in May and September, however, which are generally better times to visit the island. In May the wildflowers and birding are also excellent.

To get to Lime Kiln Point SP from Friday Harbor, head southwest on Spring St and stay on it as it turns into San Juan Valley Rd. Turn left on Douglas Rd after passing the airport and head south until it turns to the west and becomes Bailer Hill Rd. Bailer Hill Rd will then turn into West Side Rd, which goes into the park. This is a day-use only park.

Another great place on San Juan Island for seeing orca from land is San Juan County Park, just up the coast from Lime Kiln. This park has developed campsites, water, flush toilets, and a boat ramp. It is popular with kayakers because you are right on the water. Just head north on Westside Rd for a couple of miles from Lime Kiln. Reservations are highly recommended in summer. This park is near English Camp with its fabulous view from Mount Young.

Travel on the ferries is much cheaper and easier if you don't take a car. Public transportation is available on San Juan Island from San Juan Transit, which goes from Friday Harbor to Lime Kiln Point SP, San Juan County Park, and the other main points of interest on the island. While in Friday Harbor, be sure to visit The Whale Museum, just a couple of blocks from the ferry. While on the island, check out the birding and scenery at both American and British camps.

You can see orcas from any of the ferries plying the waters of the Salish Sea, but your chances are best from the Anacortes–Sydney or Anacortes–San Juan Island ferries. These routes don't go on the west side of San Juan Island, however, so your odds are not great. Occasionally orcas are seen from shore throughout much of the Salish Sea, even from downtown Seattle.

▶ **ORCA BEST BETS** BRITISH COLUMBIA

Orcas are sometimes seen from the Victoria breakwater along the southeast coast of Vancouver Island at spots such as Clover Point and the Ogden Breakwater. There is always a chance of spotting them from ferries in the Strait of Georgia. But the best place in the world to see orcas is at the other end of the island, up north near Port McNeil.

Johnstone Strait is farther north than other recommendations in this book, but to not include it in a chapter on orcas would be gross negligence. The northern resident population of about 200 orcas frequent this area during the summer and into fall. A particularly favorite spot is Robson Bight (Michael Bigg) Ecological Reserve where the orcas like to rub themselves on shallow pebble beaches. No one knows why they do this, but "because it feels good" is certainly in the running for such an intelligent animal. Because this is such a sensitive site (I wouldn't want to be interrupted in the middle of a nice back rub myself), Robson Bight is closed to entry by humans, on foot or by boat. It's possible to see orcas from land near Telegraph Cove, but the best way to get a good look at these animals is by boat. Here again there is concern about whale-watching boats disturbing the animals, but the number of boats and visitors per year is much lower than it is at the southern end of Vancouver Island. There are a modest number of tour companies operating out of Port McNeil, Telegraph Cove, and Sayward that emphasize proper operating procedures for the animals' welfare.

MARMOTS AND PIKAS

Summer is time for hiking in the mountains, and journeys into the alpine and subalpine zones bring us into contact with two charming mammals that are the favorites of many backpackers—marmots and pikas. Marmots are the biggest squirrels in the world; a big, hoary marmot perched on a rock is about as impressive as rodents get. Often living near the marmots are the smaller pikas. A common misconception is that pikas are also rodents, sort of a North American Guinea pig, but they are actually small relatives of rabbits (lagomorphs). Both these mammals are notable because they live year-round in one of the harshest environments on Earth. Much of their range is essentially uninhabitable for half the year, and surviving the winter is their greatest challenge. Interestingly, the two animals take completely different approaches in adapting to this harsh climate.

To survive a hard winter, a mammal can migrate, hibernate, or accommodate. Elk are a good example of a mammal that migrates, marmots are champion hibernators, and the pika accommodates with a unique behavioral adaptation it shares with humans.

Like all lagomorphs, pikas don't hibernate. Their small size makes migration impractical. They have adapted to the harsh alpine winter by living in a microhabitat that provides excellent shelter and by storing food. Pikas live in rockslides and talus slopes that border mountain meadows. The pile of rocks provides excellent shelter and the meadows provide the food. Storing food is common in rodents, but it's not done by any of the pika's relatives, so this behavior is unusual. Some foods, such as seeds, are easily storied but the pika eats greens—grasses, sedges, and herbs. How are these stored? The same way we humans store grasses and certain herbs—by drying the plants to make hay.

All summer long the busy little pika gathers favorite food plants and lays the plants on the rocks to dry in the sun. When the hay is ready, it is moved down into the chambers and passageways between the rocks or piled under large overhanging boulders. When snow covers the rocks the pika remains active, moving through its territory of tunnels under the snow and eating its hay. Pikas are very territorial and defend their hay stacks from others who try to raid their stores.

Marmots store food also, but in a different way. Marmots eat like crazy all summer long, building up large fat reserves in their eventually quite rotund bodies. A large adult marmot can be 50% body fat at the beginning of hibernation. Then they do that slickest of endotherm tricks, they "go ecto" (ectothermic, that is). Their body temperature drops to just above freezing and their breathing, heart rate, and metabolic processes slow dramatically. In this torpid state the marmot uses very little energy, and with enough stored fat it can remain in hibernation for seven, eight, or even nine months. The main cause of marmot mortality is the winter death of the young marmots born the previous spring. It is much more difficult for a smaller animal to conserve body heat and store enough fat; three out of four marmots don't make it through their first winter. To help conserve heat a colony of marmots may hibernate together in a large clump.

Marmots also live in large rocks near mountain meadows, so it's not uncommon to see both marmots and pikas living close to each other. Both are also diurnal and quite vocal, making them much easier to find and to watch than most other mammals. Marmots whistle and are often called whistler, whistle pig, or siffleur (French-Canadian for whistler). The hoary marmot

makes a loud, shrill, human-like whistle that startles (or greets) many hikers in the subalpine meadows. The call of the pika is also whistle-like but is
better described as a high bleat, with a bit of a nasal character. It doesn't take
long to tell the two apart and they both become welcome sounds of the high
country. Both can get acclimated to people and become quiet tame, making
it possible to watch pikas making hay and marmots chowing down or basking in the sun.

Unfortunately, marmots can get too tame and many get fed by hikers along
busy trails. Such artificial feeding by people can lead to a number of problems
and park managers in Canada and the United States are constantly pleading
with visitors to not feed the wildlife, including those adorable rodents. It is
illegal in both countries to feed wildlife in national and provincial parks, but
of course no one is going to get hauled off to jail for giving gorp to a chip-
munk. It is up to us to resist the urge to feed those cute little critters.

Marmots and pikas both have an interesting distribution that can only
be explained by the climactic changes that took place during the Pleistocene Epoch (also known as the ice age). Pikas are found on mountaintops
throughout the West from British Columbia to New Mexico. Many populations are on the peaks of mountains in the Great Basin that are isolated from
each other by miles of desert. Biologists who study animal geography have
been fascinated by the pika's distribution for years. It now seems accepted
that about 10,000 years ago pikas were widely, and more evenly, distributed
throughout the West, south of the glaciers. As the glaciers retreated and the
climate got hotter and drier, the pikas retreated northward with the glaciers,
except for some populations that retreated up the slopes to the subalpine zone
in the higher mountains. Populations of pikas that didn't make it into areas
with sufficient habitat became extinct. Isolated populations of the same species are a classic setup for the evolution of new species, so scientists are now
studying the genetics of these Pleistocene pockets of pikas.

Marmots are thought to have a similar history, except that the four kinds
of marmots in our area (and a fifth nearby) are currently considered separate species by most biologists. The yellow-bellied marmot is by far the most
widespread and abundant marmot in the West and occurs from the Cascades
east in our region. It lives in a much wider range of habitats and elevations
than other marmots, in many kinds of rocky situations from near sea level to

alpine areas and even around old log piles and buildings. It can be common in rimrock in the eastern part of our states.

The other three marmot species are all alpine specialists, living only near timberline or above in Northwest mountains. The hoary marmot has the largest range of the three, from Alaska to the Cascades and Rockies in Washington, Idaho, and Montana. Where the ranges of the yellow-bellied and the hoary overlap, the hoary seems to displace the yellow-bellied in the higher elevations. The Olympic marmot is found only in the Olympic Mountains and the Vancouver marmot, probably North America's rarest mammal, is found only in a small area on Vancouver Island. The Olympic and Vancouver marmots are believed to be very closely related to the hoary marmot and to represent two island populations that became isolated by the retreat of the glaciers. Some biologists feel that all three are really one species (as with the pika populations), and it's situations like this that challenge our ideas about what constitutes a species.

Regardless of their fascinating evolutionary history, these animals are two of the most pleasant companions a hiker in the high country could have. Certainly either one would be a good candidate if one were to choose a totem of the high places in western mountains.

▶ MARMOTS AND PIKAS BEST BETS OREGON

The first time I was hiking in the Columbia River Gorge and heard a pika bleat I couldn't believe my ears. I had never seen nor heard one below 6000 feet before and there I was at only about 400 feet. What was going on? I looked around and sure enough the habitat looked great, a huge talus slope of large chunks of Columbia River basalt. And there it was—a pika in a classic pose on the edge of a large boulder. It gave another bleat and disappeared into the cracks in the rocks. I didn't know it then, but I had just seen one of the lowest pikas in the world. The Gorge is a slice through the Cascades and the steep cliffs of the Gorge are just 20 miles from the top of

Mount Hood, the highest spot in Oregon. This steep and short descent from the alpine zone has allowed pikas to colonize good habitat almost to the river. From the Multnomah Falls visitor area you can hike to the top of Multnomah Falls on the Larch Mount Trail (#441) or to Oneonta Gorge and Horsetail Falls on the Ak-Wanee Trail (#400). Within the first two miles of both trails you traverse some large rockslides, which have traditionally been home to some pikas.

The only species of marmot in Oregon is the yellow-bellied marmot, which can be found from subalpine meadows to desert rimrock, from the Cascades to eastern Oregon. I have found yellow-bellied marmots to be less predictable and less conspicuous than the hoary. I have most regularly seen them in rimrock areas near good forage, specifically around Malheur NWR.

▶ **MARMOTS AND PIKAS BEST BETS** WASHINGTON

Hoary marmots and pikas are frequently seen, and heard, by those hiking near or above timberline in the Washington Cascades. The Hart's Pass area in the North Cascades is great for finding both and is covered in September (Raptor Migration). To the south both Mount Adams and Mount Rainier have trails that circle the peaks, and it would be hard to spend much time hiking either one without seeing both animals. In Mount Rainier the eastern section of the Wonderland Trail, which goes through Summer Land and Ohanapecosh Park, is loaded with marmots and a smaller number of pikas but requires a backpacking trip. To see both animals on a pleasant day hike you can't beat the Sourdough Ridge Trail out of Sunrise. You'll also see lots of mountain wildflowers and possibly mountain goats on this trail, as well as some of the most awesome scenery in the Northwest, making the Sunrise area one of the must-see places in this part of the world.

The Sourdough Ridge Trail starts between the ranger station and restrooms at Sunrise and there is self-guiding brochure for the trail. The trail goes west 1.5 miles to a major trail junction just past Frozen Lake. Pikas can usually be seen in the section just before Frozen Lake and marmots are often seen around the trail junction. From the junction trails go to Mount Fremont, Burroughs Mount, and Berkeley Park, and both animals can be seen from any of these routes. The most popular area in Mount Rainier NP is Paradise, on the south side, where there are a number of trails and visitor services. Paradise is a good spot for marmots and is well known for its wildflowers, but can be very crowded on summer weekends.

The Olympic marmot is found only in the Olympic Mountains and can easily be seen in Olympic NP. Hurricane Ridge is a developed visitor area that is very popular and Olympic marmots are regularly seen there. Hurricane Ridge is reached by a main park road from the park headquarters and visitor center in Port Angeles. A map of the Hurricane Ridge nature trails actually shows the location of a marmot colony on the High Ridge Trail. If you don't see them there try the Hurricane Hill Trail or the road to Obstruction Point. You will probably see deer begging for food. Please remember it is important not to feed them.

▶ **MARMOTS AND PIKAS BEST BETS** BRITISH COLUMBIA

The North Cascades of Washington continue into Canada's Manning PP. Here is another area that combines the pleasures of mountain wildflowers with the charming company of these two mountain mammals. The Heather and Paintbrush trails in the Blackwall Peak area are well known for marmots and pikas, as well as for the spectacular floral display. Naturalists conduct guided walks in this area in summer. The marmots here have become incorrigible beggars and the park staff would really appreciate your help keeping these guys on a natural foods diet.

FALL SHOREBIRD MIGRATION

It's hard to get used to the idea that fall for shorebirds starts at the end of July. Shorebirds typically spend a very short period of time at their northern breeding grounds. In some species, the adults of one sex will actually head south soon after the eggs hatch and leave the other parent to take care of the babies. It is also common for the adults to leave before the young have fledged and the juveniles left behind may arrive in our area as much as a month later. For many species, these juveniles have a plumage that is distinct from the adults.

Shorebirds migrating in fall travel at a more leisurely pace than they do during the spring. Because different age groups, and sometimes different sexes, migrate at different times, fall migration is spread out over a much longer period of time than in the spring. Each species generally has about a three-month migration period sometime between September and October. A much greater variety of species in any one area occurs during fall migration, in part because some, especially inexperienced juveniles, wander and get lost. Fall is also the time when most rarities, like lost Asian peeps, show up along our coast. This means that for shorebirds, fall migration provides more birding excitement than the spring.

Shorebirds present some really tough identification problems, especially the smaller sandpipers, often called peeps. During fall migration, adults may be in breeding plumage, winter plumage, or somewhere in between. Add to this the juvenile plumage and the difference between sexes in some species, and it's clear why fall is by far the most challenging for identification. There is also the undeniable fact that shorebirds are a fairly homogeneous group—many of them look much alike, especially in the nonbreeding plumages.

Dennis Paulson has some excellent suggestions for shorebird identification in his comprehensive book on Northwest shorebirds. Start in winter when the fewest species are around, and keep going into spring, adding new species one by one as they come through in breeding plumage. During May and June study the few breeders present, and by July when fall migration starts, you may be ready for the onslaught. Learn the easy ones first—killdeer, black oystercatcher, American avocet—before taking on the peeps. "Take advantage of flocks" may seem like odd advice, but shorebirds are found regularly in mixed flocks. In these situations, you can best judge the size of many shorebirds and other characteristics by comparing them with the ones you already know. I'm always amazed by how much the perceived size of a bird can change depending on what other bird may be nearby.

To see shorebirds in the Northwest, find an area with good mudflats, get there a good hour before high tide, and watch as the tide comes in. The high tide covers most, or maybe even all, of the mudflats in an estuary and sometimes you'll see shorebirds frantically trying to get a last meal before the flats are covered. Sometimes it's just as good to get to your selected spot just after high tide and watch as the tide goes out. Then you'll see them pile into the mudflat buffet as the tide goes out and exposes the feeding areas that haven't been exposed for several hours. Do not go looking for shorebirds in our estuaries at low tide; the birds could literally be miles away.

One almost essential aid for shorebird identification is a spotting scope. This is a significant expense because you need a tripod to go with the scope. You can get a good scope for a few hundred dollars. Tripods designed for cameras usually have too many adjustments and take too long to set up and move to the bird. It is wonderful if you can afford to get a Manfrotto tripod and not waste your time and money on the many worthless tripods that are out there.

The Best Bets for A Million Shorebirds (April) are also good for fall, but as you will see, fall shorebirds have more Best Bets. A few shorebirds are usually seen in the fall, but not in the spring, so be on special alert for these: the two golden-plovers; lesser yellowlegs; and a group considered rare, but regular—Baird's, pectoral, sharp-tailed, stilt, and buff-breasted sandpipers. Red phalaropes are common fall migrants but are usually well offshore and are best seen by boat.

▶ FALL SHOREBIRD MIGRATION BEST BETS OREGON

With 17 main estuaries Oregon has plenty of good shorebird habitat. Any time you are on the coast from August to October keep your eyes out for accessible mudflats and check them around high tide. The northeastern tip of the state, Clatsop Spit, juts into the mouth of the Columbia River and is the site of the South Jetty of the Columbia River, well known by birders throughout the state as "the" south jetty. This area is within Fort Stevens SP, reached from US Hwy 101 between Astoria and Seaside. Follow signs to the park and once there follow signs to the south jetty and parking lot C. During high tides birds come to the small ponds north and east of the parking lot. Use the observation tower at parking lot C to

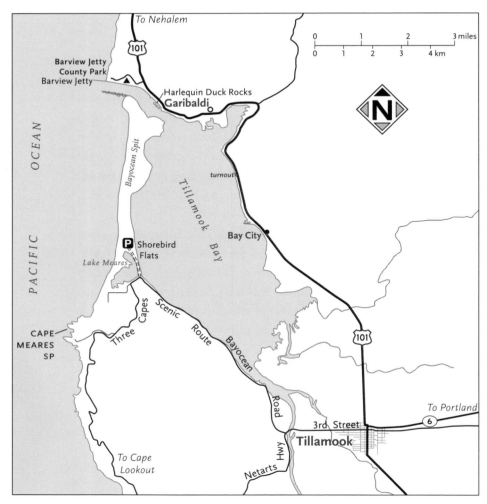

TILLAMOOK BAY AREA

get the big picture and to look in the ocean for wildlife. After checking the small ponds near C, go to parking lot D where a wildlife observation blind overlooks the Trestle Bay Wetlands. You may see birds from the blind, or you may have better luck walking along the shoreline near the blind. Trestle Bay is usually good for waterfowl and other waterbirds and can be great for shorebirds if the tide is right.

Bayocean Spit separates Tillamook Bay from the ocean and is reached from the Three Capes Scenic Route out of Tillamook, which goes to Cape Meares. Heading west on Bayocean Rd from the Netarts Highway, turn right at milepost 5 and drive north on the dirt road on Bayocean Spit. This turn is not obvious; if you get to the left turn to head up the hill to Cape Meares, you've gone too far. As you drive down the dirt road on the spit, you'll see birds along the shore of Tillamook Bay. You can often get some great looks at birds from your car this way, but watch for cars coming up behind you. If it's a good bird they'll probably stop, too, because this is one of the easiest places in Oregon to run into other birders. The parking area is as far as you can go, so park and survey the scene. You'll have a beautiful view of most of Tillamook Bay. The well-known shorebird flats are east of the parking area and along the shore to the south. Follow the main trail worn in the salt marsh toward the flats. Expect some water and mud; rubber boots are a practical choice. Regardless of your footwear, walk carefully and watch your step. When algae is growing on the mud it is very slippery.

Yaquina Bay has plenty of good birding areas that show up several times in this book. Winter Waterfowl describes the trail that starts in the parking lot of the Hatfield Marine Science Center and goes along the south shore of Yaquina Bay. This is a great area for many kinds of coastal birds and can be awesome during both fall and spring shorebird migration.

The road on the long south jetty of the Siuslaw River has several views into different habitats. This area is best for shorebirds between the high and low tide, but not at the highest tides. When the water is very shallow or not covering much of the ground, this place can be dynamite for some rare shorebirds—Baird's, sharp-tailed, and buff-breasted sandpipers.

For decades the Oregon Shorebird Festival has been held in September at the Oregon Institute of Marine Biology in Charleston. Field trips take place on weekends to several places nearby, but most agree that Bandon Marsh NWR is one of the best spots for shorebirds on the Oregon coast. Because the festival doesn't attract a huge crowd, this is a good way to learn about shorebirds in the field from experts. To visit Bandon Marsh on your own, turn west onto Riverside Dr from US 101 between Bandon and the Coquille River. In less than a mile there is a parking area near the refuge sign. A short trail leads to an observation deck and at a low tide you can walk down onto the mudflats, although this would probably not be the best time for birds. Ideally you want to be here in the morning with the sun at your back just before or after the high tide.

▶ FALL SHOREBIRD MIGRATION BEST BETS WASHINGTON

Willapa Bay has been called the largest unspoiled estuary in the Pacific states. The 20-mile Long Beach Peninsula separates the bay from the ocean and at its northern tip is Leadbetter Point, one of the best coastal birding areas in Washington. State Hwy 103 ends in Leadbetter Point SP and all land north of the park is in Willapa NWR, described in April (Brant Migration).

Northeast of Leadbetter Point on the other side of Willapa Bay is the small town of Tokeland on the end of Toke Point. Tokeland is

not known for large numbers of shorebirds, but has historically been one of the most reliable places for some of the big guys, such as marbled godwit, long-billed curlew, and willet, which all winter there. From State Hwy 105 turn south onto Tokeland Rd following signs to Tokeland. In about 1.75 miles from Hwy 105 Tokeland Rd angles off to the left, but continue straight on Fisher Ave and drive a couple of blocks to where it meets 7th St. At this corner is a small parking space and from there you can walk out onto the beach. This is the spot most frequented by the large sandpipers. Take 7th St north to get back on Tokeland Rd and continue southeast to the Tokeland Marina. Look around the shore near the public dock and the marina. To reach the small jetty, walk down to the shore by the marina.

North of Willapa Bay is Grays Harbor, the second biggest estuary in Washington. On the north side of the mouth is the Ocean Shores peninsula, considered by many to be the best fall shorebird spot in the state, especially for some of the rarities such as buff-breasted, Baird's, pectoral, and sharp-tailed sandpipers. To get to Ocean Shores, take State Hwy 109 along the north shore of Grays Harbor. This is also the route to Bowerman Basin, and in the spring you should try to visit Ocean Shores when you go to Bowerman. From Hwy 109 take State Hwy 115 south. It will take you into Ocean Shores where you'll turn right onto Damon Ave, then left onto Point Brown Ave, and then right again onto Ocean Shores Blvd. At the corner of Point Brown Ave and Ocean Shores Blvd is the visitor center with maps and information.

Head south on Ocean Shores Blvd until you get to the end of the peninsula and the parking area (with restrooms) for Point Brown. Check the rocks of Point Brown Jetty for rock-loving shorebirds ("rockpipers"), such as wandering tattler, surfbird, and black turnstone. If the weather is good and the rocks are dry, you can carefully get on top of the jetty to scan the water on the other side for seabirds and waterfowl. This is a good jetty for "walking out into the ocean;" walk out as far as you feel comfortable.

From Point Brown drive another 0.75 mile east on East Ocean Shores Blvd to the sewage treatment plant (you can see the fence as you make a turn to the north). Park where you can find space along the road and find the trails into the Ocean Shores (or Oyhut) Game Range that run along the outside of the north and south sides of the fence. These trails provide access to the mud flats, salt marsh, and sand spit to the east and north of the sewage plant. The famous spot for pectoral and sharp-tailed sandpipers is northeast of the plant at the end of the inlet near the salt marsh. This is another spot where rubber boots may make your walk more enjoyable.

Ocean Shores has a wealth of other birding opportunities and a bird list of 290 species. Another spot worth checking is Damon Point, the southeastern corner of the peninsula. Damon Point Rd goes out on this spit just south of the Ocean Shores Marina. The bay on the north side of the point, which you can see from the road, is usually a good birding area. On a clear day in the fall you can have outstanding views from Damon Point with Mount Rainier rising over Grays Harbor to the east and the Olympic Mountains looming up to the north.

The best shorebird spot in eastern Washington is the Walla Walla River delta, where the Walla Walla flows into Lake Walulla, the impoundment of the Columbia River behind McNary Dam. The delta is the westernmost part of the Wallula Unit of McNary NWR described in February (Wintering Waterfowl). This is not a stop for the casual birdwatcher; to really see shorebirds here you need a scope and rubber boots. Just across US Hwy 12 from North Shore Rd (the road to Madame Dorian Park) is a small dirt road that goes up to the train tracks. You can drive to the tracks, and then turn right and drive a bit to a parking area. A rough trail goes west from the parking area, over the tracks, and to an observation area. Needless to say, the train engineers are not looking for birdwatchers here so be very careful crossing the tracks. When the water is low enough truly dedicated birders will don their rubber boots, grab their scope, wade some shallow water in spots, and walk out along the cattails to view the farthest parts of the delta.

This may seem a bit over the edge but according to Mike Denny and other southeastern Washington experts, it's worth it.

▶ FALL SHOREBIRD MIGRATION BEST BETS BRITISH COLUMBIA

Boundary Bay and Iona Island, south of Vancouver and part of the Fraser River delta, are two of the best shorebird spots on the west coast of North America. Boundary Bay, an International Biosphere Reserve, is the stopping point for most of the world's western sandpipers. The highest number of wintering bird species ever recorded in Canada has been in the Boundary Bay ecosystem, and all but a few of the shorebirds that occur in western North American have been seen there at one time or another. Boundary Bay is described in several chapters, but here we focus on the shorebirds. There are numbered streets that go south from Ladner Trunk Rd (Hwy 10), or its continuation on Hornby, to the dike on the north shore of Boundary Bay. The area at the end of 112th St is the best and then 96th St. Park carefully so that you don't block access to driveways, roads, or farms. If you're going to stay awhile, over an hour for sure, park at the Delta Air Park at the end of 104th St. From there you can walk or ride your bike to the east to 112th or west to 96th. In either direction it's only a 1-mile round trip to either of the other two roads and back to 104th. A scope is really essential here, as it usually is with shorebirds. Plan to come around high tide when the birds are pushed in close to shore by the encroaching water.

Boundary Bay RP, at the west end of Boundary Bay, is another good access point to the shoreline. From Hwy 99 take Hwy 17 toward the Tsawwassen ferry terminal. Turn left at the traffic signal for 56th St, heading to Point Roberts. Drive south to 12th Ave, turn left onto 12th, and drive east 0.4 mile to a small parking area at the end of 12th. From the parking area take the trail east to the shore.

Iona Island, just north of the Vancouver International Airport, is the site of the Greater Vancouver sewage treatment plant and Iona Beach RP. This is the most famous spot in western Canada for rare shorebirds such as Baird's, white-rumped, pectoral, buff-breasted, and upland sandpiper, and ultra-rarities like the rufous-necked stint and spoonbill sandpiper. There are three main areas to bird here—the ponds in the area of the sewage treatment plant, the outer pond and beach area of the regional park, and the rocks on the long jetty.

Getting to Iona is bit complex, and the roads around the airport seem to be changing all the time. You can always follow any signs you see to Iona Beach. From Hwy 99 take the airport exit (Exit 39), and then follow the signs for the Main Terminal until you are on Grant McConachie Way. Soon after getting onto Grant McConachie, you'll reach a light at Templeton Dr. Turn right to go north on Templeton, which will merge with Grauer Rd. Grauer turns into Ferguson Rd. When you're on Ferguson you've got it made. After a couple of miles Ferguson turns right; drive over a slough and onto Iona Island.

The first thing you will see as you come onto Iona Island is the sewage treatment plant. You can park in the plant's parking lot and bird the sewage ponds on foot when the office is open. Check the bird sightings registration

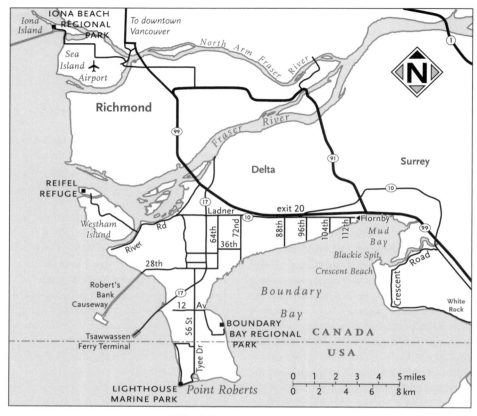

FRASER RIVER DELTA

book just outside the main door of the plant office to read what has been seen lately and to sign in. If the office is closed, you can use the special birder's entrance if you've gotten the Secret Code in advance. Instead of driving into the plant parking area, stay on the road and drive left (west). In a 100 yards or so you'll see where you can park next to a gate in the chain link fence. This is the birder's gate, and it'll have a combination lock. You can get the combination on the Vancouver Natural History Society Web site. Isn't this exciting? It's like a birding spy story. Go through the gate, and you'll see another registry and sighting

record. You will also hopefully find copies of Rick Toochin's bird checklist for Iona. After birding the sewage ponds on foot, get back in your car and drive to Iona Beach.

You'll reach the parking area for Iona Beach RP, which has a substantial restroom building. The outer pond, between the parking area and the fenced ponds in the plant, is the largest. This pond is generally better for gulls and waterfowl than for shorebirds, but you never know what may show up here. This pond is famous for the only nesting colony of yellow-headed blackbirds in coastal British Columbia. After checking the pond explore the beach and the brushy area between the beach and the parking lot, where uncommon passerines show up during migration.

The Iona Island South Jetty is a 2.3-mile long giant wastewater outflow pipe from the sewage plant into the Strait of Georgia. The jetty is one of the better places near Vancouver to see the "rockpipers," such as wandering tattler, black oystercatcher, turnstones, and surfbird. Birding is best here as the tide is rising. You can walk or ride a bicycle on the jetty's road all the way to the end. Almost any waterbird in the region is possible and rarities are frequently seen, but it can be a long, cold, windy walk. Check a rare bird alert or Web site to find out what has been seen before you decide how far you want to walk.

Two popular fall spots for shorebirds near Victoria are Esquimalt Lagoon and Witty's Lagoon RP, both described in February (Wintering Waterfowl).

AQUATIC RODENTS

It was a dark and stormy night in August 1940 when the hurricane struck Avery Island, Louisiana. A few years earlier Tabasco baron E. A. McIlhenny had imported six pairs of coypu, a large aquatic rodent from Argentina, and had them housed in a large, escape-proof pen in the marsh. It's not clear exactly what his plans were for the chunky rodents, but the little herd reproduced and grew. Then fate played an unfortunate hand with the hurricane. As the flood waters rose, they topped the fence and about 150 coypu, or nutria as they would come to be called in this country, swam off to freedom in a new world, filled with food but with few predators. It was coypu paradise and the animals spread rapidly. By 1955 they were established in the wild in 18 states. Nutria came to the Northwest in one of the great scams of the 1950s. The Purebred Nutria Associates, Inc., advertised that nutria breeding and fur production was a foolproof get-rich-quick scheme and sold breeding stock to those that fell for the pitch. In a few years there were hundreds of nutria farms in Oregon, some in Washington, and nutria ranches in California. Soon the victims of the scheme discovered there was almost no market for their pelts. The national Better Business Bureau went after the Purebred Nutria Associates, Inc., and the nutria bubble had popped. Many disgruntled nutria farmers just opened the gates and let their nutrias walk.

Nutria are currently an introduced and invasive species in many parts of the world. Oddly, this animal is called nutria only in the United States and Canada. Everywhere else it's called by its original native name, coypu (pronounced: coy-poo). Nutria is Spanish for otter: Spanish explorers mistakenly referred to coypu as nutria because they thought they were seeing otters, so using the name nutria just perpetuates an ancient mistake. Let's join the rest of the world and switch to coypu; it would make life a lot easier when talking about these animals with Spanish speakers. Coypu can now be found in many areas of freshwater habitat at lower elevations on the west side of the Cascades from the Coquille River in Oregon to the Fraser River in British Columbia.

The Northwest has two native aquatic rodents—beaver and muskrat—often confused with the introduced coypu. Beaver are one of the most well-known mammals in North America and were probably the most important animal in the European settlement of North America. The quest for beaver pelts was the greatest driving force in the early exploration of the West. Because of intensive trapping, beaver were exterminated from much of their original range but have now made an impressive comeback under modern management. Beaver are now so abundant that in some areas they are considered a nuisance, especially when they dam culverts, resulting in flooded roads. With their return to a healthy population, they are now legally trapped again and 4000 to 5000 are taken each year in Oregon alone. Beaver have shown themselves to be quite adaptable and have returned to wetlands and rivers in many of our Northwestern cities.

Beavers are often portrayed as the engineers of the animal world, and it is generally accepted that no other animal, except humans, modifies its environment as much as beavers do. By damming streams, beavers create a series of wetland habitats that are home to many other animals and plants. With time the ponds and marshes they create fill with soil and become drier, turning to meadows and eventually to forest or woodland. The industrious nature of beaver is rightfully acknowledged in the common phrase "busy as a beaver."

Beaver are found throughout our entire region, from tidal rivers to high mountain streams to desert canyons. Because their food most of the year is the cambium layer of trees and shrubs, it's unusual to find them where cottonwood, willow, alder, or aspen are not in good supply.

Muskrat are often seen as mini-beavers, but they are not closely related other than both being rodents. Muskrat have a little webbing and ridges of stiff hairs on their feet for swimming, instead of the completely webbed hind feet of beaver and coypu. The muskrat's tail is unique and very different from the famous flat tail of the beaver. Muskrat tails are flattened vertically, not horizontally like beaver. Muskrat are only half the length and a fraction of the weight of beaver, which are the second largest rodent in the world.

Muskrats are most often associated with cattail marshes and shallow, quiet waters at low elevations. They are found in this habitat throughout our region. Muskrats readily use irrigation and other ditches, as well as reservoirs, and have become quite abundant in many agricultural areas that have these features. Unfortunately, coypu prefer the same habitat as muskrat and the larger, more aggressive coypu can displace the native muskrat when they move in.

The most common question about mammals that I get as a park naturalist is, "How can you tell beaver, muskrat, and nutria apart?" I know these people mean "in the water," not sitting in the open on land as portrayed in books. If you see a beaver on land and you see its tail, it's a piece of cake to tell it's a beaver. The other two are not hard to identify either, if you see the whole animal on land. But most of the time we see these animals as brown heads moving through the water probably in dim light. I've worked on this identification challenge for years; here are my tips for distinguishing these three rodents when you see them swimming.

First be very careful about using size to separate these three—judging the size of an animal in the wild is tricky. And when all you see is a head moving in the water, forget it. There are other identifying characteristics that are much easier to see.

Muskrat swim with their tail, which is vertically flattened so that when they move it back and forth in the water it pushes them forward, like a propeller. If you see a muskrat swimming you can usually see its tail breaking the surface and whipping back and forth behind it. Neither beaver nor coypu swim with their tail, because they both have large, webbed hind feet for that purpose. Sometimes you'll see part of a coypu's tail held just above the surface, but it won't be moving back and forth and you may be able to tell that it is a round tail like a rat's. I have never seen the tail of a beaver when it was swimming, although I know some folks have. Beaver do not swim with their tail, so I think it's very unusual to see it unless they give you the alarm slap on the water.

The easiest field mark for picking out coypu are their huge, white whiskers. It's as if they have a large handlebar moustache, and you can usually see some of it even when they are swimming. Coypu also have a lot of white or gray hair around their mouth, which makes them look as if they have a gray goatee. A patch of lighter fur at the base of their ears makes their ears stand out more than the ears of muskrat and beaver. The overall impression of a coypu head is that it is not one solid color—it has patches of lighter fur in places. The heads of both beaver and muskrat are usually solid dark brown and you can't see their black whiskers. A beaver's head is large, "chunky," and fairly flat on top.

Here are a few behavioral tips. I've never seen beaver floating in the water, just hanging out. Beaver are busy and when you see them swimming it seems pretty clear that they have places to go and things to do. Muskrat are usually businesslike also and swim from point A to point B in a straight line. I've seen muskrat floating in the water while they eat, but it's much more common for them to get plants and then climb up on a log or other little feeding platform and then eat the plants. Coypu, on the other hand, regularly chow down while floating in the water. You can often watch them eating while floating in the same place for 10 to 15 minutes. Beaver are very nocturnal; you will rarely see them active during the day except around dawn or dusk. Muskrat are a bit more active during the day but are also crepuscular (active around dawn and dusk). Coypu are bold animals and can be seen any time of day. They can become tame when they are around people a lot and unfortunately people have started feeding them at some parks and golf courses. As usual, this is a bad idea.

AQUATIC RODENTS BEST BETS

Nutria are currently restricted to west-side valleys and are abundant where they occur. Beaver and muskrat are widespread everywhere in our region and are often common in the appropriate habitat, but their abundance will vary over time, so it's difficult to predict where they'll be from year to year. Ask at local ranger districts, park visitor centers, or regional offices of wildlife agencies for current information on locations. All three are most commonly seen around dawn and dusk, but nutria can be seen in the middle of the day. One of the best ways to see them is to quietly canoe (or kayak) through good habitat early or late in the day in the summer. A basic strategy for finding beaver is to locate an area with evidence of recent activity, which is about as obvious as an animal sign can get, and then come back an hour before sunset and stake it out. Find a place where you can hide with a good view of the water and wait quietly. This is a true test of patience and of how well you planned for mosquitoes.

▶ **AQUATIC RODENTS BEST BETS** OREGON

I once stood on the bank at Smith and Bybee Wetlands in Portland and saw a muskrat, a nutria, and a beaver swimming in the same area at the same time. What a great opportunity to study the difference. Working at Smith and Bybee Wetlands has allowed me to become very familiar with these three rodents and has also made me a shameless promoter of this wonderful urban natural area. This is a great site for paddling late in the day in summer when the water is still high. The water level drops in the summer so June is actually the best month; call Metro Regional Parks to check on conditions before going. Since I have been working at Smith and Bybee I have been leading sunset walks (Twilight Tuesdays) during the summer and have had many good sightings. To find out about these and other Metro Parks programs check the Web site.

The BLM has wonderful interpretive trails at its Wildwood Recreation Site 15 miles east of Sandy on US Hwy 26 to Mount Hood. The site is well signed; take the first left after you enter the area, park in the trailhead parking area, and take the universally accessible Wetlands Trail through the marshy area south of the Salmon River. This is excellent lush, low-elevation, west-side, coniferous forest with plenty of birds around the old beaver ponds. The old beaver lodges and dams are covered with plant growth now, making them difficult to see in summer, but beaver are still active in the area and fresh signs may show up at any time.

Beaver and muskrat are both seen at the McNary Nature Area, a rehabilitated wetland downstream of McNary Dam. From US Hwy 730 in Umatilla just east of Interstate 82, drive north into the main entrance for McNary Dam (large sign). Before you get to the visitor center, turn left onto 3rd St following the signs to the wildlife area. From the parking area at the end of Ferry Rd you can explore trails on both sides. This area is also good for waterfowl in the winter if the ponds aren't frozen. A map and checklist are available at the visitor center.

In the large east-side marshes of Malheur NWR, Summer Lake WA, and the refuges in the Klamath Basin muskrat habitat is excellent and they are regularly seen. The Upper Klamath NWR has an established canoe trail, starting at the Rocky Point Resort (which rents canoes), where you may find beaver, muskrat, and river otter.

▶ **AQUATIC RODENTS BEST BETS** WASHINGTON

Ridgefield NWR is one of the best areas for wildlife watching near the Portland metropolitan area. All three of our swimming rodents live here but the nutria is by far the most abundant. This could be one of the densest populations of nutria in the West. Chances are good you will see nutria anytime you're at Ridgefield.

The Selkirk Mountains of northeastern Washington appear to be loaded with beaver. Two beautiful areas to see beaver and lots of other wildlife are the Little Pend Oreille NWR and Big Meadow Lake. Little Pend Oreille NWR is described in May (Songbird Migration) and McDowell Lake has beaver and muskrat. From the north end of the lake walk down the road on the east side of the lake to where you can look over the lake.

Big Meadow Lake is 8 miles west of Ione.

Go west on Main St through the center of Ione, and then turn right at the train tracks. At the stop sign turn left, go two blocks, and then turn left again. Drive south one block, and then turn right following signs to Smackout Pass and Big Meadow Lake. Two miles after the pavement ends, turn left and stay on FR 2695 to the lake. Big Meadow Lake has a good variety of habitats so wildlife is plentiful. Beaver and muskrat are regulars and moose are becoming more common. The wooden observation tower on the Meadow Creek Trail gives a great overview of the area.

▶ AQUATIC RODENTS BEST BETS BRITISH COLUMBIA

Yet another reason to go to Manning PP in the summer is for beaver. Beaver activity is high along the Similkameen River and its tributaries in the center of the park near the visitor center. Naturalist programs during the summer include walks in these areas and discussions about beaver. The self-guided nature trail around Beaver Pond has interpretive signs about beaver and is an excellent example of an old beaver pond that is now abandoned and changing into a meadow. Rein Orchid and Twenty Minute lakes, both with short, easy trails around them, have current beaver activity.

AUGUST'S NATURE NUGGETS

BERRIES One of the benefits of living in Paradise (also known as the Pacific Northwest) is the bounty of wild berries every summer. Almost half of the bushes or shrubs found west of the Cascades have fleshy fruits, and most of these are considered edible by humans, not to mention the hundreds of animals that eat them. The abundant berries were a major food resource for Native Americans, who ate them straight off the bush in season or dried them, often blended with other ingredients, to make a variety of storable foods generally called pemmican.

Two families dominate the list of choice berries in the Northwest—the rose family and the heath or heather family. The rose family includes the various types of blackberries and raspberries (including dewberry and blackcap), thimbleberry, and salmonberry. Thickets of these plants are usually called brambles, an old English term for thorny shrubs. Two blackberries, the evergreen and the ubiquitous Himalayan, are introduced and very invasive. Many Northwesterners have fought losing battles with brambles of these two. Most of these blackberry-type plants are common at low elevations, like lots of sun, and grow just about anywhere on the west side, especially at the edges of fields and woodlands, and along streams.

The other large berry family, the heaths, includes the blueberries, huckleberries, and salal, one of the most abundant plants in coastal coniferous forests. There is no reason why some of these plants are called blueberry and others are called huckleberry, so don't worry if you call a huckle a blue or vice versa. Many forest understories are dominated by members of this group as are unforested habitats high in the mountains. Some of the mountain blueberries and huckleberries form solid thickets between about 2000 and 4000 feet in elevation. Two of the best know areas for these are around Lolo Pass and the road to Cloud Cap in the Mount Hood NF and the Indian Heaven berry fields on Mount Adams in Gifford Pinchot NF. The Indian Heaven fields are along FR 24 but the area to the north or east of the road are reserved as traditional berry-harvesting areas for Native Americans. Good picking and may you be blessed with a blue tongue.

METEOR SHOWER The largest meteor shower of the year visible during warm months is the well-known Perseid Meteor Shower. This celestial event is best around 8 p.m. between August 11 and 13. There will often be small newspaper stories about the Perseids coming with recommendations about where and when to go to see them at their best. There may also be predictions as to how good the show is going to be. Sometimes astronomy clubs in cities will have a Star Party on a particular night, and if you have never been to a Star Party, you owe it to yourself to check out this unique scene. The meteors appear to be coming from the constellation Perseus, hence the name *Perseid*, so get out your star chart if you're going out on your own. Lucky observers with good conditions sometimes see 50 meteors an hour.

SUMMER BUG SAFARI: A CLOSER LOOK

The large female sank its feeding tube deep into the vessel of its food source. While she slowly sucked the life-giving nutrients, her abdomen began to ripple with contractions. Slowly, out of her reproductive opening, a new daughter started to emerge. In a few minutes, its legs were wiggling in the air and then it was out, standing next to its mother. The large female repeated the process every two hours and was soon surrounded by a small herd of her daughters, all with embryos already starting to develop in their reproductive systems. Males were not seen for months as females produced females that produced females, on and on, until finally eggs were laid that hatched into winged males and females. They mated, the females laid eggs, and then all adults died. The entire population of this beast survived for months only as fertilized eggs in suspended animation. Then their food again became available and they underwent another females-only population explosion.

A scene from *Aliens V*? Nope, just aphids on your rose bush. Yes, aphids give live birth to little female babies that start to eat and grow immediately and are soon reproducing themselves. No males and no fertilization are involved. This process is called parthenogenesis (which means virgin birth) and you can watch it happen in your own backyard or even right in your hand. This is just one of many interesting and sometimes bizarre insect life cycles taking place right under your nose. Just step outside into your yard where you can see lots of amazing animals with almost no effort. Even with a modest variety of plants you'll have dozens of fascinating insects at your fingertips. I'm still astonished that just about every time I go on a bug safari in my yard, I find yet another new insect that I've never seen before. And I still haven't figured out what some of them are! No matter how you figure it—in total numbers, in numbers of different species or in biomass—insects rule the world. More different kinds of insects exist than all other animals put together. Life's never dull for naturalists on their hands and knees.

The joys of backyard bugs have been promoted by naturalists for years and there are some great books to help you decipher the astonishing lives of insects. With these books, a magnifying glass, and a couple of field guides for identification, you'll be all set to make sense of the jungle out there. There are also plenty of good bug books for kids, so check your local library.

My cedar fence has small, shallow grooves between the lines of grain in the wood. It looks like someone may have taken a sharp fingernail and scraped out a very thin layer of wood. Who would do this? I wondered for years. Then one summer's day I saw yellow jackets landing on this area of the fence. I watched closely and sure enough, the yellow jackets were chewing on the fence. Of course! Yellow jackets are members of the paper wasp family, and paper is made from wood. Since then I have seen other paper wasps also chewing on my fence as a source of pulp for making their paper nests. Another backyard insect mystery solved.

I've been using "bug" and "insect" interchangeably but just what is a bug? Bug is about as vague a word as you can get. Almost any small animal, including even protozoans and bacteria, are sometimes called bugs. When most people use the word, however, they are usually referring to insects, and maybe spiders. Let's be precise about these beasts because they are usually easy to tell apart.

Usually the animals called bugs are arthropods. Arthropods have no bones, but instead have a tough, usually hard skin that supports their body. To be able to move, they have joints in this hard skin or exoskeleton. It is from this characteristic that arthropod, or "jointed leg," comes and the main groups of arthropods can easily be told apart by the number of legs. If it has six legs, it's an insect and will also have three body segments and a pair of antennae. If it has eight legs, it's an arachnid and will not have wings or antennae. If it has more than eight legs and has two pairs of antennae, it's a crustacean. There are two groups of arthropods that are long and skinny with many distinct body segments. If one of these arthropods has one pair of legs on each segment, it's a centipede and if it has two pairs of legs on each segment, it's a millipede. Most adult insects have wings and can fly, but no other arthropods ever do.

In your backyard are representatives of all five of these arthropod groups. Insects are by far the most numerous and are the ones you know best. The biggest and most common arachnids are the spiders. Everyone recognizes almost every spider they see as a spider and many people know a few kinds by name, such as black widows, wolf spiders, jumping spiders, and crab spiders. There are lots of other arachnids in your yard, but you will very rarely see them unless you're looking very hard because they are so tiny. These are the mites, close relatives of ticks, and many kinds live in soil.

Many people are shocked to learn that they have crustaceans in their yard, but isopods, also called sow bugs, pill bugs, roly-polies, or potato bugs, are actually terrestrial crustaceans. Think of them as little land shrimp. You have also probably noticed millipedes and centipedes in your yard. It is easy to confuse the two, but here's an easy, usually accurate way to tell them apart. If you can catch it, it's a millipede. If it's fast and very hard to catch, it's a centipede. This rule works because centipedes are predators and have to be fast to catch their prey, but millipedes are slow, gentle vegetarians and don't need to be fast to catch a dead leaf. Neither one is dangerous to people in the Northwest, although some centipedes in the Southwest are large enough to bite people.

Here are some of the most common and conspicuous arthropods that people regularly find in their yards in the Northwest. This list may be a bit biased for the west side and others may be equally common in some areas east of the Cascades.

Grasshoppers are familiar insects but will usually be common in your yard only if you have or live near some grassy fields. Their relatives the crickets and katydids may show up from time to time and are usually noticed later in the summer when they start to sing. Male crickets and katydids sing by rubbing their wings together in order to attract their mates. Their ears are on their legs, and each species has its own unique song that identifies the male as Mr. Right for the female.

Leave a light on outside at night in the summer and you're sure to get some interesting insects. Various moths are common and some neat beetles will show up, but one of my favorites is the jewel-like green lacewing. I love the shiny golden eyes on these delicate and beautiful creatures. Lacewings are beneficial because their larvae are voracious predators of aphids and, indeed, are often called aphid lions.

The most famous aphid predator is, of course, the ladybug. Books always give the proper common name for these attractive beetles as ladybird beetles, but I've never heard that name used in the western United States. This name, by the way, can be traced back to the middle ages when these insects were dedicated to the Virgin Mary. I guess she disliked aphids as much as modern gardeners do. Ladybugs gobble up large numbers of aphids as larva and as adults. They also like to eat scale insects, nasty pests of citrus trees. Ladybugs are so beneficial from an agricultural standpoint that they can be bought at nurseries in the spring for release in your yard. Much to everyone's surprise the first time it happens, ladybugs can bite people. It certainly isn't painful or dangerous, but that little pinch seems to be some kind of betrayal after all the wonderful things we've heard about them.

In contrast, earwigs are clearly unpopular insects, probably because they have little pincers that look pretty nasty, they emit a foul odor when bothered (or smashed), and they often show up in large numbers inside things left lying around the yard. They occasionally do eat flowers, but they are primarily predators and scavengers and are therefore beneficial. The females will guard her eggs and tend her babies for a short time, unusual behavior for an insect. The most common earwigs are introduced from Europe.

Beetles are the largest group of insects. One large family that has lots of gardener's helpers is the predaceous ground beetle family or the Carabids. There are probably 600 or so species of these in the Northwest, but most can be recognized as members of this family by the flattened edges to their squarish thorax. These guys are usually nocturnal, but are easy to find hiding under rocks and logs or hanging out at the compost pile. The adults and larvae are predators of many types of caterpillars, including many of the worst pest species. Two genera of the large ones, *Calosoma* and *Scaphinotus*, are famous as the slug and snail killers of the Northwest. One with a reddish iridescence has the fantastic name "the fiery hunter."

Unfortunately, many people are as afraid of spiders as some are of snakes. Once again, the fear is totally out of proportion with any real possible danger. Rod Crawford, curator of arachnids at the University of Washington's Burke Museum, created the Spider Myths Web site to help dispel the misinformation and mythology about spiders. Use your search engine for "spider myths" and you'll find it. You'll be shocked at the truth.

One kind of spider that everybody notices are those large ones, hanging in the middle of the large, round webs in your garden, that seem to show up in the fall, but in fact have been around, growing, all summer. Two of these are very common species, the cross spider and the black-and-gold argiope, both of which are also called orb-weavers or the generic garden spider. I've heard some called Halloween spiders, which really shows you when people notice them and what they associate them with. Some of the better books on insects or bugs of the Northwest include these most common spiders.

There is almost no end to insects and other arthropods you can find around your home. Start looking in natural habitats and you'll find even more. You can find them where ever you go when it's warm enough. One of my favorite types of bug hunts is looking through streams and ponds for aquatic beasties. It's a whole other world. Happy hunting.

The magnificent snowy owl is one of the grand prizes of a winter birding trip and is seen annually in the Boundary Bay area of British Columbia.

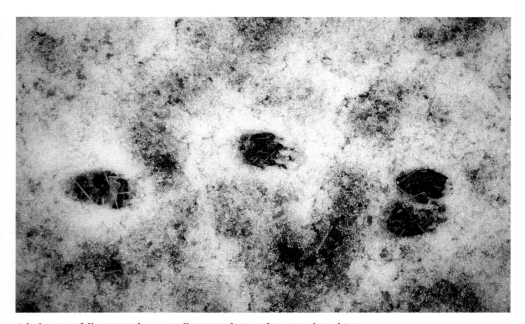

A light snowfall can produce excellent conditions for animal tracking.

When the weather gets cold enough, waterfalls can present a fantasy in ice crystals.

Hundreds of tundra swans can regularly be seen during the winter at Ridgefield National Wildlife Refuge, Washington.

Bald eagles are one of the great success stories of the Endangered Species Act and are now nesting in our largest Northwest cities.

What a handsome duck! Common goldeneyes are abundant in winter
in the waters around Vancouver, British Columbia.

The range of plumages in these glaucous-winged gulls is the result of
different ages, making gull identification a major challenge. My advice is
to work first on mature adults, like this big fellow in the middle.

Indian plum (or osoberry) is one of the first plants to bloom in spring and the new leaves look like strange, bright green flames in the still drab winter woods.

Grass widow is another of the earliest bloomers. You can easily find these beauties in the grasslands of the eastern Columbia River Gorge and The Rogue River Valley.

Charles Darwin described how nightcrawlers make these worm piles. The piles build as the big worms drag food into their burrow at night.

The large nests of great blue herons are easy to spot in bare deciduous trees.

To find roosting great horned owls during the day, look in bare trees for "a rugby ball with horns." Also scan old red-tailed hawk nests in February for the tell-tale tufts sticking out of the nest.

It's easy to see how the light strips on the top of the head and the back of a Wilson's snipe are great camouflage in the wet meadows and marshes where they nest.

Both spring and fall shorebird migration can be spectacular with flocks of thousands of birds (dunlin shown here) stopping at key feeding areas like Bowerman Basin.

Camas and sea blush (*Plectritis congesta*) often grow together in soils that are wet in spring but dry out quickly.

The white fawn lily is one of our many beautiful members of the lily family. It blooms early in open forests at low elevations west of the Cascades.

Camas was an important staple food of indigenous people who managed their camas prairies with fires (here with buttercups).

Truly among the most bizarre courtship displays you can easily see in our region—the "booming" of sage-grouse on a lek.

Thousands of brant funnel up the Strait of Georgia during their spring migration and are celebrated in April at the Brant Wildlife Festival on the east coast of Vancouver Island.

They sure are cute, but give baby harbor seals a wide berth; Mom is nearby and your presence could keep her from her pup.

Wild turkeys are now regularly seen in mid-elevation mountainous areas and coulees because of successful reintroductions.

The only place in our region where Steller's sea lions give birth on the mainland is below the viewing area at Sea Lion Caves, Oregon.

A little frog with a big voice, heard in dozens of movies and TV shows—the Pacific chorus frog, until recently called the Pacific treefrog.

Just looking at them you know something is weird about cobra lilies and you're right—they eat insects!

Yellow-rumped warblers ("butter butts" in birder's slang) are the warblers most frequently seen in large flocks (hundreds) during spring and fall migrations.

"It's not their spit, it's their pee," is one of my favorite lines when we find spittlebugs on a school field trip. I follow up with, "Why would an animal build a little pee foam nest to live in?" The kids figure it out.

The short blooming season in arid lands often results in spectacular displays of wildflowers—yellow evening primrose in a drying lake bed near Malheur National Wildlife Refuge.

Rough-skinned newts are one of our most common amphibians. Although they are docile and many youngsters do handle them, you should be cautious of their poisonous skin.

If you pick up these harmless millipedes carefully and sniff them you can smell the "bitter almond" aroma of cyanide gas. If you are a robin and eat one, you won't die but you won't eat another. Good protection for a slow animal.

For decades Elsa Lloyd tended the mountain lady's slippers, our showiest orchid, growing on the family's Flying L Ranch near Mount Adams.

This common murre, at the Oregon Coast Aquarium, flies through the water with its wings as all alcids do.

Puffins are the most well known of all alcids because of their stunning appearance. Yes, this tufted puffin is real, not made up by Lewis Carroll.

Western painted turtles are much more colorful than the drab western pond turtle, the only other freshwater turtle native to the Northwest. Smith and Bybee Wetlands, Portland.

The beautiful black-collared lizard is one of the Alvord Desert's lizard specialties.

The conspicuous anise swallowtail is one of the Northwest's most widespread butterflies.

This bold gray jay or "camp robber" is trying to find the gorp in my backpack. Nothing surprising here.

Beargrass in bloom on Mount Hood—a summer floral spectacle.

A friendly greeter to the alpine world—a robust hoary marmot in Manning Provincial Park, British Columbia.

Windows into another world—tidepools at Pacific Rim National Park, British Columbia.

The Holy Grail of any tidepool exploration, an octopus, the smartest invertebrate animal on Earth.

A lone mountain goat surveys the William O. Douglas Wilderness Area from Timberwolf Mountain, Washington.

Pikas do not hibernate so these tiny rabbits make hay all summer long for the winter and store it in their labyrinth of tunnels under boulders.

You may not see them but you know they are there when you find fresh beaver chew like this.

Compare the almost solid dark brown body and the inconspicuous whiskers
of this beaver with the coloring of the nutria (also known as coypu).

The easiest way to identify nutria is by their huge, white whiskers and patches of lighter hair around their mouth and at the base of their ears. These field marks can be seen on just a floating head, which is often the only look you get at any of the aquatic rodents.

Those funny little scratch marks on your old cedar fence are where your local paper wasps have been getting their wood pulp for their nests.

The ancient forests of the Northwest are more threatened than tropical rain forests.

The classic trail through a mossy ancient forest, Hall of Mosses Trail in Olympic National Park.

This young red-tailed hawk doesn't have a red tail yet, but you can easily identify it by the dark head–white breast–dark belly band pattern and the black leading edge of its inner wing (the patagium).

Perched on top of Red Top Mountain, this lookout provides a spectacular spot to watch for migrating raptors in autumn.

Chapman School in Portland is believed to have the largest swift roost in the world. The nightly fly-in watch of the Vaux's swifts has become a September cultural event.

Sandhill cranes regularly stop to feed in fields and pastures during migration making some agricultural areas the easiest places to see hundreds of cranes at a time.

Snow geese migrate in huge flocks during both spring and fall migration. It is common to see 10,000 to 20,000 at a time.

The bright golden leaves of black cottonwoods line most northwestern rivers in the fall.

More bright golden leaves—the needles of a larch tree. Larches are the only deciduous conifers in North America.

The famous *Amanita muscaria* or fly agaric is the most familiar mushroom image in North America and Europe because of its distinctive appearance and rich history in human culture.

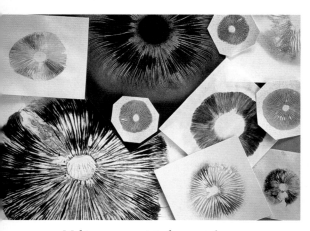

Making spore prints from mushrooms is not only helpful for identification but is also a fun art form.

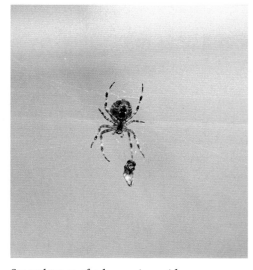

Several types of orb-weaving spiders—here a cross spider with a fly—become conspicuous in fall and are sometimes called Halloween spiders because they reach their maximum size about that time before laying their eggs and dying.

One of a kind, the pronghorn is the only living member of a unique family
of hoofed mammals and is the fastest land animal in the Americas.

Bighorn sheep can be very hard to find because they blend
in so well with the cliffs on which they live.

Say, could you show us your tail so we can see how you got your name?
A Columbian white-tail deer at Julia Butler Hansen Refuge.

A foggy winter's day in the Coast Range is a typical backdrop for a herd of elk cows.

Beautiful harlequin ducks are easy to identify and usually easy to find along the rocky shores of the Salish Sea in winter.

The largest slug in the world and it's all ours. Their slime contains a mild poison which numbs the mouth of predators, protecting banana slugs from all predators except garter snakes.

A ball o' bushtits on a suet feeder can warm your heart on a winter's day.

Ahoy matey! Ever wonder how the little lookout at the top of a mast got its name? People were familiar with crow's nests long before there were sailing ships.

The typical drey or nest of gray and fox squirrels looks like a soccer ball made out of leaves stuck in a tree.

The famous black squirrels of Stanley Park, Vancouver, are not a different species but are descendants of the black eastern gray squirrels introduced from Ontario.

SEPTEMBER

PELAGIC BIRD TRIPS

I thought a person turned green when seasick only in cartoons. But there he was, a seasick birder, and his face was actually a pale, waxy green. I was on a pelagic birding trip off the Oregon Coast and had already joined many of my fellow passengers at the rail for a little "chat with Neptune." Of course, it was also raining, which seemed odd because we were sure it was cold enough to snow. "Yeah, it just doesn't get any better than this," came the sarcastic comment from one of the cold, wet birders huddling under the tiny wheelhouse overhang, which gave little protection because the wind drove the rain horizontally into our faces. Why were we putting ourselves through this torture?

"Shearwater. Black-vented. Maybe. Coming in at eleven o'clock," shouted our leader. The deck was immediately transformed into a beehive of activity, and the boat leaned as a wave of people hit the port rail. This was it, the reason these people were putting themselves through the rigors of a pelagic birding trip. Nobody on the boat, including the guides, had ever seen a black-vented shearwater before, and many of us didn't even know they existed. All eyes were glued on the small dark bird as it few quickly by the boat and was gone. "Did anyone see if it had a black vent?" asked one of the superbirders on the trip. "Its vent? I couldn't even tell if it had a head!" came the reply from a neophyte to the wonders of pelagic birding. So was it a black-vented or an even rarer Manx shearwater? No one will ever know because both are rare in our region and almost impossible to tell apart.

Previous page:
The quickly
changing
day length of
September
triggers many
other changes.

Such are the joys and demands of pelagic birding. After an exhausting and challenging 8-hour day we had a trip list of 23 species, a fraction of what would be expected from a hard day of birding almost anywhere on land. But a third of those species were brand new "life birds" for half the people on the trip, and we all knew that this was the only way we would ever see many of these birds. This tale illustrates the essential characteristics of pelagic bird-ing—hard work for few big rewards. Pelagic birding is definitely birding on the edge. It's birding both on the edge of the continent and on the frontier of our knowledge of birds. Of course, conditions are not always unpleasant on all boat trips. I've been on trips in California when the sun was shining, the sea was like glass, and people were wearing T-shirts, but in the Northwest, you've got to be prepared for the worst.

What's all the hubbub about pelagic birds? Why bother? Well, because they're there. At some point, every serious birder just has to put to sea because pelagic birds can be seen only by boat—unless you spend hundreds of hours perched on rocky headlands during fall and winter storms. *Pelagic* means liv-ing in the open ocean and pelagic animals are hard to study because they roam over its vast expanses. Many marine animals, like seals and gulls, are actually coastal, coming out of the water regularly for various purposes. Truly pelagic animals, on the other hand, spend their entire life in the open oceans. Some travel fantastic distances as they roam the oceans. The short-tailed shearwa-ter, for example, nests in Tasmania and winters (our summer) near Alaska, traveling 20,000 miles every year!

Marine mammals like whales never have to come to land because they are viviparous ("live birth"). One group of marine reptiles, the sea snakes, are similar to mammals in that they do not lay eggs, also completely freeing themselves from the land. But bird and reptile eggs can drown so birds and sea turtles have to come to land to lay their eggs, even if they spend the rest of their lives at sea. To be precise, no birds are truly pelagic because they all, even penguins, have to come to land to lay their eggs and raise their young to a certain age.

Like *seabird*, *pelagic bird* is not an exact term, resulting in some variation in usage. The most pelagic of all birds, and always called pelagic, are the tubeno-ses. This group has no regularly used common name because most people will never see them. The only tubenoses most people have heard of are alba-trosses, sometimes called gooney birds in old travelogs and nature shows. The tubenoses include the albatrosses, shearwaters, petrels, storm-petrels, and fulmars.

By far the most common and abundant tubenose is the sooty shearwater, seen on just about every boat trip off our coast and often seen from shore. In late summer and early fall, hundreds of thousands of sootys migrate north along the Pacific Coast. Sometimes huge flocks will pass by shore for hours at a time, close enough to be easily seen with the naked eye. For most people, such a sighting will be the greatest number of animals of one species, seen at one time, in their lives! The sooty shearwater may be the most abundant bird in the world, with estimates of up to a billion individuals world-wide. If you're at the coast in August or September, scan the ocean with binoculars or a scope just outside of where the farthest waves are forming. With patience and practice you can usually find sootys zipping around out there, looking like giant sea swifts with their long, stiff, arched wings.

No other tubenose is remotely close to the sooty shearwater in numbers. The others that you'll usually see on pelagic birding boat trips are black-footed albatross; northern fulmar; pink-footed, flesh-footed, short-tailed, and Buller's shearwaters; and fork-tailed storm-petrel.

The other group of birds usually described as pelagic is the family of alcids or auks, discussed in June (Nesting Seabirds). The species most commonly seen on boat trips are common murre, pigeon guillemot, tufted puffin, rhinoceros auklet, and marbled murrelet. The tubenoses and the alcids are clearly the most pelagic birds in North America. However, other birds that belong to different families are usually included in lists of pelagic birds, even though they may spend more time on land or actually be more coastal than these two hard-core pelagic groups.

The gull and tern family has several species that we see almost exclusively offshore while they are migrating or wintering here. Pomarine and parasitic jaegers are seen quite regularly. Black-legged kittiwakes, Sabine's gulls, and arctic terns are regular and fairly common migrants with many of the kittiwakes staying for the winter. The red phalarope is the most pelagic of all shorebirds and large numbers migrate offshore. Of course, birders see other aquatic birds on boat trips, but these are not usually considered pelagic: cormorants, gulls, loons, grebes and sea ducks.

Any time you are at sea also watch for marine mammals. On pelagic bird-watching trips you may see harbor seals, Steller's and California sea lions, gray whales, harbor and Dall's porpoises, Pacific white-sided dolphins, orcas and occasionally minke whales and elephant seals. A pelagic birding trip requires much more preparation than your average birding trip. Organized trips require registration, often in advance, because space is limited. You will have to meet at the boat very early in the morning, which often means staying in a nearby motel the night before. Trips usually last 8 to 12 hours. Be sure you have the clothing necessary to keep warm and dry under any weather conditions you may encounter (it's hard to overdress). Dress for wind and wear your grippiest shoes. Bring enough food and drink for the duration of the trip—keep in mind that most people eat lightly to avoid motion sickness. Leave your scope on shore; it's useless on a boat. Bone up on your seabird identification because many of your sightings will be brief and under poor conditions.

Motion sickness is the biggest problem facing many pelagic birders and can really ruin a trip. Common sense tells you to get plenty of sleep and don't drink alcohol the night before or the day of the trip. Eat a light breakfast and have lots of little snacks during the day, high in carbohydrates and low in fats. Drink plenty of liquids. Stay standing and active on the open deck in the fresh air. Lying or sitting down inside usually makes things worse. Watch the horizon and move with the boat as if you were surfing. Stay in the middle or toward the aft where the boat is the most stable.

I believe the best thing you can do for seasickness is take preventative medication. Of all the over-the-counter medications available for motion sickness I have seen the best results (myself and others) with meclizine, available as a generic or as brand name Bonine. I have not seen meclizine make people sleepy or cause any other side effects, and it comes in chewable tablets. Take your first dose an hour before departure. No really, I don't own any stock, I've just seen it work.

What seems to be the ultimate remedy for many is "the patch," a small disk you stick behind your ear that delivers scopolamine transdermally to your inner ear, for as long as three days. The brand name is Transderm Scop, available by prescription only. It is not for children, but then neither is pelagic birding. Significant side effects are possible; follow your doctor's directions carefully. For the patch to work properly, put it on the night before the trip. With any seasickness medication, and the patch especially, try it out on land before your trip to be sure you don't have any negative side effects.

Many who desire a more natural alternative to the standard medications have success with ginger, an ancient herbal remedy for nausea and upset stomach (there really was a reason your Mom gave you ginger ale when your tummy was upset). People will eat ginger snaps or ginger candy, drink real ginger ale, or take capsules of powdered ginger. Ginger has no side effects, and some scientific evidence shows that ginger is effective. Even if it isn't the greatest cure, a box of ginger snaps makes a fine onboard snack.

Fall is the traditional time for most pelagic trips with October being the month for the biggest variety. However, birders have wanted to get more data on pelagics throughout the year, so some trips are now available almost every month except December. If tours are unavailable, ferries can provide a taste of pelagic birding in comfort and at low cost (without a car), and they sail every day.

PELAGIC BIRD TRIPS BEST BETS

These are the most regularly run pelagic birding trips in the Northwest. Schedules are always changing, so contact each operator to get the latest information. Other trips are run by local Audubon chapters, museums, and natural history associations, but they're not predictable and can be difficult to locate. The best single source for information on pelagic trips in North America is the Web site of the American Birding Association: www.americanbirding.org/resources.

▶ PELAGIC BIRD TRIPS BEST BETS OREGON

Greg Gillson finally made pelagic birding predictable and reliable in Oregon with his business, The Bird Guide, Inc. Trips leave from Newport for Perpetua Bank in the spring and fall and most are 10 hours long. www.thebirdguide.com.

▶ PELAGIC BIRD TRIPS BEST BETS WASHINGTON

Terry Wahl, one of Washington's top birders, has been running pelagic trips out of Westport since the days of sailing ships. Well, it seems like that long ago. Terry started in 1966 and Westport Seabirds trips have produced the longest running database of birds counted at sea in the world. In some years, he has offered 15 different trips from nine to fourteen hours long. www.westportseabirds.com

▶ PELAGIC BIRD TRIPS BEST BETS FERRIES

You can see our regularly occurring seabirds (loons, grebes, cormorants, waterfowl, gulls, terns, and alcids) from the ferries that ply the Salish Sea. You also might see some of the tubenoses and jaegers, but ferries are not the way to see the truly pelagic species. Ferry schedules change during the year so always get the current schedule.

The *M.V. Coho* goes back and forth between Port Angeles, Washington, and Victoria, British Columbia, with two departures a day from each city in October and November. The hour-and-a-half crossing of the Strait of Juan de Fuca is by far your best chance to see pelagic birds from a ferry. Sooty and short-tailed shear-waters, northern fulmars, and forked-tailed storm-petrels occur most frequently making this ferry ride a mini-pelagic trip. The Tsaw-wassen–Swartz Bay ferry and the Sydney–Ana-cortes ferry are considered good all-around ferry rides for wildlife and will usually have plenty of the regular seabirds and bald eagles. Always be on guard, however, you never know what might show up.

ANCIENT FORESTS

Often called the crowning glory of a land filled with superlatives, the ancient forests of the Pacific Northwest are certainly one of our greatest natural, and national, treasures. The unique climate west of the Coast Ranges, Cascades, and Coast Mountains from northern California to southeastern Alaska has created the greatest coniferous forests in the world. The main factors causing these lush forests are moderate temperatures and lots of rain—the heaviest precipitation in North America. This combination sounds great for any plant, but the most rain falls during the coldest part of the year followed by a significant summer drought. These are tough conditions for broad-leaved trees. Conifers, however, with their needles or scale-like leaves, can thrive in this environment, and it is here that they reach their greatest glory.

How great is great? About half of the 25 tallest species of trees in the world grow in this forest. For every genus of coniferous tree represented in the Pacific Northwest, the largest species in that genus is found here (except for the junipers). In eastern North America only one tree gets over 200 feet high, while in our forests thirteen different species regularly grow over 200 feet—the tallest reaching almost 400 feet. The redwoods are, of course, the most famous of these Pacific giants and just make it into the southwestern corner of Oregon from their stronghold in northern California. Close behind the redwoods in height and mass are Douglas-fir, Sitka spruce, western red-cedar, western hemlock, grand fir, Pacific silver fir, Port Orford cedar, sugar pine, and ponderosa pine.

Biomass is the total amount of all the living and once-living material in a particular area and is sometimes used to compare the productivity of two ecosystems. We frequently hear about the diversity, productivity, and importance of tropical rain forests, but the biomass of the richest tropical rain forests is about 180 tons/acre while the biomass of the average Pacific Northwest old-growth coniferous forest is around 400 tons/acre. The biomass of old-growth redwood forests can get over 1,500 tons/acre, the highest biomass of any ecosystem on Earth.

This great forest developed after the last ice age and for 10,000 years covered a 2000-mile stretch with an almost unbroken blanket of giant conifers. Native Americans used the western redcedar extensively, but their impact on this primeval forest was miniscule. Things changed dramatically in a geological wink of an eye when the new Americans and Canadians started to settle the West. With their advanced technologies and insatiable demands for building materials and fuel, they made short work of what was treated as an inexhaustible resource. Today in the United States only about 10% of this original ancient or old-growth forest is left and in Canada maybe as much as 40% remains. This is a much greater percentage of habitat loss than the often deplored current destruction of tropical rain forests. This loss seemed to go on for so long before being noticed because few people were aware of the differences between the old-growth forests being cut down and the younger forests that replaced them.

An old-growth or ancient forest is a special type of forest very different from the new forest that replaces it. Several characteristics make a forest old growth. As the name implies, there must be old trees. For the primary species in west-side forests—Douglas-fir, Sitka spruce, western hemlock, and western redcedar—"old" starts around 200 years, and 400 to 500 years is considered a good, healthy middle-age. But the big guys aren't the only trees living in an old-growth forest. Indeed, one of the most important characteristics of old growth is the presence of trees of all ages, and of a variety of species, creating a multi-layered canopy. Where the ancient giants have finally fallen, they have made openings in the canopy, letting light into the forest. This unevenness is one of the glaring differences between an ancient forest and a new forest planted in its place.

When these giants die, they remain as important to the forest as when they lived. A standing, dead tree is called a snag, and as many, possibly more, animals use snags as use living trees. Studies in Oregon have found that 60 species of birds and mammals use snags regularly for food, shelter, or both. Snags can remain standing and serve the forest for 100 years. A fallen tree is as important as a living tree; large fallen logs may last as long as 400 years on the forest floor. As many as 130 species of vertebrates may utilize a fallen log as it slowly decays, returning nutrients to the soil and to other plants. A very common sight in the Northwest is the nurse log, an old log with a garden of plants, especially young hemlocks, growing on it. Fallen logs act as giant sponges, serving as reservoirs of water for plants and animals during the summer drought.

Fallen logs in streams create the pools, falls, and riffles that are habitat for many aquatic animals. They shade the stream and help keep the temperature low, resulting in the higher oxygen content that trout and salmon need. Fallen logs, and organic debris on the ground, play an absolutely critical role in maintaining the quality of watersheds by preventing soil erosion, abating floods, and acting as filters, keeping silt out of streams. It is for these reasons that ancient forests make the greatest rivers and streams for salmon, and why logging kills fish. The presence of many snags and fallen logs is an essential characteristic of old-growth forests.

Scientists have only recently begun to understand the extreme complexity of ancient forest ecosystems. *Lobaria*, a common lichen growing on trees, plays a critical role in the forest's nitrogen cycle by fixing nitrogen from the air, making it eventually available to other plants when it falls to the ground. Tiny rodents called voles spread spores of fungi in their droppings that are essential for establishing symbiotic mycorrhizae in the roots of plants, greatly enhancing root function. Many animals utilize old-growth forests, and some are completely dependent upon this specific type of habitat.

Not many birds have made the cover of *Time* but the spotted owl's appearance in 1990 made it by far the best known denizen of the ancient forest. The marbled murrelet became the next well-known species dependent on old growth. The little voles so characteristic of old-growth forests (California redback, red tree, and Pacific voles) don't make exciting copy, so we hear little about them, or about other unpopular animals such as salamanders, but they are all unique species that play important roles in the ancient forest ecosystem. The majority of animals found in old-growth forests are also found in other forest types but old growth is their preferred habitat and the one in which they do best. Some of the other animals most closely associated with our ancient forests are Roosevelt elk, American martin, Sitka black-tailed deer, chickaree or Douglas squirrel, bald eagle, osprey, pileated woodpecker, Vaux's swift, brown creeper, hermit warbler, red crossbill, pine grosbeak, tailed frog, Olympic salamander, Pacific giant salamander, and seven bat species.

The controversy over the fate of the remaining ancient forest fragments in the Northwest has mellowed in recent years, overtaken by the immediate seriousness of salmon issues and most recently global climate change. The issues are interrelated, as are all the parts in an ecosystem.

▶ ANCIENT FORESTS BEST BETS OREGON

A small but nice sample of ancient forest close to the Portland area is in Oxbow RP, 7 miles east of Gresham. In Gresham drive east on Division St from 257th Dr (or Kane Dr) for 2.7 miles, and then angle to the right onto Oxbow Dr. Drive another 2.2 miles, and then turn left onto Oxbow Pkwy and drive another 1.6 miles to the park entrance. At the entrance station (fee) you can get a park map. The old-growth forest is south of the park road near trail markers D and E and is shown on the map. Oxbow Park is also the site of a salmon festival in October.

Another beautiful example of old growth with easy access is the Salmon River Trail in Mount Hood NF. About 18 miles east of Sandy and past the traffic signal in Welches, turn right off US Hwy 26 onto Salmon River Rd, FR 2618. Go south about 5 miles to the Green Canyon Camp Ground and just after the campground, but just before the road crosses the Salmon River on a bridge, you'll see a parking area on the left with a trailhead for the Salmon River Trail (#742).

Trail #742 heads south and immediately goes up a steep hill for a short haul, then levels out and is easy going from then on. While the trail is high on the canyon wall you can look right into the middle of some huge old maples, which are totally fuzzy with moss and ferns. You'll also get a good look at some of the birds that usually stay high in the trees. The trail drops to the river and across a small side channel is a river bench with a very scenic old-growth grove. The trail continues upstream into the wilderness area, but the forest does get a bit younger.

Some of the biggest and most accessible old-growth Douglas-firs and western hemlocks in the Columbia Gorge National Scenic Area are in Multnomah Basin, also called the Larch Mountain Crater. This is basically the area between Multnomah Falls and Larch Mountain, which has no larches, by the way. You can combine several trails in this area to make different loops; a good map or guide book is essential. William Sullivan describes a good route through the basin in his hiking guide for northwest Oregon and southwest Washington.

Opal Creek is probably the most famous ancient forest site in Oregon and was still threatened with logging when I wrote the first version of this book. But positive changes have occurred. Different parts of the area are now protected as Opal Creek Wilderness, Opal Creek Scenic Recreation Area, and the Elkhorn Creek National Wild and Scenic River, all within the Willamette National Forest. The Scenic Recreation Area protects the area that could not qualify as wilderness because it had roads, old mines, and an old mining camp—Jawbone Flats. In 1992 the Shiny Rock Mining Company made an astounding donation and gave Jawbone Flats to the private, nonprofit Friends of Opal Creek and its remaining acreage to the federal government for its eventual inclusion in the wilderness and recreation areas. The Friends are now the Opal Creek Ancient Forest Center, primarily an educational organization based at Jawbone Flats. It offers a variety of programs for different ages and interests. You can stay at Jawbone Flats for the classes and programs or as a private individual in the old cabins.

To reach Opal Creek from Interstate 5 near Salem, take State Hwy 22, the North Santiam Highway, 22 miles east and turn left (north) onto the North Fork Rd, at a flashing yellow light and across from the Swiss Village Restaurant. There is also a sign for the Elkhorn Recreation Area. Boy, you can't miss this turn. Head northeast on North Fork Rd. In about 20 miles it enters the Willamette NF, turns to gravel, and becomes FR 2209. In just over a mile turn left to stay on FR 2209, and drive another 4 miles until you reach a locked gate. Park near the gate, but do not block it or the road. Everyone must park at the gate and then walk the 3 miles to the Ancient Forest Center (Jawbone Flats). You can also ride a bike on the road from the gate to Jawbone, and if you're spending the night at the Center you can arrange to have your gear brought in for you while you're hiking or biking. There is an alternative trail to Jawbone Flats if you don't want to walk on the road.

The Aufderheide National Scenic Byway is the original section of what is now the West Cascades National Scenic Byway, a longer route. The Aufderheide is FR 19 between Oakridge and McKenzie Bridge in the Willamette NF. The Shale Ridge Trail (#3567) is an easy hike through some of the best ancient forest in the southern part of the Willamette NF. At 2 miles, inside the Waldo Lake Wilderness Area, the trail enters a grove of enormous western redcedars mixed with big leaf maples and magnificent Douglas-firs. From here trails head farther into the wilderness area. The trailhead for Shale Ridge is near milepost 30, about midpoint on the Aufderheide Byway, which is also described in October (Autumn Color in the Mountains), all the more reason to take this scenic byway.

Oregon's Coast Range has been so heavy logged that only a few tiny remnants of the once solid ancient forest remain. One of the few places to see old-growth Sitka spruce forest is in Oswald West SP, named after Oregon's governor from 1911 to 1915. Oswald deserves our eternal gratitude for making Oregon's beaches public, one of Oregon's greatest claims to fame. This state park is a fitting tribute. A section of the Oregon Coast Trail goes the length of the park, which runs between Arch Cape and Neahkahnie Mountain.

In the middle of the park are several parking areas. From the main parking area, the one with the restrooms, east of US Hwy 101 a wonderful trail goes through a great Sitka spruce forest to Short Sands Beach in Smuggler's Cove, one of the most beautiful little coves on the coast. Short Sands Creek is famous for its dippers, the beach is famous for its surfers, and the charming walk-in campground is famous for its little wheelbarrows used to haul your stuff to the campsite. The segment of the Oregon Coast Trail that goes north from the Short Sands area to Cape Falcon and eventually Arch Cape goes through some more fabulous Sitka spruce forest.

Many Oregonians have heard that redwoods, to many the ultimate ancient forest tree, grow in Oregon but few have seen them. Few redwoods remain in Oregon, and the general public is astonished, and conservationists are dismayed, when they learn that only two small stands of redwoods in the state are formally protected. The easiest way to see some of Oregon's giant redwoods is on the Redwood Nature Trail in the Siskiyou NF, adjacent to Loeb SP, about 9 miles northeast of Brookings on North Bank Chetco River Rd.

For a different mix of old-growth species, typical of southwestern Oregon with its heavy California influence, try the Big Tree Trail in Oregon Caves NM. You'll see giant white firs, incense-cedars, and the rare Port-Orford-cedar, as well as one of the contenders for the biggest Douglas-firs in Oregon. The trails are also good for wildflowers and begin at monument headquarters. Oregon Caves is 20 miles from Cave Junction, at the end of State Hwy 46.

The Northwest's east-side ancient forests are not as well known and, at this point, are not as protected as the ones of the west side. The Metolius River Trail, in Deschutes NF, goes through an excellent example of old-growth ponderosa pine forest. A 9-mile stretch of this trail runs along the west side of the Metolius River from Lower Canyon Creek CG to Candle Creek CG. You can take the trail from either end, or you can access it in the middle from the Wizard Falls Fish Hatchery (ODFW). Many consider the southern section from the hatchery to Lower Canyon Creek CG the most scenic. The Camp Sherman and Metolius River areas are reached from FR 14, about 9 miles west of Sisters on US Hwy 20.

In the Fremont NF are the last two large, unroaded stands of old-growth ponderosa pine in Lake County. Intermingled with these magnificent "yellow bellies" (a nickname for the large, old ponderosas), are old-growth white fir, western white pine, western juniper, and some beautiful meadows and aspen groves. Coleman and Dead Horse rims are northeast and southeast respectively from Gearhart Mountain Wilderness Area. Conservationists have been advocating wilderness status for these two areas for many years, but they remain unprotected. Both areas are fairly large with several parts to explore and not all trails are on maps, so use Wendell Wood's *Walking Guide to Oregon's Ancient Forests* to explore these and other forests in the state.

▶ ANCIENT FORESTS BEST BETS WASHINGTON

The ultimate temperate rain forest in the lower 48 is found in the Hoh, Quinault, and Queets river valleys in Olympic NP. Hiking up the Queets is difficult because you currently have to ford the river, but the Hoh and Quinault rainforests have outstanding trails. The Hall of Mosses Trail in the Hoh Rain Forest has the classic scene of bigleaf maples draped with mosses that you often see in photographs, but the Quinault Valley is equally impressive. Either one is a must see for anyone visiting the Pacific Northwest. The Quinault Loop Trail, near Lake Quinault Lodge, and the North Fork Quinault and Enchanted Valley trails are all well-marked, fantastic hikes. Access to both the Hoh Rain Forest Visitor Center and the Quinault area are from US 101 on the west side of the park.

Another equally impressive ancient forest is in the Soleduck Valley in the northwest corner of the park. At the end of the Sol Duc road (two spellings) are a campground, lodging, and a hot springs resort. The trail from the campground to the end of the road is 1.5 miles through ancient forest. From the road's end and parking area the trail continues another mile to Soleduck Falls through awesome old growth. You'll swear you are seeing gnomes and fairies out of the corner of your eye.

Some of the finest ancient forests in the Cascades are preserved in Mount Rainier NP. The Grove of the Patriarchs trail at Ohanapecosh, in the park's southeastern corner, is a self-guided nature trail through classic old growth with trees 500 to 1000 years old. Ranger and naturalist walks take place in summer. In the opposite corner of the park the Carbon River Rain Forest Trail, a bit wetter and less visited, allows solitude among the giants. While visiting Mount Rainier be on the lookout for mountain goats, marmots, and pikas and spectacular mountain wildflower displays in July and August.

A small but excellent example of Cascade ancient forest, and one convenient to the Emerald City megalopolis, is the Asahel Curtis Nature Trail near Snoqualmie Pass. This may be the last old-growth stand in the Interstate 90 corridor and makes a great stop any time you're passing through or going to nearby Gold Creek, with its migrating salmon, beaver, and possible mountain goats. This is a great drive in October when fall colors are peaking

and the salmon are running. The Asahel Curtis Trail has interpretive signs and is an easy hike for all ages. From I-90 take the Asahel Curtis/Denny Creek exit (Exit 47), and then turn right at the first stop sign. Turn left at the second stop sign, drive to the end of FR 55, and park. Pick up the trail (which actually starts at the picnic area) just east of the parking lot.

National wildlife refuges are rarely known for their forests, but a unique ancient forest is protected in Willapa NWR. Long Island, the largest estuarine island on the Pacific Coast, is in the southern end of Willapa Bay. On the southern end of this island is the 274-acre Long Island Cedar Grove. It is estimated that there have been no major changes to this grove in 3000 years. This grove has co-dominant western hemlock and western redcedar trees 500 and 1000 years old, respectively. Access to this island is only by private boat and depends on the tides. A boat launch is available near refuge headquarters on US 101. The island has five primitive campsites, but drinking water may not be available during the driest months. It's important to plan your trip to the island around the tides. Check with refuge staff before planning an overnight trip. If you camp on the island, be sure to take normal precautions for black bear by hanging your food.

▶ **ANCIENT FORESTS BEST BETS** BRITISH COLUMBIA

West Vancouver's Lighthouse Park is an almost-wilderness park of 185 acres within half an hour of downtown Vancouver. The heavily forested park on Point Atkinson is almost entirely original ancient forest. To reach the park drive west on Marine Dr for about 5 miles from the Lions Gate Bridge, and then turn left onto Beacon Ln at the large wooden sign for the park. Many trails crisscross the park; finding your way can be confusing. Start at the gate

at the end of the parking area and head east toward the park's summit. From here make a clockwise loop by continuing east, then driving south, and then west intersecting the road to the lighthouse. You can then drive south on the road to the lighthouse, with its scenic views of Burrard Inlet, or return to the parking area by driving north on the road.

The best examples of ancient forest still

standing in southwestern BC are on Vancouver Island. The Rain Forest Trail in the Long Beach Unit of Pacific Rim NP is two short loop trails in temperate rain forest that is so lush you'll think you'll sprout or decompose if you stand still too long. Most of the trails are on boardwalks that ramble over the forest floor and let you appreciate how dense the vegetation really is. If this doesn't make you feel like an Ewok, nothing will. The well-marked parking area is off Hwy 4 just about 4 miles north of the main visitor center at Wickaninnish. Loop A is on the north side of the highway, Loop B begins in the parking lot, and both are under a mile long. The trails go through similar habitat and have interpretive signs, but each area has its own character and the signs cover different topics, so hike both trails.

For an instant ancient forest experience, stop at MacMillian PP, usually called the Cathedral Grove, which is on Hwy 4 between Combs and Port Alberni. Park on the highway and step right into old-growth forest on either side of the road; the biggest trees are south of the highway. You can hear traffic from the highway and this well-used area is obviously not a wilderness experience, but the trees are impressive, you'll see snags loaded with old woodpecker nests, and it certainly makes a great break on the way to the west coast.

Carmanah Pacific PP was established in the nick of time in 1990 when the lower valley become protected to stop the logging of one the most spectacular stands of Sitka Spruce remaining in Canada and home to the world's tallest known Sitka Spruce, 312 feet high. Upper Carmanah and Walbran Valleys were added in 1995, and the park's name was changed to Carmanah Walbran PP. The Randy Stoltman Commemorative Grove in Carmanah Valley honors the man who tirelessly worked to protect this area since 1988 and died tragically in 1994, before the additions that had been his goal.

To me, Carmanah Walbran PP is the ultimate mysterious, lost-in-time, hidden valley of giant ancient trees. Travel is on dirt logging roads with no facilities or services within 20 miles. Be prepared and have a good map, such as the *Vancouver Island Backroad Mapbook*. Access is by one point on the western edge where you'll find some walk-in campsites with tables, tent pads, and fire rings. It's a short walk from the parking area to the sites and drinking water is nearby. The ranger station may not be staffed, but recent notices will be posted. It will take hours of rough driving on dirt roads to get here, so I recommend driving to the park one day and camping at the top that night. The next morning you can head down into Carmanah Valley and leave the modern world behind. From the camping area the trail descends 0.75 mile to the valley floor, where most of the trail is a fairly level boardwalk winding through the forest. Distances are not long, the entire trail in the valley is 6 miles, making this an area to leisurely explore in a day.

Three routes are available to get to the Caycuse River Bridge, and from that point there's one way to the park. The BC Parks Web site gives directions from Port Renfrew and Port Alberni. Here are the directions from Honeymoon Bay (great for flowers). From Honeymoon Bay on the shores of beautiful Lake Cowichan, the warmest and sunniest place on Vancouver Island, head west on the South Shore Rd. Just after the end of the lake South Shore becomes Nitinat Main, which you take southwest until it intersects South Main. Turn left onto South Main (go past the fish hatchery), and drive south until you come to the Caycuse River Bridge, 35 miles from Honeymoon Bay. Cross the bridge, and then immediately turn right onto Rosander Main. Drive another 18 miles on Rosander Main and into the park. The black bear scat we saw on Rosander Main is the most I've ever seen in my life. Be sure to leave your food locked up in your car while camping at Carmanah.

RAPTOR MIGRATION

For years they searched, hitting one dead end after another. Would it ever be found? Could there be another one? Where was the Hawk Mountain of the West?

Hawk Mountain Sanctuary in Pennsylvania could easily be the most famous birdwatching site in North America. Starting in 1934 there has been an annual count of the raptors that pass overhead during fall migration. The average count has been about 18,000 with a record high of 40,000 birds, making this one of the best-known wildlife events in the eastern United States. Was this happening in the West? Like the search for the Northwest Passage, western birdwatchers had been on a quest for the Hawk Mountain of the West for decades.

In 1977 Steve Hoffman and Wayne Potts began counting raptors in the Wellsville Mountains in Utah. In 1979 Steve shifted to the Goshute Mountains, just across the border in Nevada. An annual, systematic migrating raptor count has taken place in the Goshutes since 1983 with counts over 22,000 some years. So there is indeed a Hawk Mountain of the West: the Goshutes Mountains of Nevada. We don't have any place in the Northwest with numbers like that, but our states and our province each have one noteworthy raptor migration lookout that makes for great fall birding.

What's the big deal with counting raptors? Of course, humans have an ancient fascination for birds of prey, and raptors tend to be large and easier to see than most birds. However, there is a much more important reason to have regular, scientific counts of raptors. Birds of prey, being at the top of food webs, are sensitive indicators of ecosystem health over wide areas. Raptors are an essential part of healthy, functioning ecosystems upon which we depend. It's an "eagle in a coal mine" warning system, several layers up the food chain from the canary. In 1983 Steve Hoffman and his colleagues formed Hawkwatch International as a private, nonprofit research, education, and conservation organization. Research continues at 14 sites, including two here in the Northwest, plus partnership sites in Texas, Florida, and Mexico. Talking about numbers; each year the count at Veracruz, Mexico, is between 4 and 6 million.

What makes a hawk mountain? Hawk-watching sites are places where two things happen—the hawks from a large area become concentrated, and people can get close enough to see them. Most great hawk-watching spots are on mountains because this is where people can get closer to the birds. But the topography of the mountain must play a role in concentrating birds over a particular spot. The key for the birds is that they can soar. Soaring is flying without flapping and it provides tremendous energy-savings for birds, especially during long flights. It only works, however, when the air in which the bird is flying is rising—either (1) when wind hits a mountain or cliff and the air is deflected upward, creating a steady updraft that lifts the birds, or (2) when the air gets heated and rises, creating a thermal. Skillful soarers can remain aloft for hours without flapping their wings, if conditions are right.

Migrating hawks commonly follow ridgelines because when the wind blows from the right direction, an almost continual updraft off the ridge allows them to soar for long distances. Some of the best hawk-watching sites are on such ridges at points where the birds get closest to the land and are funneled into a smaller area because the ridge narrows or even ends. This is the situation at Hawk Mountain and the Goshutes. Good hawk-watching sites are sometimes a corridor of good habitat in a large area of bad habitat. This is another reason birds fly over the Goshutes, to avoid the Great Salt Lake Desert.

A common situation where thermals become important is when there is a large body of water. Because land near water will usually get hotter than the water during the day, thermals rise over the land. If raptors have to cross a particularly large body of water, they can save a lot of energy if there is a point of land near a crossing that has strong thermals. The birds can catch the thermals, ride them as high as they can, then glide across the open water, slowly losing altitude but greatly reducing the amount of time in which they'll have to actively flap. This is the situation at the tip of Vancouver Island, site of the best hawk migration spot currently known for British Columbia.

Because the Pacific Northwest is relatively mild, there simply are not as many birds passing through our region during migration as occur in the east. In fact many raptors from farther north stop to spend the winter here and many of our raptors don't leave. In our region the most common migrating raptors are the sharp-shinned and Cooper's hawks, red-tailed hawk, turkey vulture, and golden eagle. Regular in smaller numbers are bald eagle, northern harrier, American kestrel, and merlin, with a few peregrine falcons and osprey.

With some of our nicest weather in September and early October, hawk watching in the Northwest can be very pleasant. The best time to watch is usually in the middle of the day from about 10 a.m. to 2 p.m. Because lookouts are usually on high points of land, hawk watching usually provides some fantastic scenic vistas. The best conditions are usually when it's clear with moderate winds from the west or southwest, especially before a storm front coming from the north. Be sure to dress warmly; standing on a mountain top in the wind can be more than bracing. Scopes are rarely useful for watching flying hawks, and with the hiking involved at most of our spots, it's best to leave the scope behind (but not in your car at a trailhead.) Binoculars with a wide field of view, rather than compact models, are advantageous when trying to find birds in the sky.

The hawk-watching sites in the Northwest are relatively new, so we're still learning about what species fly when and the best dates and conditions for the maximum numbers of birds. Generally the best period is mid-September to mid-October. You may be able to make a significant contribution to our knowledge of raptors by recording your observations of fall hawk migration and contacting HawkWatch International with your information. Better yet, you can become a volunteer counter.

▶ RAPTOR MIGRATION BEST BETS OREGON

At this time the two best spots for hawk watching in Oregon are Bonney Butte and Green Ridge. HawkWatch International has been doing regular counts at Bonney Butte in partnership with the Mount Hood National Forest since 1994, and that site now has Hawk-Watch staff camping there for the entire count period—September and October. The site also now has an excellent interpretive sign, a staff educator, and a portable toilet there for the count period. To get to Bonney Butte, head east from Government Camp on US Hwy 26 to State Hwy 35 and take Hwy 35 east 4.5 miles to the White River East Sno-Park. Go south on FR 48, also called White River Rd and signed for Rock Creek Reservoir and Wamic. In 7 miles turn left onto FR 4890, which is paved and has a sign on it after you turn. Go 3.7 miles and you'll come to a well-marked intersection with FR 4891.

Following signs to Bonney Meadows, go north 4 miles on the rough, dirt FR 4891 until you reach the campground. Cars with average to high clearance should be able to make it driving carefully, but forget about bringing your '66 Impala low-rider. From the campground drive another 0.25 mile, and you'll see a parking area on your right and a gated road on your left. Leave your car in the parking area and walk up the gated road one mile to the

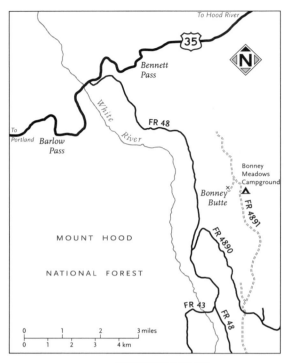

BONNEY BUTTE

ridge that is often a raptor migration route. It is also almost exactly 50 miles due south of Bonney Butte, as the merlin flies, so it was a logical place to look for another hawk mountain.

In the last couple of years the East Cascades Bird Conservancy (ECBC), based in Bend, has started regularly counting the birds passing over the site of the old Green Ridge Lookout on weekends from mid-September to mid-October. The species and numbers of birds have been very similar to Bonney Butte, no surprise given how close the sites are, although Bonney Butte is about 1000 feet higher. The surrounding forests are great for seeing typical ponderosa pine birds, such as white-headed woodpecker, Williamson's sapsucker, white-breasted and pygmy nuthatches, green-tailed towhee, Cassin's finch, red crossbill, dusky grouse, and, if you're very lucky, a northern goshawk.

The ECBC would love your help counting raptors on their organized count days. You would be among some awesome birders and would learn a lot about raptor identification. Contact the coordinator through the ECBC Web site (www. ecbcbirds.org) for meeting time and place.

If you want to go to Green Ridge Lookout on your own, it's about an 18-mile drive from Indian Ford Campground. Half of the road is dirt in decent shape but a higher clearance vehicle would be best. It's also a good idea to have the official forest map of the Deschutes NF. Start at Indian Ford Campground, 5 miles west of Sisters, and drive north on FR 11 about 10 miles until the pavement ends and the road forks. Take the left fork onto FR 1150 and continue north approximately 6 miles. Always follow signs for Green Ridge Lookout when you see them, but they won't be at every junction and turn.

hawk-watching site. You may be at the top for a couple of hours. One reason the birds are there is because it's windy, so take warm clothing, as well as food and water. During the September through October 31 (weather permitting) count period, the Hawkwatch staff stays at a campsite part way up the road. The views are awesome. When you visit you may have the chance to see birds of prey in hand from the trapping station near the top.

Green Ridge runs from Black Butte to where the Metolius River flows around its northern end. It makes up the eastern edge of the first 20 miles of the Metolius and rises steeply above the river to 4500 feet. Green Ridge is the classic north–south-running mountain

Turn left onto FR 1154 and in less than a mile, turn left onto FR 1140. Go south only 300 yards and then turn right onto FR 600, which is a single lane. Go west on FR 600 a little over 0.25 mile. Park where the road makes a 90° left turn, in a clear-cut near the ridge top. After parking walk about 5 minutes north to the survey site. If you see any blue ribbons on the north side of the road at the turn, follow them to the north, across the clear-cut and then through a narrow strip of trees into the top of the next clear-cut. This is the place. If it's a weekend you will probably see some other cars parked on the road, and as you walk north and listen carefully, you may hear voices in the distance.

▶ RAPTOR MIGRATION BEST BETS WASHINGTON

After trying several places in Washington, HawkWatch, in partnership with the Okanogan and Wenatchee national forests, has settled on Chelan Ridge, starting their counts there in 1997. This site is perched on top of the ridge that is northeast of Lake Chelan and has a full-time, on-site educator for the season. Visitors are welcome any time during September and October, unless snow causes everyone to leave sooner. Some of these hawk counters live through some pretty outrageous weather before they leave. This site is also unique because the Methow Valley Visitor Center in Winthrop displays the daily bird tallies. The number of birds seen is in the same 2000 to 3000 range as Bonney Butte and the species are the same.

This site also requires a short hike, just 0.75 mile from the parking area on a Forest Service road. To get to the Chelan Ridge count site take State Hwy 153 west from US Hwy 97 at Pateros, the route to the Methow Valley and State Hwy 20. Six and a half miles from Pateros turn left from Hwy 153 to head south on Black Canyon Rd, FR 4010. Drive 9 miles up the canyon to the intersection with FR 8020, sometimes called the Copper Mountain Rd. Turn left here to head southeast on FR 8020. In 3.5 miles is a parking area with portable toilets and some flagging. Park here, and then hike 0.75 mile to the northwest, following the flagging, to the observation site. Enjoy the birds and the view.

One of the early sites explored for raptor counting is Red Top Mountain in the Wenatchee NF, between Wenatchee and Ellensburg. This site is not used for any organized hawk watching or census work now, but it's an awesome spot with a spectacular view. The last stretch is a steep and rocky 0.5-mile hike up a craggy old volcanic peak to the abandoned fire lookout on the top. Take US 97 south from US Hwy 2 between Leavenworth and Wenatchee for 29 miles. Just before you reach the Mineral Springs Resort, turn right onto FR 9738 following signs to Red Top Mountain. The route is well marked, so just keep following the signs. In a little over 2 miles take a left fork onto FR 9702, and in 7 miles you'll be in the parking area at the top. The trail to the lookout starts at the northern end of the parking area. The trail is slippery with loose rock near the top, so watch your footing and take the most gradual trail to the top, avoiding the worn short cuts. You'll have a spectacular panorama with the Stuart Range in the Alpine Lakes Wilderness to the northeast and Mount Rainier looming up in the southwest. In the past Red Top has been a good place to see prairie falcons and Swainson's hawks, in addition to the regular sharp-shinned, Cooper's, and red-tailed hawks, golden eagles, and turkey vultures.

The road to Hart's Pass and Slate Peak is the highest in the state of Washington and provides a fairly convenient, and very dramatic, route for exploring the subalpine zone. The road is steep and narrow with turnouts, but the gravel is well maintained. Just don't let the driver do any birdwatching, especially in the last few miles. In summer this area is great for mountain flowers, high mountain birds, pikas and marmots, and provides access to the Pacific Crest Trail and the Pasaytan Wilderness Area. If you drive the North Cascades Highway in the fall, include a good part of a day for a trip to the top on this road. From Hwy 20, 16 miles northwest of Winthrop, follow signs to Mazama which mainly consists of the Mazama Country Inn and the Mazama Store. From the Mazama Store take Mazama Rd northwest following the signs to Hart's Pass, about 21 miles away. At Hart's Pass there is a sign for Slate Peak, the best hawk-watching site, in another 3 miles.

▶ RAPTOR MIGRATION BEST BETS BRITISH COLUMBIA

Beechey Head in East Sooke RP is the rocky headland on the southern-most tip of Vancouver Island and was first discovered by local birders in 1990. David Allinson, one of the first to report the great sightings there, told me about this spot when it was still new. I had the pleasure to meet David on top of the lookout on a beautiful October day when we saw one kettle of 200 turkey vultures.

Beechey Head is a classic example of a place where migrating birds pile up as they gain altitude over the last point of land before trying to cross a major water barrier, in this case the ten-mile-wide Strait of Juan de Fuca. Thermals rise as the land heats, and the birds rise to high altitudes before starting a long southbound glide to the Olympic Peninsula. In March the same thing happens in the opposite direction with birds piling up over Cape Flattery before heading north.

Fourteen species of diurnal raptors have been seen from this point, all the species that would be considered normal for southwestern British Columbia plus rough-legged hawk and at least one broad-winged hawk almost every year. Record daily highs for the most abundant species are 1000 turkey vultures, 101 red-tailed hawks, and 56 sharp-shinned hawks. Other migrating birds are seen and the Beechey Head lookout appears to be on a main migration route for band-tailed pigeons and Vaux's swifts as well. The best time for viewing is the typical mid-September to mid-October with the rarest sightings tending to be right at the end of September. Here are directions to East Sooke RP from downtown Victoria that avoid the Trans-Canada Highway 1. The traffic congestion on Hwy 1 leaving Victoria has gotten so bad that it's rarely the fastest way. This more interesting route will take you through Victoria West and parts of Esquimalt and View Royal to Colwood. If you want to take Hwy 1 you can easily pick up this route on the Old Island Highway in Colwood. This route also goes by Esquimalt Lagoon and Witty's Lagoon RP, excellent places for shorebirds and waterfowl in the fall.

In downtown Victoria get on Bay St heading west and drive over the Point Ellice Bridge to Victoria West. Bay St makes a couple of bends and does some short name changes before becoming Graigflower Rd. Continue northwest on Graigflower Rd and, lo and behold, in 3 miles it changes names again and becomes the Island Highway, also known as Hwy 1A. This sounds confusing, but just stay on the obvious main road as you drive through the various eras of its history. In 1.5 miles is a confusing series of intersections; stay on Hwy 1A heading to Colwood. You'll pass the Six Mile Pub, an old landmark from the days when miles were used in British Columbia.

If you don't want to go to Esquimalt Lagoon stay on Hwy 1A and go 2.5 miles south of the Six Mile Pub to Metchosin Rd. Turn left on Metchosin and proceed to Witty's Lagoon.

To make a side trip through Esquimalt Lagoon turn left onto Ocean Boulevard one mile south of the Six Mile Pub and follow signs for Fort Rodd Hill Park. Drive past Fort Rodd Hill Park staying on Ocean Blvd and follow signs to Esquimalt Lagoon. About 2 miles from Hwy 1A you will drive out on the sand spit that separates the lagoon from the Strait of Juan de Fuca. Drive down the spit and carefully pull over any place that looks interesting and scan both sides of the spit. From Esquimalt Lagoon you continue on to Witty's Lagoon and then to East Sooke RP.

To continue to Witty's Lagoon, drive south on Ocean to the end of the spit and turn right onto Lagoon Rd. In about 0.5 mile turn left onto Metchosin Rd and head south. In a little over 2 miles you'll reach the parking area and entrance for Witty's Lagoon RP, which is described in February (Wintering Waterfowl). A stop at Witty's takes longer than going to Esquimalt because you'll need to hike down to the lagoon.

To proceed to East Sooke RP and Beechey Head drive south less than one mile to the little town of Metchosin, which has a store and school, and turn right onto Happy Valley Rd. Drive just 0.5 mile on Happy Valley, and then turn left and head south on Rocky Point Rd. In 3.3 miles you'll come to a major fork; turn right onto East Sooke Rd—not left to the Rocky Point military facility. In 3 miles turn left onto Becher Bay Rd, there is a small sign for East Sooke RP, and drive one mile to the park. Don't take any of the driveways that fork to the left, but drive straight into the parking lot.

The trail to Beechey Head is about 2 miles one way, and the last part is rough and requires scrambling up Beechey Head itself. I would give the hike an intermediate rating, and when standing atop Beechey Head, you are totally exposed to the weather. You'll want to make this trip only when the weather is dry, clear, mild, and not very windy. Okay, so that's pretty rare in the Northwest, but in September near Victoria your chances are pretty good. An acceptable alternative to hiking out to The Head is to hang out in the parking lot and adjacent beautiful prairie and watch the sky from there. This setting is nowhere near as spectacular as Beechey Head and you won't see as many birds as close, but on a good day you'll still see plenty of the action overhead.

Onward to Beechey Head. The way is tricky because there are so many junctions and you can't really see where you are supposed to be headed, so you'll need to take these directions with you; maybe make a photocopy for the trail. The park map helps until the very end. After you've parked, walk back toward the entrance road and walk south on the dirt road that would be the continuation of Becher Bay Rd if it went straight. Go straight south on this trail, and when you come to any unmarked trails heading off to the left, stay to the right on the dirt road.

You'll encounter seven trail junctions and eight trail signs. The signs are so frequent that mileage isn't important for the route. Two general rules: (1) Always take a trail to Beechey Head (seems obvious, eh?), and (2) Never take a trail that goes to Babbington Hill, Interior Trail, Cabin Point, or Petroglyphs. Ready?

FIRST TRAIL SIGN Go straight to the Coast Trail.

SECOND TRAIL SIGN Go left to Beechey Head and the Coast Trail.

THIRD TRAIL SIGN Go right to Beechey Head, not left to Petroglyphs. You will go up and down a hill.

FOURTH TRAIL SIGN Go straight to the Coast Trail; not right to the Interior Trail.

FIFTH TRAIL SIGN Go left to Beechey Head and don't worry about the others.

SIXTH TRAIL SIGN. Tells you Beechey Head is ahead and Aylard Farm is behind you.

SEVENTH TRAIL SIGN Go right to Beechey Head and you'll quickly reach the eighth and last trail sign.

EIGHTH TRAIL SIGN Tells you that the Coast Trail is to the right or left and that Beechey Head is straight ahead.

The last time I was there it wasn't clear where to go next. Walk around the sign and go to the other side of the large Douglas-fir behind the sign. This is where you'll find the trail to Beechey Head. Aren't you glad you have these directions? Follow this trail south, more or less, about 20 paces and you'll come to a huge rock with a large crack, which the trail goes through. A yellow patch on the rock indicates the way. Keep going until you reach a humongous rock with a sign on it for Beechey Head. You made it. Now all you have to do is climb up the rock to the top. On top of The Head, you'll find a small concrete obelisk marking the international boundary line between Canada and the United States, which is out in the Juan de Fuca Strait (the Strait of Juan de Fuca for you Americans who don't speak Canadian).

On a clear day you'll be able to see Cape Flattery, the Olympic Mountains, Port Angeles, and the Washington Cascades as far north as Glacier Peak. On a very clear day you can even see Mount Rainier. You'll feel as if you're standing in the middle of the Salish Sea. The scenery is breathtaking to the south, but for birds you'll want to watch to the north and overhead. Vancouver Island works like a funnel and the migrating raptors, mainly turkey vultures, move south down the island and concentrate right over your head. Kettles of 100 to 300 vultures are regular. Anytime there are a lot of birds soaring together overhead, look them over carefully because mixed groups are common. It's not as hard as you might think to pick a Cooper's hawk out of 100 turkey vultures. The few that are different from the masses will usually stand out to you after awhile. Also watch for flocks of Vaux's swifts and band-tailed pigeons which seem to use the same route on their journeys south. Return the way you came and have fun in Victoria that night.

SWIFT ROOSTS

Swifts are one of those tiny plain birds that are unknown to most folks. Once you get to know them well, however, hardly a summer day goes by without seeing or hearing them. To me their high-pitched little chittering calls are one of the sounds of summer in Portland. To know they exist you need to recognize their sound or spend time looking up at the sky, which most people don't do because they are walking around looking at the ground talking on their cell phones. However, in September they form large communal roosts in chimneys, becoming so noticeable that they end up in the news.

These are the Vaux's swift, smallest of North American swifts. Swifts are among the world's fastest birds, constantly zipping through the air catching insects. Vaux's swifts are present in small numbers in almost all older forests throughout the Northwest during their short summer stay. You'll regularly see them over parts of many towns either over water or in areas with lots of trees, including older neighborhoods with lots of old street trees. They are here only from the second half of April to October making their visit to the Northwest for breeding one of the shortest of all migrating birds. They spend the rest of the year in the tropics, from central Mexico to northern South America.

Before migrating south in the fall, these speedy little birds start gathering together in huge numbers for communal roosts at night in preparation for migrating south together. Many types of birds migrate together in large groups for protection from predators, and this is probably true for swifts. Group migrations also help young birds learn routes and feeding stops from the old timers. Swifts probably conserve energy by roosting in groups, because those hot little bodies together in a chimney reduces an individual's heat loss. The term *roosting* describes when birds are sleeping or resting for an extended period, usually at night because most birds are strongly diurnal.

By large communal roosts I mean thousands of birds at one time. Roosts of 2000 swifts are not uncommon and some have been estimated at 30,000 birds. To see that many birds close together at one time is definitely a wildlife spectacle, and when it occurs the word usually spreads quickly through the birding community and sometimes even makes it to the evening news, or at least into newspapers. In Portland the nightly viewing of the swifts at Chapman School has become an established cultural event with hundreds of people arriving well ahead of time with lawn chairs and picnics. More than one Portland romance has started at the swifts, and a new condominium complex is called The Vaux.

These folks are there to watch the swifts gather into an increasing swarm swirling over the area and then descend into the chimney for the night. Arrive at least half an hour before sunset to select the best viewing site, trade bird stories, and generally get into the mood.

The size of the roost at any one site, and the time in the month with peak numbers, will vary some from year to year. Sometimes the swifts will stop using a site for no obvious reason and start a new one. Many small, scattered sites exist thorough our region, and you may discover one on your own. These sites may have just a few hundred birds, which often goes surprisingly unnoticed by people living nearby.

If you visit a large roost you'll first see individual birds zipping around, and then small groups starting to form. Gradually more and more birds will arrive, and they'll begin to fly together more and more. Then the flocks will grow larger and begin to join together until there are one or two huge flocks swirling in large circles over the area. The birds may disperse suddenly and then reform. Eventually, one huge tornado of swifts will be circling over the chimney, swooping closer and closer. The sounds of the crowd are pretty funny at this point as people "ooooh" in unison like a group watching fireworks.

Rather suddenly the birds will begin to drop into the chimney. To me it looks like the chimney has become a giant vacuum cleaner and is sucking the birds out of the air. Others have described the sight as looking like a black cloud of smoke going back into the chimney in reverse. What is amazing is how quickly the birds are gone and the sky is suddenly empty and quiet. If you're at a roost that has a crowd, expect applause after the last swift has disappeared.

The swifts cling onto the sides of the chimney with their tiny feet (with large claws) and hang closely packed together, looking like feathery shingles. They sleep in this position all night and leave at dawn (when there are never groups of people standing around watching). This may go on for several weeks and then the number of birds will start to drop dramatically until they are all gone.

By now you might have asked yourself, What did these birds do before there were chimneys? In times past, the vast forests of the Northwest were full of old, dead trees, called snags, some of which were hollowed out at the top from decay or fire. Some of these large natural chimneys were the sites of communal roosts. Swifts also nest inside hollow trees, but as individual pairs, not in groups. As the forests were cut down, the swifts were forced to try to find other spots for nesting and roosting. At the same time, chimneys started to appear and slowly these birds have adapted and learned to use chimneys, and a few similar structures, as substitutes for hollow snags. Most authors describe the Vaux's swifts' use of chimneys as a recent development. Its close relative, the chimney swift of the eastern United States, has been regularly using chimneys for a longer period of time, presumably because Europeans started altering the landscape and building chimneys there earlier.

Vaux's swifts have also started using chimneys for nesting. If you hear little cheeping noises coming from your chimney during July, the peak of their nesting season, you've got swifts. Close the damper so they won't get into your house, and for goodness sake don't build a fire. If a baby swift happens to fall into your fireplace, you can try putting it back up in the chimney on one of the ledges around where the damper is. Its parents will find it and feed it there if they are still using the chimney. Alternatively, contact a wildlife rehabilitation center if you have one in your area.

Don't worry about the swifts moving in; they'll be gone in at most a month. Their delicate little nest of sticks and dried saliva will quickly fall apart or go up in flames with your first fire, so don't worry about it blocking your chimney. If you are so blessed as to have your chimney chosen for a communal roost (it does happen), you will need to have the fireplace and chimney thoroughly cleaned after they are gone. Cover your chimney with a screen if you don't want a repeat performance next year, or you may decide to leave your chimney as a swift roosting refuge.

▶ SWIFT ROOSTS BEST BETS OREGON

The most famous swift roost in the West is at Chapman School, located in northwest Portland near the intersection of NW 25th and NW Raleigh. The large brick chimney at the back of the school, near the end of NW 27th is now dedicated to the swifts. This has been a festive scene since the late 1980s. It is the largest swift roost of any kind in the world and estimates have run as high as 30,000 birds in the best years.

Another roost in the Portland area is at Oregon City High School, which hasn't gotten much attention so far. I estimated 1000 swifts one night and I was the only person there watching them. How different from Chapman. The school is at 1306 12th St in the older part of Oregon City. This is another old school with a large chimney in the back, and the best place to view the chimney and the birds is from the back of the school on 10th St just before it intersects Harrison St. There is room to park along 10th where you're above the school, looking almost right at the top of the chimney. It'll be interesting to see if this develops into a major roost and becomes a tourist attraction like Chapman School.

Agate Hall on the campus of the University of Oregon has had an active roost for years. Agate Hall is in the southeast corner of the campus at the intersection of E 18th Ave and Agate St.

Continuing south on Interstate 5 is the Roseburg roost. This is an old chimney on the clay studio of the Umpqua Valley Arts Center, which used to be part of the veteran's hospital complex. Driving south on I-5 take the Harvard Ave exit (Exit 124), and then drive west on Harvard to Fir Grove Park. The chimney is obvious; to reach it turn right toward the Veteran's Hospital, and then in half a block make a quick left. You'll have to look for the best parking and access to view the chimney because the Umpqua Valley Arts Center seems to be a growing and changing place. You can call the center at 541-672-2532 to check on the chimney and roost before making a trip. No one seems sure how long swifts have been using the chimney but its use goes back at least 20 years.

▶ SWIFT ROOSTS BEST BETS WASHINGTON

The little town of Klickitat is on the Klickitat River about 12 miles upstream from the Columbia River. A mile northeast from Klickitat on State Hwy 142, near milepost 14, is the Mineral Springs Unit of the Klickitat WA managed by WDFW (fee). In the camping area is an old abandoned ice house. It was sold for salvage, but then WDFW found out it was a swift roost and bought it back for the swifts. Way to go, WDFW! Numbers are not known here, but for years folks have been saying thousands. Incidentally, the canyon of the Klickitat is beautiful and farther up Hwy 142 near the Glenwood Highway it's possible to see turkeys among the oaks.

Sumas is a port of entry on the Canadian border. The historic Sumas Customs House, built in 1932 and now a registered historic building, is just 200 yards southeast of the current inspection station. One of the chimneys on the building is a false chimney added later to provide symmetry. For decades, no one is sure when it started; at least 3000 swifts have been using the false chimney for roosting. The building has an interesting tale. A new customs building was built in 1990, and the old one was slated to be demolished. Some people expressed concern about the swifts; many others wanted to preserve the historic building. Eventually the building was saved, then moved and renovated for office space. Let's hope the building and its swifts survive another period of uncertainty.

What some claim is the largest swift roost in Washington is at the Frank Wagner Elementary School in Monroe, east of Snohomish on US Hwy 2. The school is right in the middle of town on Main St at Dickinson Rd, about 12 blocks from US Hwy 12. As with most of these roosts there isn't any kind of a real census, but the word on the street is 5000.

SEPTEMBER'S NATURE NUGGETS

FLYING ANTS AND TERMITES Ant and termite colonies produce winged adults only once a year, and for many species this happens during September, often just after some rain. When conditions are right, the air in some places can be filled with thousands of flying termites or ants. You can see flying ants at different times between spring and fall because different species have different flight times, plus species of ants outnumber termites in the Northwest. Flying termites are more noticeable because most of them are flying at the same time, they are large, and they attract plenty of birds, which gobble them up as fast as they can. Sometimes on the coast in September you'll see lots of gulls flying in fairly small circles over a certain spot. They are eating flying termites that are swarming up out of the ground under where they are flying. You can tell when this is going on because the gulls will be making little jerking movements with their heads as they grab the termites out of the air. See if you can find the termites on the ground. These winged termites are the new "princes and princesses" making their mating flights. It's no fun being an ant prince. After mating, the males die and the fertilized females go on to become the queens of new colonies. Better to be a male termite. The termite queen and her king start the new colony together. Awww.

PELICANS As summer wanes many brown pelicans start moving north up the coast from their breeding grounds in California and Mexico. Some pelicans arrive earlier in the summer but most don't show up until the end of breeding season. They always come as far as Oregon and many can be seen as far north as Cannon Beach. How far north they travel each year varies with weather and ocean conditions. During strong El Nino years they have gone as far as Vancouver Island. Elegant terns breed on islands off the Baja Peninsula and also wander north in the fall after breeding. They had never been recorded in our region until 1983, the year of a dramatic El Nino effect, when they were seen even off the coast of Washington. Be on the lookout for unusual terns when you see lots of pelicans or migrating common terns (which occur regularly in September) along the coast.

> An amazing bird the Pelican,
> its beak can hold more than its bellican.
> And to this day I still must say:
> I don't know how the hellican.
> OGDEN NASH

SHINE ON, SHINE ON ... Harvest moon. For centuries the full moon closest to the Autumnal Equinox has been called the Harvest Moon in North America. It is the full moon that stays low in the sky the longest, making it a perfect backdrop for scenes of harvested corn, migrating geese, and other autumn motifs. The next full moon is the Hunter's Moon, and these full moons are special because for several nights in a row they rise before the sky is completely dark and the reflected sunlight from them prolongs twilight. This extra light extends the time available for harvesting and hunting, important preparations for winter.

BIRD MIGRATION: A CLOSER LOOK

The regular disappearance and reappearance of many kinds of birds has puzzled people since ancient times. It took a surprisingly long time for people to accept the idea of birds making long migrations, and only in the last 100 years have humans begun to understand what's going on. The term *migration* refers to any regular extended movements by animals, usually between an animal's breeding and nonbreeding range. Birds are rightly famous for their amazing migrations, but they are certainly not the only animals that migrate. Some mammals, reptiles, amphibians, fish, insects, crustaceans, and mollusks migrate. However, many more birds migrate than do any other group of animals, and they travel some of the greatest distances at the greatest speeds.

A round trip migration of several thousand miles is common, even for small songbirds and some hummingbirds. The record holders are the shearwaters with their 20,000-miles-a-year journey and some shorebirds and terns that make 10,000 to 15,000 miles in a large loop each year. What is really impressive is how far some birds fly without stopping. Many birds regularly fly 300 to 500 miles at a time, but some shorebirds and waterfowl have been known to fly 2000 miles nonstop. That's around 80 to 90 hours of continual flying—the equivalent of a human runner doing five-minute-miles continually for four days. It has been called the greatest physiological feat of any vertebrate. Such multiday nonstops are, however, the exception and not the rule. Most birds stop regularly to rest and refuel by eating.

Why in the world would they do that? There's no question that making such long flights is dangerous in many ways. The common belief is that birds have to migrate to get away from cold weather. This is partially true, but a number of birds do live year-round in some of the harshest weather. After all, birds are endotherms (warm blooded) and have feathers, the greatest insulation around. The key to survival is food—getting enough calories to produce plenty of internal heat. This becomes impossible for birds that feed in the water when the water freezes. When cold weather comes, insects and other invertebrates become extremely limited and hard to find, so most insect eaters also have to depart. Amazingly, some birds such as chickadees, nuthatches, and woodpeckers have adapted to find enough arthropod eggs, larvae, and pupae in trees and shrubs to be common winter residents in the north. Go out some winter's day and see how many insect eggs and larvae you can find on a bunch of tree trunks, and you'll be very impressed by this feat.

Three-fourths of North America's birds are considered migratory and about 200 species winter in the American tropics, also called the Neotropics. If they go down there because food is abundant and the climate is less stressful, why don't they just stay? Why go back north? The big problem is that when it is time to breed, there is a huge increase in the demand for food to feed the babies. The traditional thinking is that our birds leave their homes up here in the northern, temperate zone to escape the cold and winter someplace warmer, only to return home in the spring. However, many of these birds spend more time in their winter range than they do up here. Another way to look at it is that these birds are tropical birds that take a quick trip north in summer to take advantage of the long days (day length doesn't change in the tropics) and exploit the massive explosion of insect life that makes raising their babies much easier than in the overcrowded, highly competitive tropical forest. As soon as the young are on their own (or even before, in some cases), these birds return home to their tropical habitats. This portrays Neotropical migrants not as helpless wimps fleeing their homes until they can come back, but as bold marauders exploiting the brief but plentiful bounty to the north for as long as it pays well.

These birds have additional reasons to head north besides longer hunting hours and tons of food. In general, the farther north you travel from the tropics, the fewer animals there are, which means fewer predators and less competition for food and space. Another advantage might be reduced parasites and germs in the far north because those nasty organisms are wiped out each winter by the cold. It's also possible that by moving north for awhile birds get a change in diet that provides some essential micronutrients harder to get in the tropics. Although possible, these last two theories have yet to be proved.

Given this point of view, the question might be, Why don't more birds migrate north? This gets down to some very tricky and highly complex risk-benefit analysis for both options based on the life history of each individual species. For birds that have a reliable year-round food source, the risks of migration rarely pay off. Then there is The Really Big Question—how did this migration business get started in the first place? The history of glaciations has been the most popular explanation, but right now science can't really answer that question. Isn't that great? Some great natural mysteries are still unsolved.

Another question that always arises about migration is, How do the birds know where to go and how do they find their way? Here, science has some answers.

Birds use several techniques to find their way during migration. The easiest to understand is one humans use—learned landmarks. Birds see and memorize features on the land below. On migrations most birds migrate in flocks, and on their first migrations the young birds just go with the flow and learn the route. This is typical of waterfowl, which most often migrate during the day. Conveniently, many of the main geographical features in North American happen to run north and south which gives a strong indication of the right general direction.

Some birds, like shorebirds, can't follow the leader because the adults actually leave for the south before the young can fly. Hard to imagine, but at a certain point the adults can't do anything more for their young and are just competition for food. Yet when the young can fly and the time is right, they just take off and go to the right place—even if it's Argentina. We now know that some birds are born with an accurate star map in their brain. This means, of course, that these birds migrate at night, which is an excellent way to avoid predators. Yes, there are hundreds of birds that are excellent celestial navigators at night! Wait a minute; the stars appear to move in the sky during the night. This means that in addition to their star map, these night-migrating birds also have an accurate biological clock in their brain that allows them to compensate for the earth's rotation. Experiments in planetariums, where scientists can manipulate the sky, have documented these abilities. Other birds fly during the day and navigate using the sun, an equally amazing ability.

These first two methods of navigating require that the birds be able to see the ground, sun, or stars. What happens when the ground is covered with fog or they have to fly through clouds? For years scientists suspected that birds might be able to sense the earth's magnetic field, and now experiments have demonstrated that this is indeed true. It turns out that some birds are very sensitive to minor variations in magnetic fields and that minute magnetic particles in their brain may play a role in this sense. Such iron particles have been found in other animals that use the earth's magnetic field for navigation, and there is now even a bit of evidence that some humans have these magnetic particles also. One scientist has even suggested that this may partially explain why some people have a better sense of direction than others.

Two more senses may play a role for some birds. Because most birds have a very poor, possibly nonexistent sense of smell, it is unusual that a few actually do use smell for navigation. Storm-petrels nest on islands and can apparently smell their island while at sea and locate their burrows by smell alone. Some other birds might be able to smell better than we think and might also use scent to some degree in finding their way. Lastly, birds can hear very low frequencies of sound, called infrasound, which are way below human hearing. Very low sounds like this are made by ocean waves, wind blowing against mountains, and thunderstorms. Because birds can hear these sounds, do they use them to help find their way? Another unsolved mystery.

The final answer to how birds navigate is that each type of bird uses some combination of all these possible techniques. As with all advanced animal behavior, multiple interacting elements are involved and no one simple answer applies in all cases. As any birdwatcher knows, birds are complex animals with some of the most finely developed senses in the world. Despite our knowledge, a few experiments are still mind-boggling and hard to explain with what we know. Manx shearwaters can be taken from their burrows at night in Wales, placed in a lightproof box, and flown 3200 miles to Massachusetts and released. In less than two weeks the birds will be back in their burrows in Wales. White-crowned sparrows have been similarly kidnapped in California and released in Maryland. Some have found their way right back where they started from, but it has taken them a year. Unless these birds have learned how to use our global positioning satellites, how they do this remains yet more unsolved mysteries of migration.

OCTOBER

AUTUMN COLOR IN THE MOUNTAINS

The changing colors of leaves in the fall must surely be one of the most powerful symbols of seasonal change, at least in the temperate zone. Even the most isolated-from-nature urban dweller knows that changing leaves means winter is on its way. Transplanted easterners may consider our colors ho-hum compared to the spectacle of the eastern hardwood forests, but I guess that's the tradeoff for having the most magnificent coniferous forests in the world. Despite the abundance of evergreen conifers, we have plenty of color to get us in the mood for jack-o'-lanterns and turkeys with cranberry sauce.

Many of North America's large families of common deciduous trees are represented in the Northwest, even if they are overshadowed (literally) by the evergreens. We have maples, willows, oaks, black cottonwood, quaking aspen, Pacific dogwood, two birches and their close relatives the alders, and Oregon ash. Then there are the many species of smaller fruit trees and shrubs, such as crabapple, chokecherry, osoberry, and huckleberries. These may not be as conspicuous, but they contribute to the colors and textures of the fall palette. Most folks would consider the maples, quaking aspen, and cottonwoods the most spectacular. The vine maple, a common understory and edge species on the west side, is among the first to change and has the brightest and richest reds, making it really stand out.

Both aspen and cottonwood turn bright yellow, but it's the effect of seeing a large mass of either one that makes an impression, not just the color. Black cottonwoods, the tallest and most massive broad-leaved tree in the Northwest, grow along rivers and streams and the golden outline of cottonwoods winding through arid land is a beautiful sight east of the Cascades. Aspens are also found on the east side and also stand out from their often duller sur-

Sandhill cranes arriving at Sauvie Island near Portland

329

roundings. Aspen leaves range from yellow to orange to even red, but it's the striking contrast between their colored leaves and their bright white trunks that is so appealing. One characteristic of aspen is that in a particular grove, all of the trees will have leaves the same color; they are unusually synchronized in their turning. This is quite different from the normal variation you see among a group of trees, but it makes sense when you know that the grove is actually composed of clones, all the trees having started from runners of an original tree. The whole grove is essentially one plant.

An unusual tree that adds interest and color to the coniferous forest is the western larch. Larches are the only deciduous conifers in North America. In fall the needles turn a bright yellow and the sight of golden larches standing among their evergreen relatives is a special sight on the mountain slopes where they occur. Most folks usually use "evergreen" and "conifer" interchangeably, but the larches demonstrate that not all conifers are evergreen. Conversely, there are broad-leaved or hardwood trees that are evergreen, such as madrone, chinkapin, rhododendron, and California laurel (also known as Oregon myrtle).

Most people know how leaves change color. Each leaf actually has several different pigments of different colors present all the time, but the other pigments are masked by overwhelming amounts of green chlorophyll. As winter nears, the chlorophyll starts to break down and the tree starts to absorb some chlorophyll into the trunk and roots, letting the other colors show through. The proportion of the different pigments and the amount of sugar present in the leaves determine whether the leaf is yellow, brown, red, purple, or combinations of these colors. Weather, especially nighttime temperatures, greatly affects these chemicals, resulting in the great variation from tree to tree and from year to year in the same tree. The trees are preparing for winter when the value of the leaves as food producers falls far short of their risk as water losers and energy consumers. The leaves become liabilities instead of assets and the tree drops them.

Because weather conditions vary from year to year, so does the timing and the intensity of fall foliage colors. Interestingly, despite our detailed knowledge of the processes at work, humans have not yet been able to accurately predict what the changing leaves of a particular year will be like. The first leaves begin to change in September, but it isn't until October that we start to see big changes in our deciduous trees. Of course, winter comes sooner the higher the elevation, and the color change starts high in the mountains and works its way down as fall progresses. One of the most pleasant ways to enjoy our fall colors is to take scenic drives in our spectacular mountains in October. This is great in combination with visiting ancient forests, watching migrating raptors, and looking for spawning salmon. And when it comes to scenic mountains, easterners who gloat about their colorful hardwood forests can eat humble pie.

In the last 10 years the National Scenic Byways and All-American Roads program has been growing, taking shape as a kind of paved national park system. The program is part of the Federal Highway Administration, working with communities across the country. If you ever want to get from one place to another in the United States without the usual mind-numbing freeway, take any of these roads. Hey, if you have to drive you might as well get as much nature as you can while on the road. You can get a free map of the system and more information from www.byways.org. Any of our Scenic Byways going over mountains will be awesome in autumn.

► AUTUMN COLOR IN THE MOUNTAINS BEST BETS OREGON

Steens Mountain rises above the surrounding Great Basin in southeastern Oregon and is one of the most dramatic fault block mountains in the West. Near the top of the mountain in the dramatic gorges carved by Pleistocene glaciers are huge groves of aspen. They have one of the most spectacular displays of fall color in our region. Unfortunately, Steens Mountain gets more than its share of strong winds; the trick is to see the leaves after they have turned but before they have been blown off the trees. A call to the Burns BLM office might help determine the best timing. Be sure to ask for whatever maps and brochures are available on "the Steens" as it's usually called. The trees seem to be at their best during late September. Steens Mountain Loop Rd heads up the mountain near Page Springs CG, about 2.5 miles east of Frenchglen. The best aspen groves are toward the top of the mountain, above Lily Lake. Although the road is a loop, the southern half, after the trail to Wildhorse Lake, is very rough. Stop at the Kiger Gorge Viewpoint for an incredible view down a glacial cirque.

Two popular scenic trips in the central Cascades are the Cascade Lakes Scenic Byway and the McKenzie–Santiam Pass Scenic Byway. Both loops provide access to many popular recreation sites and are also great in June for mountain birds. The Cascade Lakes Scenic Byway starts in Bend and follows the Cascade Lakes Highway, which begins as Century Dr or State Hwy 372, then becomes FR 46. The Bend Visitor and Convention Bureau has good information about this route.

The McKenzie–Santiam Pass Scenic Byway

is essentially a loop around Mount Washington. Starting at Sisters it heads west on US Hwy 20 to where State Hwy 126 splits off and heads south. The route heads south on Hwy 126 following the McKenzie River to State Hwy 242. Highway 242 then goes up and over McKenzie Pass and takes you back into Sisters. Special places on this route include Indian Ford and Cold Springs campgrounds for birds, Koosah and Sahalie Falls on the McKenzie River Trail, vast lava flows with strange shapes, and the amazing Dee Wright Observatory at McKenzie Pass—built out of lava rocks.

For a drive through lush lower-elevation forest on the west side, try the Aufderheide National Scenic Byway in Willamette NF. This section of road just became incorporated into the much longer West Cascades National Scenic Byway, but that is just too much road to comprehend at once. The Aufderheide is a nice chunk to handle (barely) in one day and I love the name. This route is the same as FR 19 and goes from Oakridge on State Hwy 58 to Hwy 126 near McKenzie Bridge. There are numerous recreation sites along the route including hiking trails into wilderness areas and ancient forests. Just before FR 19 meets Hwy 126 is the Delta Old Growth Grove, a famous stand of huge ancient trees accessed by a nice trail from the Delta Campground. The campground is reached by turning left onto FR 400, as you head north toward Hwy 126.

▶ AUTUMN COLOR IN THE MOUNTAINS BEST BETS WASHINGTON

The North Cascades Scenic Byway, State Hwy 20, goes through part of what is often called the North Cascades Complex—North Cascades NP, Ross Lake and Lake Chelan NRAs, and parts of Mount Baker-Snoqualmie and Okanogan national forests. This scenic drive offers access to many fabulous hiking trails and several wildlife-watching opportunities mentioned in this book. The drive is not necessarily better for fall colors than other mountain pass roads in the Cascades, but it's the only place I know of in the United States where a certain rare tree can be seen from a paved road. Just on the east side of Washington Pass you'll see a few small groups of larches—not the common western larch but the subalpine larch—which stick out dramatically when yellow in the fall.

The subalpine larch (also called alpine larch) has a very small range, growing only in the highest mountains of the interior Northwest. It grows near timberline in conditions considered too severe for the few other trees that hang on at these altitudes. Given these limitations, few people have seen or even heard of them. Washington Pass and the road to Hart's Pass give tree enthusiasts (arbornauts?) a chance to see these rare trees without some serious backpacking.

Nearby to the west is Mount Baker, third highest peak in Washington. State Hwy 542, the Mount Baker Scenic Byway, winds up the Nooksack River, and then climbs the northeast side of the mountain ending at Artists' Point at about 5000 feet. On this road and on Hwy 20, in areas without trees at higher elevations, you'll see the vivid yellows, oranges, and reds of mountain ash and the various huckleberries. Trails from Artists' Point to the Table Mountain and Ptarmigan Ridge areas are good places to look for white-tailed ptarmigan, rosy finch, pikas, marmots and occasionally mountain goats. All in all, a great fall trip.

Due east 150 miles from Mount Baker, Hwy 20 goes over Sherman Pass, which at 5575 feet is the highest road in the state kept open all winter. This section of Hwy 20 is the Sherman Pass Scenic Byway, and in October it's at its most scenic with lots of golden western larches. You'll also be able to see beaver activity in Sherman Creek from the road on the east side of the pass. As you come down off the pass into the valleys, you'll see the river of gold created by the cottonwoods. Most of the valleys in eastern Washington will have beautiful displays of cottonwoods along the rivers and streams.

Although low in elevation, the Chuckanut Dr, State Hwy 11 between Bow and Bellingham, is a favorite for the red and yellow maples and the gorgeous madrones with their red bark and red berries. It's also known for the good restaurants on the route. Across Samish Bay are scenic views of the San Juan Islands, and Larrabee SP is a good spot to see waterbirds from the beach and forest birds on the trails.

The section of US Hwy 2 between Stevens Pass and Leavenworth is another excellent route convenient to the Puget megalopolis. This is part of the Stevens Pass Greenway and a fall trip is a good time to take in the annual Wenachee River Salmon Festival, one of the best places to see salmon spawning in the wild. You could also drop by Red Top Mountain for some migrating raptors and make a return loop over Snoqualmie Pass, also scenic and near Gold Creek Pond, an excellent place to see kokanee salmon spawning. Another great fall trip, fueled by Bavarian pastries from bakeries in Leavenworth.

Another great scenic loop through the Cascades goes through the east side of Mount Rainier NP. This loop is also in the best area in the Northwest for seeing mountain goats. You can enter the loop at any point, but let's start near the Ohanapecosh Entrance at the Grove of the Patriarchs, an outstanding ancient forest experience. From the Grove of Patriarchs head north on State Hwy 123 to Cayuse Pass, and then turn right onto State Hwy 410 and head to Chinook Pass. Sometimes you'll see marmots along the side of the road between the two passes. Stay on Hwy 410 as it follows the American River and then the Naches River toward Yakima.

Just before you get to Naches you'll come to the junction with US Hwy 12, often called the White Pass Highway. Turn right and take US 12 west to White Pass, going by Rimrock Lake (check to see if the kokanee salmon are running). US 12 between Rimrock Lake and White Pass has western larches, and Clear Creek Falls, just east of Dog Lake, has a great scenic overlook. Just before you get to White Pass are some awesome views of The Big One, Mount Rainier. Once over the pass and back to Hwy 123 completes the loop. You could drive north back into Mount Rainier NP or head west to Packwood.

ARRIVAL OF THE GEESE

One of the most dramatic and romantic harbingers of fall is the arrival of large flocks of honking geese. I think the first wild goose calls you hear in the fall cause the release of an "autumn" hormone, which makes you smell imaginary smoke from a fireplace and think of pumpkin pie. We're lucky to live in a main flyway and winter home for hundreds of thousands of geese, giving us a spectacular display every fall when the first flocks begin to arrive.

Ducks, geese, and swans are close relatives in the order of birds called Anseriformes, which means "looks like a goose." Geese share certain characteristics with swans that are different from ducks. In geese and swans the males and females look alike and can be told apart only by their behavior, which includes their calls. All geese make honking, cackling, whonking, or cronking sounds, which experienced birders can use to separate different species. Unlike ducks, but like swans, geese mate for life, share care of the young, and both sexes are very territorial about their nest site. Geese are generally intermediate in size between ducks and swans, and geese spend much more time on land eating plant material, including grass, than either swans or ducks.

Most geese we see in the Pacific Northwest are migrants, passing through on their way from northern breeding grounds to southern winter ranges. An increasing number are spending the winter here, and some of the migrants stop for a month or more on their way through. Canada geese are by far the most abundant goose in the Pacific Northwest and in North America as a whole. Hundreds of thousands winter here and they are the only goose that breeds in our region. You will often hear Canada geese give a definite two-part "honk, honk" call, the second honk being a higher pitch than the first. This two-part call is actually done by a mated pair of geese singing a closely timed duet.

Good news for birders who keep a life list. There is a new species of goose in North America. Those who keep track of this sort of thing will suspect right away that this isn't really a new species that has arrived, but rather a species that has been split. Now and then the AOU (American Ornithologists Union) decides that what has long been considered one species with different subspecies is actually two, sometimes more, separate and distinct species. In 2004 the AOU split the Canada goose into two species, the Canada goose and the cackling goose. For those of us who have gotten used to seeing thousands of cackling geese every winter during the last several years this is no surprise. It's easy to tell them apart by their sound. Canada geese honk and cackling geese, what else, cackle. Cackling geese are strictly winter residents and nest in the far north. The cackling goose population in Oregon has increased greatly and in some areas near Portland they are now more abundant than Canada geese. Cackling geese are smaller than Canada geese with short necks and small beaks. When you see a cackler standing next to a big honker the difference is striking, but when they are flying the best way to tell them apart is by their calls.

Snow geese are the most spectacular bird to see during migration because they usually travel in huge flocks. A flock of 20,000 or 30,000 white geese taking off at once while making their loud houck-houck calls is an overwhelming experience. Snow geese nest in Arctic tundra, and most fly through our region on the way to California. However, tens of thousands remain in the Northwest all winter. In British Columbia and Washington snow geese tend to stay on the west side, but in Oregon they are more common east of the Cascades. The population of wintering snow geese in the Midwest has exploded recently causing concern not only for agriculture but also for the impact of the increased populations on tundra plants during the nesting season.

There are two kinds of white geese. Ross's goose is smaller than the snow goose, but it's tough to tell them apart. Sometimes they are seen in mixed flocks, most notably in the Klamath Basin, where you can do a one-to-one comparison. Both the Ross's and the snow goose populations have increased, but the snow goose population is still 10 times that of their smaller relative. A significant proportion of the world's Ross's geese migrate through Oregon to California, but not many remain in the state for winter. They are most abundant in the Klamath Basin during spring migration.

White-fronted geese also nest in the far north. Most of these geese migrate through the Northwest on their way to California, with only a few staying behind for the winter. They are the first of the geese to pass through in the fall, providing one of the most sublime signs of fall. White-fronts fly at night and if you're outside on a crisp, clear night near the end of September, you can hear them calling as they fly overhead. It's so cool knowing what animal is flying hundreds of feet over your head, even when you can't see it. On the ground they are often overlooked because their color and markings blend in well with plowed fields, which is where you'll often find them. Like snow geese, white-fronted geese move through the Northwest on their way to California, with a few staying behind for the winter, although these numbers are much lower than the number of wintering snows. In general, they fly along the coast of Washington until they get near the Columbia River, then most go over the Cascades and down the east side. They are uncommon in British Columbia.

Migrating geese will begin to arrive in September with the first white-fronted geese, slowly building in numbers until the population of migrating and wintering geese hits its peak sometime in November. Timing of peak migration differs from species to species and is affected by weather. It's common to notice large numbers of geese just before waterfowl hunting season begins, usually the second weekend in October. This makes early October the best time to get out and see fall movements of geese before hunting season spooks the birds and causes closures and restrictions in refuges. Once hunting has started, many people like to wait until the waterfowl seasons are over in January before heading out to see swans, geese, and ducks. Because the National Wildlife Refuge System in the United States was developed to protect waterfowl habitat, just about any national wildlife refuge will be a good spot to see geese outside of hunting season.

▶ ARRIVAL OF THE GEESE BEST BETS OREGON

Oregon presents the best opportunities to see the greatest numbers of all four species. Three eastern Oregon areas—Klamath Basin, Harney Basin, and Summer Lake—have some of the greatest concentrations of white-fronted, snow, and Ross's geese in the west. Klamath Basin, which has six national wildlife refuges and the state's Klamath WA, is truly one of the West's finest places for waterbirds and raptors. It is described in February (Bald Eagles), which also includes a map of these areas. The best areas in the basin for geese are Lower Klamath and Tule Lake national wildlife refuges and Klamath WA. Large concentrations of white-fronted geese are here in late October and early November. These three areas are the only places in our region where you can regularly see Ross's geese. Harney Basin is home to Malheur NWR, which has its own chapter, and the fields south of Burns are described in March (Spring Waterfowl Migration). Summer Lake WA is smaller than these first two areas, but just about as exciting.

North of these three super spots are Umatilla and Cold Springs national wildlife refuges. Birds often travel between these two refuges, which are only 20 miles apart, and it's possible to check them both in one day. More information on these refuges appears in February (Wintering Waterfowl). To get to Cold Springs NWR from downtown Hermiston, take Main St east until it angles off to the northeast and becomes State Hwy 207. Go 3 miles and just past the fire station turn right and head east on Punkin Center Rd (also called County Road 1250) following signs that read Cold Springs Res. In 2 miles the road turns to dirt and then splits. Turn right, over the train tracks, and into the refuge. Take the road that travels over the dam and follows the south shore of the reservoir.

The easiest viewing in Umatilla NWR is the auto tour route around McCormack Slough. Leave Cold Springs by returning the way you came on Punkin Center Rd and when you get to Hwy 207 take a right-angle turn to head north on Craig Rd (also known as County Road 1259). When you reach US Hwy 730, the Columbia River Highway, turn left and head west to Irrigon. When you get to Irrigon, bear to the right onto Columbia Ln and take it to where it ends at Paterson Ferry Rd. The auto tour route begins just uphill to your left.

The Willamette Valley has four major wintering sites for Canada geese and are regularly used as stopping places by white-fronted and snow geese. The three national wildlife refuges—William Finley, Ankeny, and Baskett Slough—are managed together, primarily as wintering habitat for the dusky Canada goose. Maps to these areas are available from the Willamette Valley National Wildlife Refuge Complex in Corvallis. Geese are best seen from the roads that travel through the refuges because trails are closed during the winter and the geese are easily frightened by people on foot. The fourth area is Sauvie Island WA near Portland, which ODFW manages.

▶ **ARRIVAL OF THE GEESE BEST BETS** WASHINGTON

Washington rarely has any Ross's geese, and white-fronted geese are uncommon and fairly restricted to the southwestern part of the state, Willapa Bay in particular. However, Washington plays host to the Northwest's best known population of snow geese. Western Skagit County may be the best area in the state for winter birdwatching in general. Waterfowl favor the delta of the Skagit River, especially Fir Island, and the state has established the Skagit WA to protect prime habitat for the lesser snow geese that winter there. The lesser snow geese that winter in the Skagit and Fraser River deltas nest on Wrangel Island off the north coast of Siberia and are the last breeding population of this species in Asia. The geese start arriving in October and have become a big tourist attraction in the area, helping small towns like La Conner, Conway, and Mount Vernon.

This is one of the most intensely hunted areas in Washington, and the state has had to start a new program with special regulations for snow goose hunting. Many people just wait until hunting is over at the end of January before visiting the Skagit Flats area looking for snow geese and the swans, raptors, and other birds that make this area so great. A Snow Goose and Birding Festival takes place in Port Susan, which is wisely scheduled for the end of February (www.snowgoosefest.org).

To get to the Skagit Flats, Fir Island, and the Skagit WA, leave Interstate 5 at Conway, Exit 221. Head west through Conway and continue west on Fir Island Rd. In less than a mile you'll have crossed the South Fork Skagit River and you'll now be on Fir Island. Geese and swans are often in the farm fields on Fir Island and in other parts of the Skagit Flats. Using the map in January (Wintering Raptors) you can cruise Fir Island, mainly on Fir Island Rd and Dry Slough Rd. Check out the Skagit WA, and then work your way north to the Skagit Flats. You may want to make the Skagit WA your first stop if you have the required parking permit.

To get to the Skagit WA from Conway, drive west 1.5 miles on Fir Island Rd, turn left onto Wiley Rd, and then drive 0.75 mile to the headquarters. A bulletin board has maps and information, and staff may be available to give you the latest news on snow geese and other birds in the area. Trails near the headquarters lead to the dikes.

To visit more of the wildlife area, drive back to Fir Island Rd and turn left to head west again. Fir Island Rd makes a large curve and heads north, but continue straight (west) on Maupin Rd. Just before Maupin takes a right turn, a dirt road on your left heads to a small parking area at the dike. This is called Jensen Access; take this road and park at the dike. Be very quiet and sneak up onto the dike, peering carefully over the top. There may be thousands of waterfowl on the shore or in the bay just on the other side. After checking out Jensen Access, get back on Maupin. Head west and then north as it turns and drive to Rawlins Rd. Turn left and head west on Rawlins until it ends at the dike. Sneak up on the dike again for another peak into Skagit Bay. If birds are scarce, you can walk along the top of the dike back to the southeast. Over 100,000 ducks have been seen in Skagit Bay at a time. Viewing at all areas is best at high tide.

If you don't have the vehicle use permit, an alternative is to drive the public roads through the farmlands, where you can usually see the same birds that you would find in the wildlife area. After cruising Fir Island take Fir Island Rd north to Best Rd, turn left onto Best Rd, and then take it north across the North Fork Skagit River to enter the farmlands of the Skagit Flats. The roads in this area are arranged in a grid pattern, so you can just cruise the area looking for snow geese, swans, and raptors. These are busy farm roads; watch carefully for other cars and pull far over to the side if you stop. Birders can drive local residents crazy with thoughtless driving.

▶ ARRIVAL OF THE GEESE BEST BETS BRITISH COLUMBIA

In British Columbia white-fronted geese are scarce and Ross's geese are almost unheard of. Canada geese and snow geese, however, are abundant in the Fraser River delta, the winter waterfowl Mecca of Canada. Indeed, the Fraser delta has the only wintering population of snow geese in Canada and the George C. Reifel Migratory Bird Sanctuary is the best place to see these birds. The Reifel Refuge, as it's often called, has the same Fraser-Skagit subpopulation of lesser snow geese that breed on Wrangle Island and winter in the Skagit area. The geese tend to first arrive at Reifel Refuge in mid-October, then quickly spread out until distributed about evenly between the Fraser and Skagit river deltas. From mid-December through February almost all of the birds are in the Skagit Delta. In March many begin to show up again at Reifel Refuge, building in numbers until mid-April when they all take a little 2500-mile flight to Siberia. Some have been banded and later been found to have flown 1500 miles nonstop in 36 hours. In the winter of 2006–2007 this wintering population was about 80,000 and their numbers are on the rise just like the mid-continent snow geese. The best time for snow geese at Reifel Refuge is November, a great time for waterfowl.

Reifel Refuge is easy to find. Ladner Trunk Rd heads west through the town of Ladner, becoming 47A Ave in the center of town. Head west on 47A Ave and stay on it as it turns into River Rd West. Drive 1.8 miles and turn right onto the Westham Island Bridge. Drive through Westham Island following signs for 3.5 miles to the refuge. The farm fields are often full of geese and tundra and trumpeter swans during late fall and winter. The refuge visitor area has parking, a book and nature store, restrooms, a sanctuary office, and the manager's residence. A small admission fee supports this private nonprofit sanctuary. The staff and volunteers here are usually full of birding news about the Vancouver area. Allow plenty of time to visit Reifel; an avid birder can easily spend most of a nice day here.

FALL SALMON RUNS

The largest number of Pacific salmon return to spawn in fall, creating one of the greatest seasonal spectacles in the natural world. The return of the salmon was one of the most important events in the lives of the Native Americans living in the Northwest, not only because it was their single greatest source of food, but also because it was a sign that things were right in the world.

The Pacific salmon fisheries of the Northwest were among the greatest fisheries on the planet, with the Fraser and Columbia rivers being two of the greatest salmon producers in the world. Such a bountiful resource was quickly exploited by settlers and the Columbia suffered the most. Salmon canning on the Columbia started in 1866 and by 1883 there were 39 canneries on the Columbia River. The fish were caught every way imaginable but the great fish wheels were the most effective. One fish wheel in 1882 took 6400 large chinook out of the river in one day.

At this rate it was inevitable that populations would begin to drop, and by 1900 it was clear that a great decline was underway. Over harvesting can be a relatively easy problem to correct, however, and with the banning of fish wheels and other regulations in the early 1900s it appeared that the Columbia River salmon might be able to recover. But then came the big dams on the Columbia and its largest tributary, the Snake River.

Starting with Rock Island in 1933 and ending with Lower Granite in 1975, the Army Corps of Engineers, the Bureau of Reclamation, Idaho Power, and several public utility districts in Washington built a system of dams that have been the single greatest cause of the dramatic collapse of the Columbia River Basin salmon fishery. At present there are 66 major multipurpose dams on the Columbia and its main tributaries. It has been estimated that historically the Columbia River system had an annual run of salmon between 10 and 16 million. The average annual run from 2002 to 2006 was under 600,000 wild salmon. It is clear that in the last 200 years the salmon population of the Columbia River has declined more than 90%, regardless of some error in the population estimates. Our impact has been devastating. Many populations in the Snake River system are extinct. Well over half of all runs in the rest of the Columbia River system are listed as threatened or endangered, as are populations in many other Northwestern rivers.

Habitat destruction and pollution have also contributed to the loss of salmon in the Columbia. Urbanization has destroyed many streams outright and added to pollution. Logging practices have damaged riparian vegetation, causing increased erosion into streams and the silting of spawning areas, significantly affecting fish in many areas.

Agricultural practices have also caused a variety of problems. Overgrazing causes erosion and siltation, and freely roaming livestock trample stream banks. Unscreened irrigation ditches and pipes have sucked salmon to their death, and irrigation has left some streams with little or no water. Pesticide and fertilizer runoff from agricultural land is a major source of water pollution. Fish hatcheries, which were once seen as the solution to the dams, have caused problems of their own by replacing the wild native stocks with hatchery fish that are not as well adapted for survival and reproduction in the wild. Hatchery programs are very controversial—some biologists fear they can lead to genetic contamination and loss of diversity.

This has been the hardest chapter to write because it feels like an overwhelming challenge to make any progress in the restoration of salmon runs in the Northwest. However, salmon are part of the soul of the Northwest and thousands of people—in their jobs, as volunteers, and as individuals—are working hard to bring salmon back. One bit of encouraging data that Seth Zuckerman shows in *Salmon Nation: People, Fish, and Our Common Home* is that the number of civic groups organized to protect and restore salmon habitat increased from 94 in 1989 to 369 in 2002. The salmon issue is as complex as the relationships between salmon and their ecosystem and will continue to be one of the biggest environmental issues of this century in the Northwest. Fortunately, there are still places where you can go this month to see salmon in the wild, making their final journey upstream to spawn.

▶ FALL SALMON RUNS BEST BETS OREGON

It gets scenic and wild right away on the Wild and Scenic Rogue River. The Rogue River was one of the eight original Wild and Scenic Rivers designated back in 1968 and is among the most famous rafting rivers in the world. The biggest rapid in the lower river is the rightfully respected Rainie Falls, 2 miles downstream from Grave Creek Bridge, the start of the wild and scenic portion. As much a barrier as it may be to rafters who have to float over it, think what the salmon and steelhead coming upstream have to deal with. They have to jump the falls to get to the rest of the river and Rainie Falls may be the best place in Oregon to see this spectacle. Depending on the year and your timing you could see chinook salmon, coho salmon, or steelhead, the latest of the three to arrive. Best of all, you don't have to take the plunge over Rainie Falls in a raft to see the fish, although that would be a great start to a fabulous trip down the Rogue. You can park at Grave Creek Bridge and hike 1.75 miles on a trail to the falls. The trail is rough in spots and in the open, so it can get hot in October—usually a sunny, warm month in southwestern Oregon. Take plenty of drinking water and avoid the poison oak. You may want to be prepared for swimming because you'll pass some nice still pools. From the little hamlet of Galice, northwest of Grants Pass, drive north on Galice Rd for 7 miles to Grave Creek Bridge. Before driving over the bridge, park on the south side of the Rogue River, on the left side of the road. There is no overnight parking, by the way, in case you were thinking of a nice little backpack trip to the falls. The trail follows the river west from this point and it'll be quite obvious when you get to Rainie Falls. Although not high in elevation, the waterfall is scary enough if you have to go over it.

Kokanee salmon have an interesting evolutionary story. Kokanee are a type of sockeye salmon that do not go to sea. Sockeye usually spawn in lakes or the streams that feed lakes, live a couple of years in the lake, go to sea for two to four years, and then swim back to the lake to spawn. This is a variation on the typical anadromous pattern of salmon. At some point in their ancient past, some sockeye just stayed in the lake and never went to the ocean, living out their whole life cycle in the lake and usually going up the small streams feeding the lake to spawn. In some cases a lake can have a population of both sockeye and kokanee, the sockeye going to sea and returning and the kokanee staying in the lake. Each type will then have

their own spawning areas, some along the lakeshore, and others upstream.

When lots of landscapes got moved around during the Pleistocene, some lakes got cut off from their outlet to the ocean, or at least they got blocked enough that the sockeye couldn't make it back to spawn, and that was it for the sockeye in that lake. You know what's coming, don't you? Kokanee were trapped in the lake, but they didn't care because they weren't going to the ocean anyway. Okay, so that's too anthropomorphic, but the result is the same no matter how they felt about it. There are naturally occurring populations of kokanee (native word for red fish) in lakes from Alaska to Washington, east to Montana, in Siberia, and in Japan. They have been widely introduced into lakes throughout the west and the world, even New Zealand. (What hasn't been introduced in New Zealand?) Because kokanee are not affected by dams, except maybe a few beaver dams, they are some of the most abundant salmon still around and easy to see.

A large population of kokanee lives in Lake Billy Chinook and swim up the Metolius River into the Camp Sherman area to spawn in late September or early October. You can look for fish in the river by going to Wizard Falls Fish Hatchery, 4 miles north of Camp Sherman on FR 14, and walking either north or south from the hatchery on the beautiful Metolius River Trail. You'll probably have better luck at a spot recommended by Jim Yuskavitch in *Oregon Nature Weekends*. From the post office and store in Camp Sherman drive 1.5 miles north on the Metolius River Rd and turn left onto FR 1217, right after the Allingham Campground. Cross over the Metolius on the Allingham Bridge, and then pull over and park on the left side of the road. You will be parked at the edge of a meadow. Here, a small spring is the source of a short creek that flows down to the river. Kokanee congregate in the Metolius where the creek enters and they also swim up this creek to spawn. Check out the area where the creek flows into the Metolius, and then carefully walk along the creek to look for fish. Be sneaky and get down on all fours to get a good look at any fish you see. Polarized glasses, often called fish glasses or fishing glasses, are an effective aid for viewing fish in the water because they allow you to see through the reflections. You'll usually find them where fishing gear is sold.

Multnomah Falls and Eagle Creek are two popular areas in the Columbia River Gorge near Portland where you can often see chinook or coho. Multnomah Falls is the most visited tourist attraction in Oregon, so you'll have no trouble finding that. What most of the visitors don't know is that a small population of coho and a few chinook swim up Multnomah Creek from the Columbia and spawn in the stretch of the creek that can be seen at the touristy area. A sign about these fish has been posted near the stream as you take the trail that goes under the Historic Columbia River Highway to the parking area between the lanes of Interstate 84. Look for fish any place where you can get next to the creek. You also can ask at the visitor center for fish-spotting tips.

East of the Bonneville exit on I-84, take Exit 41 for Eagle Creek and the Cascade Fish Hatchery (ODFW) and drive 1.5 miles to the parking area for the Eagle Creek Trail. Instead of taking the trail, find a good place to work your way down to Eagle Creek and see if you can find any of the coho or chinook that spawn in the creek. The bridge that crosses the creek may give you good views into the water. Again, fish glasses will help a lot.

▶ FALL SALMON RUNS BEST BETS WASHINGTON

The Wenatchee River Salmon Festival takes place at the end of September at the Leavenworth National Fish Hatchery, just outside of the Bavarian theme town of Leavenworth. To see chinook salmon spawning in the wild, however, you need to look in the Wenatchee River in Tumwater Canyon, upstream from Leavenworth. The chinook can be seen any time between mid-September and mid-October. After getting supplied with Bavarian pastries in Leavenworth, drive toward Stevens Pass on US Hwy 2, past the road to the hatchery, and up Tumwater Canyon. Look for good turnouts where you can park and scan the river from the roadside anywhere along the first 3 miles from the hatchery. One good spot is the Swift Water Picnic Area, 6.5 miles up the canyon. To avoid having to park on one side of US 2 and cross it to look into the river, drive straight to the Swift Water Picnic Area, see what you can find there, and then drive back down US 2 (south) with the river on your side of the highway, where it will be much easier and safer to pull off the road. Wildlife watching need not risk lives. The drive over Stevens Pass from the west side to Leavenworth on a clear, crisp October day is stunningly gorgeous.

Gold Creek Pond and Rimrock Lake are two well-known places in Washington to see kokanee spawn. Gold Creek Pond is a wonderful example of a restoration project for wildlife habitat. The area around Gold Creek was used as a gravel quarry for the construction of Interstate 90 and was left as a wasteland. Years later, in a massive cooperative effort involving state and federal agencies, conservation organizations, school kids, and other volunteers, the area was rehabilitated to provide wildlife habitat and a universally accessible interpretive trail. It worked and now there's a nice spot right off I-90 near Snoqualmie Pass where you can possibly see beaver, mountain goats, Canada geese, osprey, and spawning kokanee salmon. I watched a dipper get so fat gorging on salmon eggs that he had to crawl out of the water onto a log because he couldn't fly.

Just east of Snoqualmie Pass take the Hyak-Gold Creek exit (Exit 54), and then follow the signs to Gold Creek Pond. You'll parallel the interstate on the north side, heading east on a frontage road, FR 4832. In 1.5 miles turn left on Gold Creek Rd (FR 142), drive another 0.75 mile, then turn left onto FR 9080 where you'll reach the parking area. I saw plenty of kokanee and the fat dipper in the stream just west of the parking area. Universally accessible paved trails lead to the pond and to other spots to see salmon in the spawning channel. You'll need a Northwest Forest Pass to park here. You might find mountain goats on the distant mountain sides with a spotting scope, but it's a long way away. Interstate 90 makes a great drive for fall colors, and you can stop at Asahel Curtis Nature Trail for an ancient forest hike.

US Hwy 12 is another great auto route for fall colors and Rimrock Lake is a great stop for viewing a big kokanee run. In October the kokanee swim up the tributary streams that flow into the lake. The easiest place to see them is in the short section of the North Fork Tieton River that runs between Clear Lake and Rimrock Lake. From US 12, about 0.75 mile west of Indian Creek Campground, head south following signs for Clear Lake or Tieton Rd. In less than 0.5 mile go left to Clear Lake Campground and just after you pass the North Clear Lake Campground sign, turn left again onto a campground loop road. Go to the end of the campground loop and park at or near the last site, and then make your way down the informal trails to the north bank of the river.

Chinook and coho come right into Capitol Lake in Olympia, swim up the Deschutes River into Tumwater, and can be seen in Tumwater Falls Park, under the shadow of the old Olympia Brewery (closed). Coming from south of Olympia it's easy to reach, but trickier coming from north of the capitol. Coming into Olympia from the south, take the Deschutes Pkwy exit (Exit 103), and then turn right into the park's parking lot just a few blocks after exiting. Didn't I tell you it was easy?

Coming from the north take Exit 103, but get on 2nd Ave and drive south about 5 blocks to Custer Way. Turn left onto Custer Way (at the fire station), and then immediately turn right onto Boston St after you cross the river. Take Boston back over the river until it ends at Deschutes Pkwy at the Falls Terrace Restaurant. Turn left onto Deschutes Pkwy, and then immediately turn left again into the park's parking lot. From trails along the river and a footbridge you can see fish in the river and sometimes you can see them jump Tumwater Falls. A small WDFW hatchery near the parking lot has information and exhibits.

▶ FALL SALMON RUNS BEST BETS BRITISH COLUMBIA

Fisheries and Oceans Canada produces a brochure for British Columbia titled *Where and When to See Salmon*. It includes 31 sites in the range covered by this book. They are free and you can sometimes find them at hatcheries, nature centers, or Travel Info Centres. You also can order them by mail or online. If you're from the United States and you get one of these little gems, the first thing you'll say to yourself is, Why don't we have these for our states?

On Vancouver Island, Goldstream PP provides one of the most spectacular salmon runs with convenient access and viewing. From mid-October to mid-December thousands of chum salmon, with some coho and chinook, spawn naturally in the Goldstream River where they can easily be seen from the trails. The Freeman King Visitor Center, open every day during the run, has exhibits, programs, printed information, and staff on hand to answer questions and give directions to the best viewing spots. Goldstream PP is 10 miles northwest of Victoria on the Trans-Canada Highway 1. Park in the main parking and picnic area near the north end of the park and take the Lower Goldstream Trail to the visitor center. The eggs and the carcasses of spawned-out salmon provide a rich bounty for a number of predators and scavengers including gulls, bald eagles, and dippers during the day and raccoons, river otters, mink and even black bear at night.

Stamp Falls PP on Vancouver Island offers a chance to see wild fish jumping falls in a dramatic setting. A run of sockeye moves up the Stamp River from mid-July through August, as described with directions in July (Summer Salmon and Trout). Coho move up August through September, and then the chinook in September and October. Stamp Falls PP is west of Port Alberni off Hwy 4 and Beaver Creek Rd. Take the main trail to the overlook at the end. You'll see a large pool where the fish pile up waiting to go up the falls or the ladder built to make the trip easier.

Back on the mainland, the Chilliwack River, which flows west from Chilliwack Lake on the US border near Manning PP, is a good spot to see salmon. Before it gets to the Fraser River, however, it gets a new name—the Vedder River. The point where this identity crisis takes place is south of the town of Chilliwack where Vedder Rd crosses the river at Vedder Crossing. This is our first spot to try and see

fish in the river. Heading east in the Fraser Valley on Hwy 1, take the Vedder Rd exit (Exit 119), and then head south. In 2.7 miles you'll reach the area where Vedder Rd crosses the river and just before the bridge, on the right side as you're headed south, is a small parking area. Turn right into this dirt parking area where you'll see a trail that goes along the top of a dyke on the north bank of the Vedder River. Walk the trail looking for salmon in the river; you might see chum, coho and chinook salmon.

To try another stretch of the river upstream, return to your car and cross Vedder Rd to get on Chilliwack River Rd, the road that travels east on the north bank of the river, which from this point on is called the Chilliwack River. As you drive east on Chilliwack River Rd you'll see turnouts where you can pull over and look for fish in this section of the river. After 6 miles you'll reach a bridge where Chilliwack River Rd crosses the river. Cross the bridge, turn right, and then cross another bridge. You'll drive into a small park where Tamihi Creek joins the Chilliwack. This is a much more pleasant place to search for fish in the river than stopping on the road. We have one more place to try.

Go back to Chilliwack River Rd and continue east, only now you'll be on the south shore of the Chilliwack River. In another 6 miles you'll reach the Chilliwack Hatchery at Slesse Creek. Here your chances are good for seeing salmon in both the Chilliwack and probably Slesse Creek, too. You can look around the hatchery and see fish in the holding tanks and possibly see some hatchery operations underway. This hatchery was built in a scenic location and it blends in with the landscape. Return the way you came unless you're up for adventure and want to take the road until it ends at the US border beside Chilliwack Lake.

For a more subdued salmon-watching trip, visit Kanaka Creek RP in Maple Ridge, about 30 miles east of downtown Vancouver. From Vancouver head east on Hastings St, which soon becomes Hwy 7A. Continue east on Hwy 7A as it goes through many local name changes until it joins with Hwy 7, the Lougheed Highway, in Port Coquitlam. Go southeast on the Lougheed Highway through Pitt Meadows to Haney. Just less than 2 miles south of Haney, turn left onto Kanaka Way and drive east to 240th St. Turn right and head south on 240th St until you can pull over on your right just before you cross Kanaka Creek. This is the location of the fish fence and you can often see chum salmon in the creek. To visit the small Bell-Irving Fish Hatchery in the park, return north to 112th Ave and head east until you cross the creek and see signs to the hatchery.

SANDHILL CRANES

Cranes have always made a big impression on people. They are among the tallest birds in the world and with their upright posture they have an air of nobility. They also have powerful voices that typically can be heard from a mile or more, the result of a special coiled trachea that has been likened to a French horn. Added to this, they have very elaborate, dramatic courtship displays that are usually referred to as dances and, indeed, have inspired human dances. Cranes are represented in ancient Egyptian wall paintings and have popped up frequently over the centuries in a variety of art forms from different cultures. Cranes are often powerful symbols in the mythology of people who live near them, especially in Asia.

Longevity and fidelity are two characteristics that have led to their high status among humans. Cranes can live a long time, over forty years, and as a result are prominent symbols of long life in China and Japan. Cranes mate for life and are usually seen in pairs when not in a flock, making them symbols of a happy marriage. If fact they serve as an example that fidelity and a happy marriage lead to a long life. In the past thirty years they have taken on a new meaning because of the book *Sadako and the Thousand Paper Cranes*, the heartbreaking story of Sadako Sasaki, a Japanese girl who died from leukemia caused by the atomic bombing of Hiroshima. Every year Japanese children make thousands of origami cranes in memory of Sadako and as a demonstration for world peace.

North America has two cranes: the whooping crane and the sandhill crane. Whooping cranes are one of North America's rarest birds and one of our most famous endangered species. As far as we know, whoopers have never occurred in the Pacific Northwest. Sandhill cranes have always been much more numerous than whoopers, and despite past population reductions from hunting and habitat loss, their population is increasing and they are now common in many western states. They occur regularly in our region with a breeding population of about 2300 sandhills east of the Cascades, the majority in southeastern Oregon. Another small population winters in the Portland area. However, the largest numbers of cranes by far are seen during migration as birds that breed in Canada and Alaska travel to and from California.

Fall crane migration starts in September, peaking in October in Oregon. As expected, birds arrive earlier farther north. By November most have left with the only regularly wintering population being the 1000 or so birds that stay in the Sauvie Island–Ridgefield area near Portland. As is typical for many birds, the spring migration is more condensed with most arrivals in March in Oregon and Washington, a bit later farther north. Thousands migrate on both sides of the Cascades, but the biggest numbers are seen on the east side during the spring migration, primarily in Harney County, Oregon, and the Columbia Basin in Washington. When you are visiting the Best Bets for Spring Waterfowl Migration (in March), you should see plenty of these cranes.

Sandhill cranes can be mistaken for great blue herons (GBHs), and the much more common GBH is sometimes misnamed blue crane. A GBH and a sandhill do look a lot alike, but telling them apart is easy. Just remember the expression "crane your neck." Cranes usually stick their necks out straight. This is especially apparent when they are flying with their long neck out in front and their long legs out in back. Herons often hold their neck at least partially folded into an S shape when standing around. This becomes really obvious when they fly with their necks so folded that their head is back over their body. Another dead giveaway is the crane's voice, a very unique musical rattling sound that most people can quickly learn to recognize. Cranes will call like crazy when they are flying and can be heard a mile away. Herons sometimes make a loud "skwack" when disturbed, but no one would every say it's musical and they don't do it very often or repeatedly.

Cranes are social; they are either in a flock or, during breeding season, in a pair. Herons are solitary animals, and the only time you see them together is when they nest in colonies called rookeries or heronries. Sometimes you may see a lot of herons in the same area, like a shallow bay, but that's because food is plentiful in that area. You'll notice they are spread out and have their personal space. A good field mark for separating them is the monochrome coloring of cranes. Sandhills vary from grayish to brownish (the young are brown), but they are basically one color. Great blue herons are blue-gray and have white and black on them. These other colors are most apparent on adults in breeding plumage, when they also have plumes on their heads. Another interesting field mark for cranes is their rear end, which looks like a bustle.

Cranes nest in shallow marshes and well-flooded fields and hunt for food in almost any open, grassy habitat from marsh to flooded pasture to dry grain field. They are omnivorous and opportunistic (the two go together) and eat lots of plant material in the winter. You have a chance to see cranes doing some of their courtship dance early in the morning in the spring, even among migrating birds.

▶ **SANDHILL CRANES BEST BETS** OREGON

Sauvie Island, the large island at the confluence of the Willamette and Columbia Rivers, is the most famous place for cranes in western Oregon. As many as 3000 lesser sandhill cranes can be on the island at one time during the peak in October. Some birds may arrive as early as the end of August and for many years 200 to 300 have stayed through the winter. Estimates for this wintering population are now 1200! This is the only consistent winter population of cranes in the Northwest. These cranes will rejoin their buddies when they come through in the spring migration, breeding much farther north. The spring migration on the west side is not as noticeable because fewer cranes stop and for a shorter time than in the fall.

Sauvie Island is about half private farmland and half state land managed by ODFW as the Sauvie Island WA. It is probably the most popular birding area near Portland because it has good habitat, is close to town, and has a great variety of bird life—about 250 species visit the island at some time during the year. A parking permit is required to park on state wildlife area land. Permits can be purchased at the small store near the east end of the bridge as you first come onto the island. Most of the wildlife area is closed during the hunting season (except for hunting) which is generally mid-October to late January. However, some of the best birding is from the public roads through the private farmland, where you can see many birds from your car. Hunting in the Sauvie Island WA is on an every other day schedule, but hunting can occur any day on private land. Because it's illegal to shoot cranes, they do not seem to be disturbed by the hunting. You can usually find flocks of sandhill cranes if you go on a no-hunt day for the wildlife area and drive on the public roads where no shooting is going on.

To get to Sauvie Island, drive 10 miles

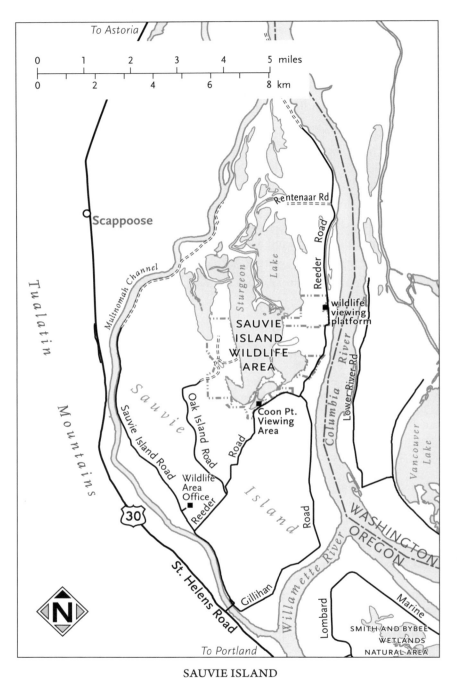

To Astoria

0   1   2   3   4   5 miles
0   2   4   6   8 km

Scappoose

Rentenaar Rd

Reeder Road

Tualatin

Multnomah Channel

Sturgeon Lake

Reeder Road

wildlife viewing platform

SAUVIE ISLAND WILDLIFE AREA

Mountains

Sauvie

Oak Island Road

Road

Coon Pt. Viewing Area

Lower River Rd

Columbia River

Vancouver Lake

Sauvie Island Road

Wildlife Area Office

Reeder

Island

Road

30

St. Helens Road

Gillihan

Willamette River

Lombard

WASHINGTON
OREGON

Marine

SMITH AND BYBEE WETLANDS NATURAL AREA

N

To Portland

SAUVIE ISLAND

northwest of downtown Portland on US Hwy 30 toward Astoria. Watch for signs for the bridge, and cross it onto the island. If you go north from the bridge on Sauvie Island Rd, past Reeder Rd, you'll reach the wildlife area headquarters where you can usually get maps and information on current closures. Cranes are often seen from the paved portion of Sauvie Island Rd past ODFW's office in the fields near the county line (a sign for Columbia County is next to the road).

Another good place to look is along Oak Island Rd. Oak Island itself is in the wildlife area and closed during the hunting season, but the private land along Oak Island Rd, between Reeder Rd and the wildlife area boundary, is very good for cranes and waterfowl. The other great stop is at the end of Rentenaar Rd, on the east side of the island off Reeder Rd. Walk up onto the dike at the end of Rentenaar Rd for a view of a wide area. Often from this vantage point you can see cranes, swans, and geese, including snow geese in recent years. Throughout the winter Sauvie Island is an excellent place to view waterfowl, raptors, gulls, and wintering sparrows.

The breeding greater sandhill cranes in Oregon are concentrated in the Harney Basin. The fields and pastures south of Burns and the marshes of Malheur NWR host 3000 cranes during October but have over twice that many in April.

▶ SANDHILL CRANES BEST BETS WASHINGTON

If closures are getting you down on Sauvie or things are just too slow from hunting and other human activities, zip on over to Ridgefield NWR. Cranes could be out in the fields anywhere but are often south of the southernmost part of the auto tour route. The northern section, the Carty Unit, never has hunting and is always open for birding; the River S Unit is open for birding on no hunt days. Check with the refuge for the hunting schedule but for a few years hunting has been on Tuesday, Thursday, and Saturday. The other four days are for wildlife watching. Ridgefield has recently started collecting an entrance fee, but it's worth paying because this is one of the better refuges for accommodating wildlife watchers and other nature lovers who don't hunt.

Ridgefield is also a great place for waterfowl, including swans, which will begin to arrive in late October or November. Ridgefield is also well known for bald eagles and from the end of waterfowl hunting season through March it's simply a great winter birding spot very convenient to the Portland metro area.

The Carty Unit has the wonderful Oaks to Wetlands Wildlife Trail, and now there is an awesome, authentic, huge reproduction of a Chinook-style cedar plankhouse at the townsite of Cathlapotle, a Chinook village. The mix of habitats on the Oaks to Wetlands Trail means bird diversity and in the spring, some great wildflowers.

The directions and a map to the River S Unit in the refuge are in January (Swans). To get to the Carty Unit, if you return to the town of Ridgefield from the River S Unit on Hillhurst St, turn left onto Pioneer St, the continuation of State Hwy 501, and then go west through town until the road ends at Main St. Turn right and go north on Main St just over a mile, and on your left you'll see the parking area for the Carty Unit. The 2-mile Oaks to Wetlands Wildlife Trail begins on the other side of the bridge over the train tracks.

The Othello Sandhill Crane Festival was one

of March's Nature Nuggets because of the thousands of cranes that stop in that area during spring migration. Cranes also stop there during their fall migration, but in much fewer numbers. The strategy remains the same. From Othello drive west on State Hwy 26 to Columbia NWR, exploring roads along the way that go south from the highway. A series of roads southwest of Othello, in particular McKinney and Bench roads, are another area to cruise with the windows down listening for that distinctive, melodic rattling call.

OCTOBER'S NATURE NUGGETS

WOOLLY BEARS Those big fuzzy caterpillars that you start noticing this month are woolly bears. You see them a lot in fall because they are big, and because they are roaming around looking for a place to hibernate. Almost everyone knows these brown and black beasts are called woolly bears, but few know that woolly bears are the larvae of the Isabella moth, one of the plainest of the usually colorful tiger moths. You may see the adult around lights on summer nights. And by the way, you can't predict the weather from the width of the colored bands of hairs.

SPIDERS Fall is spider time. All those babies that hatched out in the spring and summer have been porking up on insects and are now really noticeable as they weave webs all over your yard. Most dramatic are the large members of the orb-weaver family, usually called garden spiders or argiopes. These are the spiders that weave your classic large, circular, spiral webs and then usually hang upside-down in the middle. Spiders are tough to tell apart and the only reasonable book for amateurs is the classic Golden Guide *Spiders and their Kin* from 1968. Another fabulous spider event that takes place in the fall is ballooning. Young spiders climb to the top of a plant, stick their abdomen into the air, and shoot out a strand of silk. When the silk is long enough to catch the wind and lift the spider, it lets go and off it goes, drifting over the countryside to a new home. This is the way most spiders disperse, and it's extremely effective; ballooning spiders are seen on high mountains and remote islands, although most travel short distances. Where millions of spiders have landed, the ground or vegetation can become covered with masses of these threads—called gossamer. A field of dry grass, covered with gossamer reflecting the sunlight of a bright fall day, is one of the most beautiful and ethereal sights I've ever seen.

PLANT YOUR SOCKS Autumn is also about seeds. Plants have been blooming since spring, and the purpose of flowers is to make seeds. By fall seeds have matured and await dispersal by wind, water, hitchhiking on animals, passing through animals when they eat fruit, being carried off and stored (and hopefully forgotten) by animals, or just dropping from the parent plant. There are a lot of seeds out there waiting for a ride. Here's an experiment—a great demonstration about seeds—to try with kids. Put a pair of old socks over your shoes, the woollier or fuzzier the better, and then run or walk through a field of dry grass and weeds. When your outside socks are well covered with sticky seeds, remove them, and take them home. Leave them with the seed-side out, put them in a pan that has an inch of dirt in the bottom, then cover them lightly with about a half inch of more dirt. Gently water them, keeping the ground moist but not too wet. Keep them in a warm sunny place while you watch what happens. You can really get a feel for seed dispersal when you see it in action.

THE RAIN PROMISES MUSHROOMS: A CLOSER LOOK

You can find mushrooms just about everywhere, but some places are much better than others. Fungus likes it wet and warm, and we live in mushroom heaven, especially from the Cascades to the coast. The wet coniferous forests of the Northwest are some of the best mushroom habitats in the world. Millions of dollars worth of wild mushrooms are harvested here and shipped throughout the world. At least a dozen mushroom shows or festivals take place each fall, listed at the end of this chapter. The fall rains initiate a magnificent mushroom season that goes from September to December, varying somewhat from north to south, and, of course, depending on when the rain starts. Freezing temperatures mark the end of the first fall flush, but warmer weather later in winter will bring a second, much smaller round. The smaller spring mushroom season is famous for the morels, which occur then.

The greatest interest in mushrooms is in finding the choice edibles that the Northwest is famous for: chanterelle, matsutake, morel, porcini, Oregon truffle, lobster, oyster, and others. Some people just want to know what these weird, mysterious, sometimes abundant organisms are and what they do. Let's face it, when a bunch of big colorful mushrooms just appears overnight it does seem magical. Who hasn't seen drawings of mushrooms with little gnomes sleeping under them or fairies flying around them? Mushrooms come loaded with mythology, mystery, and misinformation.

For years I had been trying to get a handle on identifying mushrooms with continuing frustration until I found David Arora's *All That the Rain Promises, and More: A Hip Pocket Guide to Western Mushrooms*. At last I had the book that could help me learn about the complex world of fungus.

The problem with trying to identify mushrooms is that it is difficult. Sorry, but there's no way around the fact that there are thousands of different kinds of mushrooms, and most of them are very hard to tell apart. It's not hopeless, however. Some mushrooms are quite distinctive and easy for most people to identify. These are the "bald eagles" of the mushroom world. No one asks me, "How can you tell it's a bald eagle?" once they've gotten a good look at one on a bird walk. Similarly, everyone recognizes a skunk when they see one. So it is with some mushrooms, such as morels, lobsters, fly amanitas, and shaggy manes. It's wonderful when a mushroom is easy to identify and happens to be delicious, like morels and lobsters. It's also very helpful when a poisonous one like the fly amanita is obvious. Don't worry, if your true desire is to just find tasty mushrooms to eat, you can learn to identify some of the world's choicest edibles growing here in the Northwest and forget about the rest. But once your appetite is satisfied, you may not be able to ignore the thrill of the hunt.

As a beginner, start with the ones that are the easiest to identify, and don't worry about the rest. That may sound obvious, but it is difficult and frustrating for most people to be unable to identify most of the mushrooms they find—a common situation on a mushroom hunt. You have to be ready to struggle trying to identify a mushroom only to say, "I haven't a clue" and to move on. Of course, over time you will have a clue and then eventually a good idea, and a few will become easy, just as with recognizing bald eagles and skunks. Becoming familiar with your local fungus requires patience and a lot of field experience. The bright side of taking on the fungi, however, is that you'll never run out of new stuff to find and to try to identify. Most fungus fanciers, however, learn how to find and identify their favorite yummy mushrooms, and how to recognize poisonous look-alikes, and leave it at that.

More common and widespread than the interest in edible mushrooms is the fear of poisonous mushrooms. True, the most poisonous mushrooms in the world grow here, and people have died eating them. But they can't hurt you if you don't eat them. Many people think if they just touch a poisonous mushroom they'll drop dead on the spot. The toxins in mushrooms cannot go through your skin, even if you crush the 'shroom in your hand. So keep them out of your mouth and no mushroom can hurt you; it's that simple. However, if you're afraid that if you pick wild mushrooms to eat that you might eat the wrong kind and poison yourself—good, that is entirely possible and a healthy fear. You do need to be very careful about eating wild mushrooms, but don't worry about touching any of them.

Much to everyone's disappointment, there's no simple or easy way to tell an edible mushroom from a poisonous one. If you have heard any general rules, such as "if it grows in wood you can eat it" or "if it's red it's poisonous," forget them. There are no such rules. None. Period. The only way to know if a mushroom is edible or poisonous, or harmless but insipid, is to identify exactly what kind of mushroom it is. Or at least identify it precisely enough to know that it is one of a few species that are edible and which have no poisonous look-a-likes. There is no division between mushrooms and toadstools. In fact, there are no fungi named toadstool.

Eating wild mushrooms is not something to be done casually. The most common phrase you hear experienced 'shroomers say to newbies is "When in doubt, throw it out." Another general rule is never eat wild mushrooms raw. Sometimes a mushroom that most people eat without any problems can cause digestive discomfort in a few. Cooking greatly reduces the chance of any individual sensitivity or reaction. Always eat a small amount of any wild mushroom (cooked) when you eat it the first time to make sure you're not sensitive to it. Remember, start by learning the easiest, most obvious, and tastiest mushrooms first.

In addition to studying *All That the Rain Promises, and More,* going on mushrooms walks or taking classes at parks and nature centers can be helpful, especially if a program is billed for beginners. Mycological societies also offer these activities. However, sometimes the leader can be so knowledgeable that beginners are left in the dust, even more confused. Don't be afraid to speak up and ask questions such as, "What do you mean it's a bolete?" Compared to most other areas of nature study, mushrooms seem to have a larger gap between those in the know and beginners. Try to find the right mushroom mentor for you. Mushroom shows can be a good introduction, but you probably won't come away knowing how to identify many mushrooms. Mushrooms are so widespread it's not practical to list specific locations, and it's unnecessary. It's also important that areas don't become overharvested and abused, which unfortunately happens too much already. In general, the best habitats are the various coniferous forests, from western hemlock and redcedar in the Coast Range to pines and firs in the Cascades. Oak woodlands are very rich in fungi and often have a longer season than the conifers. Unless you get permission from landowners, stick to public lands for collecting or harvesting. Picking mushrooms for personal use is allowed in US national forests but often a permit is required, which is free for non-commercial picking. No collecting of any kind (outside of the gift shop) is allowed in US and Canadian national parks. In addition to individual national forests, always check on the regulations in any state, provincial, regional, or county park.

Exactly what are mushrooms? Many people know that mushrooms are fungus but when asked what fungus is, lots of folks are at a loss. Most people think of fungus as a kind of plant because that's what they were probably taught in school if they're over 40. However, in the early 1970s biologists reclassified the fungi as a distinct kingdom of living things, as different from plants as they are from animals. Although many fungi grow out of the ground much like plants, no fungus can use the sun's energy to photosynthesize and no fungus has flowers, seeds, leaves, roots, or any of the other specialized structures that plants have. Because fungus doesn't photosynthesize, it must get its energy and nutrients the way animals do, by eating.

How fungus "eats" or gets its nutrients is different from how animals eat. The fungus organism is not just the thing we call a mushroom. The fungus is a mass of thin fibers growing in soil or in its food. The food can be parts of dead plants and animals or inside the tissues of living plants and animals. The huge diversity of fungi and their different foods gets complicated, let's just talk about the fungi we usually call mushrooms, like the little brown ones that pop up in your lawn. The fungus organism started as a microscopic spore that blew into your lawn and then grew into a mass of threadlike fibers. The fibers are called hyphae; the whole mass of hyphae is called a mycelium. Sometimes you can see the mycelium of a fungus in soil—it looks like a spider web in the dirt. The mycelium is the "body" of the fungus, and it grows through the dirt eating the dead organic material in the soil. The fungi that get their nutrients this way are called saprophytes, and this way of eating makes the fungi critically important to the earth as decomposers.

Let's say the mycelium grows around a dead earthworm. The fibers (hyphae) surround the worm's body and start to grow through it. The hyphae secrete a mix of enzymes and other digestive juices into the worm's body. These juices digest the worm into a gushy blob of broken-down nutrients. Then the hyphae absorb the nutrients, which spread to the cells of the mycelium. The fungus has digested the worm outside of its cells and soaked up the nutrients. This is called extracellular digestion and is very different from the way we animals eat. Imagine what's left of the worm— not much. What is left gets decomposed further by more fungi and bacteria until the nutrients are in the soil ready to make your lawn look better than your neighbor's. That is, if you haven't killed your earthworms, fungus, bacteria, and helpful bugs with nasty chemicals.

The fungus keeps growing through the soil digesting organic matter as it goes. Or maybe it grows in a dead tree or log where it is really growing in its food. This goes on for years, hundreds of years for some, although the growth rate varies with temperature and moisture. When the conditions are right, the fungus changes its growth and sends up a fruiting body, the thing we call the mushroom. As with the flowers of plants, the only purpose of the mushroom, the fruiting body, is to reproduce. Instead of seeds, fungi produce spores, which spread vast distances in the wind to grow new funguses. So when you pick mushrooms, it is like picking apples off an apple tree, the fungus remains. That's why you can find mushrooms growing in the same place year after year. And that is why they seem to appear out of nowhere; the fruiting body is just a small part of a much larger organism that you don't see. But it's still like magic, isn't it?

Mycorrhizal fungi, a name that means *fungus root*, get their nutrients in a different way than the saprophytes described above. The hyphae of mycorrhizal fungi grow around or actually in the roots of plants in a symbiotic relationship that benefits both. An estimated 80% of plants, especially trees, have mycorrhizal fungi that help them extract key nutrients from the soil. The fungus in return gets water and organic compounds like carbohydrates from the plant's roots. Mycorrhyzal fungi are vital to the health of forests, which helps explain why so many grow in the richly forested Northwest, including some of our favorite edibles such as chanterelles.

When you identify mushrooms, you are identifying the fruiting bodies; you don't dig up the mycelium. In fact, you should carefully cut mushrooms at their base when you harvest them so you do not disturb the mycelium and its habitat. What do you look for to identify your carefully harvested fruiting body; that is, the mushroom? Most folks think of the obvious characteristics such as size, color, shape, and maybe texture. But for most mushrooms you really need to look carefully at how they are built, their structure, and that means learning the names of parts and a few descriptive terms.

Does the cap have gills or pores? Are the gills decurrent (attached to the stem) or free? Is there a ring on the stalk? Is the cap convex or depressed? You will get used to the names and terms; it's just part of the learning curve. One of the most important clues is the color of the spores. Sometimes you can make a good guess at the color of the spores by the color of the gills. But more often, you'll have to take the mushroom home to determine the color. To find the spore color, you can make a spore print.

Separate the cap from the stem of a fresh, completely opened mushroom. Sometimes you can just pop the cap off; other times you have to cut it off. Place the cap, gill-side down, on a piece of paper, and cover it with a bowl so no air currents disturb it. Use white paper if you think the spores are dark and black paper if you think they are lightly colored. Don't touch your set up for about 12 hours (you'll learn what's best with experience), and then carefully lift off the bowl and then the mushroom cap. Presto; it's gorgeous. The spores will have dropped onto the paper and made a print that is a copy of the gill structure. It looks like a bicycle wheel with lots of crowded spokes. Let the paper dry completely; the spores will stick to the paper. If you want to make the print durable and permanent, spray the dry spore print and paper gently with a matte fixative or lacquer. You can experiment with different finishes. Spore prints are beautiful and unique. If you've never seen one, try it out with a big portabella from the grocery store. Aside from the artistic thrill of making spore prints, this will accurately show you the color of the spores. But it's lots of fun regardless; it's another one of those magical things about mushrooms.

The bottom line is that you'll often have to collect the mushroom in the field and then take it home to try to identify it. Eventually you'll learn how to use identification keys, the real tool in *Mushrooms Demystified* for the "not obvious" mushrooms. As time goes on you'll build up your repertoire of mushrooms that you can identify in the wild because you have done the homework. However, you'll have to decide just how far into mushroom identification you want to go because some will just be too hard. Knowing when to give up, or to not even start, is the wisdom of the experienced 'shroomer. Avoid the dreaded LBMs. Even David Arora, The Man Himself, says in *Mushrooms Demystified,* "The fact is, Little Brown Mushrooms (LBMs) are so overwhelmingly abundant and uncompromisingly undistinguished that it is more than just futile for the beginner to attempt to identify them—it is downright foolish." Can you imagine a bird book that said, "All the sandpipers are too hard to identify so just forget about them?" With mushrooms, you'll always find some that you won't be able to identify so just get used to it and let it go.

The culinary reputation of some of our mushrooms fuels some people's desire to find "the big strike," the mushroom gold mine. Finding both gold and edible mushrooms, however, requires some knowledge, work, experience, and good luck. Learning how to identify mushrooms and where to find the treasures is a challenge, no doubt about that. Slow down, look carefully, take your time and enjoy the wonderful places where you find mushrooms. The rain will fulfill its promise, and the fungi will be there for a lifelong adventure.

Mushroom Shows

You will be astounded at the number and variety of different fungi at your first mushroom show. October is mushroom show month. These are the most established annual mushroom shows as of this writing, but more are popping up, just like the mushrooms. Be sure to check each year for the correct time and place, some are very regular and others bounce around a bit. Almost all are organized by a mycological society (abbreviated M.S.) and are listed in approximate chronological order for each state or province.

OREGON
Breitenbush Mushroom Gathering
Breitenbush Hot Springs Retreat & Confer-
ence Center; www.breitenbush.com
Early to middle of October, several days

Yachats Village Mushroom Festival (not just
mushrooms)
Yachats Area Chamber of Commerce,
Lincoln County M.S., Cascade M.S.;
www.yachats.org/events.html
Saturday and Sunday in mid-October

Portland Mushroom Show
Oregon M.S.; www.wildmushrooms.org
Third Sunday in October

Mount Pisgah Mushroom Festival, Eugene,
OR
Mount Pisgah Arboretum; www.efn.
org/~mtpisgah/
Last Sunday in October

WASHINGTON
Bremerton Mushroom Show
Kitsup Peninsula M.S.; www.namyco.
org/clubs/kpms
First Sunday in October

Seattle Mushroom Show (the largest; two
days)
Puget Sound M.S.; www.psms.org
Second weekend in October

Everett Mushroom Show
Snohomish County M.S.; www.scmsfungi.
org
Second Sunday in October

Olympic Peninsula Mushroom Show, Port
Angeles and Squim
Olympic Peninsula M.S.; groups.yahoo.
com/group/olypms
Second Sunday in October

BRITISH COLUMBIA
Bamfield Mushroom Festival
Bamfield, BC; www.bamfieldchamber.com
Second or third Saturday in October

Vancouver Mushroom Show
Vancouver M.S.; www.vanmyco.com
Third Sunday in October

Swan Lake Mushroom Show, Victoria
South Vancouver Island M.S.; www.
swanlake.bc.ca/
Last Sunday in October

NOVEMBER

PRONGHORN

"Oh give me a home, where the buffalo roam, where the deer and the antelope play." What? Antelope? On the range? In America? Most folks have no idea what the last animal referred to is in "Home on the Range." The name *antelope* conjures up images of the African plains and animals looking like impala or gazelles. Actually, those are the correct images because the true antelopes, members of the Bovidae family, all live in Africa, Asia, and Europe and are the animals one sees in scenes of the African plains. However, we do have an animal usually labeled with the misnomer "antelope," the pronghorn. Pronghorn are not, however, really antelopes but something much more special.

The pronghorn is the world's only living member of a family of hoofed mammals called the Antilocapridae. More members of this family existed in North America during the Pleistocene Epoch and before, but they are now only fossils. The family Antilocapridae is something very rare, a whole family of animals completely restricted to North America. This makes the pronghorn a truly unique animal of the American west. But whereas everyone knows about the American bison or buffalo, pronghorn are surprisingly unknown and definitely under appreciated. They truly are a unique symbol for our American west and deserve to at least grace the back of a nickel.

One very unusual feature of pronghorn is the horn that gives them their name. They are the only animal in the world with a branched horn, not antlers. Their horn is also unlike that of other animals in that the horny outer sheath is shed every year leaving a bony core. Both males and females have horns but the females' are small and inconspicuous.

Previous page:
Another cycle
of orb-weaving
spiders draws
to an end.

I advocate increased pronghorn awareness and believe these animals should really be appreciated for the amazing animals that they are. They can make a solid claim to the title of the most highly adapted animal for running in the world. Right away most will think, Oh yeah, what about cheetahs? It's very hard to accurately measure animal speeds and you can find a variety of top speeds given for cheetahs and pronghorn in different books. It does seem to be universally accepted, however, that cheetahs can beat pronghorn with a top speed of possibly 70 mph while pronghorn appear to reach a maximum more around 60 mph. But cheetahs are sprinters and can hit their top speeds for only a few seconds. Pronghorn, on the other hand, can maintain top speed for longer and apparently can cruise along for miles at over 40 mph. When it comes to sustained high speed running, pronghorn are the champs.

How pronghorn can maintain such high speeds is a marvelous study in adaptation and evolution. Pronghorn anatomy and physiology have been studied quite closely because they seem to represent a limit in evolution for running. Like other ungulates or hoofed mammals, pronghorn have legs that are highly specialized for running. Their legs and feet are very long and thin and highly modified compared to more average mammal legs. This gives them a very long stride, the most basic requirement for a fast runner. One of the main limiting factors in how fast and how long an animal can run is its ability to get oxygen to its muscles, an area where the pronghorn has some of its most extreme adaptations. Compared to a goat, which is about as close a living relative as you can find, pronghorn have five times the lung capacity, a heart three times larger, a larger windpipe, and more hemoglobin in their blood. This all goes toward making the pronghorn the super runner of the American plains.

Pronghorn, and other ungulates, developed their running abilities to escape predators on the emerging grasslands of a drying world. Their habitat has remained the prairies and sagebrush plains of the American West. They truly are animals of the wide, open spaces and will not seek shelter in trees. They once ranged from Canada to Mexico in most western states in numbers estimated as high as 50 million. As happened to their close associate on the prairies, the American bison, pronghorn numbers were decimated by settlers. But their numbers never got as critically low as the bison's, probably because they were able to retreat more to the periphery of human activity, particularly in the sparsely settled sagebrush lands of the Great Basin and Wyoming, lands frequently referred to as "nowhere." Starting around the turn of the century, they were completely protected for about 25 years and then managed as a big-game species. Today there are about 500,000 living over much of their former range where the habitat is still suitable and human disturbance is minimal.

If running away is their means of escaping predators, pronghorn must be able to detect predators well in advance. They usually don't have to worry about predators sneaking up on them because they stick to open spaces. Pronghorn have the keen senses of smell and hearing typical of ungulates, but they mainly depend on their exceptional eyesight to spot predators two or three miles away. Their eyes are very large and are unusually high and far back on the head, giving them an almost turreted look. They have an interesting way of signaling each other visually in times of danger. When frightened, pronghorn erect the white hairs on their rump as they run away. Other pronghorn see these white patches disappearing into the distance and take off themselves. Pronghorn rule number one: you see white butts disappearing in the distance—you follow 'em. Their excellent eyesight and cautious nature can make pronghorn difficult to see except at long distances. Fortunately, some pronghorn seem to have accommodated to traffic along certain Oregon roads and not all viewings are dots in the distance.

Pronghorn historically ranged throughout the Great Basin and in our region we find them most easily today in Oregon's Great Basin country. The Great Basin does not extend into Washington and British Columbia and there are no pronghorn in those areas, although there was an unsuccessful attempt to introduce pronghorn into eastern Washington. The only practical way to see pronghorn is to carefully drive the roads mentioned in the areas below, watching for their distinctive white and tan color in the distance. As with many animals, some pronghorn may actually allow a vehicle to pass fairly close but will immediately run off when they see a human on foot. Stay in your car, it's your traveling observation blind.

▶ PRONGHORN BEST BETS OREGON

The sagebrush plains and grasslands of the southeastern quarter of Oregon is the heart of Northwest pronghorn country. The best place is Hart Mountain National Antelope Refuge, about 45 miles northeast of the town of Lake-view. From Lakeview go 4.5 miles north on US Hwy 395 to the junction with State Hwy 140. Go east on Hwy 140 toward Adel, but after 15 miles turn north on the Plush Cutoff. After 17 miles on the Plush Cutoff you'll come to the tiny town of Plush. This is your last chance for gas and supplies for awhile. It's your only chance for some cool pronghorn hats and T-shirts. Continue north and east following the signs to the refuge as the road makes a few right-hand jogs. Just outside of town you'll come to a BLM interpretive area on the Warner Basin, worth a quick stop. Hart Mountain will have been looming in the east for some time, and it's obvious where you're headed.

Hart Mountain is a classic fault block mountain. Layers of basalt flowed over the area making a flat landscape. Then a major fault developed, and the land east of the fault was pushed up to become Hart Mountain while the land west of the fault dropped and became the Warner Basin, filled with a huge lake during the Pleistocene but now containing a chain of shallow lakes.

You will start driving along the base of the escarpment and will come to the end of the paved road (there are no paved roads in the refuge). Soon after you'll see a sign about bighorn sheep. From this point until the road begins to climb up the mountain is a good area to look for bighorn sheep. Bighorns are harder to see than pronghorn, and it's unlikely that you would spot any without getting out and carefully looking over the best habitat with binoculars or a spotting scope. Easier places to see bighorn sheep are described in their chapter. Continue up the mountain and then to refuge headquarters, which has a small visitor center with a restroom and information. Check with the refuge staff for the latest tips on locating pronghorn and on road conditions. The register of wildlife sightings may also provide location information on pronghorn and other wildlife.

You'll usually see pronghorn from the main road that crosses the refuge in the stretch from headquarters to the eastern boundary and from the Blue Sky Rd. The Blue Sky Rd goes south from headquarters to Blue Sky, a beauti-

ful grove of ponderosa pine and aspen. Check to be sure the Blue Sky Rd is open, although it's rarely closed except in winter. To take the Blue Sky Rd, start at headquarters and drive south following the signs. After 1.5 miles the road forks. The right fork goes to Hot Springs Camp (more later) and the left fork goes to Blue Sky. Watch carefully along the Blue Sky Rd for pronghorn and other wildlife. Blue Sky itself is a beautiful place to get out, walk around, and hang out for awhile. This groove of trees can sometimes attract some interesting migrating birds.

For more scenery, possible wildlife, and adventure you can drive the other roads on the refuge if you have a high-clearance, all-wheel or four-wheel drive vehicle. In the southeastern corner of the refuge are a series of lakes where pronghorn often congregate. The route to this area is the South Boundary Rd which takes off from the Blue Sky Rd at its southernmost point. Do not take this road without a good map and a spare tire. A consultation with a refuge staff member also is a good idea, especially when traveling midweek and off season. Most people get plenty of good views of pronghorn from the main roads.

Back to Hot Springs Camp mentioned above. After a dusty day of wildlife viewing, what could be better than a nice soak in a hot springs? South of headquarters take the right-hand fork to Hot Springs Camp which is well signed. After 2.5 miles you'll see the cement pad built around the hot springs that are down a side road to your right. The parking area for the springs is open to anyone. The water is not real hot; I couldn't stay for a long soak with freezing air temperatures and snow starting, but it is very pleasant.

While looking for pronghorn, keep your eyes out for some of the common fall and winter birds of the refuge: rough-legged hawks, northern harriers, golden eagles, horned larks, Townsend's solitaire, and mountain bluebirds.

You may see sage-grouse in the sagebrush and chukar on rocky slopes.

Malheur NWR and the adjacent BLM lands provide plenty of good pronghorn habitat, and it's unusual to spend several days in the area and not see a few. The drive from Burns to Brothers on US Hwy 20 is another good place for finding pronghorn—many birdwatchers see them along this stretch of highway when traveling between Malheur NWR and Bend. You might also spot pronghorn when traveling any of the roads through the sagebrush and grasslands of eastern Oregon.

WINTERING BIRDS IN THE SALISH SEA

If you are asking yourself "Where is the Salish Sea?," check back in the Introduction for a more complete explanation. Briefly, it's the name that more and more people are using to describe the complex inland sea consisting of Puget Sound, the Strait of Georgia, the Strait of Juan de Fuca, and the numerous other interconnected bodies of water. The Salish Sea was formed in an appropriately dramatic manner during the Pleistocene Epoch. The whole Salish Sea area, parts of which are now called the Georgia Depression or the Puget Trough, was entirely covered by a large lobe of the Vashon glacier. Imagine a solid sheet of ice 3000 feet deep over what is now Seattle. The ice gouged out the land between the Cascades and the Olympics, and when the ice melted, in came the ocean.

The Salish Sea today is a rich ecosystem, inhabited by an estimated 2000 different species of invertebrates and at least 200 species of fish. Such a large and varied food resource allowed the Coast Salish people to develop a very rich, elaborate cultural life and has since continued to support many additional people. This bounty provides for many other predators as well, making the Salish Sea a haven for many marine mammals and birds, despite the fact that the most heavily populated part of the Pacific Northwest is on its shores. Every winter, vast numbers of waterbirds, representing 10 different families, converge on the Salish Sea to escape the much harsher weather in their breeding grounds. The first winter visitors start arriving during September, but numbers don't get large until November. Most of these winter visitors will remain into March, some even to April. Although most people don't think of the dead of winter being the best time for many outdoor activities, it is the best for seeing the biggest variety of seabirds.

Who are our winter seabirds? The closely related loons and grebes are well represented. Common, Pacific, and red-throated loons occur regularly, and the yellow-billed and even the Arctic loons show up now and then. Similarly, western, red-necked, and horned grebes are all common with eared and Clark's grebes being seen in much smaller numbers. The pied-billed grebe is not usually considered a seabird because it's a common year-round resident in freshwater.

Three of our most common year-round seabirds or waterbirds are the cormorants—double-crested, Brandts, and pelagic. Gulls are another well-represented family with six species common most of the year. The waterfowl are a huge group and have the greatest number of birds and species in the Salish Sea in winter. The wintering waterfowl you can expect to see are the sea ducks: the surf, white-winged, and black scoters; the harlequin duck; and the long-tailed duck (formerly the oldsquaw). You can also easily see just about any duck that occurs in the Northwest. The alcids discussed in June (Nesting Seabirds) are possible, especially the common murre, pigeon guillemot, and marbled murrelet. The rhinoceros auklet and the tufted puffin are much more commonly seen during the breeding season, when they come to nest on islands in the Salish Sea and along the coastline.

Several birds of prey like to eat waterbirds and shorebirds and start showing up when their potential prey start gathering. Bald eagles will regularly congregate during the winter around a reliable food supply, such as a nice big population of wintering ducks. Two other birds of prey that become more common along shores in winter, but in much smaller numbers than bald eagles, are the peregrine falcon and merlin. Peregrines can take a wide range of birds and will eat alcids, ducks, and shorebirds while the much smaller merlin is pretty much restricted to shorebirds. Watch for these falcons along shore, especially near mud flats where shorebirds gather.

▶ WINTERING BIRDS IN THE SALISH SEA BEST BETS

BY BOAT A boat provides many opportunities to view marine wildlife, often at close range. Sea kayaking has become popular in recent years and outfitters offer a variety of services, but few public trips take place during the winter. If you have access to a boat, you can head out during good weather in October or early November. Just about every wintering species will be in the Salish Sea by October, only their numbers may still be small. Otherwise, a trip on a ferry can provide some wildlife-viewing opportunities. The best ferry lines are Anacortes–Sydney, Tsawwassen–Swartz Bay, and Port Angeles–Victoria.

Wildlife watching from a ferry, however, has some disadvantages compared to watching from a smaller boat. On the ferries you are high over the water so your views of birds are distant unless you have one fly right over you or hover over the boat. Does the image of gulls off the stern come to mind? You've got it. Identifying birds from big boats is a specialized skill that will take more patience and practice than many other types of birding situations. You'll need to focus on the key field marks that you can see at a distance and the basic patterns of the birds. You'll generally get plenty of practice because it's common to see the same species over, and over and over again. Then sometimes you'll sail right through a massive swarm of 100,000 fishing seabirds and it's breathtaking, even if you aren't sure what they all are.

Proper clothing is essential. You'll need to be outside a lot because you won't be able to see birds well from inside. The most important factor for your comfort is having clothes for the strong wind from the ferry's motion. Explore the outside decks looking for the spots where the wind isn't as bad. There are some great little spots here and there behind bulkheads or braces or whatever they call that stuff on boats. Often right behind the bow is good because the wind goes right over your head. When you are outside birdwatching on a ferry in cold weather you will notice that many of the people inside are looking at you in total bewilderment. Some of the greatest people you'll meet on your travels are the other folks that you run into outside on the ferries.

The Port Angeles–Victoria ferry is described in Pelagic Bird Trips (September) and is different from the others described here because you have a better chance of seeing truly pelagic birds.

The Tsawwassen–Swartz Bay (Vancouver–Victoria) ferry goes through Active Pass between Galiano and Mayne islands. The portion of the trip between Swartz Bay (Vancouver Island) and Active Pass is also good. Active Pass is famous for the massive flocks of fishing seabirds, which are there when the tides are turning and the currents churn up fish for the birds to eat. It's of course hard to time this just right because the ferries don't go when you want them to, so here's my plan for hitting the pass at about the best time. Find the time for the high tide at Point Atkinson in Vancouver, this is the location most commonly given in newspapers or in tide tables. Then take the first ferry leaving after that time from either departure port. The earlier in the day the better, but that won't be too early because the days are so short in winter. From mid-October to Christmas there will usually be a departure every odd hour, but be sure to check the current schedule.

The cost for two people to go as foot passengers is about a fifth the cost to take a car (round trip). You can leave your car in the day parking area near the terminal (have Loonies for the meter) and walk on. Each ferry makes a round trip so you can drive to the terminal, park, walk on board, ride to the other terminal, stay on the ferry watching the gulls and crows forage on the upper deck, and then take the same ferry back. It's a four-hour round trip through beautiful scenery in great comfort on one of the most luxurious ferries in the world (with a cafeteria).

The San Juan Islands Ferry from Anacortes, Washington, to Sidney, British Columbia, is one of the best all-around ferry trips for wildlife and scenery. Unfortunately, there is only one daily departure during the winter. However, a shorter trip that goes through the best areas for birds is the Anacortes–Friday Harbor route, which has two additional daylight departures.

▶ WINTERING BIRDS IN THE SALISH SEA BEST BETS WASHINGTON

FROM SHORE With its thousands of miles of coastline, the Salish Sea provides many excellent opportunities to see marine animals from shore, making any undeveloped section of coastline with public access worth checking out. All areas below are generally best at or near the high tide because the high water will bring birds closer to shore. Some of the best areas, starting at north for noon and going clockwise are Point Roberts, Birch Bay, Kayak Point County Park, Port Townsend, Dungeness NWR, and Ediz Hook. Ediz Hook, Dungeness NWR, and Padilla Bay are covered in other chapters.

Point Roberts is the end of the small peninsula that's the western border of Boundary Bay in British Columbia. It really should be part of Canada, but a mistake was made

SALISH SEA

in the 1872 negotiation of the international boundary so Point Roberts, a four-square-mile chunk of Washington, hangs out there by itself attached to British Columbia. Regardless of its geographical oddness, the southern tip of Point Roberts is one of the best spots in the Salish Sea to see wintering waterbirds. You'll be crossing the international border from Canada to the United States and back, so be sure you have the proper documents.

From State Hwy 99 near Ladner, take State Hwy 17 south following signs for Point Roberts. Turn left onto 56th St (also called Point Roberts Rd) and take it south to the border. Once you cross into the United States you'll be on Tyee Dr. Just keep going south on Tyee until it intersects APA Rd. Continue straight ahead as the road curves to the right and becomes Marine Dr. Stay on Marine Dr as it curves around the marina, and then turns into Edwards Dr. Take Edwards Dr west to Lighthouse Park where you can park (fee) and scope the surrounding waters. All the regulars are usually present including numerous harlequin ducks and long-tailed ducks, and harder to find birds, such as black scoter and ancient murrelet. And, for a special bonus, this is considered the most consistent spot in Washington for the elusive yellow-billed loon!

Birch Bay SP, just south of the Canadian border, is another excellent spot that is easy to find. Take Exit 266 from Interstate 5 and head west 7 miles on Grandview Rd, turn right onto Jackson Rd, and in less than one mile turn onto the park road and drive down to the shore. Birch Bay Dr goes along the shore for one mile in the park, and then continues into the cute little town of Birch Bay. There are many places in the park to stop and scope the waters of Birch Bay. Here I once had beautiful males of all three scoters in one scope view.

The pier at Kayak Point RP has good views of wildlife in Port Susan Bay. Although best

for birds, some marine mammals are also seen from the pier, including gray whales on occasion. Heading north from Marysville on I-5, take Exit 206 and head west on 172 St, which is also called State Hwy 531 and Lakewood Rd (jeesh, how many names can a road have?). The road twists and turns a bit but just stay on Lakewood and follow signs for Kayak Point Park. At Goodwin Lake do not take Hwy 531 as it heads south. About 8.25 miles from I-5 you'll come to a stop sign at Marine Dr. Head south on Marine Dr, making a little jog that's signed, and you'll reach the park. You'll have no trouble finding your way to the waterfront and pier.

Port Townsend, with more authentic Victorian buildings than any place north of San Francisco, is picturesque and a popular tourist destination. I'll bet it has one of the highest densities of fancy bed and breakfasts and country inns in the States. Going in winter is great, all the charm and no crowds. The Keystone Ferry from Port Townsend to Whidbey Island has already been mentioned as a short, inexpensive ferry ride that provides good wildlife viewing. Two spots in Port Townsend that provide excellent viewing of seabirds from shore are Point Hudson and Point Wilson.

Point Hudson is in the historic district right near downtown. The area is privately owned by the Point Hudson Company which runs a motel, marina, and RV camp. Birders are welcome to park in the motel parking area and walk to the shoreline. To get there drive northeast on Water St, go left two blocks on Monroe St, then turn right onto Jefferson St and take it to its end at the motel.

Point Wilson is in historic Fort Worden SP. In Port Townsend get onto Cherry St headed north and take it into the park. Just after you enter the park, turn right onto Pershing Ave and take it until it ends at Defense Way. Go left on Defense (no choice) and take it until it ends at the lighthouse. You have to stay out of the lighthouse area; walk north over the dunes to the beach and from here you can watch the channel. All the regular wintering seabirds are possible with a chance of seeing ancient murrelets. Fort Worden is also home to the Port Townsend Marine Science Center, worth a visit. Maps of Port Townsend are available at the visitor center as you come into town on State Hwy 20.

▶ WINTERING BIRDS IN THE SALISH SEA BEST BETS
BRITISH COLUMBIA

FROM SHORE Iona Beach RP is described in August (Fall Shorebird Migration). The south jetty that sticks 2.5 miles out into the Strait of Georgia is one way to "walk out into the ocean" and see waterbirds from land. This jetty is very safe to walk on but you'll only want to do that when the weather is conducive to standing out in the middle of the ocean. Cars are not allowed on the jetty so you either walk or you can ride your bicycle. You usually won't have to go very far before seeing a variety of waterfowl, seabirds, and gulls. In addition, the rocks of the jetty itself are good for rock-loving shorebirds such as tattlers, turnstones, and surfbirds. In the fall, truly pelagic species are sometimes seen from the end of the jetty. I've never done it, but a bicycle does seem like the ideal way to bird this jetty once you figure out how to carry your scope on your bike. Wait a minute, doesn't Yakima have a scope rack for bikes in their system? Anytime you are at Iona, be sure to check the other areas for gulls, waterfowl, shorebirds, and raptors.

The southern end of Vancouver Island is surrounded by the Salish Sea and, as one would expect of an island, has many good spots for seeing seabirds. The protected waters of the Strait of Georgia host huge numbers of waterbirds during winter and migration. Any of the spots described for seeing brant are good bets as are most provincial or regional parks on the coast or on the Gulf Islands. Some of the best spots are conveniently right in Victoria, along the breakwater on the southeast corner of the city. The scenic marine drive, including Cattle Point, Clover Point, and the Ogden Point Breakwater are excellent places for scanning the ocean. Ogden Point Breakwater, at the mouth of Victoria Harbor, gives you an opportunity to "walk out into the sea" a bit. As you can imagine, this is not one of the places on all the tourist maps of Victoria that you'll get on the ferries and at Travel Infocentres. The base of this jetty is about 10 blocks northwest of Beacon Hill Park. Go west on Dallas Rd from Douglas St and park as close as you can to where Pilot, Dock, or Montreal streets intersect Dallas. You'll be able to find your way to the big concrete pier that is the breakwater.

BIGHORN SHEEP

Here it is, the hardest challenge in the book. Seeing bighorn sheep in the wild often tests the limits of patience, eyesight, optics, and determination. Unless you're seeing them at one of the winter feeding stations or the Interstate 84 spot, the beasts will most likely be far away, blending in with the rocky cliffs they prefer. Often you cannot see them at all with the naked eye, but will find them only after careful searching with binoculars. Get the best information you can on their location, and be prepared to spend some time. These sheep have exceptional eyesight and will usually know you are there long before you see them. Sometimes this will cause them to start moving away and your eyes may catch their movement. In general you'll want to search where there are ledges between sections of steep cliff face. Think of looking up at a stairway and looking for the sheep on the treads or steps, not on the risers. If you see what appear to be trails along the cliffs, they probably are and you should try to follow them. If the sheep are lounging about, lying on the ground, think of where the most comfy places would be that you would use and look there. The most common way to find them is to spot their white rump; in good light it often stands out against the dark basalt typical in the Northwest. Another way to find them is to see their silhouette on a ridge top.

Your efforts may be rewarded by the sight of one of the West's most charismatic animals. Rams have been popular macho symbols of strength, stamina, and determination for centuries. Think of the sports teams named after them. Much of their reputation is deserved, for the males engage in spectacular bouts over the ewes during the winter rut. Rams charge at each other with all their might and crash their huge horns against each other so hard that the sound can be heard for miles. Rams need big horns even if there are no fights because the ewes go for the guy with the biggest curls.

Bighorn sheep, sometimes called mountain sheep, were once widespread and common throughout western North America in mountains and canyons. Now just a fraction of the original population lives in scattered and often isolated pockets in some of the West's most remote country. Their near elimination from the United States had three main causes. Over hunting and habitat destruction clearly played a big role in the bighorn's decline. But the third factor was more insidious and deadly—disease. Just as European people brought new diseases to America that decimated the Native Americans, European domestic sheep brought new animal diseases that spread to the nonresistant native bighorn. The number one killer was *Pasteurella,* but scabies and lung diseases also took their toll. By the 1920s bighorn sheep had been completely eliminated from Oregon and Washington.

Because bighorns are highly valued as big game and legally classified as such, there was a great deal of interest in, and money for, reintroducing the sheep in the Northwest. Starting in the 1950s bighorns from Canada and California, which still had healthy populations, were reintroduced into parts of their former range where there were absolutely no domestic sheep. The introductions have continued and have been successful enough to support limited hunting of bighorns in both states.

Bighorns in our region comprise two subspecies or races. The California bighorn originally ranged from the lava plateaus and canyons of the Great Basin, up the east side of the Cascades, and into the Okanagan region of British Columbia. Rocky Mountain bighorn sheep lived—you guessed it—in the Rocky Mountains and their related ranges such as the Selkirks in Washington and the Blue Mountains in SE Washington and NE Oregon. Wildlife managers have been careful to introduce the appropiate subspecies into their proper historical range.

Like all ungulates, bighorn sheep are vegetarians—grazers actually, eating grasses and sedges. They are adaptable, however, and will eat a variety of other plants when necessary. Like their relatives the mountain goats, they live on steep, rocky slopes and cliffs and use their phenomenal climbing ability to avoid most predators. Look for them in proper habit, where they are known to occur, by carefully scanning rock cliffs—particularly at the base of cliff faces and in patches of grass. When snow is on the ground, they will usually be found on steep or southern-facing slopes where the snow cover is lightest.

▶ BIGHORN SHEEP BEST BETS OREGON

California bighorns have been successfully reintroduced to three classic examples of Great Basin fault-block mountains in Oregon—Abert Rim, Hart Mountain, and Steens Mountain. Finding bighorns on Steens Mountain is difficult, but the sheep are there. Hart Mountain is within Hart Mountain National Antelope Refuge, described in November (Pronghorn). Bighorn sheep are most commonly seen along the western escarpment, usually in the steepest spots. From the tiny settlement of Plush on Hart Mountain Rd, you'll reach an appropriately placed sign about bighorn sheep soon after the old CCC camp. From here to where the road begins its steep assent up the mountain is the easiest place to spot sheep, if they are there. Stop along the roadside at regular intervals and scan the cliffs. Afternoon lighting is a tremendous advantage; in the morning you may be able to see sheep only if they are silhouetted against the sky.

The northern portion of Hart Mountain is called Poker Jim Ridge, and sometimes people get views of sheep by hiking out to this ridge from Poker Jim Rd and sneaking up on the sheep from above. It's always a good idea to talk to refuge staff for the latest information on bighorns. If no one is available at headquarters, consult the wildlife sightings register in the visitors' room at headquarters. Hunting is finished by mid-October, and from then until the first snow is the best time to look for sheep, as well as pronghorn. Changes in road access can happen at any time so be sure to get the latest information before heading out to this rather isolated area.

Another big fault block just west of Hart Mountain is Abert Rim, where I've seen bighorns several times. State Hwy 31 and US Hwy 395 meet at Valley Falls, south of Lake Abert. Head north on US 395 from Valley Falls, and in 5.5 miles you'll see a pullout sign about wildlife watching. Remember this spot, but don't stop here yet. Continue another 3 miles north, and on the right you'll see a pullout for a geologic marker. Park here and scan the cliffs rising up in front of you. Bighorns frequent this escarpment but as usual they can be very hard to find. Once we were alerted to their presence by some falling rocks from a herd of about 20 that had started to move away from us. I wouldn't give up until you've

searched carefully for half an hour. If you don't find sheep here, go back toward Valley Falls to the wildlife-watching pullout, and try looking from there. The sheep range between these two points, but I have always had the best views from the geologic pullout.

Rocky Mountain bighorn sheep have been successfully introduced into the Blue Mountains of northeastern Oregon. The best way to see them is to call the manager of the Wenaha WA and find out if any have been seen lately and where they are. It's also a good idea to find out about road conditions and make sure there isn't any hunting when you are going. One spot the sheep frequent is the cliffs above Sawmill Flat. From the town of Troy take the "low bridge" over the Grande Ronde River toward Elgin and Wallowa. In just 0.2 mile, before you come to the first signed intersection, a small dirt road takes a sharp, hairpin turn to the right. Take this road for just under 0.5 mile to where it comes out into a flat, open area which is Sawmill Flats. Get out and scan the cliffs that rise above you to the south. Occasionally some of the sheep are actually seen down on the flats. You may also see bighorns when you are driving through other parts of the Wenaha WA looking for elk.

An unusual situation has resulted in the easiest way yet to see bighorn sheep. ODFW trapped some bighorns on Hart Mountain and released them in the canyon of Thirtymile Creek, a tributary of the John Day River. Some of these sheep decided they didn't like it there and moved about 40 miles north to the steep slopes of the Columbia River Gorge, right next to Interstate 84. This herd eventually increased to about 90 animals and people were regularly seeing them while traveling east on I-84. Stories about Freeway Bighorns appeared in newspapers, and people began to stop on the interstate to look at the sheep and take photos. Does this sound like a safe way to watch wildlife? Needless to say, there were safety concerns.

ODFW has started to trap and relocate some of these animals to reduce the risk of accidents and to prevent the herd from growing too large for the area to support. It's not clear what the future holds for these sheep, but there will probably be some in the area for awhile into the future. Be on the lookout when you drive through the area, but exercise good judgment and extreme caution. Wouldn't it be nice if money was available to build some kind of "bighorn sheep–watching lane" or pullout to safely view these animals? The sheep are on rocky cliffs on the south side of I-84, about 35 miles east of The Dalles. They are seen between exits 123 and 137, the Arlington exit, but I've seen them the most often between exits 123 and 129. Don't let the driver look.

▶ BIGHORN SHEEP BEST BETS WASHINGTON

Near Yakima are two good areas for seeing reintroduced California bighorns. The Yakima River has carved a beautiful canyon through the basalt ridges coming off the east side of the Cascades. State Hwy 821 parallels the river as it winds 20 miles through the canyon between Ellensburg and Yakima—a much preferred scenic alternative to traveling Interstate 82. About 5 miles from the northern end of the canyon is the Umtanum Recreation Site where a trail goes up Umtanum Creek, considered a great area for a variety of wildlife. The best area for finding sheep is just north of Umtanum around mileposts 18 and 19. Unfortunately, this stretch of road has little room to pull over, so you'll have to be creative in finding a safe spot to park for scanning the cliffs. As usual, the sheep will probably be far away on the cliffs and hard to find. The best lighting is at midday, but this is usually a period of low sheep activity. Overcast conditions, where harsh shadows or glare are eliminated, would probably be a good time to look, as well.

Also near Yakima is a feeding station for bighorns operated by WDFW as part of the Oak Creek WA. Some people call an artificial situation like this zoo-like, but it does provide some outstanding views of the animals fairly close. On your way to see the elk at Oak Creek WA, stop by the Clemen Mountain feeding station. Timing is great for this because the sheep are usually fed mid-morning and the elk early afternoon. About 13 miles northwest of Yakima, US Hwy 12 and State Hwy 410 split with US 12 heading south to the elk feeding area. At this split, instead of turning left on US 12 or straight on Hwy 410, turn right onto the Old Naches Rd that heads back toward Yakima. Drive 0.5 mile, and you'll reach the conspicuous "Mountain Sheep Winter Feeding Station" sign and parking area. Search the cliffs surrounding the feeding station if sheep are not right there waiting for you and your camera. Contact the WDFW Region 3 office in Yakima to make sure they are feeding the sheep and elk and to check on the times because this varies with the weather. Feeding generally starts in December and continues through February.

HARLEQUIN DUCKS

Try to find an article about harlequin ducks that doesn't use the word *turbulent*. Fat chance. This duck is born to bob—in the rapids of mountain streams and the churning currents around rocky ocean shores. Despite being common winter residents in the Salish Sea, harlequin ducks are just unusual and scarce enough that they are much sought after by birders visiting the Northwest. They are certainly unique in appearance, even the restrained authority Frank Bellrose calls them the "most bizarrely colored waterfowl" and many consider them one of our prettiest birds.

Separate populations of harlequin ducks occur in Iceland, Greenland, Siberia (wintering in Japan and Korea), and North America. Two distinct populations live within North America—an eastern one centered around Labrador and a hundred-fold greater population ranging from Alaska to Oregon and the northern Rockies. The eastern population had declined so much that the harlequin was listed as endangered in eastern Canada for a few years. Fortunately, the eastern Canada population has increased and their status was improved but harlequins in eastern North American are still species of concern in the United States and Canada. The western North America population is considered healthy despite increasing threats to both nesting and wintering ranges.

No other duck in the Northern Hemisphere is dependent on turbulent mountain streams for part of its life. Harlequins spend most of their life in the ocean close to rocky shores. In May they fly up into the mountains and nest on rocky shores next to the rapids of streams. Once the female starts incubating, the male leaves and goes back to the coast, which can be as early as the end of June. Females do not return to salt water until their young can fly in September.

It is the unique lifestyle of the harlequin duck that makes it both interesting and an indicator species—an animal that gives early warning of disturbance to an ecosystem. The majority of harlequins nest in remote areas that are still free of much human activity. It is in their nesting habitat, however, where harlequins are very sensitive to disturbance. The riparian zone can easily be damaged by logging, and females can be frightened into abandoning their nest if hikers, anglers, rafters, and kayakers repeatedly come too close. The males leave when incubation begins, eliminating the chance for a second brood to replace a first one lost to flooding or other causes. When human activity increases near nesting areas, harlequin numbers start dropping.

Harlequin ducks are a good example of how the terms *winter range* or *winter visitor* can be misleading because harlequins are actually residents in salt water for most of the year and only leave for nesting, a very short time indeed for the males. But tradition treats the nesting range as the bird's "home" and the area where it doesn't breed as temporary winter range. Regardless of terminology, harlequins along ocean shores are very vulnerable to pollution. These ducks were one of the species hardest hit by the Exxon Valdez oil spill in 1989 and there is still almost no reproduction by harlequins in the spill area.

Because harlequins are sensitive to disturbance while nesting, they should be left alone during that time. The place to see them is in their "wintering range," from about September through April. Look for them close to rocky shores, especially where the water is—I have to say it—turbulent. It's fun to watch harlequins feed because they eat almost any animal they can get down their throat and it's often amusing to see some of their struggles with a beak full of legs and claws flailing about. They eat lots of crustaceans, including many types of crabs and barnacles, and plenty of mollusks, shells and all. One animal they eat in numbers and few else do are chitons, which are extremely hard to pry off the rocks. But these buoyant little sea ducks manage it some-how, grinding them up with everything else in their powerful gizzard. In their freshwater habitat they forage underwater for aquatic insects, swimming with both feet and wings and walking on the bottom like a dipper, a common asso-ciate in mountain streams.

You'll see less of these northern ducks, by an order of magnitude per state, the farther south you go. Estimates of the number of harlequins in the win-ter in British Columbia are in the thousands (15,000), in Washington in the hundreds (800), and in Oregon in the dozens.

A closely related duck sometimes found wintering with harlequins is the long-tailed duck, formally called oldsquaw. The long-tailed duck is actually the most abundant nesting duck in the high arctic but even fewer of them get down into the Northwest, their abundance following the same pattern as the harlequin, only at much lower numbers. The long-tailed duck is the only duck where the male has two different bright plumages in addition to a drab eclipse plumage. Long-tailed ducks are also well known for being one of the noisiest ducks, constantly making loud calls to one another.

▶ HARLEQUIN DUCKS BEST BETS OREGON

Inside the mouth of Tillamook Bay, just west of Garibaldi, are some picturesque rocks just offshore that are locally called the Three Graces (at least that's what they're called on postcards). But Northwest birders know them as the harlequin duck rocks, a deserving name. This is one of the most reliable and accessible places in Oregon to find harlequins.

Going west on US Hwy 101 from Garibaldi you'll go around a corner, passing Pirate's Cove restaurant, and reach a straight stretch of highway with a large wall of riprap running along the west side. You'll see the tall rocks (the Three Graces) in the bay; park near them on the west side of the road. Drive past the rocks until you can find a good place to make a U-turn to cross US 101, and then go back the way you came. Yes, that does sound a bit tricky so the best strategy might be to drive to the tiny settlement of Barview, turn left onto the road going to Barview Jetty County Park, turn around by the store, and then head back (south) on the west side of US 101. If you are coming from north of Barview you're already on the correct side.

As you near the rocks, you'll see where cars have pulled over on the side of the road and you should do the same. Be sure to park completely off the highway. Cross the railroad tracks (excursion trains occasionally use these tracks), and then walk behind the big rocks on the riprap until you can find a good place to peep over the riprap at the big rocks in the bay. Search the waters around the Three Graces for harlequins. If you can't find any standing behind the riprap, you can climb up on the rocks with binoculars and search the water from that vantage point. The rate of success here is very high so don't give up; keep searching around the rocks on shore and in the channel. You'll see other birds here and you can work on the gulls and cormorants while you wait for the ducks to show themselves.

Toward the mouth of the bay (on your right) from the Three Graces is another rock in the channel that is roughly pyramid-shaped. This is where I learned how to tell the three cormorants apart in the winter because all three can be regularly be seen on this rock at one time. This is also a great area for black oystercatchers. At times this spot can be as good for birds as any rocky place on the coast.

The city of Newport is built around Yaquina Bay, an all-around fabulous birdwatching destination. The south jetty of Yaquina Bay is one of the few jetties that you can actually drive on for awhile. An excellent variety of waterbirds can be seen here throughout the year. Head south on US 101 out of Newport, drive over the bay on the Yaquina Bay Bridge, and as soon as you come off the bridge, turn right following the signs for the Oregon Coast Aquarium and the Hatfield Marine Science Center. As you come off US 101 you'll curve around to your right and head back north. Do not stay on this road as it goes under the bridge and to the science center and aquarium, but instead turn left onto 26th St. Drive west on 26th St and it will become the road going out onto the jetty. Decide when you've had enough of the rough surface, and then park and walk. Be sure to park out of the way of any other vehicles and in a way that you can get out easily. When driving stop now and then and check out the whole channel. Don't forget to look over the rocks of the jetty itself for "rockpipers" (rock-loving shorebirds) and resting birds. The harlequins are usually close to the jetty, and you can miss them if you don't look far enough over the jetty to see the shoreline of the other side from the road. While you're in the Newport area be sure to check out Yaquina Head, Yaquina Bay, the Oregon Coast Aquarium, and the Hatfield Marine Science Center.

▶ HARLEQUIN DUCKS BEST BETS WASHINGTON & BRITISH COLUMBIA

In Washington and British Columbia any rocky coastline with turbulent water in the Salish Sea is good harlequin habitat and many possible places are mentioned elsewhere in this book. Harlequin ducks are common throughout the sea, although you rarely see more than a few in any one place. All the Best Bets from shore in Wintering Birds in the Salish Sea (November) are good except for Dungeness Spit, which is sand. Salt Creek County Park, west of Port Angeles, is one of the best in Washington. The Victoria breakwater is loaded with harlequin ducks. If you could ever get tired of seeing these little Italian clowns, which is what their name means, the rocky shoreline of Victoria would be it.

NOVEMBER'S NATURE NUGGETS

SAMHAIN During November we really make the change from fall to winter, and it seems illogical that the official first day of winter is on the Winter Solstice near the end of December. Once again, the ancient Celtic calendar makes more sense because Samhain, the beginning of winter, falls in the first few days of November. Samhain was a major festival for the Celts with harvest feasts and celebrations. It was also an important time for Druids to perform sacred rights in preparation for the coming season of darkness. In typical fashion, the early Catholic Church used Samhain as a basis for creating a Christian holy day and the modern result of this unique blending survives today as Halloween in North America and Los Dias de los Muertos in Mexico.

BANANA SLUGS Banana slugs are common year-round residents in our moist forests but are usually seen out and about only when the humidity is high—100% does nicely. Like all mollusks, banana slugs will dry out quickly in dry air so they are active on moist nights or rainy days. They use a lot of water to make their famous slime and must be able to soak up enough from their environment to replace the lost water if they are to be able to crawl about. Such conditions are indeed common much of the year west of the Cascades, and in November, when rain is common and temperatures not yet too cold, there is plenty of slug activity. Banana slugs are actually quite famous in the Northwest, which is very unusual for a mollusk. This is as it should be for an animal that is common yet fairly unique to the region, and the biggest land mollusk in the world. You can even buy a number of interesting souvenir items featuring banana slugs. Many kids know that if you lick a banana slug, your tongue will become numb. It's actually a very weird and fairly unpleasant feeling that lasts all day and is apparently the reason so few predators ever eat this slow and apparently defenseless beast.

SNOWBIRDS These days "snowbird" is commonly used to describe retired people who spend the summer up north in a cool, green place and the winter in a warm, sunny place. Of course, this word came into use long ago when people noticed that certain birds always showed up in winter and then left for the summer. West of the Cascades we have four classic snowbirds: varied thrush, dark-eyed junco, pine siskin, and evening grosbeak. All are common nesting birds in coniferous forests in our mountains. When winter arrives, instead of flying long distances to the south, most of them just start dropping down in elevation until they can find enough food. Chances are good that backyard feeders will be that special place, and juncos and siskins in particular can be the most common winter birds in some people's yards. Juncos are the most common and abundant by far; the others vary more with weather and location. You'll never forget it when you get visited by a big flock of evening grosbeaks on a late winter's day.

BIRD-FEEDING BASICS: A CLOSER LOOK

Sitting by a window, feeling the glow from the hearth, a hot latte in hand, and watching the juncos, song sparrows, towhees, siskins, and goldfinches scratching around the snow-capped feeder—a perfect winter's day in the Northwest. Colder temperatures mean hot-blooded endotherms need more calories just when food is most lacking. Many birds will come to a feeder for those extra calories allowing for some great, up-close birdwatching. Many an active birder got started by putting out a feeder. Feeding birds has always been popular in this country, but the level of interest has skyrocketed in recent years. It is now estimated that around 70 million Americans regularly feed, watch, or photograph birds at their homes every year. Here are the basics of bird feeding for those who haven't yet taken the plunge.

To attract birds to your yard, provide them with the basics all animals need to survive: food, water, and shelter. The best way to provide these elements on a year-round basis is by managing your habitat; that is, landscaping your yard for wildlife needs. The greater the diversity of plants and habitats in your yard, the more diverse your backyard wildlife will be. Plants and the insects they attract will provide birds with their natural foods and provide the natural shelter they seek. In the last 20 years landscaping for wildlife has become a well-established practice and is now often called naturescaping. Both the Oregon and Washington departments of fish and wildlife have publications on naturescaping or landscaping for wildlife that are very specific for the Northwest. You can order these publications from the agencies on their Web sites.

Here we will not take on the complex topic of naturescaping, but we'll discuss "artificial feeding." That may sound as if we're going to put feeding tubes down the throats of birds in the hospital. What it refers to, however, is feeding birds commercially produced food that is a good substitute for the natural wild food they would find in their habitat. In this part of the country we offer birds two main types of artificial food: seeds and suet. Many of our winter residents are seed eaters because seeds are a food that is naturally available during the winter. By offering certain seeds we are simply providing supplemental food that is very similar to the birds' natural diet. Suet functions as a "bug substitute," a pretty odd concept. The number of insects is drastically reduced during the winter, and suet can serve as supplement or a substitute for the fat that birds get in insects. You can feed both seeds and suet year-round. However, suet will spoil much faster in warm weather, and as insects become more abundant, the birds' interest in suet wanes. In warm weather suet can also get rancid and have strange fungus growing on it. Yeech. Many people stop artificial feeding in the summer. During the warmer months birds have a much bigger variety of foods available to them and the number and variety of birds at feeders decrease significantly.

Some bird-feeding myths, believe it or not, have survived for decades. One states that if you begin feeding birds during the winter and then stop for some reason, like a holiday vacation, the birds will perish because they have become dependent on the food you supply at feeders. It is widely accepted that such interruptions in feeding birds are not usually a problem. After all, with 70 million people feeding birds, your birds can just go down the block if you're gone. In general, the artificial feeding of birds by people has little overall impact on bird populations. Another myth is that if peanut butter is made available to birds, they can get their mouths gummed-up with it, choke, and die. Talk about anthropomorphic. Just because our mouths get sticky and gooey doesn't mean birds will have similar problems. There is no actual evidence that peanut butter hurts birds.

Three types of seed will attract and satisfy our local seed-eating birds: sunflower, millet, and cracked corn. Sunflower seeds are the most preferred seed of most seed-eating birds, especially finches, grosbeaks, chickadees, nuthatches, jays, and even smaller woodpeckers. The black oil type is a highly favored seed. Birds that lack beaks adapted for opening sunflower seeds favor millet and will eat cracked corn. All types of millet are good, but the best is white proso millet, which is the type usually used in mixes. Birds especially fond of millet are the sparrows, including juncos and towhees, and mourning doves. These birds will also eat cracked corn, but usually show a preference for millet.

Cracked corn deteriorates quickly in wet weather and can cause problems in some types of hopper feeders where it easily molds and cakes, resulting in a clogged feeder. The advantages of cracked corn are that it is inexpensive and eaten by many birds, even if it isn't their favorite. Larger ground-feeding birds, such as quail, pheasant, dove, and many waterfowl, relish whole corn kernels, which are much more water resistant and last longer in feeders. Other seeds such as peanut pieces and nyjer seed (often called thistle) are highly rated for some birds but are not regularly selected over black oil sunflower and both are much more expensive. However, some people report that goldfinches, including siskins, go totally nuts for nyjer seed and provide some of the best entertainment as they swarm over feeders with this imported seed.

For the Northwest a basic mix of black oil sunflower and white millet, with maybe a little cracked or whole kernel corn, will keep the local birds happy, healthy, and coming to your feeders for more. A word of warning. Most wild bird food mixes sold at supermarkets and big-box retailers contain other seeds added as cheap filler that are either not eaten by birds or are favored by such generally unwanted guests as starlings, house sparrows, and blackbirds. The most common filler is milo, a type of sorghum. It is a round, reddish seed that looks like a B-B pellet or radish seed. If you buy mixed seed with much milo, you're wasting your money. Quality seeds and mixes without milo or other useless fillers are available at bird stores and at many pet and feed stores. Avoid the cheap mixes of seed, which may contain the seeds of plants that are invasive weeds in some areas.

Seed is best served in some type of elevated feeder. Feeding on the ground can give local cats a big advantage, attract rodents and opossums, and can lead to problems with unwanted birds such as starlings. Don't worry, ground-feeding birds such as juncos, towhees, and sparrows will get plenty of seed spilled on the ground by other birds on the feeder. And if the feeder is big enough, sometimes called a feeding table, these ground-feeding birds will land right on the feeder. Feeders can be mounted on a pole, hung from a tree limb or roof, or mounted against a window. Some newer plastic feeders can be mounted right on the window pane with suction cups. A feeder should be located with enough clear space around it so that the birds can easily see if any cats or other predators are within striking range.

Feeders need not be fancy or expensive. All that is important is that the birds can get the seed and the seed does not get too wet. Even on the rainy west side you don't need a roof on your feeder if you put out a couple of hand-fuls of seed each day and the birds eat it before it gets soaked. Most people, however, prefer a feeder that has some type of hopper to hold more than one day's supply of feed and these do need a roof to keep the seed dry. You'll find an almost endless variety of commercially made feeders available and almost as many plans in books for making your own.

Suet is technically the hard fat from around the kidneys and thymus glands of cattle and sheep, but it's sometimes used to refer to other clean, hard fat from other parts of these animals. Why would birds like chickadees and bush-tits eat suet? Have you ever seen a flock of bushtits kill and eat a cow? Of course not. Suet is a much more artificial bird food than are sunflower and millet seeds. Suet is essentially a bug substitute and attracts birds whose natu-ral diet includes lots of insects and spiders, particularly the sedentary eggs, larvae, and pupae that are available during the winter. The fact that beef fat can serve as a substitute for insect larvae seems rather odd, but there is no doubt about the popularity of suet among chickadees, nuthatches, woodpeckers, bushtits, pine siskins, and warblers.

Chunks of raw suet can be offered without any preparation. It can also be ground, melted, and formed into suet cakes to fit feeders and for convenient storage. It isn't necessary to add anything to suet, but many people believe that adding a little peanut butter makes the suet more attractive to a wider variety of birds. Some people even have recipes for suet cakes that are more elaborate than those for cookies. Many types of commercially made suet cakes are now available with a wide range of ingredients, but many people believe that seeds should not be added to suet because this mixes two very different types of food that are best offered separately. The greased seeds in the suet may be harder to open for some birds. Simplicity is the best approach for feeding birds. Remember, they didn't grow up eating blueberry-pecan-suet pop tarts.

Suet is best offered in hanging and dangling plastic mesh bags, wire baskets, or suet logs. Do not feed suet on the ground or on a feeding table unless you want to fill your yard with starlings.

Water is not usually a limiting factor for birds west of the Cascades. On the east side, however, the addition of water to your yard can make a big difference and, depending on your location, your yard may become a true oasis, attracting many birds from a large area. A shallow birdbath, not more than two or three inches deep, will provide water for many birds and will help attract those species that do not usually come to feeders. Place rocks in the bird bath that provide places to perch at different water depths. As with feeders, there are many types of manufactured bird baths available, and it's easy to make your own. Water should be offered off the ground and in the open to make things tough on cats. Commercial birdbath heaters are available to keep bird baths ice free during freezing weather. Some birds will bathe during even the coldest weather.

Few bird-feeding topics generate as much controversy as hummingbirds. Most authors encourage the planting of plants that provide hummers with their natural foods: nectar and insects. Some people feel that the use of feeders and sugar water can harm hummingbirds. If you are compelled to use a hummingbird feeder, follow these general guidelines. Use only sugar; never use honey, which promotes dangerous fungus growth. Sugar should be dissolved in boiling water in a ratio of one part sugar to four or five parts water. Store the unused mixture in the refrigerator. Feeders should be thoroughly cleaned weekly in hot water. It is unknown whether red food coloring is potentially harmful or not. Red is attractive to hummingbirds, and red objects, such as plastic flowers on feeders, may help attract them, but it's unnecessary to add red coloring to the water.

Should you leave your hummingbird feeder up all winter? There is no correct answer because there has been no research on the effects of winter feeding of hummingbirds. It's common to hear people say that hummingbirds should not be fed in the winter because it will stop them from migrating, but there's no evidence of this happening. Anna's hummingbirds live in parts of the Pacific Northwest all year. These birds are here regardless of whether people are feeding them or not, and many of them will perish during the coldest weather even if extra food is available. The rufous hummingbird, our common summer resident, will migrate south on schedule regardless of the presence of feeders. The artificial feeding of hummingbirds during the winter will probably have no effect on the hummingbird population as a whole, but in some cases may allow an individual bird to survive a bit longer than it would otherwise.

As much as people feel that they are helping the birds by feeding them in the winter or that they need to feed the birds if the birds are going to survive, the main reason to feed birds is because you like to do it. Evidence suggests that the artificial feeding of birds has very little impact on the long-term populations of birds. Habitat protection is much more important. The reasons to feed birds are because you can observe them closely, you get to know your local birds, you learn bird behaviors, you make connections with seasons and weather, you appreciate their beauty, and you just feel good doing it. Enjoy your backyard birds!

DECEMBER

DEER

Deer are by far the most familiar large, wild mammal to most North Americans. Anyone who has spent any time outdoors has encountered these common animals. The deer family also is well known throughout the world with about 40 species living from the arctic to the tropics. These animals have always been highly revered game animals by humans. After all, some of our earliest art is cave paintings of deer. Aside from their value as food and clothing, deer have always been very popular animals. The does and fawns are frequently described with endearing language, and the bucks are symbols of animal machismo at its finest.

Unlike much North American wildlife, deer are actually more abundant now in many areas than they were before the European invasion. Ironically, overpopulation is one of the problems sometimes facing managers of deer populations. One reason for this increase is that their predators have been removed in most of their range. Deer also prefer forest edges and successional stages of forest growth, habitats caused by some of our land uses such as clear-cut logging. Another factor in their success is their desirability as a game animal, resulting in lots of sportsmen's money going into intensive management of deer populations. In addition, deer have shown themselves to be more adaptable than many other hoofed mammals.

The deer family is one of the main families of ungulates, mammals with unique legs that are highly adapted for running. Ungulates have long legs to increase their stride and a simplified skeletal structure to reduce the weight of the leg so it can be moved faster by the muscles. The most striking result of this simplification and elongation in the leg and foot is that ungulates actually stand, and run, on their tippy toes, which are few in number and are capped

A young black-tailed deer is ready to face its first winter. Stick with Mom.

385

with an incredibly large, strong toenail called a hoof. Most ungulates walk on only two toes (per foot); others, like the horse, walk on just one big toe. The evolution of ungulate anatomy has many interesting details that have resulted in mammals that use running fast as their main defense against predators. As discussed in November (Pronghorn), some ungulates have reached what may be the limit for land speed in animals.

As with most other ungulates, deer have exceptionally keen eyesight, as well as sensitive hearing and a highly developed sense of smell. Let's face it; it's really hard to sneak up on an ungulate. The most likely situations for seeing deer are in places where the deer have become acclimated to people being nearby and do not feel threatened. Like many other animals, deer may tolerate your being close while you're in your car, but as soon as you step out—off they go with a bound.

Deer are browsers, an animal that eats the tender, most nutritious parts of trees and shrubs. This term *browser* is often used in contrast to a *grazer*, who eats primarily grass. Deer do eat some grass, but even when you see them out in the grassy meadow eating, they are usually picking out the more tender broad-leaved plants, like dandelions, which biologists call forbs.

Members of the deer family are the only animals in the world with antlers. People often get antlers and horns mixed up, but the differences are clear. Antlers are shed and regrown every year, while animals with horns have them their whole life, and the horns continually grow as the animal ages. Antlers are usually found on only the male of a species. Caribou and their domesticated variety, reindeer, are an exception, which is why you can't tell if Santa's reindeer are boys or girls. Animals with horns, however, usually have horns on both the male and female, although the male's are usually quite a bit bigger.

Antlers are usually branched and horns never are, except for the unique horn of the pronghorn, which is the only branched horn in the world and the only one that is partially shed each year. Antlers and horns are also made out of different materials. An antler is bone, which is covered by a thin layer of skin while the antler is growing. The skin falls off when the antler is fully grown, leaving bare bone. A horn has a continually growing bony core covered with living skin and then an outer layer of keratin or "horn," the tough protein found in your fingernails.

In the Pacific Northwest we have both white-tailed deer and mule deer. The white-tailed deer is the most widespread deer in North America, living in almost every state, but they are most abundant east of the Mississippi. The mule deer is very common throughout the West. White-tailed deer prefer thick forest interspersed with some grassy openings and are often found near water. Mule deer live in a wider range of habitats and are often found in more open and drier habitats than white-tails and are much more common at higher elevations. Mule deer are much more abundant and widespread throughout our region than white-tails, which are localized and in smaller numbers.

You can recognize white-tailed deer by their fairly large tail, which is brown on top and bright white underneath. They often flip their tail up when running away, exposing the white underside that gives them their name. A mule deer's tail is either black on top (the black-tailed race), or light with a distinct black tip, and they usually do not flip up their tail like white-tailed deer. You can also tell the two species apart by their antlers. The antlers of white-tails have a main beam that sweeps forward with tines coming up from it. Mule deer have antlers that stick more straight up. They divide evenly or fork into two main branches, which then each divide evenly again on mature bucks.

Each of our two species of deer has two subspecies or races found in our region: basically one race found on the east side and one found on the west side, for each species. The two types of white-tailed deer in the Northwest are the Rocky Mountain subspecies, known as the Idaho white-tailed deer, and the Columbian white-tailed deer. Idaho white-tails are most common in the Blue Mountains in northeastern Oregon and adjacent parts of Washington and in the Selkirk Mountains in northeastern Washington. These east-side white-tails are scattered and difficult to see predictably.

West of the Cascades is an endangered subspecies of deer, the Columbian white-tailed deer. This deer used to be abundant west of the Cascades from the Umpqua River to Puget Sound, but by the 1930s they were thought to be extinct. However, two small populations were discovered, one near Roseburg, Oregon, and the other in the lower Columbia River near Cathlamet, Washington. In 1972 a national wildlife refuge was established for the Columbia River population. The Roseburg population has also been protected, although not with a refuge. Both populations have grown so large that the Columbian white-tailed deer may be taken off the endangered species list in the near future.

East of the Cascades mule deer are abundant and easily seen. Found west of the Cascades is the race of mule deer called the black-tailed deer, once considered a separate species. Black-tailed deer act a little like white-tailed deer in that they hide in thick forest more than other mule deer, which are often seen out in the open, including mountainous areas with steep slopes. Because mule deer live at higher elevations, they migrate more during the year because of snow conditions and food supply. They also tend to gather more in big groups on winter ranges.

Deer breeding season, or rut, begins in September or October and runs through December, with November being the peak. During this time bucks travel a lot looking for does. Sometimes bucks will fight over a doe using ritualized displays and threats, occasionally involving battles with their antlers. Deer do not, however, gather and defend harems the way elk do.

December is a good time to see deer because many of them start to gather in winter ranges, deer hunting seasons are usually over, and the bucks still have their antlers (and they look so handsome with them). When viewing deer, or any other animals on their winter range, be careful not to disturb them. If you frighten animals enough to cause them to run, they expend valuable energy during a time when they can least afford to. View from a distance, and stay in your car when possible.

Deer are commonly seen throughout the year with the possible exception of hunting season, during which time most deer wisely keep a pretty low profile. In addition to this chapter's Best Bets, you will probably see deer at any of the Best Bets listed for elk later in this section.

▶ DEER BEST BETS OREGON

Mule deer are quite common in eastern Oregon, and you'll see them even when driving many of the main highways. Two good areas are US Hwy 97 and State Hwy 31 going south from La Pine toward Klamath Falls and Lakeview, respectively. Oatman Flat Deer Viewing Area on Hwy 31 is the most famous wintering spot for deer in the state. At Oatman Flat there is an alfalfa pasture on the west side of Hwy 31, 39 miles south of La Pine and 8 miles north of Silver Lake where FR 2780 intersects the highway. The pullout has brown binocular wildlife-viewing signs, but no other signs identify the spot. When the deer are there you'll know you're in the right place because hundreds of deer will be hanging out in the pasture. Numbers sometimes approach 1000 deer according to the Oregon Wildlife Viewing Guide. Usually the deer are in the pasture early in the morning or around sunset, but on some winter days hundreds stay in the pasture all day long. Be sure to check out Oatman Flat when headed to or from Summer Lake WA or Hart Mountain NWR.

South of Oatman Flat and Summer Lake, Hwy 31 joins US Hwy 395 at the tiny settlement of Valley Falls. The stretch of US 395 just south of Valley Falls for several miles is also excellent for seeing mule deer late in the day. Another area that usually provides lots of year-round sightings of mule deer is Malheur NWR. Wallowa Lake SP is well known for its semi-tame deer which regularly come into the picnic and camping areas and eat the junk food that people give them. People have been seriously hurt by bucks here when they have walked right up to the bucks during the rut and tried to feed them. Bucks in rut are not interested in putting up with nonsense from humans, and these are the times when people learn some hard lessons about wild animals. No matter how cute they look or what a great photo it will make, please don't participate in any such feeding.

▶ DEER BEST BETS WASHINGTON

The place to see Columbian white-tailed deer is—where else?—the Julia Butler Hansen Refuge for the Columbian White-Tailed Deer. This is one of those wildlife-watching safaris that is almost too easy; usually you'll see deer in the open as you drive the road through the refuge. However, the deer are very good at hiding in the brush, and you can drive right by them if you're not watching carefully. You also have a very good chance of seeing the herd of Roosevelt Elk living on the refuge.

J. B. Hansen Refuge is easy to find and well signed. From the Longview exit on Interstate 5 drive west on State Hwy 4 for 26 miles to the charming little town of Cathlamet, a good stop for snacks or supplies. Drive another 2 miles west on Hwy 4 from Main St in Cathlamet, and then turn left onto Steamboat Slough Rd after crossing Elochoman River on a bridge. In 0.25 mile you'll reach the refuge headquarters where you can usually get printed materials and check for posted information. Look around the headquarters area because the nearby apple trees attract deer. The water channels near headquarters are a good bet for nutria.

Steamboat Slough Rd goes from the southern to the northern end of the refuge up the west side of the refuge, which is the shoreline of the Columbia or a slough. You'll usually have land on your right and water on your left creating good possibilities for different types of wildlife on each side. This is a drive to do with four wildlife spotters in the car, two for each side. Some deer may be right out in the open in the grassland, but usually they are partially hidden at the edges of the forest and brush. The elk in the refuge are usually hiding just inside the patches of forest or can be lying down in tall grass with only a few antler tips showing. On the wet side of the drive you may see nutria, muskrat, river otter, and beaver (if it's late in the day). You'll also undoubtedly have some great waterfowl and raptor sightings, including swans and bald eagles. This is the best place in Washington to see white-tailed kites near the limit of their range. A trip through the J. B. Hansen refuge is one of the best wildlife-watching drives west of the Cascades.

When you get to the northern end of the refuge you can go straight into Skamokawa or turn right onto Brooks Slough Rd and drive through more of the refuge. Either way, you'll end up back on Hwy 4. The J. B. Hansen Refuge is a good place to visit on your way to Willapa Bay or the Long Beach Peninsula. Skamokawa has an amazing history and at one time was a much bigger town. Most of the current town is now part of Skamokawa Center on the Lower Columbia River, a center for paddling the Columbia and the many sloughs and rivers by kayak or canoe. The center has a store, restaurant, lodging, rentals, lessons, and tours and is the best access point for the Lewis and Clark Water Trail. Skamokawa is one of the most unique "outdoor adventure lodges" I've ever seen.

Let's jump to the other end of the state, almost into Canada. The largest herd of mule deer in Washington winters in the Methow Valley, famous for its cross-country skiing described in January (Wildlife Watching on Skis). Mule deer are commonly seen in the valley during the winter by skiers and by people traveling any of the roads through the valley. Northeast of Winthrop and Twisp, adjacent to the Okanogan NF, WDFW owns and manages the Methow WA to protect winter habitat for the deer. WDFW biologists are concerned about the deer being disturbed in winter, so view the deer from your car.

It's a bit tricky finding your way around Methow WA. The Okanogan NF map is generally the best, but the DeLorme atlas is better for road names. During winter snow closes most roads, but conditions can vary. Two roads are usually kept plowed and open: Bear Creek and Beaver Creek. The simplest access is to go 5 miles east of Twisp on State Hwy 20 and

head north on Beaver Creek Rd (FR 1637) as far as it is clear of snow—usually about 5 miles to the intersection with Lester Rd. Lester Rd is a narrow unpaved road, steep in parts, but just fine in any vehicle when it's dry. If Lester Rd is open, take it northwest then west over the hills to Bear Creek Rd. This is a scenic route through the middle of the wildlife area. When you get to Bear Creek Rd, turn right and follow Bear Creek Rd past Pearrygin Lake SP until it intersects Eastside Chewuch Rd. Turn left on Eastside Chewuch Rd taking it into Winthrop and Hwy 20.

If either Lester or Beaver Creek road are closed by snow, you can make a short loop drive from and back to Winthrop. Take Eastside Chewuch Rd north out of Winthrop, and follow signs to Pearrygin Lake SP. Turn right onto Bear Creek Rd, and when it forks turn left on Bear Creek Rd to the Methow WA instead of turning right into Pearrygin Lake SP. Keep to the right at the next two intersections following signs to Davis Lake. Four miles from Pearrygin Lake, Bear Creek Rd becomes paved where Lester Rd intersects it from the east. Do not take Lester, but follow the paved Bear Creek Rd until it intersects the next paved road: Eastside Winthrop-Twisp Rd. Turn right and you'll end up back in Winthrop.

Another important winter range and good place to observe mule deer is the Klickitat WA between the towns of Glenwood and Goldendale near Mount Adams. About 10 miles west of Goldendale the Glenwood Highway leaves State Hwy 142 and winds its way for 22 miles northwest to Glenwood. The middle section of the Glenwood Highway passes through parts of the wildlife area, particularly the south-facing slopes, favored by mule deer. The Klickitat is a beautiful area and includes lots of oak-pine woodlands, an uncommon habitat in Washington. It is a good wildflower

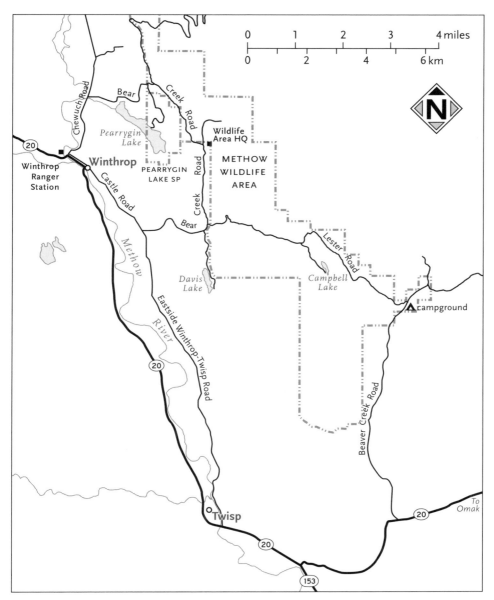

METHOW VALLEY AND WILDLIFE AREA

area in the spring and also a good place to see wild turkeys.

A good area for seeing black-tailed deer (and elk) is along the Spirit Lake Highway, State Hwy 504, which goes up the North Fork of the Toutle River to Mount Saint Helens National Volcanic Monument. Late in the day deer are common along the road from about milepost 20 until you near the Coldwater Ridge Visitor Center.

As is often the case in national parks, the black-tailed deer at Hurricane Ridge in Olympic NP have become very used to humans and, unfortunately, have learned that some people will feed them. When you visit Hurricane Ridge in the summer for wildflowers and marmots, you'll probably also get some close looks at deer. Please resist the urge to feed the adorable deer; it is against park rules.

▶ DEER BEST BETS BRITISH COLUMBIA

Deer are so widespread and common in our part of British Columbia that it's difficult to name specific sites where they are easier to see than in any big chunk of good forested habitat. In parks where deer are protected, they become more acclimated to people and less wary so people often have their closest encounters in major parks. The Long Beach Unit of Pacific Rim NP and Goldstream, Stamp Falls, and Strathcona provincial parks are probable places to see black-tailed deer.

URBAN WETLANDS

Wetlands provide needed resources for many wildlife species, and also control flooding and maintain water quality. Less than half of the original wetlands in the United States still exist, so every acre is significant. Wetlands receive special protection and landowners must get permits from the United States Army Corps of Engineers and other agencies to fill any wetlands. Some of the best conservation news stories in the Northwest are of the Local Nature Club Saves Wetlands type. All those concerned with protecting wildlife habitat must be vigilant in watching for attempts to destroy more wetlands.

Sometimes the results are rewarding. For years Portland environmentalist Mike Houck envisioned an urban wildlife refuge system in the Portland metropolitan area with wetlands and stream corridors as major components. Throughout the 1980s Mike gathered support and momentum and hundreds of active supporters. Eventually this idea found a home in the Metro Regional Parks and Greenspaces Department, part of the Portland area's unique regional government. Then in 1995 and again in 2006 the citizens of the Metro Region voted for bond measures that provided the funding to buy over 12,000 acres for parks, natural areas, and wildlife habitat. Wetlands continue to be a major focus, and the Metro Region now has one of the most outstanding systems of protected wetlands, and other natural habitats, of any city in the United States.

In Bellevue, Washington, the vision and perseverance of former parks director Lee Springgate has resulted in a system that includes large areas of protected natural habitat, with key wetlands as major components. The central piece to the system is the Lake-to-Lake Trail and Greenway, making a walking connection from Lake Washington to Lake Sammamish through the main wetlands and nature parks of the city. The largest park in the system, almost all wetlands, is Mercer Slough.

Many cities have a park pond or a river running through part of town, but if these areas don't have natural habitat around them they may not be much different from the surrounding city in terms of wildlife. Manicured lawns, sparse ornamental plantings and lots of cement are not great habitat even if they are near a pond or stream. City park departments have tended to be oriented toward sparsely landscaped and developed recreation facilities. Good wildlife habitat has often been replaced for sports fields, swimming pools, basketball courts, and picnic facilities. Recreation facilities like these are critical to the health and happiness of people and communities, but they are not enough. Fortunately, there has been a steadily growing awareness of the need and importance of natural areas ("wild places") where people can explore, exercise, wander on their own schedule, get a break from the human-built world, and—most importantly—connect with nature. This change is happening because citizens concerned about wildlife and natural habitat in their city are making their interests known to city officials and are volunteering to help park departments get the work done. Only by having regular access to nature in their own neighborhoods will people become bonded to the natural world and want to be good stewards of our planet.

Anytime of year is good for visiting urban wetlands but winter has its advantages. Fewer people go to parks, especially nature parks, in the winter, improving your chances to see wildlife. Because the Northwest is the wintering range for many species of waterfowl and other waterbirds, even the wetlands in the middle of our cities can be loaded with ducks, geese, gulls, coots, herons, and other birds in winter. Larger lakes on the west side tend to have the biggest variety and largest number of waterbirds. Most of the mammal life you'll see in wetlands are active in winter and may be easier to see because of the reduced amount of vegetation. The cold-blooded animals or ectotherms, however, will be inactive so return in the summer for frogs, garter snakes, newts, and insects.

▶ URBAN WETLANDS BEST BETS OREGON

Metro Regional Parks and Greenspaces (Metro Parks) manages a growing system of parks, natural areas and open spaces. All but a few specialized properties are areas of natural habitat within the urban environment that support wildlife and give people the opportunity to get in touch with nature. The best way to find out about nature-related programs and activities in the metro area is to visit the Metro Web site, www.oregonmetro.gov.

The largest protected, freshwater wetland in an American city is Metro Parks' Smith and Bybee Wetlands Natural Area. Access for walking is by a paved, universally accessible trail from the parking area on North Marine Dr. Entrance into the parking area is at 5300 North Marine Dr, 2.2 miles west of Exit 307 from Interstate 5. The map in the parking area shows you how to get to the Inter-lakes Trail trailhead. Smith Lake and Bybee Lake are both usually loaded with waterfowl from October into January. Fall and winter are excellent times to see GBHs, great egrets, double-crested cormorants, red-tailed hawks, and bald eagles. Check the Metro Web site for the schedule of bird walks. Boat access is available from the canoe launch to the east of the parking area. The lakes draw down in summer so the best time for boating (no engines) is from whenever it is warm enough for you in the spring until about mid-June. You may want to call Metro Parks to check on the water level before heading out to paddle.

Portland has two other wetland areas conveniently near each other that are famous bird-watching sites. Oaks Bottom Wildlife Refuge includes a remnant of the Willamette River flood plain at the base of the Sellwood cliffs. This was the first city park in the United States named a "wildlife refuge," a landmark in the recognition of wildlife habitat as a primary goal for a city park. The western boundary of Oaks Bottom is now the Springwater on the Willamette Trail, which provides excellent access and the best overview of the wetlands for birdwatching. Watch out for bicycles, however; some bike-riders tear along this trail. You can get on this section of the Springwater Trail from Sellwood Riverfront Park, the parking lot for Oaks Park, or the Eastbank Esplanade to the north. You can now start in downtown Portland, ride your bike or walk down the Eastbank Esplanade onto the Springwater on the Willamette Trail, and in a few miles be watching GBHs, a variety of ducks, and a bald eagle in a 140-acre wetland. Not bad for the middle of a city.

You can also access Oaks Bottom at the top of the Sellwood cliffs from the Oaks Bottom Trailhead on Southeast Milwaukie Ave. Head south on McLoughlin Blvd from the Central Eastside District of Portland, take the exit for

Milwaukie Ave, and then immediately after getting onto Milwaukie turn right into the parking area. From here the trail leads down to join the loop trail that you can take along the base of the cliffs, then cross over to the Springwater on the Willamette Trail to go north, and finally cross the bottoms again back to the trail at the base of the cliffs. The trail can be muddy and is uneven along the base of the cliffs. You can take the loop in either direction.

Just a mile east of Oaks Bottom is Crystal Springs Park, which includes Crystal Springs Lake and the Rhododendron Gardens on the east shore. Although this is landscaped park habitat, the lake is an excellent place to see a surprisingly large variety of ducks and other waterbirds at close range. Wood ducks are particularly conspicuous in winter to the delight of birders and non-birders alike. This is a birding site with excellent access because you can see almost everything from good, paved trails. The parking lot is on Southeast 28th Ave, just north of Southeast Woodstock Blvd and across from Reed College. There may be a small admission charge. The main trail heads south from the parking lot, and then crosses a wooden bridge. The southern end of the lake usually has the most waterfowl. I had a record day with a bird class one January morning when we saw a dozen different species of ducks in one hour here.

Jackson Bottom Wetland Preserve is jointly owned and managed by Hillsboro and Clean Water Services. One of the purposes of the preserve is to improve the quality of treated wastewater going into the Tualatin River. The preserve also functions as one of the major facilities for environmental education and interpretation in Washington County and is one of northwest Oregon's birding hotspots. Jackson Bottom is south of downtown Hillsboro along Hillsboro Highway (also known as State Hwy 219), which is the western border of the preserve. An observation platform is at the northern end, just past the water treatment plant, but the fabulous Wetlands Education Center and the trails are located 0.8 mile farther south, to your left, just before Hwy 219 crosses the Tualatin River. Jackson Bottom Wetlands Preserve is another one of the crown jewels in the Portland Metropolitan Region's system of natural areas.

Farther south in the Willamette Valley another good chunk of Willamette River floodplain is protected in Minto-Brown Island Park, just southeast of the state capitol in Salem. From downtown Salem take Commercial St south and turn right onto River Rd toward Independence. In about a mile turn right onto Minto Island Rd and follow signs to the park. The park has a mix of sloughs, channels, and riparian woodlands, providing habitat for numerous bird species.

Oregon's second largest urban area has an outstanding system of protected wetlands. The 3000-acre West Eugene Wetlands is a complex of either public land or The Nature Conservancy preserve between downtown Eugene and Fern Lake Reservoir. This system of about a dozen parcels and connecting streams is managed by the West Eugene Wetlands Partnership, a group of five public agencies and two private nonprofits, including The Nature Conservancy. The other private organization is Willamette Resources and Educational Network (WREN), started in 2000 to provide environmental education programs in the wetlands. Spearheaded by WREN, the West Eugene Wetlands Partnership is in the midst of an ambitious effort to build a state-of-the-art sustainable environmental education center. I can't wait to see it.

▶ URBAN WETLANDS BEST BETS WASHINGTON

Mercer Slough Nature Park is Bellevue's largest park and the largest remaining Lake Washington wetland. Several trails start at Winters House, the park's visitor center. To get to Winters House from Interstate 90 heading east to Bellevue, take the Bellevue Way exit and head north on Bellevue Way. In 1.3 miles you'll pass the Park and Ride on your right and then see the sign for Winters House at 2102 Bellevue Way. Turn right into the parking area. To paddle your canoe or kayak in the slough, launch your boat at Sweyolocken Park Boat launch which is the first right-hand turn immediately after you exit I-90 onto Bellevue Way. The Mercer Slough Environmental Education Center, a partnership between Bellevue and the Pacific Science Center, provides a variety of natural history programs.

The Tacoma Nature Center is a 54-acre island of wildlife habitat in the midst of Tacoma. Its central feature is Snake Lake, a shallow lake and swamp surrounded by dense vegetation. The lake is loaded with ducks, including plenty of wood ducks, and the thickets are bustling with songbird activity, especially in spring. About 2 miles of loop trails start at the visitor center. From Interstate 5 in Tacoma take Exit 132 and head west, toward Bremerton, on Hwy 16. After 2 miles exit onto South 19th St heading east. Go a couple of very long blocks, passing the Parks Department headquarters on your right, and then turn right onto Tyler St (a Fred Meyer store is on your left at this intersection). Immediately after getting onto Tyler make a left turn into the center's parking area on the east side of Tyler.

Seattle has an experiment underway that may provide some useful information for the successful restoration of landfills in the future. For hundreds of years it has been common throughout the country to use wetlands as garbage dumps. From 1926 until 1966 Seattle and the University of Washington filled wetlands along Union Bay that have become known as Montlake Fill or simply The Fill to Seattle birders. After it was closed it was covered with soil, seeded with grass, and left alone. Lo and behold, as plants started growing and ponds started forming (from settling garbage), the birds started coming. Today it is one of Seattle's most birded places and has an astounding cumulative bird list of about 200 species. Of course, the oasis phenomenon is very much at work here because it's about the only pocket of ponds and field habitat in the Seattle area and everything that flies over seems to drop in for awhile. The official name is now the Union Bay Natural Area and it's part of the university's Center for Urban Horticulture, which has undertaken the management of the habitat on The Fill. This is mainly a Herculean effort to control the vast number of non-native, invasive plants that have pretty much had their way since the Summer of Love (1967, in case you're not familiar with this term).

I hope the Center for Urban Horticulture will learn some techniques to help the hundreds of landfills in North America in a similar state. Montlake Fill is now an odd mix of grassland, shrubs, patchy wetland, ponds (some very seasonal), some stands of trees, and the lakeshore. As the rainy season progresses the seasonal wetlands get wetter and wetter, attracting more and more waterfowl and making rubber boots worth considering in winter. Finding Montlake Fill and a parking place are a bit tricky. Drive north of downtown Seattle on I-5 and take Exit 169 to head east on NE 45th St. Drive along the north edge of the campus, drive down a big hill, turn right onto Mary Gates Memorial Dr, and drive about 2 blocks. Then turn left onto 41th St. The Center for Urban Horticulture will be on your right soon after you have turned onto 41th St. Ah, parking. Drive to 36th Ave and try to park, either on 41th St or 36th Ave. From here walk over to the Center for Urban Horticulture, and at the far west end of their parking lot you'll find the start of Wahkiakum Ln, a paved (then gravel) path heading toward the main campus. You may find a trail map in a dispenser near the beginning of the trail. Explore on your own or take the main loop trail which heads to the southeast just before reaching the first large pond. Following this trail you'll make a clockwise loop, passing near the lakeshore where you can see scads of waterfowl, and then returning to join Wahkiakum Ln. You'll see the giant Husky Stadium looming in the distance. Do not try to go birdwatching here if it's a football Saturday.

Washington's second largest city, Spokane, straddles the Spokane River and has sections of good riparian habitat scattered along the river in various parks. The real gem, however, is the Little Spokane Natural Area, which is on the northwestern outskirts of town and not surrounded by urbanization. About 7.5 miles of the Little Spokane River are included in the natural area; the river is ideal for canoeing and kayaking. A good put-in spot is just west of the intersection of Rutter Pkwy and Waikiki Rd, near the trout hatchery. The well-signed, take-out spot is on Boat Launch Rd which is off State Hwy 291, just one mile north of the intersection with Rutter Pkwy. You can also explore the same stretch of river by trail. Indian Painted Rocks Trailhead is where Rutter Pkwy crosses the river right in the middle of the natural area. There is a great blue heron rookery about one mile downstream from this trailhead, and beaver are regularly seen early or late in the day. Little Spokane is in this chapter because it represents great wetland habitat very close to an urban area, but let's face it: a trip down the river by boat would be most enjoyable in the warmer months of the year. Contact Riverside State Park for more information.

▶ URBAN WETLANDS BEST BETS BRITISH COLUMBIA

Swan Lake Christmas Hill Nature Sanctuary in the District of Saanich just north of Victoria is two nature sanctuaries just 0.6 mile apart. Between the two is a mix of habitats including marshes, oak woodlands, rocky outcroppings, and the lake. The floating boardwalk crossing the lake is ideal for waterfowl watching. The lake gets considerably larger in winter offering even more room for the many waterbirds that pile in. Heading north from downtown Victoria on Blanshard St, turn right and head west one block on McKenzie, and then turn right again onto Rainbow St. Drive south on Rainbow a few blocks, and then left on Ralph St. In one block turn right onto Swan Lake Rd and drive into the parking area entrance.

Although this is the wrong time of year to mention this, Swan Lake is one of the best spots in our region for seeing western painted turtles in the summer, so come back then for a different experience.

Burnaby Lake RP and nearby Deer Lake Park are a wetland oasis surrounded by the greater Vancouver megalopolis. The 740-acre Burnaby Lake RP is part of the Greater Vancouver Regional District's park system. Out of its three entrances, the best place to start is the Nature House at the Piper Ave entrance, which has displays, trailheads, restrooms, an observation tower, and information. The lake has many marshes along the shore, especially toward the eastern end. Deer Lake, a city park, is much smaller and has little marshland. However, its good grassland habitat makes it worth a visit when going to Burnaby Lake, and you'll usually see a few bird species at one that aren't at the other.

You can reach both parks from the Kensington Ave exit (Exit 33), from Trans-Canada Highway 1. To reach the Nature House at Burnaby Lake, take Exit 33 and go north on Kensington Ave. Follow signs for Lougheed Hwy east, but as soon you cross over Still Creek, turn right immediately onto Winston St. Take Winston east to Piper Ave, and then turn right following signs for the park. To reach Deer Park take the Willingdon Ave exit (Exit 29), and then head south to the first traffic signals. Turn left onto Canada Way and drive east to Royal Oak Ave. Turn right and head south on Royal Oak, cross Gilpin at a stop sign, and in 0.25 mile from the stop, turn left into the parking lot.

ELK

Elk are big. They are often described as regal and majestic, but what it really comes down to is that these guys are big, and big is impressive. Only a few land animals in the Americas are heavier than a big bull elk at half a ton, and with their huge rack of antlers they really have a lot of charisma. Among hunters, elk are a highly prized game animal, with small wonder considering how much tasty meat one elk can provide.

The animal that we in America call the elk is called the red deer in Europe. What we Americans call the moose is what Europeans call elk. So if you're talking to Europeans about elk, moose, or red deer, be sure to get your species sorted out. Using scientific names is more precise; both the red deer and our elk are subspecies or races of the species *Cervus elaphus*. All this, of course, is of no consequence to the elk and moose themselves who have no trouble telling each other apart and call each other whatever they please. This confusion over names has caused many American naturalists and sportsmen to advocate the use of the Native American name *wapiti* for our American elk. Although wapiti is used frequently, it just hasn't quite caught on with the general public.

As one can easily see by their antlers, elk are members of the deer family. The moose is the only member of the deer family that is larger, and both animals have tremendous racks of antlers—elk can have antlers with a length of 5 feet and a spread of 6 feet. That these animals grow a whole new set of antlers every year still baffles me. I just can't see the selective advantage in having to expend all that energy and consume all those nutrients every year to grow a new rack. All that calcium is certainly utilized by rodents, who quickly eat the antlers when they are shed in late winter. New antlers begin growing within two weeks of the shed.

Unlike mule and white-tailed deer, elk are mainly grazers instead of browsers, meaning they eat more grass. Elk are, however, adaptable and they will utilize a wide variety of plant foods. Like all deer, and the majority of other ungulates, elk are ruminants—they have highly specialized digestive systems, including complex stomachs divided into chambers. Ruminants are well known for regurgitating wads of partially digested food for extra chewing, a practice commonly called chewing the cud. These adaptations allow ruminants to get the most nutrients possible out of tough, hard-to-digest plant material, particularly grass.

Elk originally occupied a wide range of habitats in North America, from the coniferous rain forests of the Northwest to the chaparral mountains of the Southwest and from the eastern forests to the Great Plains. Authorities now believe that before European contact, elk were more widespread than either species of deer, being found in every contiguous state and most Canadian provinces, and probably numbering 10 million. Elk were quickly killed off by hungry settlers in most of their range and only survived in the least accessible parts of the western mountains, their stronghold today. After intensive management for most of this century, including reintroductions, elk numbers have increased, and many areas support a healthy population, although elk are now found in only 12 states.

Unlike deer, elk are herd animals, and the females spend their whole life as part of one. Young males stay in the herd with their mothers for about the first year. The older males form smaller groups (bachelor herds) with other males, except preceding rut when they become solitary. During the rut, or breeding season, individual mature bulls attempt to gather a harem of cows that they will mate with exclusively. Competition between males is intense, and it's during this period (September and October) that males give their famous bugling call and engage in various bluffs and battles for cows. It's during some of these battles that the massive antlers become deadly weapons, although most disputes are settled without coming to blows. The unique sound of bugling elk has a mysterious and powerful quality that gives most people goose bumps. Bugling can be heard during September and October when you're in good elk habitat. However, the bulls do not bugle while the animals are gathered in wintering grounds.

Most current elk populations make regular, sometimes quite long, seasonal movements in response to food availability. Typically elk will spend the warmer months high in mountain meadows and come down into valley bottoms where food is available in winter. Unfortunately, most of the flat valley bottom lands are now intensely utilized by people for agriculture or are urbanized. This tremendous loss of winter range is the biggest problem facing elk today. To compensate for this loss, federal and state wildlife agencies, and some private conservation organizations have acquired land with critical winter range for elk. In some cases, the elk are fed on these winter ranges, not so much to keep them alive but to keep them from damaging nearby private agricultural land. These managed winter ranges provide the easiest viewing opportunities for elk, the location for most of our Best Bets. December is the earliest that elk usually start showing up in numbers on the winter ranges and when feeding programs begin, but better viewing is often in January and February.

The Northwest has two subspecies or races of elk: the Roosevelt elk, sometimes called the Olympic elk, and the Rocky Mountain elk. The Rocky Mountain elk was originally the most widespread of the elk in North America and today are found east of the crest of the Cascades and in British Columbia's Coast Mountains. The Roosevelt elk is a specialized race that lives in the moist coniferous forests along the coast, and in some parts of the western slope of the Cascades. Roosevelt elk are slightly larger and darker, with smaller antlers, than the Rocky Mountain elk, but it takes an expert's eye to tell them apart. In much of their range, where winters are mild, Roosevelt elk do not migrate.

▶ ELK BEST BETS OREGON

Oregon has the most unique elk viewing experience I've seen anywhere. ODFW manages almost 10,000 acres of land near Baker City as the Elkhorn WA. In 1991 the department started a unique program with a private concessionaire, T&T Wildlife Tours, on the North Powder Tract of the wildlife area. In the winter T&T Wildlife Tours offers horse-drawn wagon rides down into the area where 150 to 200 elk are feeding on hay. The elk have gotten completely comfortable with the wagon full of people drawn by Belgian draft horses, and you can get close looks at the elk feeding or relaxing from as close as 10 yards away. Talk about a photo opportunity. The elk seem to have accepted the horses as some distant relatives and are very mellow in their presence. You are almost tempted to try to pet the elk, but remember they are wild elk that have acclimated to the horse-drawn wagon and its unusual cargo; they are not tame or domesticated animals. Treat them as wild animals.

The wagon rides are offered for several hours a day, every weekend, from about mid-December through February. Rides are also usually offered every day between Christmas and New Year's Eve, but weather and snow conditions can affect the elk feeding and the tours so check before making the trip. Space on the wagon is assigned on a first come, first served basis when you arrive at the viewing area. Once you've signed up and been given your time, you may have to wait an hour or more. While you wait you can view the elk from the road, look for other wildlife (there are lots of hawks in the area), or huddle in your car to stay warm. There are outhouses at the waiting area; be sure to bring your own snacks and drinks.

Finding the Elkhorn wagon rides is a piece of cake. From Interstate 84, about halfway between Le Grande and Baker City, take Exit 285 for the little town of North Powder. North Powder has a motel, store, and the North Powder Cafe, which is always open and well known for vast quantities of food. Just west of I-84 take N. Powder River Ln west; do not get on State Hwy 30 to Haines. Stay on N. Powder River Ln going west and follow any brown binocular wildlife viewing signs you see. In 4 miles, at the intersection, continue straight on N. Powder River Ln. In another 3.8 miles you will come to a right hand fork to Tucker Flat but do not go that way. Instead continue straight-leftish to the feeding area. It will be obvious when you get near the feeding area and wagon rides. Contact T&T Wildlife Tours at www.tnthorsemanship.com or 541-856-3356 or call Baker County Visitors Bureau, 1-800-523-1235

Another good place for elk in northeastern Oregon is the Wenaha WA. Wenaha is not only a good place for Rocky Mountain elk but is also excellent for mule and white-tailed deer and bighorn sheep. Wenaha has a feeding program, but the feeding areas are not open for viewing. However, it's sometimes possible to go out with the staff to feed or arrange other types of tours. Call the on-site manager to find out what's possible and where the best viewing opportunities are. It's also wise to ask about road conditions. December may not be the best month to go to Wenaha because some hunting seasons continue into the month, and feeding may not have started if weather is mild.

Wenaha WA is near the tiny town of Troy, which is on the Grande Ronde River at the bottom of a beautiful canyon. It's about as out in the middle of nowhere as you can get. This is the kind of nowhere, however, where an outdoor person could spend years; the scenery in this corner of Oregon is truly spectacular. To get to Troy go north on State Hwy 3 from Enterprise for about 33 miles. Just after the Rimrock Inn is the turn-off to Flora and Troy. Take this road and head west, following the signs to Troy. This road is steep and twisty and not fun if it's snowy or icy, so get information about road conditions before heading down. A less treacherous but longer alternative is to continue north on Hwy 3 into Washington until you come to Grande Ronde Rd, and then take it back upstream, along the river, to Troy.

While I recommend making arrangements to go to the feeding areas, if you decide to head out on your own, here is the best route to find elk. I recommend a high-clearance, all-wheel or four-wheel drive vehicle for these roads. As you stand in downtown Troy you'll see two bridges that cross the Grande Ronde River. Go over the bridge farthest south or upstream, the low bridge, following the signs to Elgin and Wallowa. In just over 0.2 mile you'll reach a signed junction; turn right following signs to Elgin and Tollgate Ranger Station. In just over 2 miles you'll reach a fork in the road, turn left following the sign to Eden Bench. Slowly cruise this road for awhile and come back (10 miles should be plenty), looking carefully on both sides for elk and deer. You may see them along this road as they come and go from the feeding areas and the river.

The Jewell Meadows WA, between Portland and the coast, is an outstanding area to see Roosevelt elk. This is another ODFW site where winter feeding takes place. About 75 to 200 elk can be seen most days from November into April. To reach Jewell Meadows from Portland, head west on US Hwy 26 to Jewell Junction, just past the Elderberry Inn. Drive 9 miles north on Fishhawk Falls Highway (State Hwy 103) to Jewell. At Jewell turn left, and then head west on State Hwy 202. In 1.5 miles you'll enter the beginning of the wildlife area. The road follows the north border of the wildlife area for 3 miles, with several turnoffs and parking areas where you can stop to watch the elk.

Another choice spot for seeing Roosevelt elk is the Dean Creek Elk Viewing Area near Reedsport. Just 3.5 miles east of Reedsport on State Hwy 38 is a large wildlife-viewing and interpretive site (with restrooms). There are other places to pull over on the south side of the road and view elk for the next 2 miles.

▶ ELK BEST BETS WASHINGTON

The Cascade Mountains east of Mount Rainier NP are home to the Yakima herd of Rocky Mountain elk, descendants of elk first reintroduced 1913. Twenty-two miles west of Yakima in the foothills of the Cascades is a winter feeding area with the most visitor facilities of any wintering area in the Northwest—Oak Creek WA managed by WDFW. The headquarters of Oak Creek WA has a small visitor center and restrooms. Elk are fed at this site every day in early afternoon, usually beginning in December and continuing through February, but the feeding varies with the weather conditions so call before going. To get to Oak Creek HQ from Yakima, go west about 20 miles on US Hwy 12 to where it splits with State Hwy 410. Continue south on Hwy 12 about 2 more miles, and you'll see the area well marked with signs.

After viewing elk at the Oak Creek headquarters you might want to drive up Oak Creek itself to see elk in a less artificial setting. Just south of HQ turn right onto Oak Creek Rd. Drive up this beautiful canyon as far as you like, looking for elk on the distant hillsides and also watching for the western gray squirrel, an increasingly rare mammal in Washington that is now most abundant in the oak woodlands of Oak Creek Canyon. While you're there, stop at the Clemens Mountain bighorn sheep feeding area to look for the sheep. In these hills west of Yakima you could see elk, bighorn sheep, mountain goat, and deer in one day. It's a charismatic megafauna festival.

The largest elk herd in Washington is the St. Helens herd. A reliable way to see them is from the Spirit Lake Memorial Highway (State Hwy 504) which goes to the Johnston Ridge Observatory in Mount St Helens National Volcanic

Monument. This road is also good for spotting deer. A drive up Spirit Lake Memorial Highway to Johnston Ridge is an absolute must-do for the Northwest, but it can be closed in winter.

The 1980 eruption covered the Toutle River Valley floor with a massive mudslide. The Soil Conservation Service quickly seeded the area to reduce erosion, and the next year surviving Roosevelt elk returned to utilize the valley for winter range and to eat the new grass. The state established the Mount St. Helens WA to protect the herd and its habitat. With the forest cover removed by the blast there was an explosion of new growth by the plants elk love to eat and the population of elk in the Mount St. Helens area is now probably at an all time high. Elk are now easy to see at a number of places along Hwy 504, especially at the Forest Learning Center. Because they are often out in the open in the area devastated by the eruption, the St. Helens elk are visible, but far away; you'll need binoculars or a spotting scope to see them.

The Hoh Rain Forest in Olympic NP is famous for Roosevelt elk. Here the situation is the opposite of Mount St. Helens. The elk are not very visible because of the thick vegetation, but when you do see them they are often close by. The numerous elk in the Hoh Valley are accustomed to human activity so people sometimes see them when walking on the trails or near the campground. The Hoh is also an excellent place to hear elk bugling during the rut in fall. The Hoh Rain Forest, featured in September (Ancient Forests), is another of the must-see places in our region.

When you visit Julia Butler Hansen Refuge for the Columbian White-Tailed Deer near Cathlamet, watch for elk as well as the deer. Roosevelt elk frequent the refuge. As you drive the roads through the refuge, you'll usually see them in the wooded areas or in brush, not standing out in the open, so it often takes some effort to find them.

CROW'S NEST OR DREY?

If you live in a neighborhood with lots of big deciduous trees and you scan the bare trees in the dead of winter, what do you see? You see last summer's nests, finally revealed by the loss of their shroud of leaves. Two fairly large nests that are similar in size attract attention and start some folks wondering who lives there. Most abundant are the crow's nests which have a broad, upside-down cone shape, are almost 2-feet wide by a foot deep, and are made of small sticks. Their location makes it clear where the term used on sailing ships—crow's nest—comes from. They are usually toward the top center of a clump of trees in a substantial crotch and really do remind one of the crow's nest atop the mast of a clipper ship.

The other nest really confuses people—it looks like a soccer ball made out of leaves. It's not cup-shaped like most bird's nests and doesn't even appear to have an entrance. These are the nests made by tree squirrels, commonly called dreys in England; a name that is rarely used in North America (and here it's sometimes spelled "dray"). Although dreys do look a bit like crow's nests, here's how to tell them apart: dreys are made mainly out of leaves, not sticks, they are usually quite spherical and not conical or bowl-shaped, and they are usually lower and nearer the trunk than crow's nests.

All of our North American tree squirrels make these leafy-ball dreys, but they are not the only nests that tree squirrels use. The preferred nest for most of the year, and especially for breeding, is a cavity in a tree, most commonly an old woodpecker nest. These cavity nests (usually called dens) are more secure from predators and bad weather than are the dreys. So during the winter most tree squirrels use dens exclusively. Indeed, dreys are also called summer nests and are mainly used in the warmer months. Dreys will be used year round if weather is mild or cavities are lacking. In many northwestern neighborhoods and parks tree squirrels are abundant, but cavities are scarce because snags and dead limbs get removed. In these situations dreys seem to be used for most of the year.

Have you been squirreling away money for retirement? Have your kids been acting squirrelly lately? You know an animal must be common if there are slang terms based on its behaviors. Tree squirrels are one of the most familiar mammals in North America because they are very active during the day all year long. Some are quite adaptable and live close to people in urbanized areas, including large parks in the middle of cities. They are frequently seen visiting feeders with seeds, either feeders designed for them or at bird feeders, where they are sometimes unwelcome guests. The observation of tree squirrel behavior over hundreds of years has led to the everyday use of "squirreling away" and "squirrelly."

Tree squirrels store large numbers of nuts, seeds, or cones for the winter by either burying them or by stuffing them into hollow logs or under rocks. Squirreling away means saving for the future, but to me it has always sounded a bit sneaky, like hiding Halloween candy from your siblings. The strategy of burying lots of individual nuts, each in its own hole, over a wide area is called scatterhoarding, a technique used by the larger fox and gray squirrels. The smaller chickaree and red squirrel, on the other hand, use the larderhoarding strategy of putting a huge number of cones in one place, like a hollow log.

With larderhoarding, the squirrels must defend their precious food supply, which explains why these feisty little squirrels are so noisy and territorial. Scatterhoarding makes defending the nuts impossible, which isn't necessary anyway because other animals will never find all the cached food. Each method works for the particular kind of squirrel in its particular habitat.

People often wonder if squirrels find all the nuts they bury. It's not clear just how many of their cached nuts squirrels find or how they do it, but they do find a lot of the nuts they bury. A popular theory is that squirrels rarely remember where they have stashed their goodies, but just look in places where any squirrel in his or her right mind would hide nuts and, low and behold, there they are. They could be eating nuts buried by themselves or by other squirrels in the area. However, recent squirrel researchers Michael Steele and John Koprowski think that squirrels may have the memory abilities of jays and that their managing of caches may someday show them to be "nature's ultimate bankers."

Regardless of their potential as financial advisors, squirrels clearly do not recover all the nuts they have buried with the result that they are a "Johnny Walnutseed" of the forest. Squirrels inadvertently plant trees when they miss nuts that happen to be buried in a good spot to sprout and grow. Squirrels, and even more so jays, answer the mystery of how trees that make heavy seeds can actually spread uphill. Most walnuts may roll downhill but the jays and squirrels carry many above the parent trees.

During the mating season, which happens twice a year, tree squirrels get really wound up and chase each other all over the place. Chases are usually by males pursuing or fighting over a female. All this hubbub really does make the squirrels appear crazy, hence "squirrelly" refers to people (did I say kids?) who are whipped up and acting nutty.

Tree squirrels are common in most of the earth's forests. You can distinguish them from their close relatives the ground squirrels (including marmots, chipmunks, and prairie dogs) by their big, bushy tails. *Squirrel* comes from two Greek words that mean "shadow tail" and indeed, some do use their tails as parasols to shade their body. The tail is most important, however, for insulation, climbing, and jumping. Tree squirrels are named, of course, for their superb ability to adapt to life in the trees. Their tail is important for maintaining balance, acting as a rudder when jumping, and breaking a fall like a parachute. The ultimate arboreal rodents are the flying squirrels, which have perfected the art of gliding flight.

Five species of tree squirrels live in the Northwest, not counting the northern flying squirrel which is quite distinct. The chickaree or Douglas' squirrel is abundant and could be the mascot for the coniferous forests in the western half of our region, their loud chatter being one of the signature sounds of the Pacific Northwest. Their close relative, the red squirrel, has the largest range of any American squirrel and is found in northeastern Oregon, eastern Washington, most of British Columbia and, interestingly, on Vancouver Island. Both of these are small tree squirrels of coniferous forests and are not as common around human dwellings as are "the big guys." Their dreys are very hard to locate because they are built in the thick foliage of evergreens.

Three very closely related tree squirrels are all noticeably larger than the chickaree and red squirrel and prefer habitats with more deciduous trees than just conifers. The beautiful western gray squirrel, native only to the Pacific states, is found in oak woodlands and mixed pine-oak woodlands. Unfortunately, these habitats are highly favored by humans, and western gray squirrel populations have declined dramatically in most of the Northwest. An additional source of trouble for the western gray squirrel has been the introduction of its two eastern relatives, the eastern gray squirrel and the fox squirrel. These squirrels are more aggressive than our laid-back, mellow, western natives that are getting pushed out of good habitat. The western gray squirrel is totally gray with a bright white belly whereas eastern gray squirrels have some areas of slightly yellowish-brown fur, especially on the back and head, on their overall gray coat.

Western grays are not very tolerant of human disturbance so few people will see them around their houses. The eastern gray and fox squirrels, however, are quite adaptable and are regulars on the urban wildlife scene. Hence human development has favored eastern gray and fox squirrels; you'll see them in urban parks or running along the phone lines in your neighborhood. Because these are introduced squirrels their distribution is irregular and spotty, determined not by nature but by the whims of humans. Oregon has more fox squirrels than eastern grays, but in Washington the grays have an edge. British Columbia has no western gray or fox squirrels, so the big tree squirrels you see are eastern gray squirrels. It's shocking to see the solid black tree squirrels of Stanley Park in Vancouver for the first time, seemingly a unique and rare species. But eastern gray squirrels have several color variations in their range throughout eastern North America, and the northern populations have black or "melanistic phase" individuals. Melanistic eastern gray squirrels are most common in Ontario, and squirrels from this area were undoubtedly the ancestors of today's eastern grays in Vancouver. In fact, the majority of eastern gray squirrels in British Columbia are the black variety although you will see a range in the urban areas where they live.

Crow's nests and dreys have no specific Best Bets because they are so common and widespread. Crows are found throughout our region at lower elevations so you could see their nests almost anywhere, although their distribution is irregular east of the mountains. Eastern gray and fox squirrels are in most cities west of the Cascades in Oregon. Western Washington is eastern gray squirrel country, along with the Tri-cities area. Fox squirrels are in many of the towns near the Blue Mountains in both states and throughout the Okanogan River Valley in Washington. Then there are the black eastern gray squirrels of southwestern British Columbia. Look for the dreys of these two eastern squirrels in parks and neighborhoods with big, old deciduous trees. In just about any coniferous forest in the Northwest you'll find chickarees or, as you go east and north, red squirrels, but the dreys of these smaller tree squirrels are hard to find in conifers.

Finding western gray squirrels is, unfortunately, getting harder all the time. Western gray squirrels are a threatened species in Washington and a candidate for federal listing. In Oregon look for them in oak woodlands in the Willamette and other interior valleys and in ponderosa pine forests in the eastern Cascades. In Washington your best bet is in the pine-oak woodlands along the Klickitat River and the Oak Creek WA near Yakima (also see Elk).

DECEMBER'S NATURE NUGGETS

SASQUATCH The first serious snow in the mountains presents an excellent opportunity to see animal tracks. This may be your best chance to find Sasquatch, also known as Bigfoot because of the large tracks this mysterious animal leaves. Sasquatch is one of the main subjects of the relatively recent science of cryptobiology, the study of hidden animals. Other objects of interest in this field include the Yeti of the Himalayas and Nessie, the famous resident of Loch Ness. The Pacific Northwest is as well known for Sasquatch as it is for salmon, spotted owls, and banana slugs, so no wildlife guide for the region would be complete without some tips for finding Bigfoot. However, giving specific advice is difficult because almost all reported sightings and discoveries of tracks have been chance encounters by people who were not out looking for Sasquatch. Some areas, though, have produced more sightings than others: the Southern Washington Cascades around Mount Rainier and Mount St. Helens. This area had so much Bigfoot activity in the late sixties that Skamania County passed the world's first (and presumably only) Sasquatch Protection Ordinance, making it illegal to kill a Sasquatch under penalty of fine or imprisonment. A number of sightings have occurred in the Oregon Cascades and in the Fraser River Valley, but sites are so scattered as to be no better than chance. If you do go looking for Sasquatch remember to take a camera; you may see your photo in the periodicals displayed at the checkout stand of your supermarket. Or better yet, get *Harry and the Hendersons* at the video store and sit back with a bowl of popcorn on a cold winter's night.

CHRISTMAS BIRD COUNTS: A CLOSER LOOK

It is fitting to end the year with the biggest natural history event of the year—the Christmas Bird Count. In recent years this all-volunteer bird census has involved over 57,000 people participating in 2060 different counts. For many birders it is the highlight of the year, and for many Audubon chapters it is their biggest social event. Not bad for one guy's simple suggestion at the turn of the century.

At the turn of the 19th century many American "sportsmen" participated in a traditional Christmas hunt where teams of hunters went out on Christmas Day to see which team could kill the most animals. Many people were horrified at this slaughter so when Frank Chapman, editor of *Bird-Lore* magazine (the forerunner of *Audubon*), suggested an alternative, the idea caught on. He proposed "spending a portion of Christmas Day with the birds and sending a report of the 'hunt' to *Bird-Lore* before retiring that night." Frank received the reports of 25 counts, almost all made by single individuals. From this humble beginning in 1900, the Christmas Bird Count (CBC to birders) has become a massive, well-organized, and standardized method for censusing birds in winter.

Every year, between December 14 and January 5, volunteers record by species every individual bird they find in 24 hours within a precisely defined circle 15 miles in diameter. Because the same area is counted using basically the same method at the same time every year, CBCs show general trends in winter bird populations for the areas represented by the count circles. Although this technique is sloppy by scientific standards, the results are by far the greatest body of data on winter bird populations in North America and in many areas the CBC data is the only data on bird numbers available.

The first counts were fairly casual affairs with a few people counting for part of the day. The species seen the first years numbered in the 20s, but by 1911 the then seemingly unbelievable mark of 100 species was reached in Santa Barbara. These days at least 50 counts have species lists over 150 every year. This dramatic increase is a result of better coverage of more areas by increasing numbers of more skillful birders. In the 1920s the present rules for count circles and time of counting were established, and in 1941 the results of the then officially titled Christmas Bird Count were first published by the National Audubon Society, still the event's sponsor and organizer.

One factor that has pushed the number of species up has been the friendly competition among count areas to see which can produce the highest number of species. Every year there is close competition between the coastal areas of California and Texas for the species high for the United States. The species high has fluctuated between 225 and an astounding 250 in 2006 for two decades but the unbeatable low remains the 1981 count at North Star Island, Alaska—a big fat zero.

Christmas Bird Counts are a lot of fun, encompassing a great spirit of camaraderie, a sense of purpose (often challenged by lousy weather) and sometimes a bit of friendly competition over who will report the "big surprise" at the end of the day. The day usually concludes with a countdown pot luck dinner where the teams report their sightings for the day, grand totals are tallied, and a few wild stories are shared. Beginners are usually warmly received by count leaders and assigned to teams with expert birders. This is a great way to learn identification tips from the pros, and the CBC has inspired many novices to more serious birding.

To participate in a CBC in your area, contact your local Audubon Society chapter, local Natural History Society, or the National Audubon Society. The results are published online each year, and all the CBC records since 1900 are also available. Christmas Bird Counts in Canada are organized by Bird Studies Canada.

Counters pride themselves on going out for the count regardless of the weather, so prepare to be outdoors all day. If this sounds too brutal, certain small areas sometimes can be covered by one or two people going out for part of the day. Or consider taking part in feeder watching. Contact the count leader in advance to see where you best fit in. Happy Holidays and Good Counting.

ACKNOWLEDGMENTS

Suffer the poor writer's spouse. Unless you've been there yourself it is hard to imagine what a drag it is being married to someone as self-absorbed and unavailable as a writer working on a book. Sincerest thanks to my wife, Sally Loomis, for putting up with it all, being supportive and helpful, proofreading, and holding down the fort.

It would be impossible to write a book like this without the help of many people, and I want to express my sincerest gratitude to everyone who provided any information. I apologize to anyone I've missed or whose name I've misspelled. This book had a former incarnation as *Seasonal Guide to the Natural Year: A Month by Month Guide to Natural Events*. Those mentioned here helped me with either the earlier book or this book or both in some cases.

I never would have had the opportunity to write this book the first time if not for that fateful phone call from Dan Mathews asking if I would be interested in writing a book he had been asked to write. I was flabbergasted and greatly honored to "take his place." Another fateful meeting with Susan Applegate on Mount Adams led to this updated, rewritten, and much improved book by Timber Press. Fate works in wondrous ways. My sincere thanks to Eve Goodman and the rest of the staff at Timber Press who helped make this book real. Special thanks to Art of Geography master Erik Goetze for the fabulous maps, which add such a touch of class to the book. Mary Johnson did a fantastic job editing the manuscript.

When I decided I could take on this project, first I sat down with Harry Nehls and mapped out the year. Thanks Harry for a great start. Portland writers Judy Jewell and Phil Jones gave me encouragement and advice on business matters. The following people reviewed chapters and provided additional information: Rick Brown, Evelyn Bull, Pam Cahn, Sue Foster, Larry Hanson, Dave Helzer, Mike Houck, George Jett, Dave Marshall, Judy Maule, Lani Miller, Margaret Pounds, Jeff Smith, Maurita Smyth, Alan St. John, Walt Van Dyke, sister- and brother-in-law Barbara Loomis and Stephen Elspas, and my parents, Natalie and Luther Davis. My daughter, Risa, went on many expeditions with me and helped select photos. Good buddy Scott Bowler won the prize for returning my questionnaire jammed with the most information. Hospitality thanks to my sister, Peg, and her family for making their home my Seattle base.

I could get started rewriting this book after my colleague at Metro, Vanessa Schwab, cheerfully converted my old Mac disks into modern, Windows XP, Word documents. Thanks Vanessa. I have been very lucky to have worked for the last 10 years at Metro Regional Parks and Greenspaces with some great people. In particular I am grateful for all I have learned and the adventures I have shared with my fellow naturalists Elisabeth Neely and Deb Scrivens. I also have to say I am lucky to live in a wonderful community of many outstanding and dedicated environmental educators and naturalists; you know who you are.

It is a common tendency these days in both the United States and Canada to gripe and complain about government agencies and bureaucrats. In my research I spoke with hundreds of people working in federal, state, provincial, municipal, and other public agencies that were helpful, knowledgeable, and dedicated to managing and protecting our resources with increasingly limited funding and staff. All my thanks to these agency people who have helped me so much over the years. Let's give them a bigger budget to take care of our natural heritage.

In the US National Park Service: Paul Crawford, Ron Holms, Molly Juilleiat, Bob Kuntz, Rod Norvell and Ron Warfield. In the US Fish and Wildlife Service: Dan Alonso, Eric Anderson, Corky Broaddus, Barbara Harding, Randy Hill, Marguerite Hills, David Klinger, Lisa Langelier, David Linehan, Roy Lowe, Ed Murczek, Bill Pyle, Mike Rule and Susan Saul. In the US Forest Service: Cathy Ahlenslager, Mariann Armijo, Tom Bertram, Sally Claggett, Bob Diebel, Jeff Dose, Andris Eglitis, Pete Forbes, Mike Gerdes, Tom Horning, Martha Jensen, Virginia Kelly, Tom Kogut, Ken Kollas, Dean Longrie, Laura Potash, Scott Price, Jo Ellen Richards, Sharon Selvaggio, David Sotnik, Marty Stein, George Wooten, and Asia Young. In the Bureau of Land Management: Pam Camp, Dave Ericson, Jeanne Klein, Tara Martinak, Bob Ratcliff, Leah Schrodt, and Fred Taylor.

At the Oregon Department of Fish and Wildlife: Robin Brown, Liz Bueffel, Mike Burner, Vic Coggins, Larry Cooper, Dan Edwards, Dave Fox, Cliff Hamilton, Dave Harcombe, Bill Hastie, Mark Henjum, George Keister, Chris Kern, Dave Loomis, Bruce McIntosh, Steve Pribyl, Dan Renolds, Marty St. Louis, John Yaskovic, and my former colleague at Audubon, Claire Puchy (now with the City of Portland). Jim Ruff with the NW Power Planning Council and Dave Cantillen at the National Marine Fisheries Service helped with salmon. Other helpful folks at various agencies in Oregon were Bev Lund and Carol Walker at the Hatfield Marine Science Center, Ron Klein at Metro, Jim Sjulin at Portland Parks, Vicki Sink and Monte Turner at State Parks, and Pat Willis and Neil Bjorklund with the cities of Hillsboro and Eugene.

With the Washington Department of Fish and Wildlife: Kelly McAllister, David Anderson, Brian Calkins, John Garrett, Chuck Gibilisco, Steve Jenks, Rolf Johnson, Robert Kent, Diane Ludwig, John McGowan, Roger McKeel, Woody Myers,

John Pierce, Steve Pozzanghera, Mark Quinn, Cliff Rice, Elizabeth Roderick, Lori Salzer, Susan VanLewven, and Lee Van Tussenbrook. Debbie Hall, James Horan, and Terry Patton with Washington State Parks were helpful as were Mark Olsen at Padilla Bay and Darrel Barnes with US Customs in Sumas. Carrie Sunstrom explained the scenic byways system in Washington and Debbie Pettersson updated me on Bellevue City Parks.

Those associated with private, nonprofit conservation organizations are Bob Barnes, Bonnie Brunkow, Sarah Gage, Jeff Gottfried, Linda Hardie, Steve Hoffman, Ruthie Johns, Geoff LeBaron, Tim Lillebo, Tom LoCascio, Marie Lotz, Jim Myron, Katie Ryan, Bob Straub, Molly Sullivan, and Wendell Wood. Some of the non-agency naturalists who provided much specialized knowledge were Don Baccus, Bill Bakke, Nelsa Buckingham, Mike Fahey, John Hinchleff, Jerry Igo, Russ Jolly, Brian McNett, Bill Neill, Barbara Robertson, Maggie Rogers, Kyle Strauss, Steve Yates, and Peggy Goldie, who gave me lots of initial information on BC.

A flock of Washington birders provided information for their state: Michael Carmody, Glen Hoge, Eugene Hunn, Andy Mlodinow, Bob Morse, Dennis Paulson, Russell Rogers, Andy Stepniewski, Terry Wahl, Bob Woodley, Diane Yorgason-Quinn, and the team of Mike Denny and Ken Knittle who filled me in on the Walla Walla area. Oregon birders included Jeff Gilligan, Rick Krabbe, Tom Mickel, Owen Schmidt, and Khanh Tran, in addition to those already mentioned elsewhere.

I needed the most help finding information on British Columbia and appreciate the enthusiastic helpfulness of the Canadians I encountered. In federal agencies were Don Buxton, Joanne Day, Doug Hay, Mark Johnson, and Brian Pearce in the Department of Fisheries and Oceans; Bill McIntyre with Parks Canada and Neal Dawe with the Canadian Wildlife Service. In the provincial Ministry of Environment, Land, and Parks, BC Parks branch: Jim Cuthbert, Debbie Funk, Rick Howie, Bill Merilees, Jill Ryan, and especially Al Grass who broke all records for printed information sent. Also in the wildlife branch of the Ministry of Environment, Lands, and Parks: Syd Cannings, Don Doyle, Tom Plath, Elizabeth Stanlake, and Betsy Terpsma. With regional park districts: Jude Grass, John Heaven, and Deb Thiessen.

Other Canadian naturalists and birders were Robert Adam, David Allinson, Barbara Begg, Dick Cannings, Michael Force, Brian Gates, Richard Hebda, John Ireland, Hue and Jo Ann MacKenzie, Eric McBean, Hans Roemer, Ann Scarfe, Daphne Solecki, David Stirling, Keith Taylor, Hank Vander Pol and Beth Whittaker. Special thanks to Federation of British Columbia Naturalists manager Frieda Davidson for many answers, Sandy Bell and Michael Jansen-Reynaud for that beautiful day at Botanical Beach, and Rick Toochin for that great drive to the end of Iona Jetty.

Northwest Natural History
BIBLIOGRAPHY

These are some of the best natural history guides ever written. Many of them have been the most helpful to me in my lifetime of studying nature, from my first Golden Guide to Fiona Reid's new edition of the Peterson guide *Mammals*. This is a recommended reading list more than a citation of references. Years of teaching have shown me that these books are the most helpful to amateur naturalists and people in general who want to know more about their natural world. They are organized by topic for ease of use:

General Northwest natural history and geology
Northwest nature guides
Bird identification, field guides
Bird natural history and behavior
Birding guides—where to find the birds
Mammals
Animal tracking and observation skills
Reptiles and amphibians
Fish and freshwater life
Insects and other invertebrates
Marine life
Wildflower identification and plants in general
Trees and forests
Fungus

General Northwest natural history and geology

Alt, David and Donald Hyndman. 1995. *Northwest Exposures: A Geologic Story of the Northwest*. Missoula: Mountain Press. The most readable, easiest-to-understand book explaining our geology.

Alt, David. 2001. *Glacial Lake Missoula and Its Humongous Floods*. Missoula, Montana: Mountain Press. The best book yet explaining the Bretz Floods.

Cannings, Richard and Sydney Cannings. 1996. *British Columbia: A Natural History*. Vancouver, British Columbia: Greystone Books. *The Book* on this subject.

Kozloff, Eugene N. 1976. *Plants and Animals of the Pacific Northwest*. Seattle: Univ. of Washington Press. A good introduction to the region; best for plants. "Pacific Northwest" means the west side.

Lichen, Patricia K. and Linda M. Feltner. 2001. *Brittle Stars & Mudbugs: An Uncommon Field Guide to Northwest Shorelines & Wetlands*. Seattle: Sasquatch Books. These three outstanding books are entertaining and interesting short portraits of common plants and animals with up-to-date information.

Lichen, Patricia K. and Linda M. Feltner. 2001. *Passionate Slugs & Hollywood Frogs: An Uncommon Field Guide to Northwest Backyards*. Seattle: Sasquatch Books.

Lichen, Patricia K. and Linda M. Feltner. 2001. *River-Walking Songbirds & Singing Coyotes: An Uncommon Field Guide to Northwest Mountains*. Seattle: Sasquatch Books.

Mathews, Daniel. 1999. *Cascade-Olympic Natural History*. 2nd ed. Portland, Oregon: Raven Editions / Portland Audubon Society. An awesome all-in-one backpacker's natural history guide for our mountains; accurate and entertaining; much applies to the lowlands west of the mountains.

O'Connor, Georganne and Karen Wieda. 2001. *Northwest Arid Lands: An Introduction to the Columbia Basin Shrub-steppe*. Columbus, Ohio: Battelle Press. A great introduction to plants, animals, and habitats; also good for eastern Oregon and the Great Basin.

Saling, Ann. 1999. *The Great Northwest Nature Factbook*. 2nd rev ed. Portland, Oregon: Graphic Arts Center. Amazing facts about animals, plants, and geology.

Schwartz, Susan. 1983. *Nature in the Northwest: An Introduction to the Natural History and Ecology of the Northwestern United States from the Rockies to the Pacific*. Englewood Cliffs, New Jersey: Prentice-Hall. A good introduction to the natural history of the region; out of print, but easy to find used.

St. John, Alan. 2007. *Oregon's Dry Side: Exploring East of the Cascade Crest*. Portland, Oregon: Timber Press. At last, a great book to take the place of long out-of-print classics *The Oregon Desert* and *Oregon's Great Basin Country*.

Trimble, Stephen. 1999. *The Sagebrush Ocean: A Natural History of the Great Basin*. Rev ed. Reno: Univ. of Nevada Press. The anchor of a series of books about the Great Basin; excellent for southeastern Oregon and much of eastern Washington.

Whitney, Stephen. 1989. *A Sierra Club Naturalist's Guide to the Pacific Northwest*. San Francisco: Sierra Club Books. Another excellent, but out-of-print, introduction to our region; worth looking for.

Northwest nature guides

Butcher, Russell D. 2003. *America's National Wildlife Refuges: A Complete Guide.* Lanham, Maryland: Roberts Rinehart. This 700-page directory of all NWRs in the country includes the best descriptions of the refuges in Oregon and Washington.

Dolan, Maria and Kathryn True. 2003. *Nature in the City: Seattle.* Seattle: Mountaineers Books. An excellent, comprehensive, and fun guide to exploring nature in the Seattle area.

Goldberg, Kim. 1997. *Where to See Wildlife on Vancouver Island.* Madeira Park, British Columbia: Harbour. You have to have this book for "The Island."

Houck, Michael C. and M. J. Cody, eds. 2000. *Wild in the City: A Guide to Portland's Natural Areas.* Portland, Oregon: Oregon Historical Society Press. The most complete guide to the natural history and the natural areas of any metropolitan area in the West.

Houle, Marcy. 1996. *One City's Wilderness: Portland's Forest Park.* Rev ed. Portland, Oregon: Oregon Historical Society Press. A natural history and hiking guide.

Oregon Department of Fish and Wildlife. 2004. *Visitor's Guide: Oregon's Fish Hatcheries and Wildlife Management Areas.* Rev ed. Salem, Oregon: Oregon Department of Fish and Wildlife. A directory of state sites; brief descriptions with contact information; available from ODFW's Web site.

Plumb, Gregory. 1998. *A Waterfall Lover's Guide to the Pacific Northwest.* Seattle: Mountaineers. You'll never get to every waterfall in this book.

Tualatin Riverkeepers, Susan Peter, Shirley Ewart and Barbara Schaffner, eds. 2002. *Exploring the Tualatin River Basin.* Corvallis: Oregon State Univ. Press. A surprisingly comprehensive guide for a small where-to-go book; covers a major part of the Portland area.

Walter, Sunny and Janet O'Mara. 2001. *Washington Nature Weekends.* Guilford, Connecticut: Globe Pequot Press. Fifty-two nature adventures in Washington.

Weston, Jim and David Stirling. 1986. *The Naturalist's Guide to the Victoria Region.* Victoria, British Columbia: Victoria Natural History Society. A great "it's got it all" nature guide; out of print; if you ever see a copy for under $20—grab it.

Yuskavitch, Jim. 2000. *Oregon Nature Weekends.* Helena, Montana: Falcon. Fifty-two nature adventures in Oregon.

Bird identification, field guides

Campbell, Eileen, Wayne Campbell and Ronald McLaughlin. 1991. *Waterbirds of the Strait of Georgia*. Delta, British Columbia: B.C. Waterfowl Society. A great little booklet for one of the best waterbird areas in the Northwest.

Cannings, Richard, Tom Aversa, and Hal Opperman. 2005. *Birds of Southwestern British Columbia*. Surrey, British Columbia: Heritage House. The latest in a series of regional bird guides edited by Hal Opperman; all have outstanding photos and plenty of good natural history information; see the Morse and Nehls entries.

Davis, James L. 1990. *Familiar Bird Songs of the Northwest*. Audio cassette. Portland, Oregon: Audubon Society of Portland. Beginning guide to the most common bird songs. Available from the Audubon Society of Portland.

Dunne, Peter, David Sibley, and Clay Sutton. 1988. *Hawks in Flight*. Boston: Houghton Mifflin. Excellent for identifying raptors by gestalt.

Morse, Robert, Tom Aversa, and Hal Opperman. 2003. *Birds of the Puget Sound Region*. Olympia, Washington: R.W. Morse. The first of the Opperman series; the best photographic identification guides I have seen. Most of the birds and the photos in each of the three books are the same so just buy the one most useful to you.

Nehls, Harry, Tom Aversa, and Hal Opperman. 2004. *Birds of the Willamette Valley Region*. Olympia, Washington: R.W. Morse. See the Cannings and Morse entries; these books are excellent for beginning and intermediate bird watchers.

Paulson, Dennis. 1993. *Shorebirds of the Pacific Northwest*. Seattle: Univ. of Washington Press. Complete coverage for identification of a difficult group.

Peterson, Roger T. 1990. *A Field Guide to Western Birds*. 3rd ed. Peterson Field Guides. Boston: Houghton Mifflin. Still my all-around favorite identification guide for the West.

Sander, Thomas. 2007. *Bird Songs of the Pacific States*. Ithaca, NY, Cornell Laboratory of Ornithology. Bird songs of the designated region are organized by habitat, which is more helpful than by family.

Sibley, David. 2001. *The Sibley Guide to Birds*. New York: Alfred A. Knopf. This is "Big Sibley," the most complete, detailed identification book for North American birds. This advanced guide can be overwhelming for beginners. Bigger and heavier than other field guides, making it difficult to carry, but the ultimate identification resource.

Sibley, David. 2003. *Sibley Field Guide to Birds of Western North America*. New York: Alfred A. Knopf. This is "Little Sibley," an edited, much smaller version of "Big Sibley" for western birds. Comparable to the Peterson Guide *Western Birds* and good for intermediate birders. However, the illustrations and print are small.

Stokes, Donald and Lillian. 1996. *Stokes Beginner's Guide to Birds, Western Region*. Boston: Little, Brown. A good, small beginner's bird guide; all photographs.

Walton, Richard and Robert Lawson. 1990. *Birding by Ear: Western*. Peterson Field Guides. Boston: Houghton Mifflin. An audio CD "course" for learning how to identify bird song; excellent; one of a kind; the best for learning bird sounds.

Wheeler, Brian and William Clark. 2003. *A Photographic Guide to North American Raptors*. Princeton: Princeton Univ. Press. The best raptor identification guide.

Bird natural history and behavior

Elphick, Chris, John B. Dunning, Jr., and David A. Sibley, eds. 2001. *The Sibley Guide to Bird Life and Behavior*. New York: Alfred A. Knopf. Explains how and why birds do what they do; organized by families.

Kaufman, Kenn. 1996. *Lives of North American Birds*. Boston: Houghton Mifflin. A wonderful mini-encyclopedia with great information on habitat, diet, nesting, behavior, conservation, and more, for every species of bird in North America.

Kress, Stephen W. 1991. *Bird Life: A Guide to the Behavior and Biology of Birds: A Golden Guide*. New York: St. Martin's Press. One of those awesome little Golden Guides with the basics for beginners—adults or kids; a mini ornithology textbook anyone will enjoy.

Leahy, Christopher W. 2004. *The Birdwatcher's Companion to North American Birdlife*. Princeton: Princeton Univ. Press. A new version of the fabulous, entertaining encyclopedia bulging with fascinating information; 1050 pages, yet compact.

Marshall, David, Matthew Hunter, and Alan Contreras, eds. 2003. *Birds of Oregon, a General Reference*. Corvallis: Oregon State Univ. Press. A large, scholarly reference to Oregon's birds.

Stokes, Donald and Lillian Stokes. 1983, 1989. *A Guide to Bird Behavior*, Vols. 2 and 3. Boston: Little, Brown. Great books about the details in the private lives of common birds.

Stokes, Donald. 1979. *A Guide to Bird Behavior*, Vol. 1. Boston: Little, Brown. The first of the three-book series.

Wahl, Terence, William Tweit, and Steven Mlodinow, eds. 2005. *Birds of Wash-*

ington: A General Reference. Corvallis: Oregon State Univ. Press. Another large, scholarly reference; this one for Washington.

Birding guides—where to find the birds

Aitchison, Catherine J., ed., and Vancouver Natural History Society. 2001. *The Birder's Guide to Vancouver and the Lower Mainland.* Vancouver, British Columbia: Whitecap Books. An outstanding guide to one of Canada's best birding areas.

Rakestraw, John. 2007. *Birding Oregon: 44 Prime Birding Areas with More Than 200 Specific Sites.* Guilford, Connecticut: Globe Pequot Press. An up-to-date, concise, accurate guide to Oregon's best birding sites.

Lewis, Mark and Fred Sharpe. 1987. *Birding in the San Juan Islands.* Seattle: Mountaineers Books. An excellent local guide for a popular region with abundant waterbirds.

Opperman, Hal. 2003. *Birder's Guide to Washington.* Colorado Springs: American Birding Association. The most comprehensive bird-finding guide for one state yet published.

Taylor, Keith. 1998. *The Birder's Guide, British Columbia.* 2nd rev ed. Vancouver, British Columbia: Steller Press.

Taylor, Keith. 2000. *The Birder's Guide, Vancouver Island.* 5th rev ed. Vancouver, British Columbia: Steller Press.

Mammals

Reid, Fiona. 2006. *A Field Guide to the Mammals of North America.* 4th ed. Peterson Field Guides. Boston: Houghton Mifflin. The first new edition of this classic in 30 years; completely new book almost twice as big as previous versions; very impressive; covers the entire continent.

Eder, Tamara. 2002. *Mammals of Washington and Oregon.* Edmonton, Alberta: Lone Pine. The best complete guide to NW mammals for the amateur naturalist; illustrations and photos; good for all levels.

Hartson, Tamara. 1999. *Squirrels of the West.* Edmonton, Alberta: Lone Pine. The only comprehensive book for this large group of familiar mammals.

Maser, Chris. 1998. *Mammals of the Pacific Northwest: From the Coast to the High Cascades.* Corvallis: Oregon State Univ. Press. A comprehensive guide for west-side mammals.

Tuttle, Merlin. 1988. *America's Neighborhood Bats.* Austin: Univ. of Texas Press.

Verts, B. J. and Leslie Carraway. 1989. *Land Mammals of Oregon.* Berkeley: Univ. of California Press. The main scientific reference for Oregon; technical; 700 pages.

Zim, Herbert and Donald Hoffmeister. 1987. *Mammals: A Golden Guide*. New York: St. Martin's Press. One of those great little Golden Guides with the basics; very easy to use.

Animal tracking and observation skills

Brown, Tom and Brandt Morgan. 1988. *Tom Brown's Field Guide to Nature Observation and Animal Tracking*. New York: Berkley Books. A good start for this topic.

Elbroch, Mark and Eleanor Marks. 2001. *Bird Tracks and Sign: A Guide to North American Species*. Mechanicsburg, Pennsylvania: Stackpole Books. The only book on this topic for birds and the only one you'll ever need.

Elbroch, Mark. 2003. *Mammal Tracks and Sign: A Guide to North American Species*. Mechanicsburg, Pennsylvania: Stackpole Books. This awesome book is not necessarily the best to start with because it is encyclopedic in scope and may be too much for beginners. But it may be the only tracking book for mammals you'll ever need.

Halfpenny, James. 1999. *Scats and Tracks of the Pacific Coast*. Helena, Montana: Falcon Press. An excellent beginning tracking guide for our region.

Murie, Olaus J. and Mark Elbroch. 2005. *A Field Guide to Animal Tracks*. 3rd ed. Peterson Field Guides. Boston: Houghton Mifflin. Fabulous new update of the 1954 classic.

Young, Jon and Tiffany Morgan. 2007. *Animal Tracking Basics*. Mechanicsburg, PA: Stackpole Press. About nature awareness and wildlife observation in general, as well as tracking; very holistic, the big picture.

Reptiles and amphibians

Corkran, Charlotte and Chris Thoms. 2006. *Amphibians of Oregon, Washington and British Columbia*. Rev ed. Edmonton, Alberta: Lone Pine. Comprehensive for a large area; has photos of eggs and larva; the book the pros use.

Jones, Lawrence, William Leonard, and Deanna Olson, eds. 2005. *Amphibians of the Pacific Northwest*. Seattle: Seattle Audubon Society. Plenty of fabulous photos.

St. John, Alan. 2002. *Reptiles of the Northwest*. Renton, Washington: Lone Pine. Awesome book by Oregon's primo reptile man; you can tell how much Alan loves these animals.

Storm, Robert and William Leonard, eds. 1995. *Reptiles of Washington and Oregon*. Seattle: Seattle Audubon Society. Outstanding photos.

Fish and freshwater life

Cone, Joseph. 1995. *Common Fate: Endangered Salmon and the People of the Pacific Northwest*. Corvallis, Oregon: Oregon State Univ. Press. A history of salmon crisis politics in the 1980s and 1990s.

Fisheries and Oceans Canada. *Where and When to See Salmon*. Vancouver, British Columbia: Fisheries and Oceans Canada. A great little booklet that covers about 54 sites in BC, 31 of them in the range of this book. It sure would be nice if our states had something like this. Available printed or on line from www.pac.dfo-mpo.gc.ca or 1-604-666-6614.

Lichatowich, Jim. 1999. *Salmon Without Rivers: A History of the Salmon Crisis*. Washington, D.C: Island Press. Excellent history of the salmon crisis up to 1999.

Reid, George. 1987. *Pond Life: A Golden Guide*. St. Martin's Press, New York. Another one of those awesome little Golden Guides that has just what you will really find.

Steelquist, Robert. 1992. *Field Guide to the Pacific Salmon*. Seattle: Sasquatch Books. Great little booklet with the basics about our salmon.

Voshell, J. Reese Jr. 2002. *A Guide to Common Freshwater Invertebrates of North America*. Blacksburg, Virginia. McDonald & Woodward. The next big step up for water bugs from the Golden Guide *Pond Life*; outstanding.

Wolf, Edward C. and Seth Zuckerman, eds. 2003 *Salmon Nation: People, Fish, and Our Common Home*. Rev ed. Portland, Oregon: Ecotrust. A collection of essays that serve as a good primer; excellent portraits with maps of the different species of salmon.

Zim, Herbert and Hurst Shoemaker. 1987. *Fishes: A Golden Guide*. New York, New York: St. Martin's Press. Good general guide to the most common fresh- and saltwater fish.

Insects and other invertebrates

Acorn, John and Ian Sheldon. 2001. *Bugs of Oregon and Washington*. Edmonton, Alberta: Lone Pine. Great for beginners; an authoritative, funny, family bug book. Acorn also wrote *Bugs of British Columbia,* but you don't need both books because most of the bugs are the same in each.

Arnett, Ross H. and Richard L. Jacques. 1981. *Simon and Schuster's Guide to Insects*. New York: Simon and Schuster. A good collection of great photos and information.

Evans, Howard E. 1966. *Life on a Little Known Planet*. New York: E.P. Dutton Wonderful, classic bug book; out of print but easy to find used; any edition good.

Glassberg, Jeffery. 2001. *Butterflies through Binoculars: The West*. New York: Oxford Univ. Press. Easiest-to-use, serious butterfly identification book.

Haggard, Peter and Judy Haggard. 2006. *Insects of the Pacific Northwest*. Portland, Oregon: Timber Press. Awesome book with great photos of what we really see that is not always in other books; excellent selection of the most noticeable moth species.

Harper, Alice B. 1988. *The Banana Slug*. Aptos, California: Bay Leaves Press (booklet)

Levi, Herbert and Lorna Levi. 1968. *Spiders and Their Kin: A Golden Guide*. New York: St. Martin's Press. This book remains the best choice for amateur naturalists who want to identify arachnids.

Mitchell, Robert and Herbert Zim. 1964. *Butterflies and Moths: A Golden Guide*. New York: St. Martin's Press. Great for beginners; about the only book with moths.

Powell, Jerry and Charles Hogue. 1979. *California Insects*. Berkeley: Univ. of California Press. Most of their bugs are our bugs, making this is a great book for the Northwest; has much more natural history information on individual species than other insect identification books.

Stokes, Donald. 1983. *A Guide to Observing Insect Lives*. Boston: Little, Brown. Get the real inside story on the amazing and often bizarre life cycles and behaviors of some of our most common insects.

Teale, Edwin W. 1962. *The Strange Lives of Familiar Insects*. New York: Dodd, Mead. Another timeless American bug classic.

Wright, Amy. 1993. *Peterson First Guide to Caterpillars of North America*. Boston: Houghton Mifflin. This small book is the easiest to use for identifying caterpillars.

Zim, Herbert and Clarence Cottam. 1987. *Insects: A Golden Guide*. New York, New York: St. Martin's Press. A great way to get started on bugs.

Marine life

Fichter, George S. 1990. *Whales and Other Marine Mammals: A Golden Guide*. New York: St. Martin's Press. What could be better than a Golden Guide for the basics?

Gordon, David and Chuck Flaherty. 1990. *Field Guide to the Orca*. Seattle: Sasquatch Books. (booklet)

Kozloff, Eugene N. 1983. *Seashore Life of the Northern Pacific Coast*. Seattle: Univ. of Seattle. Classic comprehensive guide for years; more than just an identification guide.

Mohler, June, David S. Fox, and Bill Hastie. 1997. *Guide to Oregon's Rocky Intertidal Habitats*. Salem, Oregon: Oregon Department of Fish and Wildlife.

Excellent basic guide; available from ODFW's Web site. Includes list of good tidepooling places.

Oceanic Society. 1989. *Field Guide to the Gray Whale*. Seattle: Sasquatch Books. (booklet)

Sheldon, Ian. 1998. *Seashore of British Columbia*. Renton, Washington: Lone Pine. Excellent pocket field guide to the most common plants and animals, except birds, that you see while exploring tidepools and the coast; drawings are very clear and accurate for easy identification; great for beginners and good for our entire coast.

Yates, Steve. 1998. *Marine Wildlife: From Puget Sound through the Inside Passage*. Seattle: Sasquatch Books. All-in-one guide to animals and plants of the Salish Sea.

Zim, Herbert and Lester Ingle. 1989. *Seashores: A Golden Guide*. New York: St. Martin's Press. Another Golden Guide that is a great place to start.

Wildflower identification and plants in general

Atkinson, Scott and Fred Sharp. 1993. *Wild Plants of the San Juan Islands*. 2nd ed. Seattle: Mountaineers. Great guide to the flora in the rain shadow of the Olympic Mountains.

Camp, Pamela, Maggie McManus, et al. 1998. *Watchable Wildflowers, A Columbia Basin Guide*. Wenatchee, Washington: Bureau of Land Management. Brochure package available from the Wenatchee BLM office: (509) 665-2100.

Guard, Jennifer. 1995. *Wetland Plants of Oregon and Washington*. Vancouver, British Columbia: Lone Pine. "The Book" for this topic.

Horn, Elizabeth. 2006. *Oregon's Best Wildflower Hikes: Southwest Region*. Englewood, Colorado: Westcliffe. Detailed directions to the best spots for wildflowers in a floristically rich part of Oregon. This is one of a new type of wildflower book, the "wildflower hike book," that is the equivalent of a bird-finding guide.

Jolly, Russ. 1988. *Wildflowers of the Columbia Gorge*. Portland: Oregon Historical Society. I have relied on Russ and his book for much of the information about plants in the Gorge. Features 755 species, organized by family. Includes color photographs, habitat description, blooming times and specific locations. Contains lists of blooming plants by month, site descriptions, a map including habitat zones, and suggested tours from March to October. Many of the flowers covered here are found in other parts of the NW. This is not really an identification guide, but more of a catalog and a where-to-find-it guide.

Kruckeberg, Arthur, Karen Sykes, and Craig Romano. 2004. *Wildflower Hikes: Washington*. Seattle: Mountaineers. Where to find the best wildflower displays throughout Washington.

Lyons, Chess P. and Bill Merilees. 1995. *Trees, Shrubs, and Flowers to Know in Washington and British Columbia*. Redmond, Washington: Lone Pine Press.

Niehaus, Theodore F. and Charles L. Ripper. 1976. *A Field Guide to Pacific States Wildflowers*. Peterson Field Guides. Boston: Houghton Mifflin. General, but covers a wide range. Many think it has the best identification key for plant families, a basic step to learning plant identification. Works better the farther south you go in our region, but it can get you to at least the right family and often to the genus.

Pojar, Jim and Andy MacKinnon. 1994. *Plants of the Pacific Northwest Coast*. Edmonton, Alberta: Lone Pine. Popular guide; covers the areas west of the Cascades from mid-Oregon to Alaska and includes trees, shrubs, flowers, mosses, and lichens. A Canadian book that works better the farther north you are in our region.

Ross, Robert A. and Henrietta L. Chambers. 1988. *Wildflowers of the Western Cascades*. Portland: Timber Press. Includes a great selection of the most typical flowers of the western Cascades; essentially a guide to Iron Mountain in Oregon.

Strickler, Dee. 1993. *Wayside Wildflowers of the Pacific Northwest*. Columbia Falls, Montana: Flower Press. Includes impressive, large photos of the most commonly seen wildflowers in a wide range.

Taylor, Ronald J. 1992. *Sagebrush Country: A Wildflower Sanctuary*. Helena: Mountain Press. An essential wildflower book for the east-side, sagebrush steppe ecoregion.

Taylor, Ronald J. and George W. Douglas. 1995. *Mountain Plants of the Pacific Northwest*. Missoula: Mountain Press. Excellent photo guide organized by plant families with good family keys in the back; covers all vascular plants.

Turner, Mark and Phyllis Gustafson. 2006. *Wildflowers of the Pacific Northwest*. Portland, Oregon: Timber Press. Easy to use, with a fairly comprehensive photo identification guide.

Wuerthner, George. 2001. *Oregon's Best Wildflower Hikes: Northwest Region*. Englewood, Colorado: Westcliffe. Directions for getting to the best spots for wildflowers and descriptions of what you will see.

Trees and forests

Arno, Stephen and Ramona Hammerly. 1977. *Northwest Trees*. Seattle: Mountaineers. Best information on our trees, but not for identification; awesome drawings.

Cissel, Diane and John Cissel. 1993. *50 Old-Growth Day Hikes in the Mount Hood National Forest*. Eugene, Oregon: Old-Growth Day Hikes. Includes good maps with extensive information.

Cissel, Diane and John Cissel. 1996. *50 Old-Growth Day Hikes in the Southern Washington Cascades*. Eugene, Oregon: Old-Growth Day Hikes. One of a series.

Cissel, Diane, John Cissel, and Peter Eberhardt. 1991. *50 Old-Growth Day Hikes in the Willamette National Forest*. Eugene, Oregon: Old-Growth Day Hikes. One of a series.

Dittmar Family for The Wilderness Society. 1996. *Visitors' Guide to Ancient Forests of Washington*. 2nd ed. Seattle: Mountaineers. Where to go to walk in ancient forests.

Eifert, Larry. 2000. *Field Guide to Old-Growth-Forests*. Seattle: Sasquatch Books. A great booklet that sums up the basics nicely for Northwest ancient forests.

Maser, Chris. 1989. *Forest Primeval: The Natural History of an Ancient Forest*. San Francisco: Sierra Club Books. A classic.

Norse, Elliott. 1990. *Ancient Forests of the Pacific Northwest*. Washington, DC: Island Press. Another landmark classic on old-growth forests.

Petrides, George and Olivia Petrides. 1992. *Western Trees*. Peterson Field Guides. Boston: Houghton Mifflin. A good general identification guide for the western United States.

Petrides, George and Olivia Petrides. 1998. *Trees of the Pacific Northwest*. Williamston, Michigan: Explorer Press. A very condensed, smaller, "mini-Petrides" backpacker version of *Western Trees* with some common introduced trees included.

Stoltmann, Randy. 1996. *Hiking the Ancient Forests of British Columbia and Washington*. Vancouver, British Columbia: Lone Pine. The only walking guide for BC's old-growth forests.

Van Pelt, Robert. 2001. *Forest Giants of the Pacific Coast*. Vancouver, British Columbia: Global Forest Society. Portraits of the biggest individual trees of the 20 largest species of conifers growing in North America, which includes many of the tallest trees in the world.

Wood, Wendell. 1991. *A Walking Guide to Oregon's Ancient Forests*. Portland: Oregon Natural Resources Council. The most complete guide for Oregon by a legendary forest conservationist.

Fungus

Arora, David. 1986. *Mushrooms Demystified: A Comprehensive Guide to the Fleshy Fungi*. Berkeley, California: Ten Speed Press. The ultimate reference for our mushrooms. Intimidating, but it does have identification keys. If you reach the point where you can use this book, you have arrived as a true fungus fancier.

Arora, David. 1991. *All that the Rain Promises, and More: A Hip Pocket Guide to Western Mushrooms*. Berkeley, California: Ten Speed Press. This is David's entertaining beginning mushroom book and the best place to start. It has a basic key for the most conspicuous and common fungi of interest. This book has given me many good laughs thanks to David's great sense of humor. He really is a fun guy—sorry, I have always wanted to put that in print.

McKnight, Kent and Vera McKnight. 1987. *A Field Guide to Mushrooms: North America*. Peterson Field Guides. Boston: Houghton Mifflin. Useful book somewhere between Arora's two books in ease of use.

Sept, J. Duane. 2006. *Common Mushrooms of the Northwest*. Sechelt, British Columbia: Calllypso. Beginner's guide with great photos of a limited number of distinctive species.

RESOURCES

These are the names, address, phone numbers, and Web sites of agencies and organizations that can be helpful for your adventures. As the budgets and staff of these agencies decreases, more information is becoming available only on Web sites, there are fewer maps and other printed materials available, and fewer personnel are available to answer questions by phone. Public agencies in both the United States and Canada are moving rapidly to self-service Internet-based public information systems that may have dated and limited information. British Columbia, in particular, has moved quickly to a Web-based public information system and clearly the easiest way to get information about parks and wildlife in BC is now by Internet. In addition to the provincial government Web sites there are numerous commercial tourism Web sites. Web sites and e-mail addresses change more often than phone numbers and mailing addresses so be prepared to do some searching on the omnipresent Internet.

Rare Bird Alerts (RBAs)

The transition from Rare Bird Alert phone numbers to Web sites may mean that some phone numbers will no longer be active when you call, and the Web sites may have changed. The trend to Web sites may be fine if you're at home and have a computer, but it's certainly not useful if you're on the road and only have access to a phone.

Here is a tip to find the latest birding reports. In the United States go to the National Audubon Society Web site: www.Audubon.org. On the navigation bar at the top, click "States, Centers & Chapters," and then "States & Chapters." On the "United States State Office and Local Chapters" page, use the "Select State to View" pull-down menu on the right to find the chapter nearest the area in which you are interested. On the chapter's Web site you'll find information on how to access and report bird sightings. For British Columbia, go to the Federation of British Columbia Naturalists Web site: www.bcnature.ca.

OREGON

Audubon Society of Portland's RBA: 503-292-0661, ext. 200

Oregon Field Ornithologists' Oregon Birders On-Line (OBAL): www.oregonbirds.org

WASHINGTON

Washington Ornithological Society's Bird-
  Box: 206-281-9172
Tweeters list serve (hosted by Burke
  Museum): www.scn.org/tweeters/
Washington, Columbia Basin: www.groups.
  yahoo.com/group/LCBirds/

BRITISH COLUMBIA

Vancouver and Lower Mainland:
  604-737-3074, option 4;
  www.naturalhistory.bc.ca/VNHS/
Victoria and southern Vancouver Island:
  250-592-3381; www.vicnhs.bc.ca

Tides and Weather

Canada tides: www.waterlevels.gc.ca
Canada weather: www.weatheroffice.ec.gc.ca
US tides: www.tidesonline.nos.noaa.gov
US weather: www.nws.noaa.gov

Ferries

These ferries take cars, foot passengers, and
bicycles. Other ferries that take only passengers may be faster, but they aren't conducive
for wildlife watching. With all ferries be sure
you have the latest schedule for the season
you are traveling and ask when you should
get in line for your departure time.

The Ferry Traveller
2250 York, Suite 301
Vancouver, BC V6K 2C6
604-733-9113
www.ferrytravel.com
This Web site is an excellent all-in-one guide to
BC and Washington ferries. The information is
also available as an inexpensive booklet.

BC Ferries
1112 Fort St
Victoria, BC V8V 4V2
888-BCFERRY (233-3779) toll free
www.bcferries.com
An awesome system; the largest ferries are

like being on the QEII. Reservations are
available for certain routes only; others are
first come, first served.

Washington State Ferries
2901 3rd Ave, Suite 500
Seattle, WA 98121
888-808-7977 (toll free)
206-464-6400 (in Seattle)
www.wsdot.wa.gov/ferries
Reservations are limited to trips between
Seattle and Sydney, BC.

Black Ball Transport
101 E Railroad Ave
Port Angeles, WA 98362
360-457-4491
Also: 430 Belleville St
Victoria BC V8V-1W9
Victoria phone: 250-386-2202
www.cohoferry.com
M.V. Coho travels between Port Angeles and
Victoria. Reservations can be made either
online or by telephone; requires extra fee.

Victoria Clipper
800-888-2535 toll free
www/victoriaclipper.com
Fast, year-round service between Seattle and
Victoria. Limited service between Seattle
and San Juan Islands, June–September.
Reservations.

US Federal Agencies

Information centers

Nature of the Northwest Information Center
800 NE Oregon St, Suite 177
Portland, OR 97232
503-872-2750
www.naturenw.org
Information and maps for national forests
in OR and WA plus USGS, BLM and state
agency maps for OR. Bookstore.

Outdoor Recreation Information Center
US Forest Service and National Park Service
222 Yale Ave N
Seattle, WA 98109
206-470-4060
www.nps.gov/ccso/oric.htm
Inside Seattle's main REI store, second floor.
Information and maps for US Forest Service
and National Park Service areas in OR and
WA and some WA state parks. Bookstore.

National Scenic Byways Program, Department of Transportation
1200 New Jersey Ave SE
HEPN-50
Washington, DC 20590
800-429-9297
www.byways.org

National Park Service (NPS)

Crater Lake NP
PO Box 7
Crater Lake, OR 97604
541-594-3000
www.nps.gov/crla

Mount Rainier NP
55210 238th Ave E
Ashford, WA 98304
360-569-2211
www.nps.gov/mora

North Cascades NP
Ross Lake and Lake Chelan National
  Recreation Areas
810 State Route 20
Sedro Woolley, WA 98284
360-854-7200
www.mps.gov/noca

San Juan Island National Historical Park
PO Box 429
Friday Harbor, WA 98250
360-378-2902
www.nps.gov/sajh/

Olympic NP
600 E Park Ave
Port Angeles, WA 98362
360-565-3130
800-833-6388
www.nps.gov/olym

Oregon Caves National Monument
19000 Caves Hwy
Cave Junction, OR 97523
541-592-2100
www.nps.gov/orca

US Forest Service (USFS)

USFS Pacific Northwest Region
333 SW 1st Ave
Portland, OR 97208
503-808-2468
www.fs.fed.us/r6/
For visitor information contact Nature of the
Northwest Information Center and Outdoor
Recreation Information Center.
Celebrating Wildflowers Web Sites: www.
  fs.fed.us/wildflowers/regions/pacific
  northwest
  www.fs.fed.us/wildflowers

Columbia River Gorge National Scenic Area
902 Wasco Ave, Suite 200
Hood River, OR 97031
541-308-1700
www.fs.fed.us/r6/columbia/forest

Colville National Forest
765 S Main
Colville, WA 99114
509-684-7000
www.fs.fed.us/r6/colville

Spokane Information Center
(Colville National Forest)
1103 N Fancher Rd
Spokane, WA 99212
509-536-1251
Bookstore with maps and other information
for national forests in the Northwest.

Deschutes National Forest
1001 SW Emkay
Bend, OR 97702
541-383-5300
www.fs.fed.us/r6/centraloregon

Lava Lands Visitor Center
(Deschutes National Forest)
58201 S Hwy 97
Bend, OR 97707
541-593-2421
www.fs.fed.us/r6/centraloregon/
    newberrynvm/lavalands

Fremont-Winema National Forests
1301 South G St
Lakeview, OR 97630
541-947-2151
www.fs.fed.us/r6/frewin

Gifford Pinchot National Forest
10600 NE 51st Circle
Vancouver, WA 98682
360-891-5000
www.fs.fed.us/r6/gpnf

Mount Adams Ranger District
(Gifford Pinchot National Forest)
2455 Hwy 141
Trout Lake, WA 98650
509-395-3400

Malheur National Forest
431 Patterson Bridge Rd
John Day, OR 97845
541-575-3000
www.fs.fed.us/r6/malheur

Mount Baker-Snoqualmie National Forest
21905 64th Ave W
Mountlake Terrace, WA 98043
425-775-9702
800-627-0062
www.fs.fed.us/r6/mbs

Mount Hood National Forest
16400 Champion Way
Sandy, OR 97055
503-668-1700
www.fs.fed.us/r6/mthood

Mount Hood Information Center
(Mount Hood National Forest)
65000 E Hwy 26
Welches, OR 97067
503-622-4822
888-622-4822

Mount St. Helens National Volcanic
  Monument
42218 NE Yale Bridge Rd
Amboy, WA 98601
360-449-7800
www.fs.fed.us/gpnf/mshnvm

Ochoco National Forest
3160 NE 3rd St
Prineville, OR 97754
541-416-6500
www.fs.fed.us/r6/centraloregon

Okanogan National Forest
1240 S Second Ave
Okanogan, WA 98841
509-826-3275
www.fs.fed.us/r6/oka

Methow Valley Visitor Center
(Okanogan National Forest)
49 Hwy 20
Winthrop, WA 98862
509-996-4000

Olympic National Forest
1835 Black Lake Blvd SW
Olympia, WA 98512
360-956-2402
www.fs.fed.us/r6/olympic

Rogue River-Siskiyou National Forest
333 W 8th St
Medford, OR 97501
541-858-2200
www.fs.fed.us/r6/rogue-siskiyou

Rogue River Smullin Visitor Center
(Rogue Wild and Scenic River)
14335 Galice Rd
Merlin, OR 97532
541-479-3735
www.blm.gov/or/resources/recreation/
  rogue/

Siuslaw National Forest
4077 SW Research Way
Corvallis, OR 97339
541-750-7000
www.fs.fed.us/r6/siuslaw

Cape Perpetua Visitor Center
(Siuslaw National Forest)
2400 US 101
Yachats, OR 97498
541-547-3289

Umatilla National Forest
2517 SW Hailey Ave
Pendleton, OR 97801
541-278-3716
www.fs.fed.us/r6/uma

Umpqua National Forest
2900 Stewart Pkwy
Roseburg, OR 97470
541-672-6601
www.fs.fed.us/r6/umpqua

Wallowa-Whitman National Forest
1550 Dewey Ave
Baker City, OR 97814
514-523-6391
www.fs.fed.us/r6/w-w

Hells Canyon NRA and Wallowa Mountains
  Visitor Center
(Wallowa-Whitman National Forest)
88401 Hwy 82
Enterprise, OR 97828
541-426-4978
www.fs.fed.us/hellscanyon/

Wenatchee National Forest
215 Melody Ln
Wenatchee, WA 98801
509-664-9200
www.fs.fed.us/r6/wenatchee

Willamette National Forest
211 E 7th Ave
Eugene, OR 97401
541-225-6300
www.fs.fed.us/r6/willamette

US Fish and Wildlife Service (USFWS)

Pacific Region Office
911 NE 11th
Portland, OR 97232
503-231-6828
www.fws.gov/pacific/

Columbia NWR
735 E Main St
PO Drawer F
Othello, WA 99344
509-488-2668
www.fws.gov/columbiarefuge/

Hart Mountain National Antelope Refuge
PO Box 111
Lakeview, OR 97630
541-947-3315
www.fws.gov/sheldonhartmtn/

Julia Butler Hansen Refuge for the
  Columbian White-Tailed Deer
PO Box 566
Cathlamet, WA 98612
360-795-3915
www.fws.gov/pacific/refuges/

Klamath Basin NWRs
4009 Hill Rd
Tulelake, CA 96134
530-667-2231
www.fws.gov/klamathbasinrefuges/

Leavenworth NFH
12790 Fish Hatchery Rd
Leavenworth, WA 98826
509-548-7641
www.fws.gov/leavenworth/
Wenatchee River Salmon Festival: www.
  salmonfest.org

Little Pend Oreille NWR
1310 Bear Creek Rd
Colville, WA 99114
509-684-8384
www.fws.gov/littlependoreille/

Little White Salmon NFH
56961 State Route 14
Cook, WA 98605
509-538-2755
www.fws.gov/gorgefish/littlewhite/

Malheur NWR
36391 Sodhouse Ln
Princeton, Oregon 97721
541-493-2612
www.fws.gov/malheur

Mid-Columbia River NWR Complex
(Cold Springs, Conboy, McKay Creek,
  McNary, Toppenish, Umatilla)
PO Box 1447
Richland, WA 99352
509-371-9212
www.fws.gov/midcolumbiariver/

Nisqually and Grays Harbor NWRs
100 Brown Farm Rd
Olympia, WA 98516
360-753-9467
www.fws.gov/nisqually/
www.fws.gov/graysharbor/
Grays Harbor Shorebird Festival: www.
  shorebirdfestival.com

Oregon Coast NWR Complex
(Cape Meares, Three Arch Rocks, Siletz Bay,
  Bandon Marsh)
2127 SE Marine Science Dr
Newport, OR 97365
541-867-4550
www.fws.gov/oregoncoast/
Oregon Shorebird Festival: www.fws.gov/
  oregoncoast/shorebirdfestival.htm

Ridgefield NWR
28908 NW Main Ave
PO Box 457
Ridgefield, WA 98642
360-887-4106
www.fws.gov/ridgefieldrefuges/

Turnbull NWR
26010 S Smith Rd
Cheney, WA 99004
509-235-4723
www.fws.gov/turnbull/

Willamette Valley NWR Complex
(Ankeny, Baskett Slough, Finley)
26208 Finley Refuge Rd
Corvallis, OR 97333
541-757-7236
http://pacific.fws.gov/WillametteValley

Willapa NWR Complex
3888 SR 101
Ilwaco, WA 98624
360-484-3482
www.fws.gov/willapa/

Bureau of Land Management (BLM)

Oregon State Office, BLM
333 SW 1st Ave
Portland, OR 97204
503-808-6002
www.blm.gov/or/

Burns District Office, BLM
(Steens Mountain, and Alvord and Malheur
  areas)
28910 Hwy 20 West
Hines, OR 97738
541-573-4400
www.blm.gov/or/districts/burns/

Medford District Office, BLM
(Table Rocks, SW Oregon)
3040 Biddle Rd
Medford, OR 97504
541-618-2200
www.blm.gov/or/districts/medford/
Table Rocks: www.blm.gov/or/resources/
  recreation/tablerock/index.php

Roseburg District Office, BLM
(Deadline Falls)
777 NW Garden Valley Blvd
Roseburg, OR 97470
541-440-4930
www.blm.gov/or/districts/roseburg/

Spokane District, BLM (all of Washington)
1103 N Fancher Rd.
Spokane, WA 99212
509-536-1200
www.blm.gov/or/districts/spokane

Yaquina Head Outstanding Natural Area
750 Lighthouse Dr
Newport, OR 97365
541-574-3100
www.blm.gov/or/resources/recreation/
  yaquina/

National Estuarine Reserve Research System

Padilla Bay National Estuarine Reserve
Breazeale Interpretive Center
10441 Bayview-Edison Rd
Mount Vernon, WA 98273
360-428-1558
www.padillabay.gov

South Slough National Estuarine Research
  Reserve
PO Box 5417
Charleston, OR 97420
541-888-5558
www.oregon.gov/dsl/ssnerr/

US National Private Nonprofit Conservation Organizations

HawkWatch International
1800 SW Temple, #226
Salt Lake City, UT 84115
800-726-4295
www.hawkwatch.org

National Audubon Society
(US Christmas Bird Counts)
700 Broadway
New York, NY 10003
212-979-3000
www.audubon.org
Great Backyard Bird Count: www.
  birdsource.org/

National Wildlife Refuge Association
1901 Pennsylvania Ave NW, Suite 407
Washington, DC 20006
877-396-6972 (toll free)
www.refugenet.org

Xerces Society
(Conservation of insects and other
  invertebrates)
4828 SE Hawthorne Blvd
Portland, OR 97215
503-232-6639
www.xerces.org

Oregon State Agencies

Oregon Department of Fish and Wildlife (ODFW)

The directory *Visitor's Guide: Oregon's Fish Hatcheries and Wildlife Management Areas,* a comprehensive listing of ODFW managed areas, is available from the main office, regional offices, or Web site.

ODFW Headquarters and Main Office
3406 Cherry Ave NE
Salem, OR 97303
503-947-6000
800-720-6339 (toll free in Oregon)
www.dfw.state.or.us

ODFW High Desert Region Office
61374 Parrell Rd
Bend, OR 97702
541-388-6363

ODFW Southwest Region Office
4192 N Umpqua Hwy
Roseburg, OR 97470
541-440-3353

ODFW Northwest Region Office
17330 SE Evelyn St
Clackamas, OR 97015
503-657-2000

ODFW Northeast Region Office
107 20th St
La Grande, OR 97850
541-963-2138

Bonneville Fish Hatchery
70543 NE Herman Loop
Cascade Locks, OR 97014
541-374-8393

Elkhorn WA
61846 Powder River Ln
North Powder, OR 97867
541-898-2826

Jewell Meadows WA
79878 Hwy 202
Seaside, OR 97138
503-755-2264

Klamath WA
1850 Miller Island Rd W
Klamath Falls, OR 97603
541-883-5734

Sauvie Island WA
18330 NW Sauvie Island Rd
Portland, OR 97231
503-621-3488

Summer Lake WA
53447 Hwy 31
Summer Lake, OR 97640
541-943-3152

Wenaha WA
85060 Grande Ronde Rd
Enterprise, OR 97828
541-828-7721

Oregon state parks

Get the latest edition of Oregon Parks and Heritage Guide from area offices.

Oregon Parks and Recreation Department
725 Summer St NE, Suite C
Salem, OR 97301
800-551-6949 (park information)
800-452-5687 (camping reservations)
www.oregonstateparks.org

Oregon State Parks, Area 1
North Coast
401 SW 9th St
Newport, OR 97365
541-265-8179

Oregon State Parks, Area 2
Willamette Valley and Columbia Gorge
2501 SW 1st Ave, Suite 100
Portland, OR 97201
503-872-5288

Oregon State Parks, Area 3
Central and Western Oregon
84505 US 101 S
Florence, OR 97439
541-997-5755

Oregon State Parks, Area 4
Southern and Western Oregon
89814 Cape Arago Hwy
Coos Bay, OR 97420
541-888-3778, ext. 26

Oregon State Parks, Area 5
Central Oregon
1645 NE Forbes Rd, Suite 112
Bend, OR 97701
541-388-6316

Oregon State Parks, Area 6
Eastern Oregon
1705 Main St, Suite 101
Baker City, OR 97814
541-523-2499, ext. 3

Silver Falls State Park
20024 Silver Falls Hwy SE (Hwy 214)
Sublimity, OR 97385
503-873-8681

Tryon Creek State Natural Area
11321 SW Terwilliger Blvd
Portland, OR 97219
503-636-4398
www.tryonfriends.org

Whale Watching Center
119 SW US Hwy 101
Depoe Bay, OR 97341
541-765-3407
www.whalespoken.org

Oregon regional, county, and municipal agencies

West Eugene Wetlands
Managed by Willamette Resources & Educational Network (WREN)
751 S Danebo Ave
Eugene, OR 97402
541-683-6494
www.wewetlands.org

Jackson Bottom Wetlands Preserve
Managed by the city of Hillsboro
2600 SW Hillsboro Hwy
PO Box 3002
Hillsboro, OR 97123
503-681-6206
www.jacksonbottom.org

Leach Botanical Garden
6704 SE 122nd Ave
Portland, OR 97236
503-823-9503
www.leachgarden.org

Metro Regional Parks and Greenspaces
600 NE Grand Ave
Portland, OR 97232
503-797-1850
www.oregonmetro.gov
Publishes the *GreenScene* newsletter four times a year.

Portland Parks and Recreation
(Forest Park, Oaks Bottom)
1120 SW 5th, Room 1302
Portland, OR 97204
www.portlandonline.com/parks
503-823-7529

Hoyt Arboretum Visitor Center
4000 SW Fairview Blvd
Portland, OR 97221
503-865-8733
www.hoytarboretum.org

Mount Pisgah Arboretum
34901 Frank Parrish Rd
Eugene, OR 97405
541-747-4110
www.efn.org/~mtpisgah/

Oregon Nonprofit Organizations

Audubon Society chapters in Oregon
All chapters of the National Audubon Society can be found on the Web site: www.audubon.org.

Audubon Society of Portland
5151 NW Cornell Rd
Portland, OR 97210
503-292-6855
www.audubonportland.org
Audubon House is a multipurpose visitor center, meeting hall, and natural history bookstore. Open every day from 10 a.m. to 6 p.m., 5 p.m. on Sundays. The trails in the sanctuary are open from dawn to dusk.

Friends of Haystack Rock
PO Box 1222
Cannon Beach, OR 97110
www.friendsofhaystackrock.org

Harney County Chamber of Commerce
76 E Washington St
Burns, OR 97720
541-573-2636
www.harneycounty.com
John Scharff Migratory Bird Festival: www.migratorybirdfestival.com

Klamath Wingwatchers, Inc.
PO Box 251
Klamath Falls, OR 97601
www.winterwingsfest.org
Winter Wings Festival: www.winterwingsfest.org

Native Plant Society of Oregon
PO Box 902
Eugene, OR 97440
www.npsoregon.org

The Nature Conservancy of Oregon
821 SE 14th Ave
Portland, OR 97214
503-802-8100
www.nature.org/oregon

Opal Creek Ancient Forest Center
917 SW Oak, Suite 412
Portland, OR 97205
503-892-2782
www.opalcreek.org

Oregon Field Ornithologists
PO Box 10373
Eugene, OR 97440
www.oregonbirds.org

Washington State Agencies

Washington Department of Fish and Wildlife (WDFW)

WDFW Main Office
Office: 1111 Washington St SE
Mailing: 600 Capitol Way North
Olympia, WA 98501
360-902-2200
www.wdfw.wa.gov
Use this Web site for regional offices and wildlife areas.

WDFW Region 1, Eastern
2315 North Discovery Place
Spokane Valley, WA 99216
509-892-1001

WDFW Region 2, North Central
1550 Alder St NW
Ephrata, WA 98823
509-754-4624

WDFW Region 3, South Central
1701 S 24th Ave
Yakima, WA 98902
509-575-2740

WDFW Region 4, North Puget Sound
16018 Mill Creek Blvd
Mill Creek, WA 98012
425-775-1311

WDFW Region 5, Southwest
2108 Grand Blvd
Vancouver, WA 98661
360-696-6211

WDFW Region 6, Coastal
48 Devonshire Rd
Montesano, WA 98563
360-249-4628

Washington state parks

State Parks Headquarters
7150 Cleanwater Dr SW
Olympia, WA 98504
360-902-8844 (information)
888-226-7688 (reservations; toll free)
www.parks.wa.gov

Winter Recreation Program, State Parks
7150 Cleanwater Dr SW
PO Box 42662
Olympia, WA 98504
360-586-6643
www.parks.wa.gov/winter/

Washington State Parks
Southwest Region
11838 Tilley Rd S
Olympia, WA 98512
360-956-4800

Washington State Parks
Puget Sound Region
1602 29th St SE
Auburn, WA 98002
206-931-3907

Washington State Parks
Northwest Region
220 N Walnut St
PO Box 487
Burlington, WA 98233
360-755-9231

Washington State Parks
Eastern Region
2201 N Duncan Dr
Wenatchee, WA 98801
509-662-0420

Riverside SP
RSP Foundation
9711 W Charles
Nine Miles Falls, WA 99026
509-465-5064
www.riversidestatepark.org

Washington State Department of Natural Resources (DNR)

Natural Areas Program
Washington Dept. of Natural Resources
1111 Washington St SE
PO Box 47014
Olympia, WA 98504
360-902-1600
www.dnr.wa.gov/nap/
Manages state land for wildlife and habitat values.

Pacific Cascade Region DNR
(Mima Mounds Natural Area Preserve and
  McLane Creek Nature Trail)
601 Bond Rd
PO Box 280
Castle Rock, WA 98611
360-577-2025

Washington regional, county, and municipal agencies

City of Bellevue
Parks and Community Services Dept.
PO Box 90012
Bellevue, WA 98009
425-452-6881
www.ci.bellevue.wa.us/parks/
Mercer Slough: www.pacsci.org/slough

Clallam County Parks
(Salt Creek County Park)
PO Box 863
Port Angeles, WA 98362
360-417-2291
www.clallam.net/park/

Discovery Park Visitors Center
Seattle Parks and Recreation
3801 W Government Way
Seattle, WA 98199
206-386-4236
www.cityofseattle.net/parks/

San Juan County Parks
350 Court St, #8
Friday Harbor, WA 98250
360-378-8420 (information)
360-378-1842 (camping reservations;
  seasonal)

Tacoma Nature Center
1919 S Tyler
Tacoma, WA 98405
253-591-6439
www.metroparkstacoma.org

Washington Nonprofit Organizations

Audubon Society chapters in Washington
All chapters of the National Audubon Society can be found on the Web site: www.audubon.org.

Audubon Washington (state office)
1411 4th Ave, Suite 920
Seattle, WA 98101
206-652-2444
www.wa.audubon.org

Audubon Society of Seattle
35th Ave NE
Seattle, WA 98115
206-523-4483
www.seattleaudubon.org

Herons Forever
www.heronsforever.org
Stewards of the herons at Black River.

Heron Habitat Helpers
PO Box 99815
Seattle, WA 98139
206-284-6489
www.heronhelpers.org
Stewards of the herons in the Kiwanis Ravine.

Methow Valley Sport Trails Association
PO Box 147
Winthrop, WA 98862
509-996-3287
800-682-5787 (recorded snow conditions,
  events, and more)
www.mvsta.com

The Nature Conservancy of Washington
1917 1st Ave
Seattle, WA 98101
206-343-4344
www.nature.org/washington/

Othello Sandhill Crane Festival
449 E Cedar
PO Box 542
Othello, WA 99344
866-726-3445
www.othellosandhillcranefestival.org

Port Townsend Marine Science Center
Fort Worden State Park
532 Battery Way
Port Townsend, WA 98368
360-385-5582
800-566-3932
www.ptmsc.org

Skagit River Bald Eagle Awareness Team
   (SRBEAT)
(Upper Skagit Bald Eagle Festival)
7460 Dillard St, #B
PO Box 571
Concrete, WA 98237
360-853-7283
www.skagiteagle.org

Washington Native Plant Society
6310 NE 74th St, Suite 215E
Seattle, WA 98115
206-527-3210
888-288-8022 (toll free)
www.wnps.org

Washington Ornithological Society
PO Box 31783
Seattle, WA 98103
www.wos.org

The Whale Museum
62 First St N
P.O. Box 945
Friday Harbor, WA 98250
360-378-4710
www.whalemuseum.org

These two institutes offer a wide variety
of educational programs about nature:

North Cascades Institute
810 State Route 20
Sedro Woolley, WA 98284
360-856-5700, ext 209
www.ncascades.org

Olympic Park Institute
111 Barnes Point Rd
Port Angeles, WA 98363
360-928-3720
www.yni.org/opi/

Canada Federal Agencies
Parks Canada (national parks)

Pacific Rim NP
Box 280
Ucluelet, BC V0R 3A0
250-726-7721
www.pc.gc.ca/pn-np/bc/pacificrim/
Pacific Rim Whale Festival: www.pacificrim
   whalefestival.org

Fisheries and Oceans Canada

Fisheries and Ocean Canada
Capilano Salmon Hatchery
4500 Capilano Park Rd
North Vancouver, BC V7R 4L3
604-666-1790
www-heb.pac.dfo-mpo.
   gc.ca/facilities/capilano

Chilliwack River Hatchery
55205 Chilliwack Lake Rd
Chilliwack, BC V4Z 1A7
604-858-7227
www-heb.pac.dfo-mpo.
   gc.ca/facilities/chilliwack

Environment Canada—Environmental Conservation Branch (Canadian Wildlife Service)

Canadian Wildlife Service
Pacific Wildlife Research Center
5421 Robertson Rd
Delta, BC V4K 3N2
604-940-4700
www.pyr.ec.gc.ca/en/wildlife

Canada National Nonprofit Organizations

Bird Studies Canada
PO Box 160
Port Rowan, Ontario N0E 1M0
888-448-2473
www.bsc-eoc.org/bscmain.html
Coordinates Christmas Bird Count

British Columbia Provincial Agencies

Ministry of Environment

BC Parks (Provincial Parks System)
PO Box 9398 STN PROV GOV
Victoria, BC V8W 9M9
www.env.gov.bc.ca/bcparks/

BC Wildlife Viewing Guide
www.env.gov.bc.ca/fw/wldview

Fish and Wildlife Branch Headquarters
PO Box 9374, STN PROV GOV
Victoria, BC V8W 9M4
250-387-9771
www.env.gov.bc.ca/fw/

Fish and Wildlife Branch
Vancouver Island Region
2080 Labieux Rd
Nanaimo, BC V9T 6J9
250-751-3100
http://wlapwww.gov.bc.ca/vir

Fish and Wildlife Branch
Lower Mainland Region
2nd Floor
10470 152nd St
Surrey, BC V3R 0Y3
604-582-5200
http://wlapwww.gov.bc.ca/sry

British Columbia regional agencies

Greater Vancouver Regional District
Parks Department
4330 Kingsway
Burnaby, BC V5H 4G8
604-432-6200
www.gvrd.bc.ca/parks

Capital Regional District
Parks Department
490 Atkins Ave
Victoria, BC V9B 2Z8
250-478-3344
www.crd.bc.ca/parks

British Columbia Nonprofit Organizations

In British Columbia local nature clubs are called field naturalists, naturalists, nature clubs, or natural history societies and all but a handful belong to the Federation of BC Naturalists. Each issue of the federation's newsletter, the *BC Naturalist*, lists member and affiliated clubs. Contact the Federation's office to get a copy or for other information.

Federation of British Columbia Naturalists
321-1367 West Broadway
Vancouver, BC V6H 4A9
604-737-3057
www.bcnature.ca

Vancouver Natural History Society
PO Box 3021
Vancouver, BC V6B 3X5
www.naturalhistory.bc.ca

Victoria Natural History Society
PO Box 5220 Stn B
Victoria, BC V8R 6N4
www.vicnhs.bc.ca

BC Waterfowl Society
(George C. Reifel Migratory Bird Sanctuary)
5191 Robertson Rd
Delta, BC V4K 3N2
604-946-6980
www.reifelbirdsanctuary.com

The Nature Trust of British Columbia
260-1000 Roosevelt Crescent
North Vancouver, BC, V7P 3R4
604-924-9771
1-866-288-7878
www.naturetrust.bc.ca
www.brantfestival.bc.ca

Swan Lake-Christmas Hill
Nature Sanctuary
3873 Swan Lake Rd
Victoria, BC V8X 3W1
250-479-0211
www.swanlake.bc.ca

INDEX

JAMES LUTHER DAVIS is a naturalist for Metro Regional Parks and Greenspaces in the Portland metropolitan area. He holds a master's degree in zoology from Colorado State University. He was the first education director of the Audubon Society of Portland and taught at Marylhurst University where he helped start the university's Head Start Summer Science Institute. During this time he wrote *Seasonal Guide to the Natural Year: Oregon, Washington, and British Columbia* (1996), this book's predecessor. He also contributed to *Wild in the City: A Guide to Portland's Natural Areas*. Davis and his wife, Sally, live in Portland. When not pursuing his natural history interests, he plays guitar in rock and roll bands, although not nearly enough these days.